D1121186

YALE HISTORICAL PUBLICATIONS

MISCELLANY 85

PUBLISHED UNDER THE DIRECTION OF THE

DEPARTMENT OF HISTORY

This Essay won the John Addison Porter Prize

Yale University, 1965

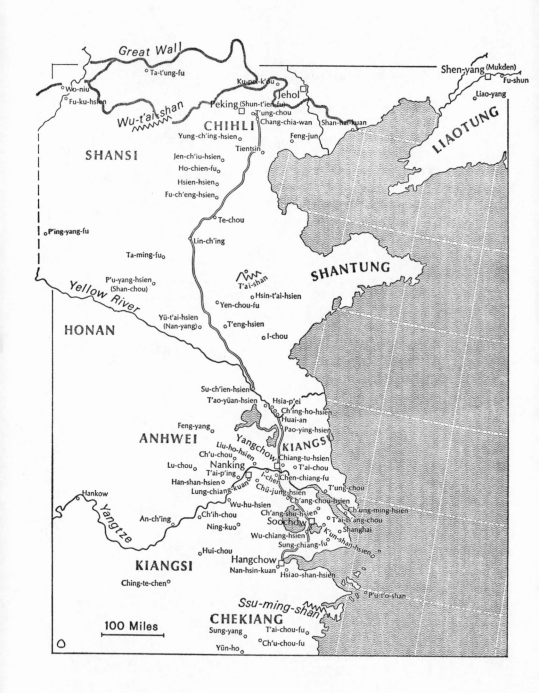

Great Wall

Shen-yang (Mukden)
Fu-shun
Liao-yang

LIAOTUNG

Ta-t'ung-fu
Ku-pei-k'ou
Jehol
Peking (Shun-t'ien-fu)
T'ung-chou
Chang-chia-wan
Shan-hai-kuan
Wo-niu
Fu-ku-hsien
Wu-t'ai-shan
CHIHLI
Feng-jun

SHANSI
Yung-ch'ing-hsien
Tientsin
Jen-ch'iu-hsien
Ho-chien-fu
Hsien-hsien
Fu-ch'eng-hsien

SHANTUNG

Te-chou
P'ing-yang-fu
Lin-ch'ing
Ta-ming-fu

Yellow River
P'u-yang-hsien
(Shan-chou)
T'ai-shan
Hsin-t'ai-hsien
Yen-chou-fu
Yü-t'ai-hsien
(Nan-yang)
T'eng-hsien
I-chou

HONAN

Su-ch'ien-hsien
T'ao-yüan-hsien
Hsia-p'ei
Ch'ing-ho-hsien
Huai-an
Pao-ying-hsien

Feng-yang
Liu-ho-hsien
Yangchow
KIANGSU
ANHWEI
Ch'u-chou
Chiang-tu-hsien
Lu-chou
T'ai-chou
Nanking
T'ai-p'ing
I-chen
Chen-chiang-fu
Han-shan-hsien
T'ung-chou
Lung-chiang-kuan
Chü-jung-hsien
Ch'ang-chou-hsien
Hankow
Wu-hu-hsien
Ch'ang-shu-hsien
Ch'ung-ming-hsien
Ch'ih-chou
Ch'ang-shu-hsien
T'ai-ts'ang-chou
An-ch'ing
Ning-kuo
Soochow
Shanghai
K'un-shan-hsien
Wu-chiang-hsien
Hui-chou
Sung-chiang-fu
Hangchow
KIANGSI
Nan-hsin-kuan
Hsiao-shan-hsien
Ching-te-chen
Ssu-ming-shan
P'u-t'o-shan

Yangtze

100 Miles

CHEKIANG
Sung-yang
T'ai-chou-fu
Yün-ho
Ch'u-chou-fu

Ts'ao Yin and the K'ang-hsi Emperor,

Bondservant and Master

JONATHAN D. SPENCE

Yale University Press
New Haven and London

THIS BOOK IS DEDICATED TO
CHARLES PARKIN
AND TO THE MEMORY OF
TIMOTHY BIRDSALL

"It's time we were starting," he
whispered, and showed the sky, whose
orange was already fading into green.
"Wish everything good night."

E. M. FORSTER, *The Longest Journey.*

Copyright © 1966 by Yale University.
Preface to the Second Printing copyright © 1988 by Yale University.

All rights reserved.
This book may not be reproduced, in whole or in part,
including illustrations, in any form (beyond that copying
permitted by Sections 107 and 108 of the U.S. Copyright Law
and except by reviewers for the public press), without
written permission from the publishers.

Printed in the United States of America by
The Vail-Ballou Press, Binghamton, N.Y.

Library of Congress catalog card number: 87–51374
International standard book numbers: 0–300–04277–9 (cloth)
0–300–04278–7 (pbk.)

The paper in this book meets the guidelines for
permanence and durability of the Committee on
Production Guidelines for Book Longevity of the
Council on Library Resources.
10 9 8 7 6 5 4 3 2

Contents

Preface to the Second Printing

In the twenty-one years since this book was published, there has been an astounding increase in our knowledge of its two main protagonists, the K'ang-hsi Emperor and his bondservant Ts'ao Yin. Multivolume compendia of the palace memorials received by K'ang-hsi, along with his appended comments, have been published in facsimile in Taiwan and in the People's Republic of China. Separate editions of the palace memorials written by Ts'ao Yin and his sons or adopted sons have appeared, along with volumes devoted to the memorials of the two bondservants who served along with him as textile commissioners and secret informants, Li Hsü and Sun Wen-ch'eng. The early Ch'ing archives in Peking are now open to scholars to complement those in Taipei, and important monographs—in Chinese, Japanese, English, and other languages—either recently published or in preparation, have greatly deepened our knowledge of the workings of the Ch'ing state and the Emperor's relations with his bureaucracy and with his own family.

But the true explosion of knowledge about the Ts'ao family has come out of the renewed fascination of Chinese scholars with the great novel *The Dream of the Red Chamber* and its author, Ts'ao Hsüeh-ch'in (Cao Xueqin in the pinyin romanization form). Two major journals devoted to the novel and its author were founded in 1979 and have issued a mind-boggling barrage of historical data, aesthetic interpretation, and learned controversy. *Hung-lou meng hsüeh-k'an* (*Hongloumeng xuekan* in pinyin), studies on *The Dream of the Red Chamber*, published under the auspices of the Chinese Academy of Arts, has been appearing quarterly with an average of 346 fine-print pages per issue. *Hung-lou meng yen-chiu chi-k'an* (*Hongloumeng yanjiu jikan*), collected studies on *The Dream of the Red Chamber*, has been producing one to three volumes each year since 1979, with most volumes, in equally fine print, running about 492 pages. This second journal is sponsored by the Chinese Academy of Social Sciences. Though

I am indebted to Ch'en Kuo-tung both for undertaking an exhaustive review of the current Hung-hsüeh literature and for generously sharing with me his wide knowledge of the economic role of the bondservants in early Ch'ing history.

many of the articles in these journals relate solely to characters within the novel itself, there are nevertheless scores of pieces each year that are in some way related to the historical background of the Ts'ao family and their friends and acquaintances.

How has this outpouring of scholarship affected the validity of my book? Though adding immensely to our knowledge of the times and of the Ts'aos, it has not, I think, altered my basic premises. Among these were four that had a central importance to me. First, that a special relationship existed between Ts'ao Yin and his Emperor, based on their youthful contacts, the Ts'ao family's bondservant status, and the fact that various imperial wet nurses were drawn from families related to the Ts'aos. Second, that this special status was important in understanding how Ts'ao Yin's career developed and why the palace memorial system grew in the way that it did as a conduit of secret information for the imperial eyes only. Third, that Ts'ao Yin moved in a curious cultural and economic world that crossed the more obvious boundaries separating the Manchu from the Chinese realms. And fourth, that the opulence of the Ts'ao mansions in Nanking, and the family's dramatic fall under the Yung-cheng Emperor, must have deeply touched Ts'ao Hsüeh-ch'in and thus colored important facets of *The Dream of the Red Chamber*.

That said, one must pay homage to the variety and importance of the new scholarship and acknowledge that if I were writing the book today it would be very different. In English-language publications Preston Torbert, Chang Te-ch'ang, and Madeleine Zelin, respectively, have transformed the way we think about the bondservant organization, the finances of the Imperial Household, and the collection of taxes in this period. Silas Wu has analyzed the whole palace memorial system and revealed unguessed dimensions in the relations of K'ang-hsi with his sons. Hilary Beattie, Jerry Dennerline, Frederic Wakeman, and others have all changed our sense of the Manchu conquest and its effect on Chinese local society. Pamela Crossley has shed a quite new light on the Sino-Manchu amalgam in individual lives, while the work of Beatrice Bartlett promises to change entirely the way we evaluate imperial decision making.

These works relate to the background of my book rather than to its heart, but that is not true of a host of recent Chinese studies. The Banner origins of the Ts'aos have been explored in depth by Ch'en Kuo-tung, Chao Tsung-p'u, and Chang Shu-ts'ai. Chu Tan-wen, in an essay he modestly called "a brief study of Ts'ao Yin" ("Ts'ao Yin hsiao-k'ao"), published in the *Hung-lou meng hsüeh-k'an* (hereafter *HH*) of August 1982, presents detailed evidence that Ts'ao Yin was a boyhood study companion of K'ang-hsi, that his mother was named Ku, not Sun, and that the well-known scholar Ku Ching-hsing was therefore Ts'ao Yin's uncle. Ku P'ing-tan (in *HH* 1984: 4) suggests that Ts'ao knew some Japanese. Wang Jen-ch'i (*HH* 1980: 4) joins the fray on Ts'ao Hsüeh-ch'in's ancestry by repeating the claim (similar to the one I made in my book) that the novelist's mother was the woman née Ma who gave birth to Hsüeh-ch'in after her husband—Ts'ao Yin's son Ts'ao Yung—had died. This would refute Feng Ch'i-yung's claim (in his book and in *HH* 1979: 1) that new genealogical evidence showed the novelist to be the natural son of Ts'ao Fu, who was in turn the natural son of Ts'ao Yin's younger half brother, Ts'ao Hsüan. Both Wang and Feng (and I myself) have been refuted in turn by the discovery in the Peking archives of a document dated 1690 that relates to Ts'ao Yin's purchase of *chien-sheng* honorific titles for members of his family before he left to take up the post of Soochow textile commissioner. This document, analyzed by Chang Shu-ts'ai and others in *HH* 1984: 2, shows that in 1690 Ts'ao Yin had one natural son, Ts'ao Yen, aged three *sui;* while Ts'ao Yin's younger brother Ts'ao Ch'üan, twenty-nine *sui* at the time, had three sons, Ts'ao Shun (thirteen *sui*), Ts'ao Ti (five *sui*), and Ts'ao Yung, then only two *sui*. Ts'ao Yin, however, had adopted his younger brother's eldest son, Ts'ao Shun, presumably fearing that his own line might die out.

Almost equally complex research has been done recently on the family of Li Hsü, perhaps the most important by Hsü Kung-shih in *Hung-lou meng yen-chiu chi-k'an,* no. 5 (November 1980). According to Hsü, Li Hsü's ties to K'ang-hsi were even more complex than Ts'ao Yin's, since Li Hsü's mother, née Wen, was one of K'ang-hsi's wet nurses, and Li Hsü's wife, née Wang, was the aunt of one of K'ang-hsi's concubines, who bore the Emperor no less than three sons. Ts'ao Yin, in turn, married Li Hsü's cousin. Such meticulous research in the People's Republic—and in Taiwan, where there has been work parallel in quality though not in volume—will doubtless gradually transform much of our thinking about the Ts'aos, though not the main picture.

In complete contrast to that kind of name-by-name burrowing in arcane texts are the hundreds of thousands of Chinese tourists who as of this year are cramming the walkways and pavilions of the *Dream of the Red Chamber*'s exquisite "Great View Garden" (*Ta-kuan yüan*). For the garden, fruit of Ts'ao Hsüeh-ch'in's fantasies and of his memories of his ancestor Ts'ao Yin's splendors, has now been lovingly recreated in cement, wood, tiles, and mortar by the Peking municipality. Another version is rising in Shanghai. Transformed into a Chinese version of Disneyland, Ts'ao Hsüeh-ch'in's dreamworld now serves cold drinks and ices on sticks.

For those who, inspired by their visit, wish to take up the scholarly cudgels and join the *Red Chamber* research fray, new tools are also at hand to aid them in their quest. The computer center of Shenzhen University, in conjunction with the Chinese literature department there, has developed the software for a computer retrieval-system covering the entire novel. The software package on diskette is operable on all IBM-PC-XT and compatible computers and can, in seconds, bring the researcher a complete run of *Dream of the Red Chamber* data on such topics as bisyllabic word frequency, auxiliary verb usage, onomatopoeia, education, garments, food and drink, medicine, ghosts, and love affairs. Ts'ao Yin never had it so good.

J. D. S.

New Haven
September 1987

Preface

This book deals with the life of the Ch'ing official Ts'ao Yin (1658–1712), but it is not a biography. It attempts to relate his life to the institutions of his time, and to give equal recognition to those institutions. Thus what is of importance to me is not so much where Ts'ao Yin was on a certain day, or what he felt at a certain time, but what it means when we read in the official Chinese histories that he was a bondservant, a textile commissioner, a salt censor. The problem of what he did is of course considered; but so are the problems of what he might have done—or more exactly what the statutes said he might do, and what his contemporaries in the same offices did do.

The span covered is greater than Ts'ao Yin's life alone. The story starts with his great-grandfather in the days of Manchu consolidation, and ends with his grandson in the reign of the Ch'ien-lung Emperor (r. 1736–96). Not surprisingly, since the Ts'ao family were bondservants of the Manchu rulers, their story is a sharp reflection of the changing faces of the Ch'ing Emperors and their modes of expression. The background to the study is the Ch'ing dynasty itself. Though there is no hope in a work of this compass of capturing all the change and vitality of the first century of Manchu rule, enough should emerge to show at least the variety.

Ts'ao Yin's great-grandfather was captured in the time of Nurhaci (1559–1626), and the new bondservant companies in which he was enrolled were one of the organizational forms developed by that tough and wily ruler, who had first consolidated his own power and then, in 1616, declared himself Emperor T'ien-ming of the Chin dynasty, staking his claim as the leading contender for the mandate still held by the Ming. Ts'ao Yin's grandfather started his career under Abahai (1592–1643), self-proclaimed Emperor Ch'ung-te of the Ch'ing dynasty (in 1636), while the Manchus, still held north of the Great Wall by the Ming, were studying and practicing Chinese bureaucratic techniques. But the Manchus conquered China in 1644 very much as Manchus, and used many of their own control devices. This we can see from the career of Ts'ao Yin's father, who served in the Imperial Household under the Shun-chih Emperor (r. 1644–61) and in the K'ang-hsi regency became the textile commissioner of Nanking, a post of which the Manchu rulers were to make special use.

Ts'ao Yin's own life, which was passed from childhood to death within the K'ang-hsi reign (1661–1722), points up the experimentation and the tentativeness that marked the government of that time. Neither he nor his Emperor seem to have taken much for granted, and both kept a close eye on the economic and the political scenes; though it cannot be claimed that they always responded constructively to what they saw, they were willing to improvise, and their flexibility certainly modified the patterns of Chinese bureaucratic tradition. For example, the K'ang-hsi Emperor used his Southern Tours to check personally on provincial conditions, and developed the system of palace memorials so that he could supplement his own observations with secret reports. He made Ts'ao Yin textile commissioner of Nanking, but did not restrict him to the statutory duty of directing the imperial silk manufactures in that city. Ts'ao Yin handled rice relief measures, purchased copper, checked grain transport, supervised literary projects, delivered Buddhist images to temples, and reported on the conduct of great officials and the yield of the local harvest. He was also appointed Liang-huai salt censor, both to direct the collection of the annual two million taels in regular taxation and to apply an additional half-million taels surplus to purposes designated by the Emperor.

The K'ang-hsi reign was not a period of stability and complacency, when change might be resisted on principle as it was later in the Ch'ing dynasty. The late seventeenth-century was a time when the Ming loyalists who might threaten the new dynasty were still occasionally vocal, when the great feudatories and border tribes who had once allied with the Manchus became bellicose, when imperial attempts at asserting prerogative were still tentative, and imperial brushes with Chinese culture were still uneasy. There may have been some deliberate calculation in Ts'ao Yin's career, but little was necessary; circumstances favored him as they had his forebears. This was not simply a time for new men, but rather a time for the old men tied to the new; what more admirable in 1675 than to be a Manchu bondservant with a classical Chinese education? This Ts'ao Yin was. Such a man could be used in many ways, and the rewards for success and loyalty were high.

But Ts'ao Yin's adopted son, Ts'ao Fu, was confronted by the centralizing tendencies—often realized through bureaucratic purges—of the Yung-cheng Emperor (r. 1723–35). His inability to adapt to the times and meet these new challenges led to the family's collapse. With Ts'ao Yin's grandson, Ts'ao Chan, the story ran to its end, in childlessness and genteel poverty amid the expansive glories of the Ch'ien-lung reign. The Ts'ao family would probably have passed into oblivion had not Ts'ao Chan conceived the grand idea of recalling the days of his family's greatness and its subsequent fall. The result was the *Dream of the Red Chamber* which, though it was never completed by the author, is generally considered China's greatest novel. The novel should gain extra poignancy now that we can see, behind the literary images of Ts'ao Chan, the actual working life and days of glory of his grandfather Ts'ao Yin.

Ts'ao Yin's personality emerges clearly when the various documents —institutional, literary, and political—are considered as a whole. He was an easygoing man who liked the good things of life; he found these good things in both the Manchu and the Chinese cultures, in horsemanship and archery as well as in poetry and intelligent conversation in the soft southern climate. His image of hard-riding aesthete pleased Manchus and Chinese alike. He was given to sudden bursts of enthusiasm and commitment, as when he tried to reform the salt administration in 1704, or leaped to the defense of those unfairly condemned in the examination-hall scandal of 1711; but in general he was content to move with the tide. Trusted by the K'ang-hsi Emperor, and given an increasing number of lucrative posts, he behaved realistically, making the most of his chances for gain but never crassly exploiting them.

No great claims need be made with regard to Ts'ao Yin's personal importance. He was not one of the great officials of the Ch'ing dynasty, nor even a major figure in the K'ang-hsi reign. His importance lies rather in what the course of his life can tell us about the society in which he lived and the institutional framework within which he operated. One purpose of this study is to show Ts'ao Yin's life as a paradigm (in the sense that the word has been employed by a historian of science) :

Discovery commences with the awareness of anomaly, i.e., with the recognition that nature has somehow violated the paradigm-induced expectations that govern normal science. It then continues with a more or less extended exploration of the area of anomaly. And it closes only when the paradigm theory has been adjusted so that the anomalous has become the expected.*

I initially undertook this study because Ts'ao Yin appeared unique and quite out of place in Ch'ing history. As the work progressed it became apparent that what had appeared to be uniqueness was merely a reflection of the fact that too much of the content of Ch'ing history, and the nature of the Chinese bureaucracy, had been taken for granted. It is now clear that Ts'ao Yin's life ran a logical course—as a bondservant in one of the Upper Three Manchu Banners he was a member of the K'ang-hsi Emperor's personal bureaucracy, and was therefore employed in certain key financial posts in the provinces over which the Emperor intended to keep control. This personal imperial bureaucracy naturally cut across the lines of the metropolitan and provincial bureaucracy, and its members were a group that can be defined, performing specific functions that can be analyzed. Since there is almost no previous Western study on any aspect of the first century of the Ch'ing dynasty, and an attempt is being made here to draw a complex period of growth and change out of the historical limbo, the findings presented must be exploratory and tentative. But if my major thesis stands, then the anomalous has become the expected, and a small discovery may be claimed.

* Thomas S. Kuhn, *The Structure of Scientific Revolutions,* International Encyclopedia of Unified Science, 2, no. 2 (Chicago, University of Chicago Press, 1962), 52–53.

Acknowledgments

My main debts of gratitude are to two people. The first is Mary Wright, who introduced me to Chinese history when I arrived at Yale, then encouraged me to write a dissertation which she directed, and finally read the whole of the revised manuscript. She has been in turn a stimulating teacher and critic. The second is Chaoying Fang who, while working in Australia, accepted me as his student and with kindness and heroic patience undertook the task of introducing me to the documents of the early Ch'ing dynasty and teaching me how to use them; after his return to the United States, he consented to be my thesis adviser. I benefited at every stage of research and writing from his comments and advice; my main regret is that this apprentice work still falls so far short of his own high standards.

Ping-ti Ho, Harold Kahn, Thomas Metzger, and Arthur Wright found time to read and comment on draft chapters of the thesis and the revised manuscript, for which I thank them. In the course of my travels many other scholars helped me with advice, references, books, and study facilities, although my visits were often unannounced and my questions inept; for their aid and their courtesy I would like to thank Charles Chu, Fang Hao, Hans Frankel, Shinichi Hyodo, Chuzo Ichiko, D. C. Lao, Owen Lattimore, Tien-yi Li, Ts'un-yan Liu, Göran Malmquist, Ichisada Miyazaki, Tomi Saeki, Dermot Spence, Denis Twitchett, Ling Wang, Silas Hsiu-liang Wu, and Wu Shih-ch'ang.

The following libraries kindly made their facilities available to me: in Australia, the Australian National Library and the Australian National University Library in Canberra, A.C.T.; in Japan, the libraries of the Toyo Bunko, Tokyo University, the Naikaku Bunko at the Imperial Palace in Tokyo, and the Research Institute for Humanistic Studies of Kyoto University; in England, the School of Oriental and African Studies at London University, the British Museum, and Cambridge University. In the United States, Columbia University allowed me to use its resources to supplement those of Yale.

At the archives of the National Palace Museum in Wu-feng, Taichung, Taiwan, permission to study the palace memorials of Ts'ao Yin and certain other officials of the K'ang-hsi period was generously granted by the acting director, Ho Lien-kwei, and the senior archivist, Chuang Yen; two assistants in the archives, Shen Ching-hung and Yü Kuo-chi, were particularly helpful to me.

The research and writing for the original dissertation were done during my three years as Yale Fellow in East Asian Studies, from 1962 to 1965. I wish to thank both the donor of this fellowship, of which I am honored to have been the first recipient, and the members of the advisory committee who awarded it to me: Professors W. T. de Bary, J. K. Fairbank, J. W. Hall, T. Y. Li, A. F. Wright, and M. C. Wright. The subsequent revision of the dissertation was undertaken at Yale University.

J. D. S.

Yenling Yeyuan
March 1966

Abbreviations

BH   Brunnert and Hagelstrom's terms in *Present Day Political Organization of China* (1911), cited by number.

CNTC   *Chiang-nan t'ung-chih* (1736).

CS   *Ch'ing-shih* (Taipei, 1961).

HLMHC   Chou Ju-ch'ang, *Hung-lou meng hsin-cheng* (Shanghai, 1953).

HT (1732)   *Yung-cheng hui-tien* (1732).

HT   *Ch'in-ting ta-Ch'ing hui-tien* (1899), references given to the Taiwan 1963 continuous pagination reprint, also citing the original *chüan* and page numbers in parentheses.

HTSL   *Ch'in-ting ta-Ch'ing hui-tien shih-li* (1899), citations as for *HT*.

PCST   *Pa-ch'i Man-chou shih-tsu t'ung-p'u* (1745).

PCTC   *Pa-ch'i t'ung-chih* (1739).

PCTC (1795)   *Pa-ch'i t'ung-chih* (undated, listing officials through 1795).

YCCPYC   *Yung-cheng chu-p'i yü-chih* (1887).

YFTC   *Yen-fa t'ung-chih* (1918).

Full references for the above, and for all other works cited by author and short title in the footnotes, are given in the bibliography.

All Chinese dates in the footnotes refer to the K'ang-hsi reign, unless stated to the contrary.

CHAPTER 1

The Imperial Household

Sometime during the Ming dynasty the ancestors of Ts'ao Yin moved from northern Chihli province to Shen-yang, the present Mukden, in the area known as Liaotung. This was a part of Ming China, but in 1621 the Manchu forces under Nurhaci captured and held the city of Shen-yang; many of the Chinese survivors surrendered and were enslaved. Among them was Ts'ao Yin's great-grandfather, who was made a bondservant in the military group known as the Plain White Banner. He thus became a member of that banner system which the Manchus made the central core of their organization before their conquest of China.

For thirty years before they captured Shen-yang the Manchus had been slowly consolidating their power north of the Great Wall: after learning to protect their scattered forces within fortified manors and towns, they moved on to adapt the Ming system of military garrisons as a model for their own banner organization, and finally deliberately used Chinese advisers to teach them Chinese bureaucratic techniques.[1]

1. The most useful introductions in English to this Manchu background (which I do not attempt to study in detail here) are: Wada Sei, "Some Problems Concerning the Rise of T'ai-tsu, the Founder of [the] Manchu Dynasty," *Memoirs of the Research Department of Toyo Bunko*, 16 (1957), 35–73; Franz Michael, *The Origin of Manchu Rule in China* (Baltimore, The Johns Hopkins Press, 1942); Piero Corradini, "Civil Administration at the Beginning of the Manchu Dynasty," *Oriens Extremus*, 9 (1962), 133–38; and the relevant biographies in *Eminent Chinese*. Many Japanese scholars have made major contributions to the study of this preconquest Manchu period, the most prolific writer being Wada Sei. A bibliography of his numerous pioneering works on Manchu and Mongol geography and history is printed in *Mem. Toyo Bunko*, 19 (1960), iii–xix. For his special studies with reference to early Manchu-Chinese collaboration, cf. his essay on Kung Cheng-lu in *Tōashi Kenkyū: Manshū Hen* (Tokyo, 1955), pp. 637–49, and also his essay on Li Ch'eng-liang in *Tōashi Ronsū* (Tokyo, 1943), pp. 362–79. Appropriately Wada Sei's essay on Li Ch'eng-liang first appeared in the congratulatory volume for another great Manchu scholar, Inaba Iwakichi (*Inaba Hakushi kanrekikinen Mansenshi ronsō*, 1938). Inaba Iwakichi's most widely influential work was probably his *Shinchō zenshi* [Complete History of the Ch'ing

But although they seemed to be increasingly sinified, and even developed Six Boards of their own in imitation of the Chinese administrative system, the Manchus kept their Eight Banner organization after they captured Peking in 1644 and subsequently became the rulers of China. They thus modified the institutional system that had prevailed in the Ming dynasty. As bondservants in the Plain White Banner—a status that was hereditary—the Ts'ao family accordingly became a part of this new order in China.

Banners and Bondservants

The Banner system was a means of both military and civil control: common soldiers were enrolled within it, but so were their families; military discipline was combined with a comprehensive registration of civilians; and the wages and grants of land made to the soldiers kept a whole people clothed and fed. Manchu historians dated the origin of the Banner system to the year 1601, when their leader Nurhaci (posthumously styled Emperor Ch'ing T'ai-tsu) organized his soldiers into groups of three hundred men called *niru,* the prototype of the companies the Chinese later named *tso-ling.*[2] In 1615 the method of grouping these companies under banners of different colors was given a settled form: there were to be eight Banners, plain yellow, plain white, plain red, and plain blue, and bordered yellow, white, red, and blue. Each Banner was to contain five battalions (*ts'an-ling*); each battalion was to contain five companies (*tso-ling*). These companies were the basic organizational unit of the Banner system and more and more were created as the Manchus attracted new adherents.[3] In 1634,

Dynasty] (Tokyo, 1914), translated into Chinese the following year and published under the same title (*Ch'ing-ch'ao ch'üan-shih*). Some of Inaba's detailed studies of the Manchus before 1616 appeared in H. Matsui, W. Yanai, and I. Inaba, *Beiträge zur Historischen Geographie der Mandschurei,* vol. 2 (Tokyo, 1912). A more recent major study of Banner organization is that by Abe Takeo, "Hakki Manshū niro no kenkyū" (On the Manchu Niru System of the Eight Banners), *Tōhō Gakuhō,* 20 (1951), 1–134.

However, none of these scholars were concerned specifically with bondservant problems, nor have I found other Japanese works dealing with this question. I have therefore concentrated on Chinese sources such as the *Pa-ch'i Man-chou shih-tsu t'ung-p'u* (PCST) and the *Pa-ch'i t'ung-chih* (PCTC), and on Chinese secondary works by Meng Sen, Cheng T'ien-t'ing, Mo Tung-yin, and others, which are cited below in the relevant footnotes.

2. PCTC, ch. 1, p. 4. Cf. also the biography of Nurhaci in *Eminent Chinese,* pp. 594–99.

3. PCTC, ch. 1, p. 4; and *Eminent Chinese,* p. 596. Only the Chinese terms are used here. An official table of the Manchu-Chinese term changes was produced in 1660, and listed in

eight Mongol Banners were set up on the same pattern, and finally in
1642 the increasing numbers of Chinese troops who had surrendered
and gone over to the Manchus were divided into eight Chinese Banners (*han-chün*).[4]

During the Shun-chih and K'ang-hsi reigns these bannermen lived
in comfortable circumstances, the majority of them being stationed
either in and around Peking (*ching-ch'i*) or in the provincial garrisons (*chu-fang*). They had lavish allotments of land—much of the
best land around Peking was made over to them after the conquest [5]
—and they were not yet suffering the awkward effects of having too
many mouths to feed from the produce of that land.[6] Moreover they
enjoyed extraordinary security of tenure. Hereditary succession to
military office did not merely develop after the Banner system had
atrophied in the eighteenth century; it existed already at the beginning of the Ch'ing dynasty. For example, the office of company captain (*tso-ling*) passed directly down the male line of a given family in
72 percent of the companies in the Upper Three Manchu Banners,
while the same family was in command most of the time in 87 percent
of the companies.[7] For the eight Chinese Banners there was a strong

the Eight Banner section of the statutes; *HTSL*, pp. 18,169–70 (ch. 1111, pp. 2b–3). Earlier changes in Chinese transcriptions for these same offices are in Meng Sen, *PCCTKS*, p. 375.
Various problems involved in the language changes are discussed at length in Nieh Ch'ung-
ch'i, "Man-kuan Han-shih" (Manchu Official Titles with Chinese Explanations), *Yen-ching
hsüeh-pao*, 32 (1947), 97–115. He concludes that though Chinese words naturally won out,
there was confusion in the transcription systems, and that there are frequent examples of
different Chinese transcriptions for the same Manchu term (pp. 114–15).

4. *PCTC*, ch. 1, p. 10b, and ch. 1, pp. 14–15. Existing Chinese units were formed into
two Banners in 1637, the number being increased to four in 1639. Details of the early
commanders and the numbers in the Banners are in Hsiao I-shan, *Ch'ing-tai t'ung-shih*
[A History of the Ch'ing Dynasty], 1 (Shanghai, 1927), 210. Cf. also the biography of
T'ung Yang-hsing in *Eminent Chinese*, p. 797; and *HTSL*, p. 18,169 (ch. 1111, p. 2). There
was also a company of Russian bannermen, in the Manchu Bordered Yellow Banner (*Eminent
Chinese*, pp. 269 and 631).

5. Liu Chia-chü, *Ch'ing-ch'ao ch'u-ch'i-ti pa-ch'i ch'üan-ti*, English abstract, p. 1.

6. As they were as early as the Yung-cheng reign. Cf. that Emperor's edict of 1730,
quoted in Meng Sen, *PCCTKS*, pp. 411–12: "The numbers in the Chinese Banners are increasing, and some way of feeding and educating these people must be devised. . . . As in the
provincial garrisons the children and younger brothers of Chinese bannermen are gradually
becoming more numerous and each man's revenue is fixed at a definite amount, they find it
hard to support their families and have to order the surplus to return to Peking and seek
appointments."

7. *Tso-ling* count of *PCTC*, ch. 3–5. The number of companies eligible for count, by
virtue of the fact that they had had at least two incumbents, was 247. "Passes directly

incidence of hereditary succession in 187 out of 270 companies, or almost 70 percent.[8] In the seventeen Mongol battalions virtually every captain had hereditary command.[9]

Manchu, Chinese, and Mongol bannermen alike shared this prosperity and stability in the early Ch'ing period, but just because of the apparent solidity of the Banner system, it is necessary to remember that throughout the seventeenth century the position of the Manchu Emperors remained insecure. The most dramatic proofs of that insecurity were the long-drawn-out wars that the early Emperors waged: against Cheng Ch'eng-kung (Coxinga) and the Southern Ming in the 1650s, against Wu San-kuei and the Southern Feudatories in the 1670s, against Galdan and the Ölöds in the 1690s.[10] Less dramatic, but equally telling, is the evidence from administrative records showing the caution with which the early Emperors appointed Manchus to major civil positions.

The Manchus, who often had a poor knowledge of the Chinese language and might arouse hostility if given the chief civil posts in the provinces, were given the major military posts instead, and appointed in a ratio of one Manchu to one Chinese in the Six Boards and the Grand Secretariat; the Chinese worked with them in Peking or in provincial posts from the rank of governor downward. The majority of governors-general in the Shun-chih and K'ang-hsi reigns were Chinese bannermen (*han-chün*), the natural intermediaries between Manchus and the mass of the Chinese people.[11] In 1647, all nine officials with the rank of governor-general were Chinese bannermen; in 1661,

---

down the male line" is used of companies in which the relationship between each member is stated (either son, grandson, brother, or nephew) and in which the line is broken in not more than *one* instance in any one company (e.g. for a dismissal, before reverting to the family line). "Most of the time" is used of companies in which the same family with stated relationships occurs regularly in command. In the first category there were 180 companies, in both categories 216. There were about 650 Manchu companies in all in the 1690s; it is assumed that the Upper Three Banner companies alone provide an adequate sample.

8. *PCTC*, ch. 13–16. These figures are too low, because there was carelessness in the compilation of the *PCTC*. For instance in ch. 13, p. 15b, Fan Ch'eng-hsün and his son Fan Shih-i are listed, but their relationship is not stated.

9. *PCTC*, ch. 11 and 12.

10. *Eminent Chinese*, pp. 108–09, 877–80, 265–68.

11. My findings on the use of Chinese bannermen as *tu-fu* in the Shun-chih and K'ang-hsi reigns have been confirmed by Lawrence Kessler. Unknown to each other, we were both working on this same problem, using different sources. I am grateful to him for taking time from his Taiwan research to send me further references.

after the number of these posts had been temporarily extended to one for each province, nineteen out of the twenty were held by Chinese bannermen; of the ten posts in 1681, seven were held by Chinese bannermen, two by Manchus, and one by a Chinese official.[12] One Manchu had been made director-general of grain transport in 1655, and was retired the next year.[13] Apart from him, no other Manchu was appointed until 1668, and it was not until the 1670s that Manchus were appointed as governors-general in any numbers; even then, they continued far fewer than the Chinese bannermen in the same posts until the end of the K'ang-hsi reign. During the same period, only a handful of non-Banner Chinese officials were appointed as governors-general. Non-Banner Chinese officials were not even given a monopoly of the governorships as a consolation; between 1644 and 1668, no less than ninety-six Chinese bannermen were appointed as governors, and after 1668 in accordance with an edict of that year, only Manchus were appointed as governors in Shensi and Shansi.[14]

The foregoing summary, though it shows some of the basic facts of the Banner organization, still does not tell the full story. The Banner system did not merely contain Manchu, Mongol, and Chinese troops, divided into the standard eight Banners, and subdivided into battalions and companies, with members appointed to the bulk of the military and a few of the key civil offices, though this certainly was the

12. Conclusion and figures arrived at by comparing the tables of governors-general, including the directors-general of river conservancy (*ho-tao*) and the directors-general of grain transport (*ts'ao-yün*) as they are listed in *CS*, pp. 2847–89, with the tables in *PCTC* (*1795*), ch. 339, which lists Manchus and Chinese bannermen who held positions as governors-general. These *PCTC* (*1795*) tables sometimes omit men who were in fact bannermen: e.g. Hung Ch'eng-ch'ou, who had been ordered to join the Bordered Yellow Banner (*Eminent Chinese*, p. 359), and in the eighteenth century Chang Kuang-ssu (ibid., p. 43).

13. This was Wu K'u-li, *PCTC* (*1795*), ch. 339, p. 3.

14. *HTSL*, p. 5350 (ch. 23, p. 8b). Almost all Kansu governors were also Manchus. *PCTC* (*1795*), ch. 340, pp. 1–9. The "Manchu" listed as being Kansu governor in 1647 (*PCTC* [*1795*], ch. 340, p. 2b) was in fact not Manchu at all, but Chinese as is shown by the Manchu genealogy which states that Chang Wen-hsing (the governor concerned) was one of the Chinese families that had been taken into a Manchu Banner without being made bondservants (*PCST*, ch. 74, p. 1b). (There is a different rendering of the last character of his name between *PCST* "hsing" on the one hand, and *PCTC* [*1795*] and *CS* "heng" on the other. But all listings agree that he was in the Bordered Yellow Banner (though *CS* lists him as in the Chinese Banner), and governor of Kansu in the early Shun-chih reign, and there is slight chance of more than one man being represented by the two names.) Manchus were not only frontier province governors; Ma Hu was governor of Kiangsu from 1669–76. (*CS*, pp. 3019–24 reads Ma Yu.)

harmonious picture presented by the first known historian of the Banners. Writing in 1715, he described their composition and formation as follows:

> T'ai-tsung . . . organized the various peoples who followed the Dragon Standard and the sons and grandsons of officials from neighboring states who submitted to him, whether officials or commoners, into the Manchu Banners. Those bowmen from the northern deserts who admired our culture and came to join us were separately formed into the Mongol Banners. The sons and grandsons of the former Ming military officials in Liaoning, Chinese officials and commoners who surrendered and those who were captured, were separately attached to him in the Chinese Banners.[15]

The author of this passage, Chin Te-ch'un, was himself a Chinese bannerman [16] and thus, though his book warned of the possibilities of military decay, was something of a propagandist. What he ignored, in describing the Chinese who were formed into their own Banners, were those Chinese who surrendered or were captured before the formation of the Chinese Banners—before 1631, that is, when the troops of T'ung Yang-hsing were used as the nucleus for the later Chinese Banner organization.[17] It was these Chinese, not discussed by Chin Te-ch'un, who were made bondservants of the Manchus, and the Ts'ao family were among them.

Nurhaci launched his first strong attack on the Chinese in 1618, when he took the city of Fu-shun and captured many Chinese troops; in 1621 he captured and held Shen-yang (Mukden) and Liao-yang. These were vicious campaigns, and the fate of the captured was not always pleasant. An edict of 1618 directed "when people are captured in battle, don't strip off their clothes, don't debauch their women, don't separate men from their wives." [18] Such an edict indicates the existence of the practices condemned. As late as 1626, a list of taxable

15. Chin Te-ch'un, *Ch'i-chün chih*, p. 1.

16. *Eminent Chinese*, p. 167.

17. T'ung Yang-hsing's biography is in *Eminent Chinese*, p. 797. Of course men were still made bondservants later on in the dynasty for criminal offences. Cheng T'ien-t'ing, *Ch'ingshih t'an-wei*, p. 60, discusses the case of Gioro Hua-t'e whose household were enrolled in a *pao-i tso-ling* after he had misappropriated military funds in 1683. He himself was later excused from *pao-i* service, since it was not fitting for a member of the Gioro clan. Other K'ang-hsi *pao-i* are listed in *PCST*, ch. 52, p. 10.

18. Quoted in Mo Tung-yin, *Man-tsu shih lun-ts'ung*, p. 137.

items included men slaves, horses, cattle, donkeys, and sheep within a single classification.[19] It is not strange that the early Manchus had slaves; for theirs was an aggressive and expanding nomadic tribal society in which farms were also cultivated, and as they grew increasingly powerful they inevitably captured many prisoners who could be put to work.

The first bondservants were slaves in private households.[20] They had either been captured in battles with hostile tribes, Mongols, Chinese, and Koreans,[21] or else they were the families of condemned criminals or men who voluntarily became slaves because they were impoverished or separated from their families.[22] Tracing and recording such slave families is almost impossible, since they were in servitude well before the Banners were organized,[23] and the families were often divided, some becoming slaves while others remained free men.[24] Once enslaved, they and their descendants remained so in perpetuity, and could be freely bought and sold by their owners.[25]

The Chinese word for bondservant, *pao-i*, was adapted from the Manchu *booi*, meaning "of the house." [26] The original bondservants were therefore probably used in menial positions in the households of their owners, though they were also widely used in agricultural work before the Manchu conquest,[27] and even after the conquest many slaves were still used both as bailiffs and workers on the farmland of bannermen.[28] The bondservants were rarely used in actual fighting.[29] But this loose system of privately owned slaves was not acceptable to

19. Mo Tung-yin, p. 139.

20. Cheng T'ien-t'ing, p. 60. *PCST*, ch. 48, p. 1, shows slaves given as presents to *tso-ling* before the conquest.

21. Mo Tung-yin, p. 136.

22. Cheng T'ien-t'ing, p. 63.

23. Mo Tung-yin, p. 136. Cheng T'ien-t'ing, p. 61.

24. Mo Tung-yin, p. 137.

25. Ibid., p. 143. Cheng T'ien-t'ing, p. 63.

26. Erich Hauer, *Handwörterbuch der Mandschusprache* [A Dictionary of the Manchu Language] (Tokyo, 1952–53). Haneda Toru, *Manwa Jiten* (*Manju Zi-ben, Gisun Kamci-buha Bithe*) [A Dictionary of the Manchu Language] (Kyoto, 1937). Meng Sen, *PCCTKS*, p. 375.

27. Mo Tung-yin, p. 141.

28. Liu Chia-chü, English abstract, p. 2. The observant Jesuit missionary Father Gerbillon saw such Chinese slaves at work on their masters' lands in 1688. Cf. Du Halde, *History of China*, 4, 327–28.

29. For instance in the lists of *pao-i tso-ling* in *PCTC*, ch. 3–10, and the *pao-i* lists in *PCST*, ch. 74–80, there are hardly any references to awards or promotions given in combat, though such references are common in the ordinary Manchu and Chinese Banner catego-

Manchu leaders with imperial pretensions, whose interests were increasingly directed toward centralized organization; [30] and besides this political consideration, as the Manchus conquered increasing amounts of territory settled by the Chinese it became a practical necessity to organize the captured men in some way that was more formal than allotting them to leading Manchus in private bondage. Accordingly, sometime between 1615 and 1620,[31] the bondservants were formed into companies and battalions on the model of the Manchu Eight Banner organization. The bondservants so organized were those belonging to the Emperor or the Manchu princes who commanded their own Banners; bondservants in private hands, owned by officials or members of the imperial clan, stayed on with their owners, though they gradually ceased to be called bondservants (*pao-i*) and were more usually referred to simply as "household slaves" (*chia-nu, chia-p'u*).[32]

This reorganization of slaves into bondservant companies was still no more than a stopgap measure. The successful Manchu campaigns of the 1620s brought increasing numbers of Chinese under Manchu control, and these men had to be treated on an equal basis, as allies. So in the late 1620s the surrendering Chinese were used increasingly in battle, under the command of Manchu or of defected Chinese generals.

---

ries. Meng Sen, *PCCTKS*, p. 375, says that in the Lower Five Banners, *pao-i* "might sometimes follow their lord in the field." In the Upper Three Banners there is the example of Han Ta-jen, *pao-i* in the Bordered Yellow Banner, who went on the campaign against Galdan, *PCST*, ch. 74, p. 8.

30. Thesis of Mo Tung-yin, p. 135: "In the *nuchen* society of Nurhaci's time, the two greatest classes already formed were those of the slaves and the slave owners; but at the same time within it was originating a feudal class and that class's concomitant peasant class." There is little doubt that Mo Tung-yin greatly exaggerates the number of slaves, yet his evidence is still relevant. Similarly on p. 146: "The Manchu rulers developing and consolidating their political power wanted not only to be able to exercise control over the great Manchu clans in the field of administration but also in the economic field they wanted to have control over them . . . by control of their household servants (*chia-jen*), that is the slaves who were privately attached to them."

31. The date of the formation of these bondservant companies is usually given in *PCTC* as "at the founding of the dynasty (or nation)"—*kuo-ch'u*—a vague term that could be applied to the beginning of Nurhaci's rise, to 1616, 1636, or 1644. The bondservant companies cannot have been formed earlier than the Banners in 1615, and were probably in existence by the fall of Shen-yang in 1621. Earlier, specialization of function had necessitated the separation of warriors from domestics, and the elevation of the former, who entered the ordinary Banners.

32. Cheng T'ien-t'ing, p. 62.

Finally in the early 1630s the first of the Chinese Banners were formed.

Important figures like Li Yung-fang and T'ung Yang-hsing, who had held Ming official positions and defected openly to the Manchus,[33] or Chinese who surrendered or were captured in the late 1620s or after, seem to have run little risk of becoming bondservants. Those in the first category were usually richly rewarded, while those in the second category were employed as soldiers in the Manchu or Chinese Banners.[34] Examination of the extant records of Chinese bondservants suggests that the misfortune of a Chinese becoming a Manchu bondservant depended largely on specific coincidence of time and place. For 813 men of Chinese nationality (ni-k'an hsing-shih) are listed as having been made bondservants, and of these men, 532 are said to have been living in Shen-yang, 83 in Liao-yang, and 66 in Fu-shun.[35] These were the three major cities captured by the Manchus between 1618 and 1621, and it is probable that the majority of the Chinese bondservants acquired their bondservant status at this time.

Ts'ao Yin's great-grandfather, Ts'ao Hsi-yüan, is listed in the genealogy of the Manchu clans as being a bondservant in the Plain White Banner, and formerly a resident of Shen-yang; the record adds that it is not known when he entered the Banner.[36] The most likely answer is that he was captured at the fall of Shen-yang in 1621. The official history of the Manchu conquests states that after the fall of the city on May 4, 1621, "those who had been captured, and the booty, were registered and distributed among the officers and men." [37] Since

---

33. Eminent Chinese, pp. 499 and 797.

34. Chinese could be incorporated directly into Manchu Banners. Cf. both tso-ling listings in PCTC, ch. 3–10, and the non-pao-i Chinese listed in PCST, ch. 74–80.

35. Count taken from PCST, ch. 74–80. The remaining 132 pao-i were from widely scattered areas in the north. Such counts from early Ch'ing compendiums can never be completely reliable, since there are often errors, and the listings can be ambiguous. For the figures here cited, men listed in PCST as being simply "Liao-tung jen," men from the Liaotung area, are not taken as being from one of the three cities, though they well might have been. The Kao and Ch'en families, later removed from the pao-i registers, are included here as pao-i; they were not freed until the 1730s.

36. PCST, ch. 74, p. 8b.

37. Huang-Ch'ing k'ai-kuo fang-lüeh [Official History of the Founding of the Ch'ing Dynasty] (Shanghai, 1889 ed.), ch. 7, p. 5, and the same work translated by Erich Hauer, Die Gründung des Mandschurischen Kaiserreiches (Berlin and Leipzig, 1926), p. 105. Ta-Ch'ing T'ai-tsu Kao huang-ti shih-lu [The Veritable Records for the Reign of Nurhaci] (Taipei, 1964 reprint), p. 86 (ch. 7, p. 16b). Those receiving slaves and booty were ordered

Ts'ao Hsi-yüan and his family were made bondservants in perpetuity, Ts'ao Yin's whole life and career were affected by this moment. But of comparable importance in shaping Ts'ao Yin's life was the fact that his great-grandfather was attached to the Plain White Banner, since the Banners of different colors were differently rated.

The basic division was between those Banners controlled by the Emperor, which were called the Upper Three Banners (*shang-san-ch'i*), and the Banners controlled by the princes, which were called the Lower Five Banners (*hsia-wu-ch'i*). These terms had arisen after the posthumous disgrace of the regent Dorgon in 1651, when the Shun-chih Emperor took Dorgon's Plain White Banner and added it to those that he already controlled—the Plain and Bordered Yellow Banners.[38] This arrangement, initially a fortuitous political accident, was later institutionalized in the Ch'ing statutes and the Banner gazetteers. This division of the Banners, which occurred twenty years after Ts'ao Hsi-yüan's capture, remained a very real one even after the 1720s when the Yung-cheng Emperor broke the last control of the princes over their own bannermen.[39]

The division of the Banners was especially relevant to the bondservants, because they were totally in their master's control, and even in the eighteenth century could be treated as chattels, being divided up and reapportioned together with the household effects when their owner was disgraced.[40] Thus those men who had been made bond-

---

to send them home at once, presumably so that they would not impede the campaign. There was therefore clearly no question at this time that the Chinese prisoners would fight side by side with the Manchus. Older Manchu chronicles also mentioned that those captured at Shen-yang were distributed among the conquerors; cf. *Tongki Fuka Sindaha Hergen I Dangse* (*Man-wen lao-tang*, English title, *The Secret Chronicles of the Manchu Dynasty, 1607–1637 A.D.*), 1 (Toyo Bunko, Tokyo, 1955), 283. PCTC (1795), ch. 61, pp. 3 and 26b, lists the *han-chün* families named Ts'ao as hailing from Shen-yang or Fu-shun. *Han-chün* might here be applied loosely to bondservants also, or there may have been many thousands of surrendered troops at Shen-yang of whom only a few were made bondservants. Though such points are important, there at present appear to be no adequate means of solving them. PCST, ch. 74, p. 3; ch. 75, p. 3; ch. 77, p. 7; and elsewhere, lists some *pao-i* families from Shen-yang entering Banners in the T'ien-ts'ung period (1627–35), perhaps transferred from private owners.

38. This process is described by Fang Chao-ying in his biography of Dorgon, *Eminent Chinese*, p. 218.

39. Also discussed by Fang Chao-ying in the biography of the Yung-cheng Emperor, *Eminent Chinese*, pp. 916–17.

40. Two examples from the Yung-cheng period are in *Yung-hsien lu*, pp. 220 and 288.

servants in what became the Lower Five Banners became the household servants of princes; even their nominal commanders, the bondservant company captains (*pao-i tso-ling*) had little or no independent power.

The descendants of those men who had been made bondservants in what became the Upper Three Banners, however, became the household servants of the Emperor. With the formation of the Imperial Household (*nei-wu-fu*) to manage the Emperor's affairs, the bondservants were also institutionalized: the former bondservant overseers (*booi amban*) became the ministers of the Household (*tsung-kuan nei-wu-fu ta-ch'en*), while bondservants in the Plain and Bordered Yellow Banners, and in the Plain White Banner, became the bannermen of the Imperial Household (*nei-wu-fu san-ch'i*).[41] This term set them apart from all other bannermen, bondservants or free, by emphasizing their role as the Emperor's personal servants. Though technically servile, their position was thus an advantageous one, for the Emperor could feel free to use them for many of the confidential or lucrative assignments that in other dynasties had been performed by eunuchs.

From the very beginning of the Ch'ing dynasty, measures had been taken to reduce the power of the eunuchs. In 1644 they were forbidden to collect rents from land, to be received in audience, or even to enter Peking from the provinces without authorization. Dorgon, who as regent for the young Shun-chih Emperor was virtual ruler of China, did not live in the inner palace, and he dispensed with eunuchs; cut off from the source of power, the eunuchs' influence dropped accordingly. Between 1644 and 1652 many eunuch offices were abolished, and eunuchs were forbidden to hold other offices such as that of textile commissioner (*chih-tsao*) which had been one of their special perquisites in the Ming dynasty.[42] After Dorgon's death in 1650, the eunuchs regained some of their lost influence, and in 1653 the Imperial Household organization was abolished and replaced by that of the "thirteen yamen" through which the eunuchs exercised considerable power. But upon the death of the Shun-chih Emperor in

41. Cheng T'ien-t'ing, p. 64. BH 75, 76, 97. This explains notes in the statutes, such as that in the Banner section of HTSL, p. 18,177 (ch. 1111, p. 18), that for *Shang-san-ch'i pao-i tso-ling* the reader should see the *nei-wu-fu shih-li*, not the *pa-ch'i shih-li*, i.e. The Imperial Household rather than The Eight Banner Sections of the Statutes.

42. Cheng T'ien-t'ing, pp. 65–67.

1661, the Imperial Household organization was restored, and the most influential eunuch, Wu Liang-fu, was executed.[43] The eleventh item in the Shun-chih Emperor's posthumous "will" (a document produced by the four Manchu regents of the young K'ang-hsi Emperor) was an expression of regret that he had appointed the eunuchs in the thirteen yamen.[44]

A number of regulations to limit eunuch influence were issued by the regents for the young K'ang-hsi Emperor in 1661, the regents insisting that they were returning to the principles of the founders of the dynasty.[45] But when the Emperor came of age, he added personal abuse to the existing institutional restriction. The eunuchs had already been shrewdly limited in influence by edicts that lowered their official ranks,[46] and forced them to apply to the Board of Revenue for their funds.[47] In an edict of 1681 the K'ang-hsi Emperor declared outright that "eunuchs are persons equivalent to the meanest of insects," and castigated them for failing to rise when ministers and guards officers came into the room.[48] The K'ang-hsi Emperor was always a stickler for palace etiquette—he also issued edicts reprimanding girls for screaming in the corridors and concubines for fraternizing with the palace workmen [49]—and in 1682 four of the eunuchs were duly given fifty lashes for sitting down before all officials were seated.[50] In 1689 the eunuch body were strongly cautioned against corruption after they had been accused of drawing excessive supplies and wages.[51] In such an atmosphere the bondservants flourished. But in fact the eunuchs proved irrepressible, and many of the sterner edicts were modified in obvious acknowledgment of the inevitable. Whereas an edict of 1665 had made it an offence for anyone to have sons or grandsons castrated, a new edict of 1684 limited the offence to those

43. HTSL, p. 18,749 (ch. 1170, p. 1). Eminent Chinese, p. 258. Cheng T'ien-t'ing, pp. 65–68. He dates the establishment of the thirteen yamen from an edict of 1653, and does not accept the dates of 1654 and 1656 sometimes given.

44. Cheng T'ien-t'ing, p. 71. Eminent Chinese, p. 258.

45. HTSL, p. 19,197 (ch. 1216, p. 11b).

46. Ibid., p. 19,192 (ch. 1216, p. 1).

47. Ibid., p. 19,195 (ch. 1216, p. 8).

48. Kuo-ch'ao kung-shih, ch. 2, p. 2b, edict dated 20/1/6.

49. Ibid., pp. 1 and 2b, edicts of 1673 and 1687.

50. Ibid., p. 2b, edict of 21/7/8. The names of the four erring eunuchs were listed, so it may be assumed that they held senior positions.

51. Ibid., p. 3, edict of 28/3/25. "A eunuch has but one body and one mouth" the Emperor sarcastically noted.

who forcibly castrated persons not in their families—in future, parents might castrate their children, or men might castrate themselves, without penalty.[52] An edict of the previous year had permitted officials of the first and second rank to have their own eunuchs.[53] By 1724 it had become necessary to forbid bannermen to make themselves eunuchs,[54] which is a clear enough statement that Manchu martial ideals were in decay. In the same year, eunuchs' wages were almost doubled.[55]

The early Ch'ing period, and the K'ang-hsi reign in particular, was an especially propitious time for those Chinese who were tied to the Manchu regime either as bannermen or as bondservants. The Manchus were as yet neither completely confident nor competent enough in language to handle provincial posts with ease; the ordinary Chinese could not yet be trusted to serve the dynasty with total loyalty; and the eunuchs were strongly held in check. It is thus no coincidence that the Ts'ao family, of Chinese origin but held in hereditary servitude in the Imperial Household as Plain White Banner bondservants, achieved their greatest affluence precisely during these years—from the 1650s when Ts'ao Yin's grandfather was Chekiang salt controller, to 1728 when Ts'ao Yin's adopted son was finally dismissed by the Yungcheng Emperor from his post as textile commissioner. But before considering the Ts'ao family history in detail, it is worthwhile examining the elusive bondservant status in more depth.

The task is difficult, because the bondservants rarely appear in official records. It is only by looking at the fragmentary data in the Manchu genealogies that some picture can be reconstructed of what the bondservants did.[56] The great majority of bondservants held no office, but served in the palace either as guards or maintenance men.

52. *HTSL*, p. 19,197 (ch. 1216, pp. 11b–12).

53. Ibid., p. 19,207 (ch. 1217, p. 16). Though the officials were expected to curb their own eunuchs' excesses. Thus in November 1712 the Manchu general Hai-shan was punished for letting his eunuch Li Huan act in a reckless manner. *Tung-hua lu*, K'ang-hsi, ch. 90, p. 8.

54. *HTSL*, p. 19,197 (ch. 1216, p. 12b).

55. *Kuo-ch'ao kung-shih*, ch. 20, p. 2. The later history of eunuchs in the Ch'ing dynasty is discussed by Cheng T'ien-t'ing, pp. 78–80. He feels that eunuchs remained under tight control through the Tao-kuang reign, and that there were no recurrences of the "Ming eunuch catastrophes" was largely due to the existence of the *pao-i* organization.

56. The crucial work being *PCST*, ch. 74–80, the sections of the genealogy of the Manchu clans dealing with Chinese clans attached to the Manchu Banners, and hence considered as Manchus by the compilers of the work.

The commonest offices for those who managed to rise out of the lowest level were either junior posts in the palace guards brigades, minor posts as clerks and secretaries in the Imperial Household, the slightly superior posts of department directors and assistant department directors or, most prestigious of all, as second- or third-class officers in the Imperial Bodyguard.[57] Those in the Lower Five Banners held similar posts in the princely households (*wang-fu*).[58]

Bondservants could also be given posts in the provincial bureaucracy, though this happened rarely. Such promotions were made without regard to the Banner involved, probably when an appointment was suddenly open; it is possible that bondservant promotions to provincial posts were made on the basis of imperial or princely recommendations, rather than through the Board of Civil Office, for not all these officeholders took the examinations. Over seventy-five bondservants served as subprefects and magistrates in the first century of the Ch'ing dynasty;[59] twenty-four were prefects.[60] Other bondservants served in a variety of provincial and metropolitan offices: in the Grand Secretariat and the Hanlin Academy, in the Medical Department and the Transmission Office, as army colonels, and as grain or salt intendants.[61] At least four bondservants obtained the *chin-shih* degree, two the military and two the civil;[62] thirty-four are mentioned as having the *chü-jen* degree, but almost all these were in the Yung-cheng reign,[63] suggesting that the system was becoming more flexible by the eighteenth century.

57. The offices were in the *hu-chün-ying, hsiao-ch'i-ying,* or *ch'ien-feng-ying* (BH 97A–C); as *pi-t'ieh-shih* and *chu-shih, yüan-wai-lang* and *lang-chung* (BH 76); and *shih-wei* (BH 99). They were almost never made first-class officers in the Imperial Bodyguard; a rare exception was Su-leng-e, a Plain Yellow Banner bondservant, PCST, ch. 78, p. 9.

58. PCST, ch. 74–80 passim, the *wang-fu* offices (BH 45–49).

59. PCST, ch. 74–80. Random examples are 74/1, 75/3, 76/2. Those roughly grouped here include *t'ung-chih, chou-t'ung, chih-chou,* and *chih-hsien* (BH 849, 851A, 855, 856).

60. PCST, ch. 74–80. Random examples are 74/9b, 75/13b, 77/18b.

61. In the order of offices mentioned, sample references are: PCST, 74/3b, 78/2, 76/9, 77/5, 77/9b, 77/11b, 78/6b.

62. Ibid., military 74/2b, 77/3, civil 77/10, 76/11.

63. Ibid., passim, examples on 74/6b, 75/2b, 77/5b. Either the degree is mentioned preceded by the word *hsien* ("at present") meaning that the holder was still alive at compilation (?1735–45), or they were usually in the fifth or later generation of their bondservant families, which meant that they were living in the Yung-cheng period, or at the earliest in the late K'ang-hsi reign. A double-check on *pao-i chü-jen* can be made through PCTC (1795), ch. 105.

Only a handful of bondservants reached important posts. Two became financial commissioners (*pu-cheng-shih*) in Fukien and Kiangsu,[64] and four became judicial commissioners (*an-ch'a-shih*) in various central provinces.[65] Two were censors,[66] and a few others were granted minor hereditary titles, or honorary titles as Board presidents.[67] Among these last was Ts'ao Yin's father Ts'ao Hsi, made an honorary president of the Board of Works. Two bondservants served as provincial governors: Lü Yu-lung in Fukien from 1718 to 1722, and in Chekiang in 1722;[68] Ch'en Ping-chih in Chekiang from 1674 to 1679.[69] One man even reached the exalted office of governor-general. This was Wu Hsing-tso, a bondservant in the Plain Red Banner, who was a licentiate with the *kung-sheng* degree. After serving for many years as a magistrate, he was promoted to the offices of Fukien judicial commissioner, Fukien governor, and finally made Liang-kuang governor-general, which post he held from 1681 to 1689.[70] His bureaucratic career was like that of any ordinary official,

64. Ibid., 75/8 and 77/18b.

65. Ibid., 75/11b in Honan, 77/6b in Chekiang, 77/16b in Kiangsu, 78/10 in Kiangsi.

66. Ibid., 75/6b, 76/15b.

67. Ibid., 74/8, Han Ta-jen given eighth-grade title as *yün-ch'i-yü* (*BH* 944) for services in the campaign against Galdan. 74/8, Sang-ko was president of the Board of Civil Office. (Many of the Chinese bondservants took Manchu names, as in less favorable times during the early seventeenth century many Manchus had taken Chinese names. Cf. Ch'en Chieh-hsien, *Man-chou ts'ung-k'ao* (Studies on the Early Ch'ing Dynasty) (Taipei, 1963), p. 28, and English abstract, p. 3.) *PCST*, 74/8b, Ts'ao Hsi was president of the Board of Works. Neither Sang-ko nor Ts'ao Hsi were listed as being substantive holders of these offices. However those of the nonbondservant Chinese listed in *PCST* as attached to the Manchu Banners who are credited with Board titles, often held them substantively: Hsing Kuei (*PCST*, 74/8b) was Chekiang governor, 1729–30; Board of War president, 1733–35; Board of Civil Office president, 1736–38 (*CS*, pp. 2893, 2621–28). Ch'o-erh-tai (*PCST*, 79/1) was vice-president of the Board of Civil Office in 1726 (*CS*, pp. 2613). Che Hsien (*PCST*, 80/1) was vice-president of the Board of Works from 1726–27 (*CS*, pp. 2613–14).

68. *PCST*, 74/9b, Plain Red Banner bondservant. *PCTC* (1795), ch. 340, p. 18 (listed as *han-chün*). *CS*, pp. 3049–51.

69. *PCST*, 74/4b, Bordered Yellow Banner bondservant. *PCTC* (1795), ch. 340, p. 9b (listed as *han-chün*). *CS*, pp. 3023–25. A third bondservant might have been a governor. The Chang Tzu-te (Plain White Banner, Shansi governor) in *PCST*, 74/1b, might be the Chang Tzu-te (two last characters different) listed in *CS*, pp. 3012–13, 3015–18, as Shensi governor, 1659–60, and Honan governor, 1662–68. The *CS* variant appears in *PCTC* (1795), ch. 340, p. 5, where he is listed as Plain Yellow Banner *han-chün*. A certain Cheng Pin (Manchu Plain Yellow Banner bondservant) is also listed in *PCST*, 74/9b, as being Kiangsu governor, but he is not so listed in *CS*, *PCTC* (1795), or *CNTC*.

70. On Wu Hsing-tso, cf. the long biography in *Ch'ing-shih lieh-chuan*, ch. 9, pp. 1–4b, giving precise details of his rise and later dismissal. Both this work and his biography in *PCTC*,

and it is impossible to say what difference, if any, was made by his bondservant status.

The careers of many men were, however, basically determined by this same bondservant status. This was especially true of bondservants in the Upper Three Banners who showed some special ability and were selected by the Emperor to carry out certain special tasks. Ts'ao Yin and his brother-in-law Li Hsü were two such men, both bondservants in the Plain White Banner who served as textile commissioners and salt censors, performed various commissions for the K'ang-hsi Emperor, and also sent in secret memorials on provincial matters. Ts'ao Yin's friend Sun Wen-ch'eng was a bondservant in the Plain Yellow Banner; he was Hangchow textile commissioner and one of the first Hoppos of Canton. Kao Pin, a bondservant in the Bordered Yellow Banner, had a career that closely paralleled Ts'ao Yin's as he rose from being a department director in the Imperial Household to become a textile commissioner and salt censor. But because of his exceptional ability, he was transferred into the regular bureaucracy as a financial commissioner; and after his daughter had been made a concubine of the Ch'ien-lung Emperor, the Kao family were officially freed from their bondservant status.[71] Yet another was T'ang Ying, a bondservant in the Plain White Banner, who was a supervisor of customs revenues and connected with the imperial porcelain manufactory in Ching-te-chen for over twenty years.[72] Many other bondservants were appointed to these important financial posts that dealt with textiles, salt, and customs revenues.[73]

By using their bondservants in these posts, the early Ch'ing Emperors ensured that they would keep a tight personal control over several large sources of revenue. Substantial sums of money flowed directly into the Imperial Household, bypassing both the provincial govern-

---

ch. 179, pp. 22–27, list him as a Plain Red Banner *han-chün*. He is only listed as a bondservant in *PCST*, 74/7, and in the *Pa-ch'i i-wen pien-mu*, 1, 10b.

71. *PCST*, ch. 74, p. 3. *Eminent Chinese*, pp. 412–13.

72. *PCST*, ch. 78, p. 10b. He was later transferred to the Plain Yellow Banner: cf. *PCTC*, ch. 4, p. 41, and ch. 5, p. 40. *Eminent Chinese*, p. 442. T'ang Ying was also a famous literary patron and a popular figure in the south; cf. Arthur Waley, *Yuan Mei* (London, 1956), pp. 159–60.

73. For detailed figures and references to the bondservants in these offices, cf. pp. 86, 174, and 104 below.

ment and the Board of Revenue. The K'ang-hsi Emperor especially relied on his bondservants such as Ts'ao Yin for money and information.
There was also the political advantage that Ts'ao Yin and the other
bondservants mentioned were Chinese within the Manchu system, and
could thus work easily with the Chinese people for the benefit of their
Manchu Emperor. Many of the bondservants picked by the K'ang-hsi
Emperor had already been captains of their own bondservant companies; he probably got some knowledge of them by seeing them engaged on their various duties in the Imperial Household.

The bondservants were a group that filled the vacancy left by the
eunuchs, and they were used accordingly by the K'ang-hsi Emperor
both as checks on the bureaucracy and as "instruments for the imple-
mentation of autocracy"; [74] they were private bureaucratic agents
whom the Emperor could use in the provinces to "withdraw, for associates of his own, some stores of strength from the field open to official
depredations." [75] They were above provincial law and untouched by
military law; when the servants of a Plain White Banner bondservant
in 1698 beat up a respected Soochow gentleman, no action could be
taken until officials from the Imperial Household had conducted an
investigation.[76] The bondservants worked for the Emperor only; just

74. Robert B. Crawford, "Eunuch Power in the Ming Dynasty," *T'oung-pao*, 49 (1961),
116, in describing the basis of eunuch power. This power in the Ming of course far exceeded
anything that any bondservant ever attained.

75. Joseph R. Levenson, "The Problem of Monarchical Decay," in *Confucian China and
Its Modern Fate*, 2 (London, 1964), 45. I disagree with Levenson's analysis that "simple
Manchus became the centralizer's tools," and suggest that the bondservants rather than
Manchu bannermen were "agents" forming a "personal corps," or "a set of instruments," or
"a 'third force.'" The bondservants were the Emperor's men in a sense that ordinary Manchus never were. On the other hand the complex of the regular Manchu Banner organization was a power center of its own, that until the 1720s was not only not subservient to
the Emperor, but was frequently in tension with him; it does not seem that Ming eunuchs
and Ch'ing Manchus were "functionally equivalent" (Levenson, ibid., p. 46). The bondservants were more nearly equivalent, but they never developed power of their own, nor
were they recklessly used. The Manchus performed a peacekeeping, garrisoning, and self-
supporting role that was largely passive yet also country-wide to an extent impossible for
palace-based eunuchs, even when on provincial assignment.

76. *Li Hsü Memorials*, pp. 4–5, both dated K'ang-hsi 37/6/–. It is probable that Li Hsü's
bondservant Li Yung-shou was the man of the same name (with different character for final
"shou") listed in *PCST*, ch. 75, p. 10b, as a Plain White Banner bondservant and storehouse-
keeper (*ssu-k'u*, a *chih-tsao* apointment like that of *wu-lin-ta* which Li Hsü mentioned as
his current post).

because they were his servants, he protected them and appointed them to lucrative office, so that at some indeterminate point servility became prestige.

The Rise of the House of Ts'ao

The Ts'ao family were originally from Feng-jun in northern Chihli, but sometime during the Ming dynasty a branch of the family moved northeast to Liaotung. It was probably here that Ts'ao Yin's great-grandfather Ts'ao Hsi-yüan was captured by the Manchus while he was living in Shen-yang and made a bondservant in the Plain White Banner. When this branch of the family crossed the frontiers into China with the victorious Manchus, the other branch of the family were not made bondservants and continued to live peacefully in their Feng-jun homes. Furthermore, some of the Ts'ao family in Liaotung avoided capture and continued to live there as free men; fifty years later, Ts'ao Yin was friendly with one of these Liaotung relations, a young cousin who had been sent south as a magistrate in Kiangsi. So it was only a section of the family that became bondservants, and, as already suggested, it was through this very bondservant status that they achieved wealth and prestige.[77]

77. Knowledge of the Ts'ao family was minimal until the classic essay by Hu Shih, "Hung-lou meng k'ao-cheng," a study of the *Dream of the Red Chamber* written in 1921. In this essay (especially pp. 586–93) Hu Shih ran down the vague existing information (and misinformation) about the Ts'ao family, and established a firm basis for future study of them on the basis of local gazetteers, the Manchu genealogy, and the literary works of Ts'ao Yin and his contemporaries. Not surprisingly he believed that Ts'ao Yin had two sons, Ts'ao Fu and Ts'ao Yung, as their names seemed to appear categorically in the available evidence. This error was rectified by Li Hsüan-po, whose essay on the Ts'ao family, "Ts'ao Hsüeh-ch'in chia-shih hsin-k'ao," appeared in 1931. Li Hsüan-po used both the selection of memorials that had just appeared in *Wen-hsien ts'ung-pien* and some further originals in the archives of the Palace Museum. His essay revealed considerable new detail about the Ts'ao family. The works of these two men were ably summarized and synthesized, and some new information added, by Tu Lien-che in her biography of Ts'ao Yin in *Eminent Chinese*.

The most important work, however, and the one most widely used in this study, is the work of Chou Ju-ch'ang entitled *Hung-lou meng hsin-cheng*, published in Shanghai in 1953. His book is a brilliant work of research on the Ts'ao family background, as well as being a mine of information. So full are the notes on Ts'ao Yin and his friends that the book is virtually a collection of documents on the literary life of the K'ang-hsi period. This section of chapter 1 and much of chapter 2 are based on his studies.

Chou Ju-ch'ang's discovery of the Ts'ao family collateral branch can stand as an example of his method. He listed every Ts'ao (it is a common name) in the Shen-yang and Liao-yang

Almost nothing is known of Ts'ao Hsi-yüan except that he had been living in Shen-yang. In 1668 he was posthumously granted the title of the second rank *tzu-cheng ta-fu,* and his wife, née Chang, was given the posthumous title of *fu-jen* at the same time. These honorary titles were granted as rewards to his grandson, so it does not follow that they had relevance to Ts'ao Hsi-yüan's actual achievements, which may have been slight since he had no official post that has been recorded.[78]

With Ts'ao Yin's grandfather, Ts'ao Chen-yen, the family began to rise. The only known son of Ts'ao Hsi-yüan, Ts'ao Chen-yen was probably born about 1610;[79] a bondservant in the Plain White Banner, he obtained a licentiate's degree which different local histories record as either *sheng-yüan* or *kung-sheng.* Others ignore it completely, merely describing him as a man from Feng-t'ien, Liaotung, or Liao-yang.[80] Whether for literary merit or because he had proved his competence in some other way, in 1650 Ts'ao Chen-yen was made department magistrate of Chi-chou, P'ing-yang-fu, in the province of

areas of Feng-t'ien, and checked them all for connections with the Ts'ao Yin family. He eventually discovered that the courtesy name (*tzu*) of a Feng-t'ien Ts'ao, Ts'ao Ping-chen, was Chih-nai, and remembered that, in the note at the end of a poem sending off a friend, Ts'ao Yin had written "my second younger brother (meaning young cousin) Chih-nai is your fellow traveler." The rest was easy. *HLMHC,* pp. 118–21.

78. It is even possible that Ts'ao Hsi-yüan's real name was Ts'ao Shih-hsüan, since this is the name written on the patent scroll (*kao-ming*) that was presented to his grandson in 1668. The name form appearing on this scroll may therefore be more accurate than the name of Ts'ao Hsi-yüan, which is found in the Manchu genealogy printed in 1745. There is no doubt that it is the same man referred to in both cases. No other references to him have yet been discovered. (Some further information may be given in a family record (*chia-p'u*) of the Ts'ao family that has recently come to light, and which was on view in a traveling exhibition of matters relating to the family of the novelist Ts'ao Chan, sent by the Chinese government to Tokyo in the winter of 1964. However, at that time exhibition authorities would allow no close examination or copying of this document, which has since been returned to China. For this information I am indebted to Professor Denis Twitchett.)

This patent for the honorary title is preserved in the library of Yenching University, where it and two other scrolls dealing with the Ts'ao family were discovered by Chou Ju-ch'ang. They are described in *HLMHC,* pp. 31–32, and the text of this one is given on pp. 213–14. The title *tzu-cheng ta-fu* is BH 945, *fu-jen* is BH 945, pt. 2.

79. And was therefore a young child when his father was captured. It is unlikely that he was born later than 1610, since his son Ts'ao Hsi was born in 1630, and bondservants rarely married young.

80. Different local history listings are detailed in *HLMHC,* pp. 41 and 210. Degrees applied to him are *sheng-yüan* and *kung-shih,* used as an alternate term for *kung-sheng.*

Shansi.[81] The Manchus never made the error for which the Ming Emperor Yung-lo castigated the Mongols:

> Discrimination was used by the Mongols during the Yüan dynasty; they employed only Mongols and Tartars, discarding northern and southern Chinese. This was precisely the cause of their disasters.[82]

But the early Manchu rulers did show their preference for military men or for Chinese from the Liaotung area north of the Great Wall in the areas where they had first consolidated their power, and bondservants could be used as well as bannermen. In the late K'ang-hsi period, around 1710, there were still a high percentage of bannermen and so-called "Feng-t'ien *jen*" (men of Liaotung) employed in civil posts in the south.[83]

Ts'ao Chen-yen must either have performed his duties well or have rendered the Emperor some special service, for in 1651 he was granted the honorary title of *feng-chih ta-fu* of the fifth rank, second class. This corresponded to his existing rank as a department magistrate. His wife, née Yüan, was granted the equivalent female title of *i-jen*. The title scroll bears only the statutory praise following his name—"You Ts'ao Chen-yen . . . careful in maintaining your dignity, intelligent in attending to your official duties," which gives no information about his actual services; while the section that was headed "Former appointments" has been left blank. Either the scroll was filled in very rapidly, or he had had no previous appointment of an official nature.[84] At the same time he paid for the repair of a temple, thus assuring himself of favorable mention in the local gazetteer.[85]

In 1652 he was promoted to be the prefect of Ta-t'ung-fu, also in Shansi. From 1656 to 1658 he served as salt taotai in Chekiang and concurrently held the higher post of salt controller of Liang-che.[86]

81. Listing of biographical sources on Ts'ao Chen-yen is given in *HLMHC*, pp. 41–42 and 206–10. His rank was *chih-chou*, BH 855.

82. Edict of November 16, 1412, quoted in Henry Serruys, *The Mongols in China during the Hung-wu period* (Brussels, 1959), p. 25.

83. *CNTC*, ch. 105–08.

84. Text of these scrolls in *HLMHC*, pp. 206–07. Titles in BH 945.

85. The *Chi-chou ch'üan-chih*, ch. 1, p. 25. Cf. *HLMHC*, p. 206.

86. His official title was a combination of the two offices, *tu-chuan yün-yen-shih-ssu yen-fa-tao*, BH 835 and 841.

The head of the salt administration in his area, salt censor Tsu Chien-ming, singled him out for special praise in a memorial to the Emperor.[87] In the year 1658 he died in office, probably shortly before the birth of his grandson Ts'ao Yin. Nearly all the Ts'ao males died before they reached their middle fifties.[88]

Salt appointments could be enormously lucrative, as an examination of Ts'ao Yin's career as Liang-huai salt censor will show. And though it cannot be known how much money Ts'ao Chen-yen made or how he lived, for the above sketch contains all the facts at present known about him, there is no doubt that he had made sufficient mark as an administrator to lift his family out of the ranks of the ordinary bondservants.

Study of the Ts'ao family is made difficult by the almost total absence of any mention of them in the various biographical collections of the Ch'ing period; if a man had no post in the provincial administration, and no literary friends, he not surprisingly disappears entirely and defies the historian's efforts to disinter him. Such is the case with Ts'ao Erh-cheng, son of Ts'ao Chen-yen and uncle to Ts'ao Yin. The Manchu genealogy records that he was grandson to Ts'ao Hsi-yüan and was made a company captain (tso-ling); [89] the Banner gazetteer lists him as the third ch'i-ku tso-ling of the fifth pao-i ts'an-ling in the Manchu Plain White Banner,[90] which can be translated as captain of a standard-bearers and drummers company in the fifth bondservant battalion.[91] From this post he was later dismissed. That is the beginning and end of all official mention of Ts'ao Erh-cheng's existence, and he could well be left out of the story entirely were it not for the fact that this promotion of his uncle probably had considerable effect on Ts'ao Yin's own career, owing to the curious principles of hereditary succession practiced in the bondservant companies.

In the regular Banner organization, described above, the heavy in-

87. HLMHC, p. 208.

88. These datings of Ts'ao Chen-yen's life and career are fairly tentative. His appointment as magistrate and prefect, and the date of the patent scroll are known. But there are contradictions in the Salt Gazetteers about the date of his appointment, which might have been as early as 1655 and run as late as 1659. These problems are discussed in HLMHC, pp. 208–09. Chou Ju-ch'ang does not find a definite answer possible on the basis of existing records. He thinks Ts'ao Chen-yen died in 1658, aged 53 sui, thus placing his birth in 1606 (p. 210).

89. PCST, ch. 74, p. 8b.

90. PCTC, ch. 5, p. 41.

91. Terms adapted from Ts'ao Yin's biography in Eminent Chinese, pp. 740–41.

cidence of hereditary succession arose because the Emperors either rewarded brave warriors with hereditary captaincies or were content to
leave trusted Banner families to run their own companies. The bondservant companies, however, had little or no hereditary succession
since the bondservants were rarely used in fighting and could not earn
the attendant rewards. In seventy-seven bondservant companies in the
Lower Five Banners, only about twelve percent show strong hereditary succession; in the thirty-three Upper Three Banner bondservant
companies there was almost no hereditary succession, either stated or
suggested by the recurrence of identical family names.[92]

Such a state of affairs is not surprising. It merely supports the conclusion that the bondservants were at the disposal of their princely or
imperial masters and had little say in the matter of their careers,
whereas in the regular Banner organization an elite had formed which
largely perpetuated itself. So it was extremely important for a bondservant family to establish its claims to any given official position.
Though he was dismissed, Ts'ao Erh-cheng's holding of the company
captain's rank in the fifth battalion was clearly an important step for-
ward for the family, and reflected their growing prestige. After two
men had followed Ts'ao Erh-cheng at this post, it was given to his
nephew Ts'ao Yin.[93] Also, in 1695 an additional company was created in the same battalion, and one of the captains appointed in the
early eighteenth century was Ts'ao I, Ts'ao Yin's younger brother.[94]

92. *PCTC*, ch. 3–10, the bondservant companies being listed at the end of each Banner. One
exception to the hereditary balance is the special company of Korean *pao-i tso-ling* in the
Plain Yellow Banner, *PCTC*, ch. 4, p. 38, which has hereditary succession stated throughout,
despite many changes of name. The possibility of further exceptions appearing cannot be
denied. For example, the Shen family of Plain Yellow Banner bondservants as listed in *PCST*,
ch. 78, p. 3, have five successive members of the family, spanning four generations, appointed
as *pao-i tso-ling*. However, this did not mean firm succession. For the first of these men (the
sixth-generation Shen Yü—his name has different homophones in *PCST* and *PCTC*) was the
fourth *ch'i-ku tso-ling* and is listed in *PCTC*, ch. 4, p. 38b, whereas the second and third (Su
Po and Ya-erh-tai) were in the first *ch'i-ku tso-ling* and are accordingly listed on *PCTC*, ch.
4, p. 40. Furthermore they were divided by another incumbent, definitely not of their family.
The fourth and fifth family members are listed in *PCTC* (1795), ch. 5, pp. 36b and 38 as
being in the fifth *ts'an-ling*; Yung Chung being in the first *ch'i-ku tso-ling*, and Cho-erh-tai
in the third.

93. *PCTC*, ch. 5, p. 41.

94. Ibid., second *ch'i-ku tso-ling*. For his relationship with Ts'ao Yin, cf. *PCST*, ch. 74, p.
8b.

The Ts'ao family were clearly on the rise: insignificant in the first generation, affluent and respected in the second, in the third generation with Ts'ao Hsi, younger son of Ts'ao Chen-yen, they achieved both wealth and prestige. Ts'ao Hsi (?1630–84) was an official in the Imperial Household in Peking when his eldest son Ts'ao Yin was born in 1658, and his successful career as textile commissioner had not yet begun; but he had already made a marriage that did much to assure his future good fortune.

Ts'ao Hsi's wife, née Sun, was born in 1632,[95] and in her early twenties was a nurse to Prince Hsüan-yeh, the later K'ang-hsi Emperor.[96] She must therefore have been among the women from the Manchu Banners, probably one of the Upper Three Banner bondservants. For a statute of 1661 (almost certainly the ratification of current practice), laid down that the Upper Three Banner captains and palace overseers [97] must send annual records of the daughters of those in their charge who had reached the age of 13 *sui* to the chief eunuch, who thereupon requested permission to bring them to the Emperor for inspection. Those selected were made female attendants on the Emperor (*kung-nü*), and could be later taken as imperial concubines.[98] They were returned to their families when they reached the age of 25 *sui*.[99] When an imperial birth was imminent, the chief eunuch instructed the captains and palace overseers to send in the names of

95. HLMHC, p. 205, prints the congratulatory essay written on her sixtieth birthday (reaching sixty *sui*) which is dated 1691.

96. This important fact is recorded only in *Yung-hsien lu*, p. 390, where in a biographical note on Ts'ao Yin is found the phrase "mu wei Sheng-tsu pao-mu"—his mother was the K'ang-hsi Emperor's nurse. This reference is taken as definite evidence because the *Yung-hsien lu* is extraordinarily accurate about all other details of the Ts'ao family, and if Yin's mother was the Emperor's nurse, many puzzling aspects of the relationship between them and the Emperor are explained. Chou Ju-ch'ang accepts *Yung-hsien lu* as one of his "major historical sources" (HLMHC, p. 35).

97. The *nei-kuan-ling*, BH 104D, who were bondservants. They are listed with the *pao-i tso-ling* and the *ch'i-ku tso-ling* in the PCTC, ch. 3–10. Up to 1685 there were twenty of them with twenty assistants. They took charge of maintenance work within the inner palaces, "sprinkling, sweeping, pasting, adorning" and had charge of materials for incense and sacrifices, some of the rice and salt storehouses for the palaces, the wine and the ice. They were in charge of some 445 artisans at the stores alone, who may well have been more lowly *pao-i*. Cf. HT (1732), ch. 126, p. 7, and ch. 132, pp. 20–22b.

98. HTSL, p. 19,212 (ch. 1218, p. 7).

99. Ibid. This statute is dated 1723, but there is no reason to doubt that it reflected existing palace practice.

women suitable for selection as wet nurses (*ju-mu*) or nurses (*pao-mu*).[100] Ts'ao Yin's mother was one of the latter, a nurse on palace duty.

If Sun were released from palace service at the age of 25 *sui*, she would have rejoined her family in 1656; shortly after this she married Ts'ao Hsi, and their first son, Ts'ao Yin, was born on October 3, 1658.[101] Prince Hsüan-yeh lived for a part of his childhood with his nurses outside the Forbidden City, in an Inner City house.[102] The Inner City was the home of the Manchu bannermen, and it is possible that Sun continued to nurse the Prince after she was 25 *sui*, or even after her marriage. After the Prince became Emperor he clearly remembered her with affection and showed her especial favor. On the death of her husband in 1684 he visited her house in person to offer his condolences,[103] and in 1699 on his third Southern Tour she was summoned in audience. One version of the Emperor's words on this occasion runs "this is an old lady from my home," [104] the type of colloquialism that matches the language he is known to have used with her son.[105] This account may be fictional, but the Emperor did then take a brush and write the three characters *hsüan jui t'ang*, "hall of celebrations for a distinguished mother," an act which various contemporaries recorded and held to be quite unprecedented.[106] The Emperor's affection for Sun cannot have had any influence on the appointment of her husband as textile commissioner in 1663, however, since though he was now the K'ang-hsi Emperor, he was only nine years old and controlled by regents. But in noting the later career of Ts'ao Hsi and following in detail that of his son Ts'ao Yin, it is important to remember that the Ts'ao family were no longer mere bondservants who had made a hard-earned name for themselves; they were also royal favorites.

Ts'ao Hsi was appointed textile commissioner at Nanking in 1663,

100. Ibid., p. 19,214 (ch. 1218, p. 11), statute of 1661. A note to the statute adds that imperial wet nurses who had to employ other wet nurses to suckle their own children were to be paid eighty taels.

101. *HLMHC*, pp. 209–10, gives evidence for the October 3 birth date, rather than the October 13 date given in *Eminent Chinese*, p. 740.

102. Fang Chao-ying in *Eminent Chinese*, p. 328.

103. *HLMHC*, p. 229, citing Hsiung Tz'u-li's eulogy for Ts'ao Hsi.

104. *Ch'ing pai lei-ch'ao*, section 10, p. 11: "tz'u wu-chia lao-jen yeh." *HLMHC*, p. 319.

105. Cf. K'ang-hsi endorsements in *Ts'ao Yin Memorials*.

106. Some are quoted in *HLMHC*, pp. 316–20.

under a new ruling that the posts were to be filled by specially selected personnel from the Imperial Household.[107] He accordingly moved south with his family to take up residence in Nanking, and he remained commissioner until his death in 1684.[108] The exact duties of his office, which involved the management of the three government silk factories in the city, the purchase of raw materials, and the dispatch of the requisite quotas of silk to the Court in Peking, will be examined in detail with regard to his son Ts'ao Yin who held the same post from 1692 to 1712.[109] No official record of Ts'ao Hsi's administration has survived, but he must have been extremely efficient, for in 1667 he was summoned to an audience in the capital and presented with a ceremonial robe embroidered with dragons (*mang-fu*) and raised one rank.[110] In January 1668 he was granted two patents awarding titles of the second rank to his paternal grandfather and grandmother, and at some stage he was given the honorary title of president of the Board of Works while his wife was made first-rank *fu-jen*.[111] These were the highest honors ever awarded to members of the Ts'ao family. These patents and honorary ranks might have been given either in recognition of his services or because he contributed to the Imperial Household Treasury; [112] in any case the office brought the wealth, and the prestige was his whether bought or earned.

Ts'ao Yin was therefore brought up in Nanking from the age of five and, together with a younger brother, received a strict Chinese classical education from his father. The Manchu Banners and bondservant duties seem very far away in the scraps of affectionate reminiscence that have survived—a tranquil record of an apparently tranquil period.[113]

The famous scholar Yu T'ung,[114] who spent twenty-two years in leisurely retirement from 1656 to 1678, as compensation for the fa-

---

107. *CNTC*, ch. 105, p. 9. *Shih-lu*, ch. 8, p. 7.

108. *chih-tsao* listings in *CNTC*, ch. 105, p. 10.

109. Cf. chapter 3 below.

110. *HLMHC*, p. 213.

111. Ibid., p. 42. The title *kung-pu shang-shu*, BH 460 and 276, is that by which he is listed in *PCST*, ch. 74, p. 8b. His wife's title is BH 946.

112. Two alternatives suggested by Tu Lien-che in *Eminent Chinese*, p. 740.

113. The many essays written about Ts'ao Hsi dealing purely in generalities are ignored here, though they do cumulatively show that he was probably an unusually good administrator.

114. *Eminent Chinese*, pp. 935–36.

tigues of his four-year stint as a magistrate in Chihli, recalls them thus:

> When Ts'ao Hsi opened up the office in Nanking, he planted a *lien* tree with his own hands in the gardens of his yamen, and there he built a thatched pavilion, with balcony railings interlacing. He sent his two sons to study beneath it. Summer day or winter night, one heard their shrill voices.[115]

In an essay written forty years later, Ts'ao Yin recalled his childhood contact with Chou Liang-kung,[116] a formidable figure who had fought the Manchus in 1642 and later in a stormy civil career was twice condemned to death for corruption, though both times reprieved:

> When my father was in Nanking, and I was just a little boy, Chou Liang-kung was grain intendant at Nanking and the two men became very close friends. Later Chou became good friends with me and often embraced me and sat me on his knee, making me run through the Classics and helping me to punctuate passages.[117]

The Manchu poet Singde,[118] in an essay written the year after Ts'ao Hsi's death, recorded one of his conversations with Ts'ao Yin. The melancholy is sincere enough, but Ts'ao Hsi emerges nevertheless as a rather forbidding person:

> Ts'ao Yin said to me: "My father was ordered to manage the imperial textiles in Nanking which he did with an integrity and kindness that was known throughout the southeast. . . . When not busy in his office he would have me and my brother at his side. When we were still young children our studies of the Classics continued through heat and cold. Outside his library Ts'ao Hsi planted a *lien* tree which is still flourishing today. Before the spring petals had blossomed, when the autumn pods were not yet scattered, he would stand there as if at Court, wearing hat and

---

115. Yu T'ung, *Ken-chai ch'üan-kao* (*wen*), ch. 5, p. 1. This is quoted in full in *HLMHC*, pp. 353–55. The *lien* tree, a recurring motif in Ts'ao Yin's life, and a part of his favorite studio name, was the *melia azedarach*, and is described in chapter 2 below.

116. *Eminent Chinese*, pp. 173–74.

117. *Ts'ao Yin Wen*, p. 13. Cited in *oratio obliqua* in *HLMHC*, p. 213.

118. *Eminent Chinese*, pp. 662–63.

sword, dignified as if on a solemn occasion. Oh, how long ago that was. The tree of those bygone days is now a tree that my hands can no longer span, the person of those bygone days is no longer a child." When he had finished speaking, Ts'ao Yin grew melancholy, recalling his father.[119]

Such, even if in rather idealized form, was the upbringing of Ts'ao Yin. And it was with a thoroughly Confucian education, though probably a good knowledge of Manchu as well, that he was sent off to Peking to seek employment in the Imperial Household.

Service in the Imperial Household

Ts'ao Yin probably went to the Imperial Household at the age of fourteen or fifteen to apply for a suitable job. In the same way, in March 1709, he was to send off his own son to Peking, mentioning the fact to the Emperor in a memorial but apparently seeking no favors and having no particular job in mind. He wrote: "I have one son, and this year I am letting him go to Peking to seek employment, and sending my daughter with him." [120]

It is unlikely that Ts'ao Yin had been back to Peking since he left with his father as a child of five. There are various hints that Ts'ao Yin may have been employed in the palace at some stage as a childhood reading companion of the young Emperor K'ang-hsi, but they are tantalizing hints and nothing more; [121] and though it is true that in some memorials late in his life Ts'ao Yin wrote that he had served the Emperor since he was a child,[122] this could equally well mean no more than that he had served in the Imperial Household since his early teens.

119. Quoted in *HLMHC*, p. 234.

120. *Ts'ao Yin Memorials*, p. 19b, dated 48/2/8.

121. Chou Ju-ch'ang discusses this point in *HLMHC*, p. 215. He states that he was told by a scholar in Peking that there was in the Yen-ta library a book in 8 fascicles (*ts'e*) dealing with administrative points arising from the K'ang-hsi reign, which mentioned that Ts'ao Yin had been a *"shih ti tu,"* reader to the Emperor. The scholar could not remember the name of the book, nor could Chou Ju-ch'ang find it, despite an intensive search. In *HLMHC*, p. 225, Chou Ju-ch'ang finds further hints, in poems, that Ts'ao Yin had been a palace reader. He in fact admits the inadequacy of the evidence by ignoring this possible occupation in his summary of Yin's life, ibid., pp. 43–45. In wealthy families, the sons did have reading companions who could be either from free or slave families.

122. E.g. *Ts'ao Yin Memorials*, p. 23, dated 50/3/9: "Since my childhood I have labored in office, and received the Emperor's favors."

It is not easy to determine exactly what Ts'ao Yin's status was at this period, and whether he could expect privileged treatment or not. His parents were both in the Emperor's favor, but their son does not seem to have had any hereditary privilege (*yin*), for which even bondservants could be eligible. Ts'ao Yin's brother-in-law and close friend, Li Hsü, for instance, was granted the *yin* privilege; and though, like Ts'ao Yin, he was a bondservant in the Plain White Banner, after a short spell as a secretary in the Grand Secretariat he was made a prefect in Kwangtung.[123] The office Ts'ao Yin finally obtained, by what means we know not, was that of controller of the sixth class in the Imperial Equipage Department.[124]

The Imperial Equipage Department (*luan-i-wei*) was one of the more or less autonomous departments, concerned with imperial regalia and ceremonies, on the fringes of the Imperial Household. The evidence that this was where Ts'ao Yin's career started comes from the funeral eulogy written at his death by Chang Po-hsing,[125] onetime governor of Kiangsu. The few sentences in the eulogy are all that we know about this stage of Ts'ao Yin's career. They run:

> In his youth he was a skillful calligrapher and adept at mounted archery. Appointed *i-yü* and transferred to be *i-cheng*, how respectfully he tended the leopard's-tail and dragon-head banners, how loftily he strode with sable hat and feathered arrows.[126]

I-yü and *i-cheng* are abbreviations of two offices that recur through the lower echelons of the Imperial Equipage Department; they may be translated here as controller of the sixth class and assistant section

123. Li Hsü's offices are listed in the biographical collection *Pei-chuan-chi*, ch. 66, p. 1, in the biography of his father Li Shih-chen. It was first cited by Li Hsüan-po, "Ts'ao Hsüeh-ch'in chia-shih hsin-k'ao," section 11 (misprinted as ch. 6). The reference to the fact that Li Hsü was appointed by *yin* privilege is mentioned in the gazetteer of Ning-po, cited in *HLMHC*, p. 231; (ibid., p. 104 cites Li Shih-chen reference correctly). The Li Shih-chen listed in the *Index to Thirty-three Collections of Ch'ing Dynasty Biographies*, p. 141, as being in the *Ch'ing-shih lieh-chuan*, ch. 72, p. 50a, is in fact a Chia-ch'ing official of the same name. Li Hsü's Grand Secretariat office was *nei-ko chung-shu*, BH 137.

124. *cheng-i-yü* in the *luan-i-wei*, BH 126 in BH 109.

125. 1652–1725, a scholar and famous incorruptible official. Biography in *Eminent Chinese*, pp. 51–52.

126. Sections of the eulogy are quoted passim by Chou Ju-ch'ang, and he cites it in full in *HLMHC*, p. 388.

chief.[127] These offices were in fact not as insignificant as they sound; they gained their value from the fact that their incumbents, like officers in the Imperial Bodyguard (*shih-wei*), had chances of contact with the Emperor and always had their appointments ratified in a formal audience with him.[128]

The Imperial Equipage Department was similar to the Ming dynasty department in organization.[129] It was given its new name *luan-i-wei* in 1645, and in 1654 the ranks and duties were fixed in the form that remained unchanged in essentials throughout the Ch'ing dynasty.[130] The basic concern of the Department was all matters relating to the concrete embodiments of imperial pomp. It was in charge of the imperial carriages, "of maintaining the distinctions of their names and types and arranging them in the correct order." [131] It sent heralds to warn people of the Emperor's approach, prepared equipages for the Empress and the concubines, and ensured that the right insignia were displayed on all occasions. On difficult questions it acted in consultation with the Board of Rites, the Court of Sacrificial Worship, and the Court of State Ceremonial. The descriptions of the Department in the statutes are full of the lavish ritual for getting the Emperor into and out of his various carriages, of horses and elephants with their magnificent trappings, of the flags and banners in embroidered silks, of the ceremonial swords, bows, and spears.[132]

There had to be completely perfect arrangements made in the four main categories of imperial journeys: processions to the Three Great Sacrifices, to the Ancestral Sacrifices, processions within the imperial city, and royal progresses to the provinces.[133] One description of the Emperor's retinue at the Three Great Sacrifices has, besides the many

127. *BH* 125 and 123. The reasons for selecting *chih-i-cheng*, *BH* 123, rather than *chih-i-cheng*, *BH* 125, are given below; and only *BH* 123 closely fits Chang Po-hsing's description.
128. Appointments to *luan-i-wei* and *shih-wei* sometimes overlapped; cf. *HTSL*, p. 18,150 (ch. 1108, pp. 10b–11), where it is also stated that sixth-class controllers and upward were received in audience to have appointments ratified.
129. *Li-tai chih-kuan piao* [Table of Official Positions in Successive Dynasties], ch. 42. The work is printed in *Ts'ung-shu chi-ch'eng*, vols. 0846–65.
130. *HTSL*, p. 18,145 (ch. 1108, p. 1).
131. *HT*, p. 0833 (ch. 83, p. 1).
132. Ibid., pp. 0833–36 (ch. 83, pp. 1–8b).
133. Ibid., pp. 0836–38 (ch. 83, pp. 8b–11). The four categories were *san-ta-ssu*, *chi-ssu*, *hsing-hsing yü huang-ch'eng*, *sheng-fang jo ta-yüeh*.

officers of the Imperial Bodyguard and other officials in attendance, over 1,700 subordinates from the Imperial Equipage Department controlled by fifty-eight Department officials.[134] All senior appointments to the Department were made on the basis of recommendations from the Board of War submitted to the Emperor; Manchus were selected from the senior officers in the Imperial Bodyguard, Chinese from military men in the provinces.[135] But the expenses, down to such details as extra funds for feeding the elephants,[136] were handled by the Board of Revenue.

Ts'ao Yin was lucky to get a post as controller of the sixth class, for in 1684, only about ten years after his appointment, it was decreed that in future only bannermen holding hereditary office or men who had passed the military *chin-shih* degree should be selected for this office.[137] As controller, Ts'ao Yin may have been employed in any of the subdepartments of the Imperial Equipage Department, since "controllers of the sixth class were not given specific appointments but were kept on call for jobs that needed doing." [138] The controllers had to keep their attention on their work, for they could forfeit six months' salary if any collisions or mishaps occurred in their section of the processions, nine months' salary if they lost any of the insignia in their care, and one year's salary if they covered up the fact than an official had hired substitutes to march in a procession in his place.[139] Ts'ao Yin apparently avoided these pitfalls, and was promoted. He may have sat for one of the special examinations held by the Department, the results of which were confidentially transmitted to the Board of War and the Board of Civil Office, who in turn submitted them to the Emperor.[140]

134. *HTSL,* pp. 18,156–57 (ch. 1109, pp. 6–9). This is in the year 1748 and may be more lavish than K'ang-hsi period parades, though the statutes show no great changes in organization since the 1670s.

135. Ibid., p. 18,150 (ch. 1108, pp. 10b–11).

136. *Hu-pu tse-li* (1874), ch. 92, p. 20.

137. *HTSL,* p. 18,150 (ch. 1108, p. 11).

138. Ibid., p. 18,149 (ch. 1108, p. 9b).

139. Ibid., pp. 18,152–53 (ch. 1108, pp. 15–16).

140. Ibid., p. 18,152 (ch. 1108, p. 15). There were also quotas for bondservants to take the civil service examinations within the normal Manchu quotas. An edict of 1733 ordered that Upper Three Banner bondservants be removed from the Manchu quotas and placed in the Chinese *han-chün* quotas. *PCTC* (1795), ch. 102, p. 12. This is an example of the growing pressures for office building up in the Banner system by the Yung-cheng period.

On the basis of Chang Po-hsing's eulogy mentioned above, it is most likely that Ts'ao Yin went as an assistant section chief in the third subdepartment, the *chung-so,* which had two sections, dealing with pennons and flags.[141] These flags were known as *fan,* and two assistant section chiefs, who were in charge of four dragon-head *fan* and four leopard's-tail *fan,* marched in the processions to the Three Great Sacrifices, in which the Emperor traveled in his "jade coach" with seven elephants before.[142] In the third subdepartment alone there were over five hundred menials whose duty it was to accompany the carriages and carry the insignia.[143] So it was perhaps in one of these splendid processions to the Temple of Heaven, at the head of his own detachment, that Chang Po-hsing portrayed his friend: Ts'ao Yin at twenty, striding out proudly with his sable hat on his head and a quiverful of feathered arrows on his back, the banners flying behind him.

While Ts'ao Yin was employed in the Imperial Equipage Department, the captain of the third bondservant company in the fifth battalion of the bondservant section of the Plain White Banner was dismissed.[144] This was the post that Ts'ao Yin's uncle Ts'ao Erh-cheng had once held, and now Ts'ao Yin himself was appointed to fill the vacancy. At times in the Ch'ing dynasty bondservant company captains came under the control of the chamberlains of the Imperial Bodyguard; [145] but between the years 1674 and 1695 they were controlled entirely by the ministers of the Imperial Household,[146] and so Ts'ao Yin became an official in that organization.

It was in service in the Household, either directly in one of its departments, or indirectly as an agent of the Emperor, that Ts'ao Yin

141. *HT,* pp. 0840–41 (ch. 83, pp. 16b–17). *BH* 120.

142. *HT,* p. 0837 (ch. 83, p. 9).

143. Ibid., p. 0841 (ch. 83, p. 17). The menials were the *min-yü* who worked with the insignia, and the *ch'i-yü* who worked with the carriages; cf. *HTSL,* p. 18,161 (ch. 1109, pp. 16–17).

144. *PCTC,* ch. 5, p. 41. The date of the dismissal is not given.

145. *ling shih-wei nei-ta-ch'en, BH* 98.1.

146. *tsung-kuan nei-wu-fu ta-ch'en, BH* 76. To be exact, it was not the *ch'i-ku tso-ling* themselves who came under *shih-wei* control, but the *hu-chün* (Guards Division privates, *BH* 734) attached to each *ch'i-ku tso-ling.* This must have made an unsatisfactory division of command, and the arrangement was abolished in 1674. But by 1695 this earlier system was reverted to, perhaps because the soldiers needed military rather than mainly civil discipline. *HTSL,* pp. 19,046–47 (ch. 1201, pp. 1–2).

was to spend the whole of the rest of his life. The term "Imperial Household," the common translation of *nei-wu-fu*,[147] is not really adequate; a nearer translation would be the "Emperor's personal bureaucracy," since this would show more clearly the scope of this large and complex organization. In the context, the *nei* means "pertaining to the Emperor," rather than being literally "inner" as in "the inner palaces" or "the inner city"; and *nei-wu-fu* is thus the "Bureau for managing the Emperor's affairs." These "affairs" of course extended far beyond the Emperor's immediate household.

The Imperial Household was a self-contained bureaucracy, "in charge of the receipt and allocation of all the wealth and resources of the Imperial Household, and of sacrifices, state feasts, fine food, clothes, and of making rewards and punishments, of maintenance, and of education." [148] The ministers of the Household were described as "being in charge of the administration of the bondservants of the Upper Three Banners, and managing the palaces and the Forbidden City." [149] They selected and promoted their own staff, the Emperor choosing the highest officers, and the Six Boards had no say in their affairs.[150]

In Ts'ao Yin's time there were six main departments within the Imperial Household, which dealt with the imperial treasures of bullion, fur, and silk; the imperial hunts; court ceremonial, and the pasturage on Banner lands; the accounts and rents from imperial land leased to the bannermen; the maintenance of royal properties; and discipline and justice.[151] All of these departments had been reorganized in 1677 with complete staff and their own official seals. In 1684 a seventh department was added to deal exclusively with pasturage, which prior to this had been concurrently managed by the Ceremonial Department.[152] For some reason this new department remained semi-independent until 1723 when it came under Imperial Household control. With this exception, the reorganization of 1677 became the set form for the remainder of the dynasty, though there were dozens of minor changes in personnel.

147. *BH* 77.
148. *HT* (1732), ch. 226, p. 1.
149. *HT*, p. 0905 (ch. 89, p. 1).
150. As is explicitly stated in *HT*, p. 0906 (ch. 89, p. 3).
151. *HTSL*, pp. 18,749–54 (ch. 1170), for histories of the various departments. As listed in *HTSL* they are *BH* 77, 80, 79, (83), 78, 82, and 81.
152. *HTSL*, pp. 18,752–53 (ch. 1170, pp. 8–9).

Besides these major departments there were all the smaller offices that dealt with specific areas—armories, stud farms, gardens and parks, the various palaces inside Peking or in Jehol, temples, libraries, dispensaries, butteries, and the imperial mausoleums at Mukden.[153] In nearly every office there were numbers of changes made in organization and personnel which show that the Imperial Household bureaucracy was kept constantly under review. The time of greatest administrative change was between 1661 and 1677, from the death of the Shun-chih Emperor to the attainment of a successful working system. Eunuch control was ended, and the places were filled by Upper Three Banner bondservants at the lower levels, and by princes or members of the Imperial Bodyguard at the top. The K'ang-hsi reign was the high point of Imperial Household independence; as early as the 1720s the Boards began to assume some control over its affairs.[154] The Chinese historian Meng Sen has pointed out how entirely different this K'ang-hsi system was from that existing in the Ming palaces, which were controlled by eunuchs. The Manchu Imperial Household was based on earlier tribal principles and (with the exception of the thirteen-yamen interlude from 1654–61) run according to military law, often by military men.[155]

Ts'ao Yin's new post as a bondservant company captain is a good example of Meng Sen's point. The organizational form of the Upper Three Banners in the Imperial Household was decided in 1644, immediately after the Manchus entered China.[156] In each of the three

153. Ibid., pp. 18,755–73 (ch. 1171–72).

154. A good case study is the *feng-ch'en-yüan*, Bureau of Imperial Gardens and Hunting Parks (*BH* 90), as described in *HTSL*, pp. 18,758–62 (ch. 1171, pp. 7–16). First managed by an early version of the *tu-yü-ssu*, Department of the Household Guard and the Imperial Hunt (*BH* 80), it was given over to eunuch control in 1656, on the grounds that it was concerned with forbidden areas. It was put under joint Imperial Guards and Imperial Household control, an obvious compromise, in 1671, before being returned in 1677 to the newly reorganized *tu-yü-ssu*. But even then there was further compromise, and Imperial Guards and Imperial Household continued to run it jointly. In 1684 it was reformed as the *feng-ch'en-yüan* and given a seal that was to be held by an Imperial Household minister. In 1726 it was decided that in future *feng-ch'en-yüan* vacancies must be reported to the Board of Civil Office, who would select candidates to fill the vacancies. This assumption of Board control shows a weakening of Imperial Household autonomy.

155. Meng Sen, *PCCTKS*, p. 376.

156. Before this date they may have been loosely organized in a similar way (and of course the Plain White Banner only became truly the Emperor's after Dorgon's disgrace). The *HTSL*, p. 12,232 (ch. 543, p. 26), records that the *nei-kuan-ling* (who equal *pao-i-ta*, palace overseers) were organized in the *nei-wu-fu* before the conquest, though there were only

Banners were placed three Manchu bondservant captains (*pao-i tso-ling*) and four other captains (*ch'i-ku tso-ling*).[157] The Ts'ao family were registered under one of the latter, and it was one of these companies that members of the family later commanded. The phrase *ch'i-ku* in fact seems to have been coterminous with the Chinese nationality of the officeholders, for a check through the names of the *ch'i-ku* captains shows that nearly every one has an ordinary Chinese name, whereas nearly all the *pao-i tso-ling* have Manchu names.[158]

Each *ch'i-ku* captain, regardless of how many actual bondservants were in his company, was also in command of fifty cavalrymen of the first class (*ma-chia*).[159] He also had six corporals[160] to help with discipline. In 1661 each captain was allotted one lieutenant to be his second-in-command.[161] There were also privates from the Guards Division (*hu-chün*), ten for each company. As was the case with the six departments of the Imperial Household, major reorganization took place in 1677. Each of the Imperial Household Upper Three Banners was divided into five battalions (*ts'an-ling*) in the care of two colonels.[162] At this time, when Ts'ao Yin was a captain, the organization remained simple and practical. The only reform that might have affected him was one in 1684, fixing that each captain should command eighty cavalrymen.[163] In the 1680s the whole process of grad-

four of them. This seems quite inadequate for the probable numbers of bondservants at that time, and there must have been many who were outside the Household organization who were brought in in 1644, the same being true of *pao-i* and *ch'i-ku tso-ling*.

157. Either *HTSL*, p. 12,232, is in error here, or *PCTC*, ch. 3, pp. 36–38b, for the latter has only three *ch'i-ku tso-ling* in the Bordered Yellow Banner dated early, then one in 1678, and two in 1695. The statutes are more likely to have back-dated the 1678 company.

158. Some random correlations are: Ch'en Ping-heng (*PCTC*, 3/38b and *PCST*, 74/4b, Manchu Bordered Yellow *ch'i-ku tso-ling* and Chinese *pao-i*), Kao Kuo-yüan (*PCTC*, 5/41 and *PCST*, 76/10, Manchu Plain White *ch'i-ku tso-ling* and Chinese *pao-i*), and Cheng Lien (*PCTC*, 5/41 and *PCST*, 77/6b, Manchu Plain White *ch'i-ku tso-ling* and Chinese *pao-i*). Also Ts'ao Yin, Kao Pin, and T'ang Ying, listed in the first part of this chapter. Naturally many Chinese took Manchu names, but cross checks back from *pao-i tso-ling* in *PCTC* not listed in *PCST* support the general conclusion that more *pao-i tso-ling* were Manchus.

159. This round number of fifty *ma-chia* per *ch'i-ku tso-ling* was fixed in 1644. At the same time the arrangements for Manchu *pao-i tso-ling* were more flexible—each had one *ma-chia* for every two bondservants in his company. Thus the largest companies, which presumably had the largest resources, controlled the most regular troops. *HTSL*, p. 19,046 (ch. 1201, p. 1).

160. *ling-ts'ui*, BH 729.

161. *hu-chün hsiao*, BH 734A. *HTSL*, p. 12,232 (ch. 543, p. 26).

162. Ibid., one colonel being *hu-chün ts'an-ling* and one *hsiao-ch'i ts'an-ling*.

163. *HTSL*, p. 19,047 (ch. 1201, p. 2).

ually swelling out practical command groups with sinecures and redundant postings had only just begun;[164] as the dynasty progressed
the system grew increasingly impractical and unwieldy.[165]

Despite this military-looking and -sounding organization, Ts'ao
Yin's basic duties were purely administrative.[166] He had to check the
family registrations of all those in his company, down to the unemployed supernumeraries. He had to receive and distribute their salaries
in rice and silver, arrange for the issuing of special awards at weddings
and funerals. Family allowances had to be paid out to widows, orphans, and those who were unemployed and childless, at the rate of
one ounce of silver a month, with an extra ounce every quarter for
buying rice, and the captain was responsible for assessing the genuine-
ness of all hardship claims and submitting them to the proper office in
the Imperial Household. He kept inventories of all equipment, arranged regular inspections of weapons, and once every five years had
to prepare his company for a full inspection conducted by an official
specially appointed by the Emperor. Lastly he had to keep some three
hundred sets of water pipes and other fire-fighting equipment in good
repair.[167]

Each of the Three Upper Banners in the Imperial Household was on
duty for one month in rotation. During his two months not on specific palace duties, Ts'ao Yin attended to his company. When his Banner was on duty, he might have been engaged either in more administrative work connected with the Imperial Household, or in guarding
one of the palaces and accompanying the Emperor on his tours, or in
training horses and cavalry. These were the different roles portioned
out among the three Household Brigades, among which the different
bondservant companies were divided,[168] so that there were in fact
nine distinct units within the Upper Three Banners of the Imperial
Household: for the Brigades cut across Banner lines but the Banners
were appointed in rotation.

It is most likely that Ts'ao Yin was in the second Brigade, the Impe-

164. For instance with the appointment of fifteen "acting-colonels" in 1681. HTSL,
p. 12,233 (ch. 543, p. 27).

165. Cf. the regulations under both the Board of War and the Imperial Household sections
of HTSL cited above: p. 12,233 (ch. 543, p. 27) and p. 19,047 (ch. 1201, p. 2).

166. Based on pao-i tso-ling duties, HT, pp. 0961–62 (ch. 95, pp. 6b–7).

167. All these duties are in ibid.

168. HT, p. 0960 (ch. 95, p. 4). BH 97A, B, C.

rial Guards,[169] who guarded the palaces and formed the Emperor's retinue when he traveled, supplementing the elite forces of the Imperial Bodyguard.[170] Since Ts'ao Yin's youngest brother Ts'ao I rose to be a colonel in this same Brigade [171] and was a *ch'i-ku* captain in an extension of what had been Ts'ao Yin's company,[172] it is probable that the company was seconded to this Brigade.

In this Brigade, too, Ts'ao Yin would have had the chance to practice his archery. Mounted archery was a Manchu speciality; there was even a special school for the crack archers of the Upper Three Banners,[173] and Ts'ao Yin's skill at this difficult art, mentioned in Chang Po-hsing's eulogy, may have brought him preferment. In the Imperial Guards he would have had a chance to join in the great imperial hunts which the K'ang-hsi Emperor led the bannermen on with such gusto. As a Chinese contemporary wrote:

> Every year in autumn and winter they had hunting exercises beyond the borders. Private soldiers, commanders, and captains were divided into groups to follow the Emperor on the hunts. These hunts were in fact a cover for military maneuvers.[174]

In the early Manchu dynasty it was unlikely that an excellent mounted archer in a Banner command position would have had a purely sedentary job. An early poem of Ts'ao Yin's shows him at Ku-pei-k'ou, a town by the Great Wall in northern Chihli through which the Emperor used to pass on his way to the northern hunting grounds, and where he paused on occasion to inspect his troops and to shoot pheasant and quail. In the poem Ts'ao Yin contrasts the frontier scenery, as typified by the little town of Wo-niu on a tributary of the Yellow River in northern Shensi, with the softer views of Shan-chou in central China:

> "At Ku-pei-k'ou, mid-autumn"

> Blue-green the mountains and white the waters at
> Wo-niu on the Great Wall,

169. The *pao-i hu-chün ying*, listed in *BH* 97A as *nei hu-chün ying*; the meaning is identical.

170. *shih-wei*, *BH* 99.

171. *PCST*, ch. 74, p. 8b.

172. *PCTC*, ch. 5, p. 41.

173. *Ch'ing pai lei-ch'ao*, section 22, p. 6.

174. Chin Te-ch'un, *Ch'i-chün chih*, p. 5.

The wide yellow banners fly and countless horses neigh.
At midnight in Shan-chou, viewing the autumn moon
River and mountain blend together, increasing each
other's luster.[175]

There was, of course, a Chinese genre of such "frontier poems";
literati sitting peacefully at home would extol the virtues of land-
scapes they had never seen. Ts'ao Yin, however, might well have written this modest verse when he was in Ku-pei-k'ou, accompanying the
Emperor to the north as a member of his retinue, a captain in the
Plain White Banner attached to the Imperial Guards Brigade. He
would have passed through Shan-chou while taking the land route
from Peking to visit his family in Nanking; Wo-niu he perhaps visited on the Emperor's Western Tour of 1683. Certainly Ts'ao Yin's
love of mountain scenery was sincere; elsewhere he wrote of it in un-
affected terms:

The border mountains stand out like clean-drawn eyebrows,
Washed by the rain their cover of foliage glistens.
When I arrived, summer was newly over;
The rocky track coiled round the lofty peaks,
A fresh breeze swept the scattered clouds,
And glinting mist brightened the face of autumn.[176]

Ts'ao Yin was a captain in his Banner, young and successful and
probably personally known to the Emperor, who might have got to
know him during his palace work—the bondservant yamen was inside
the Forbidden City [177]—or for his skill in the hunt and at archery, or
because he had been received in audience on his appointments, or be-

175. *Ts'ao Yin Shih*, ch. 1, p. 11b. The poem is also included in the anthology by Hsü
Shih-ch'ang, *Wan-Ch'ing i-shih hui*, printed in *Ch'ing shih hui* [Collected Poems of the
Ch'ing dynasty] (Taipei, 1961), vol. 2, ch. 50, p. 8.

Wo-niu was northwest of Fu-ku-hsien in northern Shensi; Shan-chou was the T'ang name
for P'u-yang-hsien, which during the Ch'ing period was part of Ta-ming-fu in southern
Chihli. (Cf. Liu Chün-jen, *Chung-kuo ti-ming ta tz'u-tien* (Peiping, 1930), pp. 783, 623,
981, and 626. The Emperor's activities in Ku-pei-k'ou are described by Father Gerbillon in
Du Halde, *History of China*, 4, 358.

176. *Ts'ao Yin Shih*, ch. 1, p. 2. For the Western Tour, cf. *Shih-lu*, ch. 107, p. 17b through
ch. 108, p. 2. The Emperor did not get beyond the Wu-t'ai-shan area in Shansi, but some
of his troops may have gone on to Fu-ku-hsien.

177. *Yung-hsien lu*, p. 67, mentions the position of the *pao-i* yamen in describing officials
privileged to ride into the Forbidden City.

cause his mother was the Emperor's affectionately remembered nurse. It was at this time that he had the best chance in his life of throwing off the family bondservant status; for though bondservants were technically the princes' or Emperor's slaves in perpetuity, they could occasionally be given their freedom.

There seem to have been three main ways in which this was effected. Firstly, one of the women from a bondservant company could become an imperial concubine, and in gratitude for service rendered, the Emperor could then free the members of her family. This happened in 1735 to the Kao family, who had been Bordered Yellow Banner bondservants, and in 1734 to the Ch'en family of the same Banner.[178] Later in the eighteenth century the famous official Chin Chien was removed from the bondservant registers partly because of his own successful career but mainly, one suspects, because his sister bore the Emperor Ch'ien-lung three sons.[179]

Secondly, those who had been enslaved at the end of the Ming dynasty could be freed on humanitarian grounds. This apparently happened to many of the earliest captured Chinese, who were made members of the regular Chinese Banners after they had been captured and enslaved.[180] A number of edicts during the seventeenth century directed that Chinese slaves of Manchus be returned to the registers as free men.[181]

Thirdly, a large number of bondservants were reallocated during shuffles of personnel within the Banner system, and since those affected were often ch'i-ku captains, Ts'ao Yin might have gained his freedom in this way. In the first century of the Ch'ing dynasty, at least eight

178. PCST, ch. 74, pp. 3 and 4b.

179. Ch'ing pai lei-ch'ao, section 27, p. 87. Eminent Chinese, p. 159. It could be extremely dangerous to use a family concubine to bring pressure on the Emperor. In Shang yü pa-ch'i [The Emperor Yung-cheng's Edicts to the Eight Banners], ts'e 4, p. 69, there is a furious edict to those trying to save the family of Acina (Yin-ssu). The concubine, his mother, had been extremely ambitious, said the Emperor, ending with a typically sarcastic flourish: "If among them there is a single man who again makes reckless proposals that might stir up trouble among the people, and I hear about it, the whole clan shall be executed. Send down this edict to them, and see if they have anything further to say." Acina's mother had been the commonborn concubine of the K'ang-hsi Emperor (Eminent Chinese, p. 926).

180. Ch'ing pai lei-ch'ao, section 22, p. 6. This may be what is referred to in An Outline History of China (Peking, 1958), p. 185: "Hongtaichi Nurhachu's son who succeeded him, released the Han from the status of slaves and organized them into civilian households to be administered by Han officers," i.e. put surplus slaves and pao-i into the han-chün.

181. HTSL, pp. 18,213–19 (ch. 1116, pp. 1–14).

new companies in the Lower Five Banners [182] and ten companies in the Upper Three Banners [183] were formed from the surplus men in various bondservant companies being joined with other surplus men from the regular Banners, and often the new commander was a former bondservant captain. Ten *pao-i* and *ch'i-ku* captains are listed as having been transferred into the regular Banners, often with the rank of regular captain in a new company.[184] Bondservant captains who had spent three years of service in Liao-ning could be made full captains.[185] Six bondservant captains in the Upper Three Banners are described simply as having been "removed from the bondservant registers." [186]

That Ts'ao Yin did not achieve freedom from bondservant status as these men did may have been due as much to luck as was the family's first capture. For the company he commanded did not have surplus men, and though his mother was a favorite, no woman in the family was made an imperial concubine. So it was that after his period as a bondservant company captain he was appointed to yet another administrative job in the Imperial Household, this time as a department director in the Judicial Department.[187] This was one of the six main departments in the Imperial Household, which dealt with criminal cases involving members of the Upper Three Banners.[188] As with his earlier appointments, the date Ts'ao Yin took up this new one is unknown. It cannot have been later than about 1687, for otherwise he would not have had the time to prove his administrative abilities before being promoted to his first important post—as Soochow textile commissioner—in 1690. That he held this judicial post at all is only proved by a fortunate coincidence that two sources supplement each other. Chang Po-hsing wrote that after being a captain Ts'ao Yin was

182. References in PCTC, 7/9b, 7/12, 8/31b, 8/32, 8/33b, 9/7, 9/16b, 9/23b.

183. PCTC, 3/26b, 3/31 (two men), 3/31b, 4/18, 4/24, 4/32, 5/24, 5/27, 5/34b.

184. Ibid., 3/38b, 4/34, 4/34b, 4/36, 4/38b, 4/39b, 5/38, 5/41, 9/31b, 9/35b.

185. *Ch'in-ting chung-shu cheng-k'ao (pa-ch'i)* [On the military Affairs of China, Eight Banners], compiled by Pao Ning (1808 ed. in 32 *chüan*), ch. 4, p. 18.

186. *ch'u pao-i chi.* PCTC, 3/36, 3/37b, 4/34, 4/36 (two men), 4/38b. PCST, ch. 56, p. 15, has another example.

187. *shen-hsing-ssu lang-chung*, BH 81.

188. HT, p. 0959 (ch. 95, p. 1). BH 81 says that this Department dealt with cases relating to the Imperial Clan Court. This is an error. HTSL, p. 5191 (ch. 10, p. 1), records that the Imperial Clan Court settled its own minor cases, and requested special edicts in all cases that called for severe penalties.

promoted to *lang-shu* (the office of a department director, *lang-chung*),[189] and a local history records that Ts'ao Yin had been the *"nei hsing-pu shih-lang."* [190] The *nei hsing-pu,* "Imperial Household Board of Punishment," clearly refers to the Judicial Department. But *shih-lang,* senior vice-president of a Board with rank 2A, is meaningless here; so Chang Po-hsing's *lang-chung* fills the gap.

Ts'ao Yin was one of three department directors in the Judicial Department; they had a staff of six assistants and fourteen clerks,[191] and directed the Police Bureau,[192] which was responsible for cases involving eunuchs. The Judicial Department did not have very wide powers. It could pass judgment and apply the penalties in all cases meriting a punishment of 100 blows or less; in such cases Department personnel did the actual beating. It had charge of the prisons for minor offenders, and had to make sure that men and women were kept in separate cells.[193] Basic rations were stipulated and had to be distributed fairly; in the hottest summer months each prisoner was entitled to two lumps of ice per day in addition to his food.[194] Furthermore, the prisoners' condition had to be checked, and those seriously ill were to be treated by a doctor sent from the Board of Punishments.[195]

But in every serious matter, the Department had to request guidance from above. Board of Punishments' personnel were brought in when it was necessary to question prisoners under torture, and their coroners came to investigate all murders.[196] The Three High Courts of Judicature took over all cases in which the death penalty was recommended. And all cases had to be tried in accordance with the existing codes of the Board of War and the Board of Civil Office.[197]

189. *HLMHC,* p. 388.

190. Ibid., pp. 231–32, citing Shang-Chiang gazetteer, and the problem is further discussed in *HLMHC,* p. 43.

191. Establishment of 1655. *HTSL,* p. 18,754 (ch. 1170, pp. 11b–12).

192. *fan-i ch'u,* BH 81.

193. *HT,* p. 0959 (ch. 95, p. 1).

194. *HT* (1732), ch. 131, p. 12. The ice suggests the grilling heat of the cells rather than epicureanism. With the passionate attention to unenforceable detail that characterizes much of the statutes, it was on record that the palace overseers should ensure that in the five ice stores there were 29,226 pieces of ice. Ibid., ch. 132, p. 21b.

195. Ibid., ch. 131, p. 12.

196. *HTSL,* p. 19,149 (ch. 1212, p. 2b), edict of 1661.

197. Ibid., p. 19,148 (ch. 1212, p. 1), edict of 1672. The three high courts were the *san-fa-ssu,* BH 215.

There was thus little room for initiative, and apparently there were not even very many duties, since several posts on the Department staff were abolished as redundant.[198] So that even if Ts'ao Yin "conducted the accounting and recording in a most devoted manner" as Chang Po-hsing assured posterity,[199] he still had a great deal of leisure time. This leisure time Ts'ao Yin passed most agreeably among his literary friends in Peking.

198. *HTSL*, p. 18,754 (ch. 1170, p. 12), in 1698, 1699, 1722.
199. In his eulogy, *HLMHC*, p. 388.

CHAPTER 2

Peking and Soochow, Poetry and Society

For fifteen years Ts'ao Yin lived in Peking, a bondservant employed in the Imperial Household and the Imperial Equipage Department. On duty, he lived and worked as a Manchu, serving in the great imperial processions, riding and shooting on the imperial hunts beyond the Great Wall. But off duty he formed part of a wide circle of Chinese friends who wrote poems together and strolled in the countryside in true literati tradition.

These disparate modes of existence do not seem to have troubled him at all. Far from being torn between allegiance to Manchu and Chinese modes, Ts'ao Yin made a harmony of the two, writing poems on the hunt and the strolls. His friends responded by praising him in terms of both worlds, the martial and the aesthetic. Many of the elderly Chinese scholars who came to Peking to take the special *po-hsüeh hung-ju* examination of 1679 became his friends, attracted either by his youth or talent, or perhaps by his father's money, since the Ts'ao family kept a lavish establishment in the capital.

The death of his father Ts'ao Hsi in 1684 seems to have made no immediate difference to Ts'ao Yin's career or way of life. But it did increase his literary reputation, since he had the happy idea of perpetuating his father's memory through the circulation of a series of albums, to which leading scholars and painters would contribute. The response was gratifying, and Ts'ao Yin collected essays and poems and paintings from many of the most famous scholars of the K'ang-hsi reign. Some of these scholars, though not active Ming loyalists, were nostalgic for the fallen dynasty and refused office in the new one; they responded to Ts'ao Yin because he offered them friendship and probably financial assistance also.

In 1690, Ts'ao Yin was sent south as textile commissioner (*chih-*

tsao) of Soochow. There he was a part of the literary circle gathered around the eminent scholar Yu T'ung, and drank and wrote with the local literati. This group included men who were officials of some stature, but also obscure scholars of whom no trace remains besides their names in the dedication to some poem. Yet they all clearly had things in common, interest and background and way of life, and might be properly termed a local elite. Even a rapid examination of this society —of the distribution of offices between bannermen and Chinese, for instance, or Ts'ao Yin's usage of the term *hsiang-shen* ("gentry"), or the number of students of the Imperial Academy (*chien-sheng*) appointed as district magistrates—shows how much it differs from accepted accounts of Ch'ing society in general. For this reason it seems worth attempting a definition of the upper class in China at this time, as a prelude to examining Ts'ao Yin's cultural and social life in Peking and Soochow.

The Upper Class

Broad criteria for membership in the Chinese upper class, as in the upper classes of other societies, may be seen as being the possession of such characteristics as prestige, political power, personal influence, functionally important occupation, substantial economic resources, advanced education, and leisure to engage in cultural pursuits.[1] This is by no means to deny the crucial role of bureaucratic office in China, nor the importance of passing the civil-service examinations as a generally necessary prelude to obtaining such office. Indeed it is evident from the above list of criteria that in China the attainment of substantive office, bringing with it prestige, power, wealth, and leisure, almost automatically made a man a member of the upper class, which of course was not necessarily true in other societies.

In attempting to describe this Chinese upper class, I start with a definition by Richard Centers:

> Classes are psycho-social groupings, something that is essentially subjective in character, dependent upon class-consciousness (i.e. a feeling of group membership), and class lines of cleavage may or

1. Adapted from Gösta Carlsson, *Social Mobility and Class Structure*, Lund Studies in Sociology, 1 (Lund, 1958), 11–12. Carlsson takes off from Richard Centers' distinctions between class and strata.

may not conform to what seem to social scientists to be logical lines of cleavage in the objective or stratification sense.[2]

What Centers is doing here is to insist on a clear distinction between stratum and class:

> Social and economic groupings and categories of people distinguished on the basis of occupation, power, income, standard of living, education, function, intelligence or other criteria are easily and properly denoted by the terms stratum and strata.[3]

Ts'ao Yin's life and career certainly point to the existence of this "feeling of group membership"; as a young man in Peking he was socially accepted by certain men, just as later in Soochow he could accept others. But in Ts'ao Yin's time, though it is clear that China was not a classless society—poor peasants and senior officials, to give an extreme example, lived in qualitatively different worlds, one of which was obviously lower class and one obviously upper class—it is still hard to draw a precise line below which a minor official was no longer a member of the upper class, or a precise line above which a peasant with some education ceased to be a member of the lower class. Furthermore I agree with Centers that narrow groupings are often better denoted as strata: in the Chinese context a licentiate's degree or an income of 200 taels a year or the holding of a title of nobility are inadequate criteria for determining precise class membership. Yet on the other hand, because of the peculiar nature of Chinese society, bureaucratic function above a certain level does seem to have played a decisive role in ensuring membership in the upper class.

For this reason, I break the Chinese upper class into four elites. The word "elite" is used in the specific sense of "functional, mainly occupational, groups which have high status (for whatever reason) in a society," and it is intended that the word connote superiority.[4] Two of these elites, the Chinese official elite and the Banner elite, are defined precisely in terms of office held; one, the imperial elite, is defined more in terms of power; and one, the local elite, is defined most broadly of all in terms of attitudes.

2. Richard Centers, The Psychology of Social Classes (Princeton, Princeton University Press, 1949), p. 27.
3. Ibid.
4. T. B. Bottomore, Elites and Society (London, 1964), pp. 8 and 12.

Firstly, the Chinese official elite, which I define as comprising all Chinese, not bannermen, who held substantive posts in the civil and military bureaucracies of the seventh rank and above. Secondly, the Banner elite, defined as comprising all members of Manchu, Chinese, and Mongol Banners with the rank of company captain (*tso-ling*) and above, or holding substantive posts in the civil and military bureaucracies of the seventh rank and above. Thirdly, the imperial elite, defined as comprising those imperial clansmen, bondservants, or eunuchs who because of imperial favor or special appointments were placed in terms of parity with members of the Chinese official elite and the Banner elite. Fourthly, the local elite, defined as comprising those Chinese and Manchus who, not being members of the Chinese official elite, the Banner elite, or the imperial elite, nevertheless, because of family ties with those elites, or private sources of wealth, or excellence in some speciality, or the attainment of examination and purchased degrees, or the holding of hereditary ranks, were able to lead a life of comparative leisure, and to expect and receive favorable treatment from the members of those elites. Within each elite there were various strata, based on determinants such as rank or wealth.

Using the same definitions, it follows that the ruling group was composed of the Emperor, the Chinese official elite, the Banner elite, and the imperial elite.

Ts'ao Yin, though a bondservant, was a member of the upper class. This appears obvious from his style of life, his education, his friends, and his tastes, though he never took an examination, nor held posts in the regular bureaucracy; he was a member of the upper class by virtue of his position in the imperial elite. His grandson, the novelist Ts'ao Chan, was also a member of the upper class, although his family had been bankrupted and dismissed from all official positions, and he never obtained a degree; his talents at poetry and his powerful friends in the ruling group elites assured him of a place in the local elite. A few of Ts'ao Yin's friends in Peking and Soochow were of the Chinese official elite, but most of them were probably of the local elite. The argument is taken from their style of life rather than their degrees. Ho Ping-ti is surely right in his reasoning that in general licentiates and students in the Imperial Academy (*sheng-yüan* and *chien-sheng*) were merely a privileged group among the commoners,[5] and did not become mem-

5. Ho Ping-ti, *The Ladder of Success in Imperial China*, p. 35.

bers of the local elite immediately on receiving their degree. They were not automatically members of the upper class. But it should be added that any young man of an upper-class family who obtained a *sheng-yüan* degree was himself upper class, as he would have been indeed even if he took no degree.

The entire career of Ts'ao Yin, now to be examined, is an example of bureaucratic life outside the regular bureaucracy, of a member of the imperial elite working in cooperation with the Chinese official elite and the Banner elite, and finding social stimulation among the local elite. Yet even though his life was curious, and he was often concerned with performing confidential imperial commissions or sending secret memorials and handling monopolies, it must never be forgotten that he was in the ruling group and comfortably in the upper class.

Ts'ao Yin in Peking

While Ts'ao Yin was living in Peking, from around 1675 until 1690, he held no very important offices and received no lucrative imperial commissions. But his grandfather had been Chekiang salt controller, and his father was Nanking textile commissioner, and the money that the family had accumulated permitted Ts'ao Yin to live in considerable style.

As a bondservant, Ts'ao Yin lived and worked inside the Imperial City; this was the walled area lying in the heart of the Inner City. In the center of the Imperial City, also surrounded by its own walls, was the Forbidden City where the Emperor lived. Ts'ao Yin's office in the Judicial Department was on the north side of the Imperial City, between the T'ai-yeh lake and the Ti-an gate.[6] The office of the Imperial Household was inside the Forbidden City itself, on the west side,[7] and he must have gone there frequently during his duties as a bondservant company captain. To outsiders he must have seemed very near the sources of power.

Ts'ao Yin's Banner, the Plain White, was allocated the area due east of the Imperial City.[8] As no law forbade bondservants from buying property, it might have been somewhere in this section of the Inner City that the Ts'ao family bought their first property, using the

6. *Tōdō meishō zue,* series 1, ch. 2, p. 1.
7. Ibid., ch. 1, p. 13, near the Hsi-hua gate.
8. Ibid., ch. 3, p. 1, general map of the Inner City and Banner areas. A detailed map of the Plain White Banner area is in ibid., p. 34.

profits from salt and textile administration to buy out an indigent bannerman. It is known that the Ts'ao family had at least two Peking houses, and that they were in the Inner City.[9] This area was inhabited exclusively by the bannermen from 1648 onward, for in that year continuing friction (including murders and looting) between the bannermen and the Chinese had led Dorgon to order all Chinese officials, merchants, and common people to move out to southern Peking.[10] Possibly the houses were former mansions of the Ming imperial family which had been in this area, for though early Banner regulations firmly stated what size house might be lived in by officials of a given rank,[11] the Ts'ao family might have acquired one through Ts'ao Hsi's combination of money and an honorary title of the first rank. Such mansions were of considerable size, with wide courtyards, lofty buildings, and elaborate gateways. Drawing evidence from various writings of the Ts'ao family, the historian Chou Ju-ch'ang places one Ts'ao family house in the northwest, near the Forbidden City, and one in the southeast, near the examination halls.[12] However, all that can be said definitely about the houses is that they had beautiful gardens, and that the garden called the Chih-yüan, containing the Hsi-t'ang pavilion, was especially loved by Ts'ao Yin.[13]

9. *Ts'ao Fu Memorials*, p. 31, in which he lists the family property as of August 4, 1714. It is of course possible that the houses were bought by either Ts'ao Yin or Ts'ao Fu, but since they spent most of their lives in Nanking, the most likely purchaser was Ts'ao Hsi, who was wealthy and did not move to Nanking until 1663.

10. *PCTC* (*1795*), ch. 113, pp. 1–2. An exception was made in the case of those Chinese who had voluntarily attached themselves (as slaves or servants) to one of the eight Banner generals. The Emperor (through Dorgon as regent) regretted the inconvenience that would be caused by the enforced move, but described it as essential to ensure lasting Manchu-Chinese peace. The Chinese were to be allowed to move their houses, or to sell them. All were to be given four taels per room moving allowance, and this money they were to collect in person from the Board of Revenue to prevent the possibility of corruption.

11. Ibid., ch. 113, pp. 2–3. At the same time prices were fixed, from a rate of 120 taels per room for the best mansions, down to 20 taels a room for unclassified houses (in 1652 this lowest price was raised to 30 taels).

12. Inner City houses are described in *HLMHC*, p. 157. The possible locations for the houses of the Ts'ao family are presented by Chou Ju-ch'ang in *HLMHC*, p. 137, after intensive research into the views described in Ts'ao Yin's poems, and descriptive matter drawn from the novel *Hung-lou meng* written by Ts'ao Yin's grandson Ts'ao Chan, which he believes was set literally in Peking. The arguments are ingenious, but not totally convincing.

13. The gardens and their location are discussed in *HLMHC*, pp. 145–51. Chou Ju-ch'ang believes that this garden is the Ta-kuan yüan of the *Hung-lou meng*, which for the purposes of his novel Ts'ao Chan situated at the northern of the two houses, which equals the novelist's Jung mansion.

Though his father was in Nanking, Ts'ao Yin had the company of other members of the family while he was living in Peking. The one he was closest to was his younger brother Ts'ao Tzu-yu. Only scraps of information have survived about this man to whom Ts'ao Yin wrote many affectionate poems.[14] He lived from about 1659 to 1705, and was an officer in the Imperial Bodyguard (shih-wei).[15] He had two literary names (hao), the commonest being Yün-shih, the other Chih-yüan from the family garden of the same name. Ts'ao Tzu-yu was also an accomplished painter; the famous scholar Chu I-tsun wrote a colophon on one of his works which was later in the collection of Weng Fang-kang, a well-known authority on calligraphy and painting in the Ch'ien-lung reign.[16] The Ts'ao family record is so incomplete that it is impossible even to document Ts'ao Yin's generation thoroughly; but besides Ts'ao Yin and Ts'ao Tzu-yu there was a third brother, Ts'ao I. Born about 1680, Ts'ao I was employed in the Imperial Household, and was still alive as a bondservant company captain in the early Ch'ien-lung reign.[17]

14. Ts'ao Yin Shih, ch. 1 and 2. All references are discussed in HLMHC, pp. 59–60.

15. On his age, cf. HLMHC, pp. 61–62. Chou Ju-ch'ang suggests that the two were twins, relying on hints found in contemporary poems. But though the arguments for the existence of this brother are convincing, the twin theory is less so. For had Ts'ao Yin and Ts'ao Tzu-yu been twins, there seems little reason for their contemporaries not mentioning it and using historical and poetical allusions to highlight the fact. The date for Ts'ao Tzu-yu's death is put at 1705 (ibid., p. 62), based on evidence from Ts'ao Yin's poems, and what is apparently a definitive poem of mourning written in 1709.

For Ts'ao Tzu-yu as an officer in the Bodyguard, cf. Yu T'ung, Ken-chai ch'üan-kao wen-chi, ch. 4, p. 26, quoted in HLMHC, p. 258.

16. HLMHC, pp. 30, 60, 223 through 226. For Chu I-tsun, cf. Eminent Chinese, pp. 182–85; for Weng Fang-kang, ibid., pp. 856–58.

17. Ts'ao Yin Memorials, p. 18, dated 47/4/3: "Sun Wen-ch'eng and my younger brother Ts'ao I . . . reached P'u-t'o shan." PCST, ch. 74, p. 8b. PCTC, ch. 5, p. 40, as ch'i-ku captain in a new company formed in 1695. The existence of two brothers is argued convincingly by Chou Ju-ch'ang in HLMHC, p. 59, on the grounds that a Ts'ao I born in 1658 (1660 at the latest) could hardly have been a bondservant company captain and a hu-chün ts'an-ling in 1735 (which he was) aged seventy-five, since such posts were active, not sinecures, and incumbents were retired when no longer active. The real Ts'ao I was probably born about 1680, shortly before Ts'ao Hsi's death.

Using the characters known to have been given by Ts'ao Hsi to his sons Yin and I, Chou Ju-ch'ang guesses the name of the missing "twin" brother as Ts'ao Hsüan. But it seems unsound on the basis of such a discussion alone to accept Ts'ao Hsüan as a historical person (as does Wu Shih-ch'ang, On the Red Chamber Dream, p. 115). The second brother's known tzu of Tzu-yu serves better as a name for him, and the youngest brother can stand as Ts'ao I. Shao Wen, "Chi Lien-t'ing t'u yung chüan," p. 23, clearly rejects Chou Ju-ch'ang, writing firmly "Yün-shih is Ts'ao Yin's brother Ts'ao I," and returning the argument to its starting point.

The fact that Ts'ao Tzu-yu was an officer in the Imperial Body-guard, while Ts'ao Yin was in the Imperial Equipage Department, misled even some of his contemporaries into describing Ts'ao Yin as an officer in the Bodyguard.[18] But it seems likely that if Ts'ao Yin had had such a prestigious post, the fact would have been mentioned openly by close friends such as Chang Po-hsing, who wrote his funeral eulogy.[19] Yet there is little doubt that his brother's being in the Bodyguard brought further luster to the family.

The officers in the Imperial Bodyguard were a group of picked men, who were much closer to the Emperor than ordinary members of the Imperial Household or the Imperial Equipage Department. There were only 570 officers in the Imperial Bodyguard at one time, divided into four classes,[20] and chosen either from the young men in the Upper Three Manchu and Mongol Banners who showed exceptional ability or from members of the Lower Five Banners, including Chinese, who for the duration of their service were divided by lot among the Upper Three Banners.[21] Their general duties were to guard the gates to the Forbidden City and the palaces within it; those showing exceptional zeal were permitted to serve in rotation within the palaces.[22] They accompanied the Emperor on all his travels, were present at all audiences and banquets, accompanied officials submitting memorials, and were divided into sections for the purpose of guarding

18. *Ts'ao Yin Tz'u*, preface by Wang Ch'ao-hsien dated 1713. The problem of whether or not Ts'ao Yin was a *shih-wei* still remains open. Though Wang Ch'ao-hsien did write that in about the year 1680 Ts'ao Yin "being one of those eligible for palace service was made a *shih-wei*" this may not be as definite as it sounds since he was not dealing with Ts'ao Yin's career and would be inclined to exaggerate. Whereas Chang Po-hsing, in writing his funeral eulogy, was summarizing Ts'ao Yin's career and would hardly have ignored one of its major achievements.

19. Chang Po-hsing did mention that Ts'ao Yin tended the leopard's-tail banners; this phrase, with the answering sentence that he strode loftily in sable hat, etc., is not a reference to Ts'ao Yin's membership in some such group as the *pao-wei pan shih-wei*, "Imperial guards wearing the leopard's tail" (*BH* 99.3). Chou Ju-ch'ang cannot decide whether Ts'ao Yin was a *shih-wei* or not. He says that he was in *HLMHC*, p. 216, in the year 1673; yet he omits *shih-wei* from the list of offices held by Ts'ao Yin discussed in ibid., pp. 43–45. Chou Ju-ch'ang reports that Ku Ching-hsing called Ts'ao Yin "*shih-chung*" on one occasion (ibid., p. 222); this was an archaic pre-Yüan dynasty term for *shih-wei*. But it can also mean simply palace official, i.e. member of the *luan-i-wei* or the *nei-wu-fu*.

20. *HT*, p. 0829 (ch. 82, p. 5). *BH* 99 lists the four classes. There were additional groups of Imperial Clan, Chinese, and *pao-wei* guards.

21. *HT*, p. 0827 (ch. 82, p. 1). "By lot" is *ch'e*, an abbreviation of *ch'e-ch'ien*.

22. *HTSL*, p. 18,122 (ch. 1106, p. 1).

the various gates, being given special lists of all officials and confidential servants who might be permitted to enter.[23] They had to be near
the palace at all times, as is shown by a domestic fragment from one of
Ts'ao Yin's memorials to the Emperor, written after his daughter had
married a *shih-wei:* "The Emperor's Bodyguard are coming and going
day and night, and as I was afraid that his dwelling was rather far
away from the palace, I planned to move my son-in-law to a house
outside the Tung-hua gate." [24]

The two brothers Ts'ao Yin and Ts'ao Tzu-yu, the one a bondservant captain in the Imperial Guards and the other an officer in the Imperial Bodyguard, must have journeyed together on some of the Emperor's tours. They may also have been accompanied by the Manchu
poet Singde, who had been given his own company with surplus men
from his father's command and had been made a *shih-wei* by Emperor
K'ang-hsi.[25] Singde was a poet of great brilliance who enjoyed a high
reputation among Chinese scholars before he was twenty-five. It is not
known when he and Ts'ao Yin became friends, but there is evidence
that both of them studied with Hsü Ch'ien-hsüeh, a famous scholar
(and noted Court intriguer).[26] Both of them loved to write *tz'u*
poems and enjoyed considerable reputation in their day.[27] And both
of them profited from the *po-hsüeh hung-ju* examination of 1679 to
extend their acquaintance among the highest strata of the Chinese
scholars of the early Ch'ing.

The *po-hsüeh* examination, an attempt to bring some of the more
aloof Chinese scholars into service under the Manchus, was announced
in 1678.[28] About 150 candidates came to Peking to take the examination, which was held in April 1679. Singde's father Mingju, at this

23. Exact details of the various duties are in *HT*, pp. 0827–32 (ch. 82, pp. 1–12).

24. *Ts'ao Yin Memorials*, p. 19b, dated 48/2/8. The Tung-hua was the southeast gate to
the Forbidden City.

25. *PCTC*, ch. 4, p. 15. Biography of Singde in *Eminent Chinese*, pp. 662–63.

26. *HLMHC*, p. 216, evidence from writings of Han T'an. Biography of Hsü Ch'ien-
hsüeh in *Eminent Chinese*, pp. 310–12.

27. Ts'ao Yin's first collection of poems appeared in 1679, when he was twenty-one,
with a preface by Ku Ching-hsing; the preface is printed at the beginning of *Lien-t'ing
chi.*

28. Preliminaries to the examination, names of candidates, and ranking order of those
successful are given in *HTSL*, pp. 17,527–28 (ch. 1046, pp. 1–3). There is a short essay
on the examination by Hellmut Wilhelm, "The *po-hsüeh hung-ju* Examination of 1679,"
Journal of the American Oriental Society, 71 (1951), 60–66.

time one of the most powerful officials in China, had been friendly to Chinese scholars, and during the examinations Singde acted as host to many of them.[29] So Singde may have been the cause of some of Ts'ao Yin's meetings with his future friends. But it seems that most of these friendships developed after casual encounters. Thus Yu T'ung, who came to Peking at the age of sixty to take the examination, which he passed, met Ts'ao Yin at a friend's house and became an admirer of his poetry.[30] The scholar Shih Jun-chang, recalled from retirement to take the examination, used to murmur one of Ts'ao Yin's poems to himself, and had an especial fondness for the line "In the winter mountains I see the men from afar"; later, Ts'ao Yin used to submit his poems to the old scholar for his criticism.[31] The scholar Ku Ching-hsing, who traveled to Peking for the examination but was unable to take it because of ill health,[32] met Ts'ao Yin soon after arriving in Peking and found him "charming and lively." They became fast friends, and Ku Ching-hsing wrote the preface for the first collection of Ts'ao Yin's poetry, which is dated 1679.[33] Ku also became a close friend of Shih Jun-chang's.[34]

This was the nucleus of a circle that steadily widened. By 1680 Ts'ao Yin was friendly with two more successful candidates of the *po-hsüeh* examination, Chu I-tsun and Ch'en Wei-sung,[35] who had both been made compilers in the Hanlin Academy. A contemporary recalled these days in a preface to another collection of Ts'ao Yin's poems dated 1713, with Ts'ao Yin on duty at the palace with his lance, marching with a leopard's tail flying behind him, or riding out in short jacket and tight leggings to hunt tigers "with the joys of a controlled touch on the taut bow." Then coming off duty, Ts'ao Yin invites the two compilers to write poetry with him and sits there sucking his brush as they pick out the rhymes and select a theme.[36]

29. Cf. *Eminent Chinese*, Mingju, p. 577, Singde, p. 662.

30. *HLMHC*, p. 231.

31. Epilogue to a poem by Mei Keng, quoted *HLMHC*, p. 219; and incident recalled by Shih Jun-chang's grandson, Shih Li, in the preface to a poem written for Ts'ao Yin, ibid., p. 219. Shih Jun-chang's biography is in *Eminent Chinese*, p. 651.

32. *Ch'ing-shih lieh-chuan*, ch. 70, p. 47b.

33. Ts'ao Yin; *Lien-t'ing chi*, first preface by Ku Ching-hsing, dated 1679, fourth month.

34. *Ch'ing-shih lieh-chuan*, ch. 70, pp. 47b–48.

35. *Eminent Chinese*, pp. 182–85 and 103.

36. Ts'ao Yin, *Lien-t'ing tz'u-ch'ao*, preface by Wang Ch'ao-hsien, dated 1713, intercalary fifth month.

Though this passage is allusive and complex in the original, and was written by someone who may not ever have known him in Peking, it still captures the mood these Chinese scholars seem to have shared in their dealings with Ts'ao Yin, and which recur in their writings. They seem to have taken a great delight in the pageantry and exuberance of this extrovert Manchu life. Another friend put these feelings into verse in a poem written for Ts'ao Yin about 1680:

> At the palace with his leopard's tail pennon, easily he sits his prancing horse, a wonderful hero. He is all the more so when he approaches the Sang-kan River, on that endless expanse of sand, when he has just loosed the falcon that will swoop down to the ground.
> The ten thousand horsemen, returning to the camp from the hunt, drink their wine while the evening sun flickers and fades.
> Jade bridles in the wind's roar, engraved bows in the night's cry. The cold soaks his wind-blown hair. Beating the whip while composing a poem, he startles a crow into wheeling away under the frosty moon.[37]

Ts'ao Yin's early life and employment revolved around the palace, the Banners, and the hunt. These hunts were vast affairs, in which thousands of Banner troops took part; the K'ang-hsi Emperor led them in person nearly every autumn, taking a few picked officers to hunt bear and tiger, or else forming great rings of soldiers to beat out and kill stags and hares. The Emperor would sit doggedly in the rain, cooking the newly killed venison over an open fire and sleeping in the chill nights in a simple tent. His entourage perforce did likewise.[38] For Ts'ao Yin's Chinese friends these must have been engaging details, and they accordingly flattered him by writing extravagantly about his hardihood and his martial prowess. Some of their admiration was probably genuine: a century later the poet Yüan Mei could still show "an awed appreciation of bluff, soldierly tales";[39] at the same time

37. Chiang Ching-ch'i, quoted *HLMHC*, p. 223.

38. There is a full description written by the Jesuit Father Gerbillon, who traveled north with the K'ang-hsi Emperor's entourage on the autumn 1692 hunt, printed in Du Halde, *History of China*, 4, 358–80.

39. Arthur Waley, *Yuan Mei*, p. 68.

Yüan was flattered in return by his powerful Manchu friends.[40] This interplay of Chinese and Manchu life is one of the most curious facets of the early Ch'ing dynasty.

Ts'ao Yin appears to have been genuinely Manchu on duty, and genuinely Chinese in his spare time. The two main authorities on the Ts'ao family, Chou Ju-ch'ang and Wu Shih-ch'ang, emphasize the strong Manchu element in the lives of these Imperial Household bond-servants, calling them "in way of life and characteristics indistin-guishable from the Manchus"[41] and "naturalized Manchus";[42] but these seem to be overstatements. In the case of Ts'ao Yin a balance had been attained between the two cultures. It is clear that he flung him-self with passion into the active horse-riding life of the Manchu mili-tary exercises, but also that he was a sensitive interpreter of Chinese culture. He could not offer to the Chinese scholars in Peking any of the hopes of political advancement that they might find in the homes of a Mingju or Singde, for though his family were wealthy members of the imperial elite, there is no evidence that they ever had any real "influence," at least outside their immediate bondservant circle. All he could offer was the sincere interest of a twenty-one-year-old poet in his elders' advice, and lavish hospitality in the family's Peking homes.

What is fascinating about Ts'ao Yin's life at this period is not that he was divided in his loyalties between Chinese and Manchu, but how successfully he made a synthesis of the two. An example is this poem in *shih* form, which Ts'ao Yin wrote in his early twenties. Despite the dutiful reference to his Emperor, and the ambiguous second verse which may be a reference to the rebellion of the Three Feudatories which commenced when Ts'ao Yin was in his teens (1673–74), the real delight in the hunt still comes through:

> When I was a young lad, aged fifteen or sixteen,
> As I grasped my bow and wheeled my horse, all ordinary
> cares were forgotten;
> I gave no thought to using my strength to serve my brilliant
> ruler,

40. Ibid., p. 187.
41. *HLMHC*, p. 129. Though on p. 13, Chou Ju-ch'ang mentions the clash between Manchu and Chinese as one of the tensions in the life of Ts'ao Chan.
42. Wu Shih-ch'ang, *On the Red Chamber Dream*, pp. 63, 109–10.

But longed only to shoot pheasants on the edge of the southern mountains.

South of the mountains the wheat was ripening, but never
reached fullness,
As soon as the green and yellow were joined, they were
quickly picked.
The mountain fields were long in drought and no man
ploughed
As the old cocks called for a mate, strutting in the pale dawn.

One on the mountain peak, advancing and posturing,
One below the summit, deep-red wattles and the strength
of a tiger.
I had no pity for the two cock-pheasants, dying for their
mate,
And thought only of taking fresh aim with my bronze-
toothed crossbow.[43]

Ts'ao Yin left no poems that give details of his northern tours, and
wrote only this one poem that gives his picture of the joys of sport.
Rather than presenting some picture of himself brooding and shiver-
ing at a northern fort, in the conventional genre of Chinese frontier
poems, he seems to have largely ignored the subject. The poem "At
Ku-pei-k'ou, mid-autumn" (quoted earlier), probably written at a
guard post on the Great Wall, is neutral in tone, though Ts'ao Yin
clearly enjoyed the scenery. Only once, as he traveled fairly comfortably from Nanking to Peking in the autumn, did his thoughts turn
northward to those areas where the Emperor was traveling on one of
his hunts:

The Tour has gone to T'ien-shan and beyond.
In the west wind the frosty tents are cold.[44]

It is not clear whether he was nostalgic or glad to be out of it.

Ts'ao Yin wrote several *chüan* of classical *shih,* and later in his life
dozens of these were clearly rattled off on suitable social occasions. But
he also concentrated on the more complex *tz'u* form (at which his

43. *Ts'ao Yin Shih,* ch. 1, p. 3.
44. Ibid., ch. 1, p. 8b.

friend Singde excelled). One of his *tz'u* was chosen by Wang Ch'ang for inclusion in his comprehensive collection of Ch'ing dynasty *tz'u*, printed in 1803.[45] Being included places Ts'ao Yin on the very edge of acceptable poets; at least he was noticed, but the inclusion of one poem only shows that he was not considered a poet of much stature. The poem was to the tune T'ung-hsien-ko, and called "On the San-t'un road, lines written on the Dragon Maid's temple." [46]

> Range upon range the hills spread green, their serpent coils blocking the traveler. The country temple is deserted, chilly, spring passed it by; spread over the wooded vista there is nothing but the myriad lengths of trailing threads, tangled catkins, and mother pigeons calling mournfully in the rain.

> The moon was bright when you left the green waters, and came to our earthly world; how many changing seasons you passed among us mortals! Yet at parting the tears fell on your dragon sleeve, turning your head to that desolate city, where a pale mist bleakly lighted the place that had bruised your heart.

> Let's not worry about the rise and fall of the world's fortunes, but help me with a favorable wind and whip my horse back to the east.[47]

Such a poem translates awkwardly, and it is hard to convey in English the attraction it must have had in the original to a Ch'ien-lung scholar surveying his dynasty's poetic accomplishment. But one of Ts'ao Yin's very early *tz'u* is less opaque: written after he had been strolling through the cheerful chaos of the festival on the fifteenth day of the first month, the first full moon of the Chinese new year, this poem is dated 1682, and the dedication shows that it was written while Ts'ao Yin was in the company of Ch'en Wei-sung, himself a celebrated writer of *tz'u* and a master of the antithetical prose style.[48]

45. Wang Ch'ang's biography is in *Eminent Chinese*, pp. 805–07.

46. The Dragon Maid's story is in E. D. Edwards, *Chinese Prose Literature of the T'ang Dynasty* (London, 1938), pp. 86–94.

47. Included in Wang Ch'ang, *Kuo-ch'ao tz'u-tsung* [The Collected *tz'u* of the Ch'ing Dynasty], *ts'e* 1, ch. 4, p. 2b, printed in *Ssu-pu pei-yao*.

48. *Eminent Chinese*, p. 103. Ts'ao Yin wrote that he was with Chia-ling (*tzu* of Ch'en Wei-sung). Ch'en died this same year.

Ch'en Wei-sung was fifty-six at this time, Ts'ao Yin twenty-three. Both were living in Peking.

> The out-of-towners are just like a flock of ducks, and at every crossroads the girls are bustling. They like to wander, and who should stop them? There may be few sports and playgrounds on earth, but on this day the festive clothes and decorated carts are numberless. Everyone is out strolling in this springtime vanity fair, with their caps awry they crowd me to a standstill; boisterously the pretty girls are playing around, reaching a turn in the road. And everywhere the Liang-chou drums are beating.

> The full moon bursts out above the city walls, whitely translucent, perfect in shape, fresh on the fifteenth day. The city colors and the lantern lights compete in brilliance. Above the streets fish- and dragon-shaped lanterns fly and dance; every single household has put them on display. A candle gutters over scented clothes, but is not yet burnt down; she with dimpled face and pretty hands clasped, tells the story from the beginning. In detail the picture unfolds: a tale of fair women.[49]

These must have been good times for Ts'ao Yin, and other poems round out the picture a little further. On his day off from work he wanders despondently round Peking, the streets almost deserted after a sudden shower of rain; no friends are with him. "One whole day off, and nothing to do; the horses are neighing at their troughs, though outside grass covers the ground. One whole day off, with nowhere to go." Then as he sits mournfully at home there is (predictably) a tap on the door; friends at last, drinking can begin, harmony is restored.[50] Or he goes off to visit his friend Ku Ching-hsing and talk books, not forgetting of course to take the money to buy his share of the wine.[51] Or a group wanders over to the Tz'u-jen temple in the west of Peking, to write yet more poems in honor of the already re-

---

49. Ts'ao Yin, *Li-hsüan tz'u*, pp. 1b–2.
50. *Ts'ao Yin Shih*, ch. 1, p. 10.
51. Ibid., ch. 1, pp. 1b–2.

peatedly immortalized pine tree there, a pastime at which any early Ch'ing scholar with literary pretensions tried his hand.[52]

This contented life was not even shattered when his father died in 1684. For, by rising to the occasion with a splendid display of filial piety, Ts'ao Yin consolidated and assured his reputation among the Chinese scholars of his day.

Conspicuous Filial Piety

While Ts'ao Yin had been living and working in Peking his father, Ts'ao Hsi, had had a long and successful career as textile commissioner of Nanking, a post he held continuously for twenty-one years, from 1663 until 1684 when he died in office.[53] Both Ts'ao Hsi and his wife, a former nurse of the K'ang-hsi Emperor's, had received honorary titles of the first rank.[54] The Emperor came to Nanking in December 1684 on his first Southern Tour and visited the bereaved family in person, presenting them with imperial calligraphy and sending a chamberlain of the Imperial Bodyguard to offer libations.[55] Ts'ao Hsi's name was entered in the Nanking temple of worthy officials, and his funeral eulogy was written by the former Grand Secretary, Hsiung Tz'u-li.[56]

Ts'ao Yin had of course returned south to take care of the funeral arrangements, and by the end of the year he had already embarked on his project to perpetuate his father's memory. What he did was to circulate a series of albums to which leading scholars and painters of the day were invited to contribute. He gave the albums the general name *Lien-t'ing t'u*.[57] The *lien-t'ing* was the pavilion that Ts'ao Hsi had

52. One of the great meeting places for Ch'ing scholars. Chou Ju-ch'ang says that nearly every collection of poems from the early Ch'ing period has some reference to this spot (*HLMHC*, p. 220).

53. *CNTC*, ch. 105, p. 10.

54. *HLMHC*, p. 42.

55. Ibid., p. 227.

56. *Eminent Chinese*, pp. 308–09. Eulogy cited in full in *HLMHC*, pp. 228–30.

57. Four scrolls of commemorative writings and paintings were found by Chou Ju-ch'ang, in a private collection in Peking, in perfect condition. *HLMHC*, pp. 33–34. The contents of the scrolls are printed almost in toto by Chou Ju-ch'ang, according to their known or probable dates of composition, in the *nien-p'u* section of *HLMHC*, pp. 231–300. Some may have beeen written after 1691, for there are twenty-one items without any specific date. The bulk of the items, however, fall within the seven-year period 1684–91. In ibid., p. 34, Chou Ju-ch'ang suggests various names of those who probably wrote on the lost scroll

built in the garden of his commissioner's yamen in Nanking, in the shade of a *lien* tree that he had planted with his own hands.[58] His children had studied there under his direction,[59] and there he loved to relax when off duty.[60] The *lien* tree (known in the West as china-berry or Persian lilac), grows to a height of thirty feet and has a thirty-foot crown spread; with its mauve flowers blooming in summer and its small yellow fruit, it is both exotic and elegant.[61] This, combined with its associations linking both father and children, made it an admirable symbol for the commemorative albums. Once the project was under way, and the name chosen, Ts'ao Yin took Lien-t'ing as his studio name, abandoning the studio name Li-hsüan under which he had written his first poetry.[62]

For the albums to get off to a good start, it was essential for Ts'ao Yin to obtain prestigious names, and in this he succeeded admirably.

(formed from lost albums). The clearest evidence for the existence of such a fifth scroll is given in Yeh Hsieh's essay, cited ibid., p. 248, which is obviously a copy of a work first written for the scrolls and later printed in the author's collection. (Works are cited here according to Chou Ju-ch'ang's listing of the scrolls.)

A special article on the *Lien-t'ing t'u* by Shao Wen, entitled "Chi Lien-t'ing t'u yung chüan," *Wen-wu*, 1963 (no. 6), pp. 23–25, was written for the two-hundredth anniversary of the death of the novelist Ts'ao Chan. Without giving any acknowledgment at all to Chou Ju-ch'ang, Shao Wen repeats many of Chou Ju-ch'ang's findings, though he also adds some interesting details. Shao Wen finds that the present scrolls are in fact composed from an unknown number of albums—the square shape of the paper and the lack of uniformity in the colors of the sheets prove this incontestably. This breaking up of the albums to create scrolls was done not once but twice, for the Ch'ing writer Lu Shih-hua described the contents of the scroll on which Yün Shou-p'ing's painting appeared; his description does not tally at all with the present scroll. If there was such reshuffling of contents, it is probable that even more of the *Lien-t'ing t'u* writings have been lost than was first supposed. The scrolls were possibly in the collection of the Hunan governor Yü Ming-chen, as they bear his seal. Cf. Shao Wen, p. 23.

58. As reported by Ts'ao Yin to Singde, *HLMHC*, p. 234.

59. As described by Yu T'ung, *HLMHC*, p. 234.

60. Yeh Hsieh, cited *HLMHC*, p. 248.

61. The tree is native to southeast Asia but will grow throughout Asia and Australasia. The description is taken from L. D. Pryor, *Trees in Canberra* (Canberra, Department of the Interior, 1962), p. 65; and by observation from Babbage Crescent, Canberra, A.C.T., Australia, which is planted with *lien* trees—*Melia azedarach*. (I am grateful to Helen Spence for this information.)

62. His collected works were called *Lien-t'ing chi*, and so were his compilations, *Lien-t'ing shih-erh chung* etc. But those who had known him in Peking as Li-hsüan continued to address him thus and only slowly adopted the new name; cf. Tu Chieh, introduction to *Lien-t'ing shih-ch'ao*, p. 2.

One of the first to inscribe a memorial essay and poem was Singde,[63] who had long been a friend of the family's. In another album the first writer was Yu T'ung, with whom Ts'ao Yin had become friends in Peking; before his long commemorative poem Yu T'ung wrote a preface:

> As soon as the funeral was over, the filial son sent me a painting. I looked and saw that it was the *lien* tree that his father had planted with his own hand. . . . So I wrote a poem to comfort him in his filial thoughts.[64]

The painting could have been the one by Yün Shou-p'ing, known as one of the "Six Masters" of the early Ch'ing, who made a speciality of detailed paintings of insects and flowers; "in this field he had no equal among his contemporaries." [65] The painting was almost certainly commissioned by Ts'ao Yin, since Yün Shou-p'ing lived by selling his work in order to support his family, which was strongly Ming loyalist. The choice of painter shows Ts'ao Yin's fine taste, for the strong yet delicately detailed paintings of branches in blossom by Yün Shou-p'ing are still immensely impressive,[66] and many of his paintings later found their way into the palace collection where the Emperor Ch'ien-lung wrote an introduction to them.[67] However, in his painting for Ts'ao Yin, Yün Shou-p'ing clearly did not bother to extend himself. A skeletal *lien* tree rises over a small thatched pavilion, and in the foreground bamboos are tossed in the wind. The picture bears no inscription, merely the title "Lien-t'ing t'u" and the painter's name. Yün Shou-p'ing made the minimal gesture consonant with his duty —or with his fee.[68]

63. *HLMHC*, p. 234.

64. Ibid., p. 33, 3rd scroll, 8th name. Cited ibid., p. 231.

65. *Eminent Chinese*, pp. 960–61. The judgment is Fang Chao-ying's, p. 960. Sirén, *Chinese Painting*, 5, 192–200, and 7, 462–66.

66. For example the "Rock and plum blossom" in the collection of Ling Shu-hua, exhibited by the Arts Council of Great Britain, May–July 1964, where I saw it and the other paintings by Ts'ao Yin's friends mentioned below.

67. *Eminent Chinese*, p. 960.

68. The picture is reproduced by Shao Wen, "Chi Lien-t'ing t'u yung chüan," as illustration no. 2, facing p. 22. Shao Wen feels, ibid., p. 25, that the painting is careless and shows both Yün Shou-p'ing's distaste for the idea of contributing at all, and also the power that Ts'ao Yin had in the Kiangsu area that could enable him to get such fine painters to work for him whatever their feelings about the dynasty. The picture that Shao Wen paints of Ts'ao Yin's power as an Imperial Household figure seems definitely

In another of the albums, Yu T'ung wrote in 1691:

> There are pictures on the right and poems on the left. Yin
> brought it to Soochow, with a pile of blank pages a hand thick,
> and said: "Write a poem for me, to continue my book of po-
> etry." I responded "Yes," took up my brush and respectfully
> wrote as follows.[69]

By this time there were many paintings in the growing albums. One
was by Yü Chih-ting, one of the K'ang-hsi Emperor's court painters,
who could, however, be prevailed upon to make paintings for friends,
and also presumably on commission.[70] He was outstanding as a figure
painter, his figures of women especially having great realism and sen-
suality.[71] Another was by Tai Pen-hsiao, one of the "Eight Masters of
Nanking," and a highly imaginative landscape painter,[72] who
painted for Ts'ao Yin a steeply roofed pavilion on the edge of a
stream, sheltering under a *lien* tree in bud. A crane has just crossed the
bridge and walks purposefully toward the pavilion; behind the building is a giant ornamental rock, and in the far distance tree-topped
crags loom menacingly over the scene.[73] One of Ts'ao Yin's close
friends, Ch'eng I, painted a simple pavilion under two tall trees, with
a rock-lined small pond in the foreground and a fence and some
shrubbery in the background.[74] Perhaps this simplest representation
was nearest the truth.

Yu T'ung, Singde, and Ch'eng I were family friends. Yün Shou-
p'ing, Yü Chih-ting, and Tai Pen-hsiao had probably been commissioned. A third category of those who contributed to the albums were
those who were caught up by the idea and felt that they ought to con-

---

overdone. Yün Shou-p'ing must have done this painting before 1690 (as he died that year),
but it was not until 1690 that Ts'ao Yin had any office in Kiangsu at all. It is hard to
believe that a department director in the Judicial Department would cow Yün Shou-p'ing.

69. *HLMHC*, p. 253.

70. *Eminent Chinese*, p. 941. Listed in *HLMHC*, p. 33. Sirén, *Chinese Painting*, 5, 92,
and 7, 457–58.

71. Cf. his "Lady and a maid perfuming clothes," British Museum, exhibited by the
Arts Council, 1964.

72. Cf. his "Fantastic landscape" in the collection of Dr. Franco Vannotti, exhibited by
the Arts Council, 1964. Tai Pen-hsiao's biography is in *Kuo-ch'ao shu-hua-chia pi-lu*
(1911), ch. 2, p. 36b. Sirén, *Chinese Painting*, 7, 401.

73. Shao Wen, "Chi Lien-t'ing t'u yung chüan," as illustration no. 1, facing p. 22.

74. Ibid., as illustration no. 3.

tribute, either because they had genuine admiration for Ts'ao Yin's filial piety, or because they did not want to be left out of a cumulative work to which some of the most talented men of the time were contributing. Two of them have left quite frank accounts of their reasons for writing in the albums.

The first of these is Yeh Hsieh,[75] a *chin-shih* of 1670 and well-known scholar and official, who later became a friend of Ts'ao Yin's. In 1690 he wrote:

> Now Ts'ao Yin has had paintings made of the *lien* pavilion, so as to preserve his father's memory. Throughout the country worthy scholars pass them around among themselves, thinking this a fine action, and all of them write poems to commemorate it. I, Yeh Hsieh, am the latest to be shown them, and am happy that their prestige and good taste are certain to be handed down to posterity, so I declaimed the following. . . .[76]

The second is Chiang Ch'en-ying,[77] an essayist and scholar of some distinction. After giving the background of Ts'ao Hsi's administration and the planting of the *lien* tree, he praised Ts'ao Yin in the already stock terms:

> Walking round and looking at the old office, he grieved that the pavilion had fallen into decay, so he took some money and rebuilt it; and as the *lien* tree planted by his father was still flourishing beside it, he called it the *lien* pavilion. He pulled down and grasped one of the branches and sighed repeatedly in affectionate remembrance. Far and near the scholars heard of this and all sent essays praising him; it was like the *kan-t'ang* thatched cottage.

(The Duke of Chou had rested briefly under a *kan-t'ang* tree, which the country folk later immortalized in song.) Chiang then gave a perfunctory history of the textile commissioner's office and the fact that the Ming dynasty fell because of the excesses of the eunuchs, repeated what he had just said about Ts'ao Hsi's administration and the scholars' response to Ts'ao Yin, and concluded:

75. *Ch'ing-shih lieh-chuan*, ch. 70, pp. 37b–38.
76. This is printed in Yeh Hsieh's works (cited *HLMHC*, p. 248) and points to a fifth scroll now lost.
77. *Eminent Chinese*, pp. 135–36.

In June 1691 I came south with subprefect Chang of Chien-
yang. The subprefect brought over this album to get me to write
an essay. We had been on board [a canal boat] for about a month
and I was exhausted; so this essay and my calligraphy are not
good enough to show anyone. But I had to obey a good friend's
request and send something to serve for Ts'ao Yin's family
record.[78]

The good friend is here rather pointedly subprefect Chang rather than
Ts'ao Yin, and though Chiang Ch'en-ying's modesty may be sincere
enough, there is also a perfunctory air about the whole performance
and even a note of exasperation. Later, however, Chiang and Ts'ao
Yin became good friends.

Of the fifty-four men who contributed to the surviving albums,
twenty-six are not listed in the usual Ch'ing biographical collections,[79] so it cannot be said that Ts'ao Yin was merely collecting prestigious names; a great many of those twenty-six were probably fairly
obscure family friends. The rest can be looked at briefly, in an attempt to gauge Ts'ao Yin's success in assembling an impressive list of
contributors.

The conclusion must be that he was indeed successful, for over
twenty of those writing in his albums were among the best-known
scholars, writers, and poets of the day. There was Han T'an,[80] who
had been placed first in the palace examination of 1673; Wang Shih-
chen,[81] regarded as the foremost poet of the Ch'ing dynasty; Hsü
Ch'ien-hsüeh,[82] teacher and politician; Sung Lao,[83] the famous judge
of awkward cases; Wang Hung-hsü,[84] a compiler of the Ming history; and Ku Ts'ai,[85] the dramatist. Continuing the tradition that
Ts'ao Yin had started in Peking, there were at least four men besides
his earlier friends who had passed the *po-hsüeh hung-ju* examination:

78. *HLMHC*, p. 33, 2nd scroll, 5th name. Cited *HLMHC*, p. 261.

79. That is, their names do not appear in the *Index to Thirty-three Collections of Ch'ing
Dynasty Biographies.*

80. *Eminent Chinese*, p. 275. 3rd scroll, poem printed in *HLMHC*, p. 300.

81. *Eminent Chinese*, p. 831. 3rd scroll, poem printed in *HLMHC*, p. 289.

82. *Eminent Chinese*, p. 310. 3rd scroll, poem printed in *HLMHC*, p. 266.

83. *Eminent Chinese*, p. 689. 3rd scroll, preface and poem printed in *HLMHC*, p. 288.

84. *Eminent Chinese*, p. 826. 3rd scroll, poem printed in *HLMHC*, pp. 250–51.

85. *Eminent Chinese*, p. 435. 1st scroll, poem printed in *HLMHC*, p. 235.

Yen Sheng-sun, Wu Nung-hsiang, Ch'in Sung-ling, and Hsü Lin-hung.[86]

The most curious thing about the contributors was that, other than Singde, there was not a single Manchu. And that in addition to the *po-hsüeh* listed above, some of whom were initially cool to the Manchu regime, there were at least four avowed Ming sympathizers. These were the painter Yün Shou-p'ing (mentioned above); Mao Ch'i-ling,[87] a bitter and unpopular figure, who after fighting in the Ming armies and wandering for many years, finally took the *po-hsüeh* exam and passed it; Tu Chün,[88] who edited the works of the Ming loyalist Mao Hsiang;[89] and Ch'en Kung-yin.[90] Ch'en Kung-yin's father and three brothers had all been killed fighting the Manchus in 1647, and he only gave up the Ming cause in 1658. He lived in retirement until 1678 when he was imprisoned on charges that he was in communication with the rebellious Three Feudatories and had written against the Manchus. On his release, he began for the first time to associate with officials of the new dynasty, but he never served them and remained classified as among the *i-min*, those whose hearts remained with the fallen Ming dynasty.

It is not easy to know exactly why such men should have consented to write pieces in the commemorative albums, or why Ts'ao Yin should have asked them. One modern writer has guessed that they were virtually forced to contribute because of the power that Ts'ao Yin exercised as a trusted official of the Imperial Household,[91] but there is no evidence that Ts'ao Yin was really so powerful as this in his youth, if ever. A more likely reason is that in many cases Ts'ao Yin bought their services, either directly in the case of some of the commissioned painters, or indirectly by giving hospitality or help to many of those who wrote short essays. The historian Chou Ju-ch'ang, concentrating on Ts'ao Yin's friendship with the crotchety brothers Tu Chün and Tu Chieh, who were forty years older than Ts'ao Yin and

---

86. All four have biographies in *Ch'ing-shih lieh-chuan*, ch. 70, pp. 34b, 46b, 34, 47.

87. *Eminent Chinese*, p. 563. 2nd scroll, two poems printed in *HLMHC*, p. 289.

88. *Ch'ing-shih lieh-chuan*, ch. 70, p. 16b. 2nd scroll, four poems printed in *HLMHC*, p. 294.

89. *Eminent Chinese*, p. 566.

90. Ibid., p. 88. 1st scroll, poem printed in *HLMHC*, p. 292.

91. Shao Wen, "Chi Lien-t'ing t'u yung chüan," p. 25.

sympathetic to the Ming, finds the answer in Ts'ao Yin's intelligence
and charm—"he was just that kind of man." [92] It is certain that
Ts'ao Yin would not have got on with them at all had he not been a
sympathetic companion, but there is also the interesting fact that in
some ways they shared a common background.

The Ts'ao family, however successful they now were, were not in a
position to forget that they had been captured by the Manchus and
made bondservants. On occasion this might have been recalled as a
humiliation suffered by a formerly Chinese family, just as former
Ming sympathizers felt humiliated to be serving the regime they had
opposed. It is known that Ts'ao Yin, either as an intellectual or as a
writer with an eye for the dramatic, was deeply interested in the problems attendant on the Manchu conquest. One of his friends who wrote
on the drama, and a Yung-cheng-period historian, both record that
Ts'ao Yin wrote a play called *Hu-k'ou yü-sheng*, "A Narrow Escape
from the Tiger's Mouth." This dealt with the collapse of the Ming dynasty and the changes that occurred in Peking, and it concentrated on
the loyalty to their dynasty of certain Ming military and civil officials,
the havoc wrought by the rebellious leader Li Tzu-ch'eng, and the sycophantic behavior of certain officials who changed sides.[93] It is quite
probable that Ts'ao Yin was torn in his admiration for the Ming sympathizers, and that, as he had done in Peking with his on-duty and off-
duty lives, he found a successful synthesis in personal friendship rather
than being tormented by conflicting allegiances.

As an exercise in conspicuous filial piety, the formation of the *lien-
t'ing* albums had been a success. They did perpetuate his father's
name, and they did enlarge Ts'ao Yin's own circle of acquaintance.
Though most of the literary offerings were heavily allusive and historical in content, they occasionally revealed some interesting details
about the family background. But it was left to Singde, the only Manchu contributor, to make the only accurate forecast about the effect
of Ts'ao Hsi's death on his son's career. In 1685 he wrote at the end of
his essay:

92. Discussed in *HLMHC*, pp. 34 and 232–33, the same remark being made on both pp.
34 and 233, with only slight word changes.

93. The two sources for this information are the writer Liu T'ing-chi and the work
Yung-hsien lu, the relevant passages from which are cited in *HLMHC*, pp. 272–73. Ibid.,
p. 271, Chou Ju-ch'ang gives references to show that the play was also called *Piao chung
chi*, but it has not survived under this or the original title *Hu-k'ou yü-sheng*.

In these days our Court places great emphasis on families with a history of government service. When the day comes for you to receive the imperial edict that will send you away from the Capital on important business, who can say that you won't be sent to take up office in the south, to follow in your father's footsteps? Then this one tree, your father's benediction, will therefore be a link with the future, and the benediction of later generations will therefore stem from this. How then can we not write a few words? [94]

In 1690 Ts'ao Yin was duly sent south, to take up office as textile commissioner in Soochow. Two years later he was transferred to be commissioner of Nanking,[95] the position that his father had held for twenty-one years. This was an important post, but before taking it up he had a last chance to pursue his social life in an atmosphere still free of grave administrative worries.

Soochow Society

Ts'ao Yin spent almost three years in Soochow as textile commissioner, from the spring of 1690 to the winter of 1692.[96] The records of this period are silent on his administrative achievements, but supply much detail about his social life and the circle he moved in. As presented in the poems written by Ts'ao Yin's circle, this social life was an ideal round of drinking and poetry parties, interspersed with well-chosen bucolic outings. Thus we find Ts'ao Yin watching the harvesting in the autumn, enjoying the snow in winter, going on the lake in summer to enjoy the lotus and the cool breezes, yearning for the simple life of fisherfolk in their little village, or traveling in spring to see the blossoms.[97] Each outing produced its poem and usually a poem in answer to the poem.

But even in this rarefied air, Ts'ao Yin still kept to his riding and archery, and we know that the poems tell only a part of the story. His self-made image of hard-riding aesthete has nowhere been better captured than by the scholar and official Han T'an, who wrote this essay

94. Singde, 1st scroll, essay printed in *HLMHC*, p. 234.
95. *CNTC*, ch. 105, pp. 9–10.
96. *CNTC*, ch. 105, p. 10. *HLMHC*, pp. 243 and 269.
97. As presented in outline in *HLMHC*, pp. 243, 251, 268.

on Ts'ao Yin's thirty-third birthday in response to requests from the
local scholars:

> He thinks that the reading of books and the hunting of game are
> not things in natural opposition. Riding a swift horse and clutch-
> ing the bow, the taut bowstring making a noise like a thunder-
> clap—that is better than being hidden away in a carriage like
> most noblemen. And then to take the remaining arrows back
> home and entertain his friends, to get in heated arguments about
> ancient and modern, the different types of writers and the source
> and history of their merits, while the seated guests are silent since
> none can oppose him. . . .[98]

Han T'an at this time was living in retirement in Soochow and had
already exchanged poems with Ts'ao Yin,[99] so the description is almost certainly a true picture based on personal knowledge, and it has
become an accepted source for biographies of Ts'ao Yin.[100]

Nothing is known of Ts'ao Yin's riding companions, who might
have been officials from the Banner garrisons in the area, or simply
members of his household. But the names of many of his literary
friends are known. These were not just men who engaged in literary
correspondence, nor were they official colleagues, nor were they men
who shared a common background in terms of the degrees they had
been awarded. They were friends of diverse origins who went on excursions together and had convivial drinking parties—even if on occasion Ts'ao Yin had to drink alone when the others weren't up to it.[101]
He had to beg forgiveness for his general euphoria; "for us northern-
ers" he wrote, "Soochow is heaven." [102] As friends they clearly
formed a compact group, and it is worth examining the composition
of this group to see if it can yield any information about the society of
the time.

Besides Ts'ao Yin, there were at least seventeen men in the group,

98. Essay quoted in *HLMHC*, pp. 257–58.

99. *Eminent Chinese*, p. 275. *HLMHC*, p. 251.

100. As in *Ch'ing-shih lieh-chuan*, ch. 71, p. 61.

101. *Ts'ao Yin Shih*, ch. 2, p. 3, poem at Yu T'ung's party, with interlinear note "this
day none of the other worthies were drinking."

102. Ibid., ch. 2, p. 2, interlinear note.

living in and around Soochow between 1690 and 1692.[103] Six of
them were scholars of considerable reputation: Yu T'ung, Han T'an,
P'eng Ting-ch'iu, Chiang Ch'en-ying, Yü Huai, and Yeh Hsieh. The
first three were all from the district of Ch'ang-chou-hsien, attached to
Soochow prefecture. Yu T'ung was made a senior licentiate in 1648 at
the age of thirty, and served for four years as a police magistrate in
Chihli. He retired in 1656 and spent the next twenty-two years in
Soochow, reading widely and gaining a solid literary reputation. In
1679 he passed the *po-hsüeh hung-ju* examination and was appointed
to the Hanlin Academy. After working for four years on the compilation of the Ming History, he retired again and held no further post; in
1704 he died at the age of eighty-six. He was a bon vivant and a favorite of the K'ang-hsi Emperor's. Of the fifty-six years of life remaining to him after his attainment of the senior licentiate's degree,
he spent exactly eight in office.[104]

Han T'an, who passed first in the metropolitan and palace examinations of 1673, when he was thirty-six, led a fuller official life, working
for fourteen years in the Hanlin Academy and the Grand Secretariat.
He retired in 1687, and was living near Soochow during Ts'ao Yin's
tour of duty there.[105] P'eng Ting-ch'iu had also passed first in the
palace examination, in 1676 at the age of thirty-one, and worked for
thirteen years in the Hanlin Academy before retiring to Ch'ang-chou
in 1689 to mourn his father's death. He stayed in retirement for the
next thirty years until his own death.[106]

103. Their names are taken from the introductory notes in Ts'ao Yin's poems, and in
Yu T'ung's various writings. These together with other relevant material have been printed
by Chou Ju-ch'ang in *HLMHC*, pp. 243–301. The thoroughness of his researches into
early Ch'ing sources is such that it can be assumed that no good friend of Ts'ao Yin's
has escaped his net, though we should acknowledge his disclaimer that in view of the vast
numbers of Ch'ing literary collections he may have missed many references to the Ts'ao
family (ibid., p. 29). The names of the friends are the twelve listed, plus the five in note
117 below. Most of the men lived near Soochow, the others came on extended visits. It is
in order to eliminate purely formal relationships that some wider list of contacts such as
those found in the *lien-t'ing* albums has not been used.

104. *Eminent Chinese*, pp. 935–36. *Ch'ing pai lei-ch'ao*, section 10, p. 8, and section
59, pp. 3–4. *HLMHC*, pp. 244–45. *Su-chou fu-chih*, ch. 63, p. 1b.

105. *Eminent Chinese*, pp. 275–76; he was recalled to Peking in 1695 and later became
president of the Board of Rites, in which post he drank himself to death. *Su-chou fu-chih*,
ch. 63, p. 8b. *HLMHC*, pp. 251, 269.

106. *Eminent Chinese*, pp. 616–17; he did return to work for one year in 1693, but

Of the other three, Yü Huai had been a student at the Imperial Academy in Nanking, but after the Manchus took that city he retired to Hsia-p'ei, returning later to live and study in Nanking. He wrote a number of short scholarly treatises but took no examinations and held no official positions. He was a close friend of Yu T'ung's, whom he used to visit in Soochow.[107] Chiang Ch'en-ying had a distinguished reputation as a scholar, but had failed to pass any advanced degree and was mistakenly overlooked at the time of the *po-hsüeh hung-ju* examination. However he was appointed to help in the compilation of the Ming History, and finally obtained his *chü-jen* degree in 1693, at the age of sixty-five.[108] Lastly Yeh Hsieh, *chin-shih* of 1670, served for two years as a magistrate in Yangchow prefecture before he retired in order to travel and write. He finally settled in Wu-chiang-hsien, another of the districts of the Soochow prefecture.[109]

Because of their literary accomplishments, all six of these men were well covered in local and national biographical collections. Four other members of the group, though not nationally famous, nevertheless have had their names and a few details preserved. Tu Chieh (1617–93) had been a licentiate at the end of the Ming dynasty, but made no attempt to pursue an official career after the Manchu conquest. He and his more famous brother Tu Chün lived quietly as scholars in Nanking; Tu Chieh often came to visit Ts'ao Yin in Soochow, as the two had become close friends.[110] Kuo Chien-lun was a serious-minded person and a good painter, who at this time was director of

---

was unhappy and retired permanently. He later worked with Ts'ao Yin on the compilation of the *Complete T'ang Poems*, cf. *Ts'ao Yin Memorials*, pp. 12b–14, dated from 44/5/1 to 45/7/1. *Su-chou fu-chih*, ch. 63, p. 9. *HLMHC*, pp. 268, 270. He and Han T'an had both passed the *chü-jen* exam together in 1672 (*Su-chou fu-chih*, ch. 64, p. 7b).

107. *Eminent Chinese*, p. 942, *HLMHC*, p. 243.

108. *Eminent Chinese*, pp. 135–36. *HLMHC*, p. 269, shows that Chiang was asked to write by Ts'ao Yin's friends, and may have been commissioned to do so.

109. *Ch'ing-shih lieh-chuan*, ch. 70, p. 37b. *Su-chou fu-chih*, ch. 64, p. 6b, and ch. 63, p. 8b, where his 1666 *chü-jen* and his 1670 *chin-shih* degree are claimed to the credit of — Wu-chiang-hsien, though Yeh Hsieh was in fact a Chekiang man who took a Shun-t'ien provincial exam. This is a good example of one danger pointed out by Ho Ping-ti in *The Ladder of Success in Imperial China*, p. 245, that local histories cumulatively will provide far larger degree totals than the official lists. *CNTC*, ch. 108, p. 21, as magistrate of Pao-ying-hsien from 1675–77. *HLMHC*, pp. 243, 247,

110. *Ch'ing-shih lieh-chuan*, ch. 70, p. 16b. *HLMHC*, pp. 232, 239, 241, 243. *Ts'ao Yin Tz'u*, p. 5.

schools in Ch'ung-ming-hsien; Yu T'ung met him while he was staying at Ts'ao Yin's house.[111] Ch'eng I was from Anhwei, and also had
some reputation as a painter.[112] Chang Ch'un-hsiu was a bondservant
in the Plain White Banner who became a senior licentiate (*kung-
sheng*) and was made a prefect; he was a good landscape painter and
the owner of a fine library.[113]

The seven remaining members of the group are nearly all untracea-
ble. Only one of them, Tung Ch'i, appears in the lists of candidates
from Soochow who passed the higher examinations; he received his
chü-jen degree in 1690 while Ts'ao Yin was living in Soochow, and his
chin-shih ten years later, being made a bachelor in the Imperial Academy.[114] The remaining six appear neither in the *kung-sheng* lists of
Soochow prefecture nor as the holders of any local office. They might
have been licentiates from Soochow, or degree holders or minor officeholders from some neighboring prefecture; again, they might have
had no place in the official hierarchy at all.[115] At least one of them,

111. *HLMHC*, pp. 268–70, 285. Ch'ung-ming-hsien was a district of T'ai-ts'ang-chou,
until 1719 attached to Soochow prefecture, *CNTC*, ch. 108, p. 31. His office was *hsüeh-
po*, rank 7A, *BH* 850.7.

112. *HLMHC*, pp. 237, 251. *Ts'ao Yin Shih*, ch. 1, p. 17b.

113. *PCST*, ch. 74, p. 1b, lists him as a Plain White Banner bondservant who became
a prefect, and as the son of governor Chang Tzu-te. His father had been a licentiate at
sixteen, and at nineteen moved from Feng-jun in Hopeh to Liaotung. Captured by the
Manchus at Liao-yang, he was enrolled as a bondservant. He took his *chin-shih* degree in
1647, and was a censor, then Shensi and Honan governors. Cf. *Pei-chuan-chi*, ch. 62, p.
2a, and *PCST*, ch. 74, p. 1b.

Chang Ch'un-hsiu has two short biographies in *Kuo-ch'ao hua-shih*, ch. 6, p. 16b (stating he was a magistrate) and in *Ch'ing hua-chia shih-shih* (i-shang), p. 49a (stating he
was Lu-chou prefect). Both of these are literary in tone and make no mention of his
being a bannerman, or bondservant. But they both state he was "governor Yüan-kung's
son," this being the *tzu* of Chang Tzu-te. Chang Tzu-te and Change Ch'un-hsiu are listed
together in *PCST*, though the Tzu-te there has different characters and the governorship
is different from those in other sources. Yet the identification seems definite, unless there
was an extraordinary coincidence of names.

114. *Su-chou fu-chih*, ch. 64, p. 11b, from Ch'ang-chou-hsien, *chü-jen* 1690; ibid.,
ch. 63, p. 12b, *chin-shih* of 1700, appointed *shu-chi-shih* (*BH* 201), his *tzu* being Kuan-san.
He appears with the group in *HLMHC*, pp. 243 and 250 (this latter reference mentioning
the identical *tzu*).

115. *Su-chou fu-chih*, ch. 64, pp. 2b–14 for K'ang-hsi *chü-jen* listings; ibid., ch. 66,
pp. 2–4 for *kung-sheng*, where apart from one Yen there are not even any family name
duplications. Ibid., ch. 55–57 for local offices; ch. 58, p. 5 for tabular listing of 1690
officials.

Yeh Fan, had the time and money to travel fairly regularly between
Soochow and Peking, as can be seen from Ts'ao Yin's poems of welcome and parting.[116] The other five have disappeared.[117]

Though it cannot be known exactly how many members of this
group held advanced degrees, and though many of them were in their
sixties and seventies, it still seems clear that their general willingness to
retire early (or even not to take office at all), and to settle in the Soochow area, is indicative of a serious wastage of talent in the early
Ch'ing dynasty. It is true that individually they may have had sound
reasons—Ming loyalist sympathies on the part of Tu Chieh, wander-
lust on the part of Yeh Hsieh, filial piety on the part of P'eng Ting-
ch'iu, or even the simple human desire for a comfortable life of leisure
on the part of Yu T'ung—but it is equally true that their withdrawal
from the bureaucracy reflected certain problems of employment in the
bureaucracy at this time.

The main problem of employment was the one that faced the early
Manchu Emperors: whom should they employ in civil office in order
to assure the stability of the new dynasty? Their answer at the highest
level, in the offices of the governors-general and governors, had been
to employ Chinese bannermen.[118] And even lower down at the provincial level there was a marked use of bannermen. These provincial
offices were not like the offices in Peking, on the Six Boards and in the
Grand Secretariat, where the Manchus merely added extra offices on a

116. Yeh Fan (tzu T'ung-ch'u), Ts'ao Yin Shih, ch. 1, p. 9b; ch. 1, p. 11b; ch. 2, p.
2; Ts'ao Yin, Li-hsüan tz'u, p. 2b (dated 1684), p. 8, p. 9b; Ts'ao Yin Tz'u, p. 4. This
is not the Yeh Fan (same characters) who appears in the Index to Thirty-three Collections
of Ch'ing Dynasty Biographies, p. 132, as having biographies in 3/237/10a and 17/7/28a.
Both these biographies deal with a Yeh Fan with a different tzu who was a Ch'ien-lung
chin-shih. There was a prominent Yeh family in K'un-shan-hsien, Soochow, at this time,
two of whom sat for the po-hsüeh hung-ju exam and failed (Su-chou fu-chih, ch. 63,
p. 1b, interlinear note). It is possible that Yeh Fan was of this family and Ts'ao Yin met
him over the exams.

117. The five being Yeh Nan-p'ing (HLMHC, pp. 268, 270), Mei Mei-ku (HLMHC,
pp. 268, 270), Mei Tzu (HLMHC, pp. 243, 244), Yen Hung (HLMHC, p. 269), and
Chu Ch'ih-hsia (HLMHC, pp. 251, 268, 270, and Ts'ao Yin Tz'u, p. 5). It is possible
that Mei-ku was the hao or tzu of Mei Tzu. It is unlikely that Nan-p'ing was an alternate
name for Yeh Fan since his common tzu of T'ung-ch'u was used regularly by Ts'ao Yin
and Yu T'ung in their poems. The same surnames of these men—Yeh, Mei, Chu, Yen—
of course occur frequently in the local history listings, but the tzu is often given, and
in no case does this or the formal name coincide with any of the above. Yen Hung might
possibly be the retired general discussed on p. 146 below.

118. Cf. above, pp. 4 and 5.

parity with existing offices, so that each post could be held both by one member of the Chinese official elite and by one member of the Banner elite. There was only one of each provincial office, and the more of these that were occupied by the Banner elite, the fewer were open to the ordinary Chinese official elite, embarking on a normal bureaucratic career through the examination system. That the shortage of lucrative senior offices may have been such as actively to discourage Chinese officials from pursuing careers in the bureaucracy is suggested by a survey of the incumbents of provincial offices in Chiang-nan (Kiangsu and Anhwei) during the K'ang-hsi reign.[119]

119. The main source is *CNTC*, ch. 105, pp. 1–6; ch. 106, pp. 1b–8; ch. 107 through 108. Under "Banner elite" are listed those given in the *CNTC* as "Feng-t'ien *jen*," since cross checks of senior officials listed as "Feng-t'ien" to the Banner gazetteer prove that the terms were usually synonymous. Thus two governors-general are listed in *CNTC* as being "Feng-t'ien *jen*" and "Shen-yang *jen*"; they are Lang T'ing-tso (*PCTC* [1795], ch. 339, p. 3b, Bordered Yellow Banner Chinese bannerman) and Fan Ch'eng-hsün (ibid., 339/7b, Bordered Yellow). Of river directors and grain transport directors listed as "Feng-t'ien," Ch'ü Chin-mei was Bordered White Banner (ibid., 339/5); Hsing Yung-ch'ao was Bordered Yellow (ibid., 339/8), as was Chin Fu (ibid., 339/6b); Yü Ch'eng-lung was Bordered Red (ibid., 339/7); and Wang Hsin-ming was Plain Blue (ibid., 339/7b).

The listing of river directors follows that of *CNTC*, which counted this as a Chiang-nan provincial appointment from 1679. Checks of the earlier directors from *CS* to *PCTC* show that of the five earlier incumbents, one was Chinese and four were bannermen. Chin Fu was reapppointed, so only eight river directors are counted, not nine. But when men were posted from a different office, i.e. from governor-general to river director, as was Yü Ch'eng-lung, they are counted once for each office.

All officials are counted as being in the K'ang-hsi period if the K'ang-hsi reign name appears in their date of appointment. This will cut off a few Shun-chih officials who ran into the K'ang-hsi reign, and add a few who ran into the Yung-cheng reign from the K'ang-hsi sixty-first year. An exception is made in the case of Lang T'ing-tso, since he was governor-general for the unusually long span of Shun-chih 13 to K'ang-hsi 10 (1656–71).

Of the ten governors listed in *CNTC* as being from Feng-t'ien, *all* were Chinese Bannermen; they are listed in *PCTC* (1795), ch. 340, from Chang Ch'ao-chen (p. 6b, Plain Blue) through to Li Ch'eng-lung (p. 18, Plain Blue). Of the two governors described as bannermen in *CNTC*, Yü Ch'eng-lung was a Chinese bannerman; Plain Blue (340/15b). He was the third senior official in this period with an identical name (*Eminent Chinese*, p. 937), and Yeh Chiu-ssu was also Chinese in the Bordered Blue. Of the six bannermen who were Kiangsu governors, only two were Manchus.

Feng-t'ien/Banner correlations are harder to trace for all the financial and judicial commissioners, but working the other way, we find that all the *tso-ling* listed in *PCTC* as having been promoted to Kiangsu and Anhwei commissioners' posts, are in fact merely listed in *CNTC* as "Feng-t'ien *jen*." Random examples are Shih Lin (*PCTC*, 14/2 and *CNTC*, 106/4) and Ts'ui Ch'eng (*PCTC*, 15/8 and *CNTC*, 106/1b). Sometimes Banners are given in neither local nor national histories; thus Ting Ssu-k'ung is listed as a Feng-t'ien

Type of Office	Chinese Official Elite	Banner Elite
Governors-general, directors-general of grain transport, directors-general of river conservancy. Ranks 1B–2A.	8	31
Governors of Kiangsu and Anhwei. Rank 2B.	14	19
Financial commissioners and judicial commissioners of Kiangsu and Anhwei. Ranks 2B and 3A.	33	39
Salt controllers and grain intendants. Ranks 3B and 4A.	28	18
Prefects of Nanking, Soochow, Yangchow. Rank 4B.	33	17
Magistrates of the seven hsien in Nanking fu. Rank 7B.	70	19

Such groupings show that the appointments were carefully regulated, with the Banner elite holding most of the senior positions (though not to the total exclusion of the ordinary Chinese); the Banner elite and Chinese official elite having virtual parity in the middle positions; and the Chinese official elite holding most of the junior positions (though not to the total exclusion of the Banner elite). That there was definite and conscious regulation of this balance is shown by approaching the same provincial listings in a slightly different way. Taking the same two provinces of Kiangsu and Anhwei, and tabulating the governors and the financial commissioners (the *pu-cheng-shih*, who are also commonly known as lieutenant-governors) of both provinces during the years 1680 to 1715, the following results are obtained: in twenty separate years there was exact parity, with two men from the Banner elite and two from the Chinese official elite holding the offices; in eight years the Banner elite held three of the offices to one held by the Chinese official elite; in eight years the Chinese official elite held three offices to one held by the Banner elite. In no single year did members of either elite hold all four offices to the exclusion of the other.[120]

---

chin-shih in both *CNTC*, 106/5, and *Ch'ing-shih kao*, 245/11a. However he appears in the Banner *chin-shih* lists as in the Chinese Bordered Yellow Banner, examination of 1652 (*PCTC* [1795], ch. 104, p. 3b). The general conclusion must therefore be that whenever possible the compilers of local histories tended to obscure the Banner origins of many of their senior officials.

120. *CNTC*, ch. 105, pp. 4–5, and ch. 106, pp. 2–3. In all, thirty-seven bannermen were appointed to twenty-nine Chinese. The few Chinese appointments are partly explained by the exceptionally long term in office of the famous Sung Lao, who was Kiangsu governor from 1692 to 1706.

In his study of social mobility in the Ming and Ch'ing periods, Ho Ping-ti has shown that the K'ang-hsi reign was a period of comparatively low mobility, a time in which it proved unusually difficult for men from obscure families to obtain the *chin-shih* degree.[121] He sees this as being largely due to the fact that the new dynasty had to win the support of the existing official class.[122] To the frustrations arising from such a state of affairs must be added the frustrations arising from the inabilities to translate even a superior degree into superior office, for a preliminary check of officeholding in Soochow prefecture during the K'ang-hsi reign suggests that such inabilities were common.

Not only did the Banner elite hold a substantial number of the more important offices, but the Chinese holders of advanced degrees often found themselves confined to junior offices as a result. For instance, among the seventy-two Kiangsu and Anhwei judicial and financial commissioners, there were not more than twenty-four holders of the *chü-jen* and *chin-shih* degrees, while among the eighty-nine magistrates of the Nanking prefecture there were at least thirty-six.[123] In the one district of Chiang-tu-hsien there were eight *chü-jen* and nine *chin-shih* as magistrates out of twenty-five incumbents; while of the thirty-three governors of Anhwei and Kiangsu over the same period, not more than twelve held these two degrees.[124]

To complicate matters further, not only did the Banner elite hold the best posts, and hold them with low degree qualifications, but in the K'ang-hsi period local offices were often given even to Chinese

121. Ho Ping-ti, *The Ladder of Success in Imperial China*, pp. 111–17. The figures in table 9, pp. 112–13, show his category A for the years 1682 and 1703 as the lowest in the whole dynasty save 1874. But Ho Ping-ti warns that had figures been available for the eighteenth century they might well have yielded totals even lower than those for the K'ang-hsi reign (p. 114).

122. Ibid., p. 185.

123. *CNTC*, ch. 106, pp. 1–6, and ch. 107, pp. 3–8b. To make the figures err on the side of moderation, commissioners' figures include all Chinese incumbents for whom no details are given, while the *hsien* figures include only those definitely described as *chin-shih* and *chü-jen*. The degrees of the highest officials could have been left out of *CNTC* for reasons now unknown—probably simple carelessness. Tung Na, for example, listed with no degree as governor-general and director-general of grain transport, was the third senior *chin-shih* of 1667 (*Ch'ing-shih kao*, ch. 285, p. 9b).

124. *CNTC*, ch. 108, p. 1b, and ch. 105, pp. 4–6. Though cf. note on Tung Na directly above; only ten are listed with the degree, but two Chinese are undescribed and given the benefit of the doubt.

who held only the *chien-sheng* degree; if for later periods *chien-sheng* degree holders were considered ineligible for office,[125] this was certainly not true for the K'ang-hsi reign. The following table of the magistrates and prefects of Soochow prefecture, with their qualifications at the time of their appointments during the K'ang-hsi reign, should prove the points mentioned above:

| | SOOCHOW PREFECTS | | THE FIVE MAGISTRATES IN SOOCHOW PREFECTURE | |
| | Banner | Chinese Official | Banner | Chinese Official |
Degree Held	Elite	Elite	Elite	Elite
chin-shih	—	4	1	23
chü-jen	—	—	1	26
kung-sheng	—	2	2	19
en-kung-sheng	—	—	—	2
pa-kung-sheng	—	2	—	6
sui-kung-sheng	1	—	—	2
chien-sheng	4	2	12	12
li-chien-sheng	—	—	3	2
sheng-yüan	1	1	—	—
yin-sheng	—	1	7	1
li-chüan	—	—	—	1
pi-t'ieh-shih, li-yüan	—	—	1	1

Even allowing for errors arising from the inconsistencies in different listings, and the fact that not all qualifications of incumbents are recorded, the table still shows the trend.[126] Furthermore, the members of the Banner elite had longer tenure of office than the Chinese official elite: during the whole K'ang-hsi reign the Banner elite averaged 4.3 years as Soochow prefects and 3 years as *hsien* magistrates, whereas the Chinese official elite averaged 2.7 years in each office.

125. Robert Marsh, *The Mandarins*, p. 56. Ho Ping-ti, *The Ladder of Success in Imperial China*, qualifies a similar point: "*chien-sheng* as a rule were unable to enter government service without further purchase of official titles" (p. 34). It is possible that many of these *chien-sheng* magistrates had bought their offices, especially since this was a period of Ch'ing financial difficulty in which degrees and offices were freely sold, the years 1678–82 being a peak of this practice (ibid., p. 47). Yet it is undeniable that some *chien-sheng* must have been employed on the basis of that degree alone: in the K'ang-hsi reign, for example, there were two *chien-sheng* and two *kuan-sheng* as governors of Anhwei; cf. *CNTC*, ch. 105, p. 5.

126. The sources are *Su-chou fu-chih*, ch. 55, p. 1b to ch. 56, p. 25b; and *CNTC*, ch. 107, pp. 9b–17. *Su-chou fu-chih* listings are much fuller than those in *CNTC*, but frequently do not give the dates of a man's tenure and sometimes have no information at all on a given man. So a composite list has to be composed from the two sources, which

Inequalities in appointments were of course not confined to the offices of prefects and magistrates at the local level. It must have been equally hard for the seven Chinese *chü-jen*, who all served long terms as the district director of schools in Ch'ang-chou-hsien (with rank 8A, the office itself being considered an insignificant one), to see the justice of the situation in which their contemporary incumbents as subprefect of Soochow (with rank 5A) numbered six *chien-sheng*, five *kung-sheng*, one *yin-sheng*, and only two *chü-jen*.[127]

The bannermen of course took provincial and metropolitan examinations, as did the Chinese, but they did so with their own quotas which fluctuated considerably. The earliest Banner exams for the *chü-jen* degree were held long before the conquest, in 1634, 1638, and 1641. In 1651 the *chü-jen* quota was set at fifty for Manchus, twenty for Mongols, and fifty for Chinese bannermen, with *chin-shih* quotas being half those amounts.[128] This gave bannermen an extraordinarily favorable ratio between the two examinations, and it was exceeded in practice. For these quotas were for the senior Manchu examination (*Man-chou chin-shih*), and in both 1652 and 1655 fifty bannermen accordingly received *chin-shih* degrees. But in the same years another fifty-six bannermen received the normal *chin-shih* degree, so that the Shun-chih reign saw ninety-eight Manchus and Mongols and fifty-eight Chinese bannermen receive *chin-shih* degrees;[129] this put the Banner organization on a par with the larger provinces as far as over-

still may not be completely correct. The complete correlation between Feng-t'ien listings and Banner membership, found above for senior ranks such as governors-general and financial commissioners, does not always hold at this lower level of prefects and magistrates. For instance, one Soochow prefect and one Wu-chiang-hsien magistrate, listed as Feng-t'ien in CNTC, are also Feng-t'ien without Banner in *Su-chou fu-chih*. But the majority are listed as having been bannermen, and on one occasion (a K'un-shan-hsien magistrate) a Chihli *sheng-yüan* turned out to be a bannerman. The only conclusion from such listings is that any definitive count of qualifications and status of provincial officials at the junior level will have to be made by correlating two (or preferably more) local histories.

127. The *chiao-yü* (BH 857) in *Su-chou fu-chih*, ch. 57, p. 7b, and the *tsung-pu t'ung-chih* (BH 849) in ibid., ch. 55, p. 9. Ch'ü T'ung-tsu, *Local Government in China under the Ch'ing*, p. 9, includes these directors of schools in his section on insignificant subordinate officials.

128. PCTC (1795), ch. 102, pp. 2–4b. HTSL, p. 9690 (ch. 348, p. 3b) and p. 9717 (ch. 350, p. 1b) which shows that the *chin-shih* quotas were immediately increased, though they were later reduced, and finally brought far below the original level.

129. PCTC (1795), ch. 104, pp. 1b–7, examinations of 1652 and 1655; and Fang Chao-ying and Tu Lien-che, *Tseng-chiao Ch'ing-ch'ao chin-shih t'i-ming pei-lu* [List of Recipients of the *chin-shih* Degree in the Ch'ing Dynasty] (Harvard-Yenching Index Series, 1941), pp. 13–18.

all quotas were concerned.[130] The extra Banner examinations were twice abolished, from 1657–69 and from 1676–90. Despite this fact, and excepting a special examination of 1663 in which 118 Chinese bannermen were awarded the *chü-jen* degree, the Manchus produced ninety-five *chin-shih* and the Chinese bannermen forty-seven; both groups maintained a ratio ensuring that one out of every three *chü-jen* holders received the *chin-shih*.[131] Even if a Chinese official saw an office that might have been his held by a bannerman degree holder, he might still have been sceptical about the rigors of that bannerman's path to advancement. And there is the further point that bannermen and bondservants gaining degrees were listed under their own companies; it was their company captains' names and not their place of origin that was important; so it is quite possible that a whole network of personal allegiances subsisted among members of the Banner elite who were untouched by the laws of avoidance and the other checks that the Chinese had built into their bureaucracy.[132]

130. If the hundred Manchu *chin-shih* holders are added to the fifty-six regular *chin-shih* in table 28, p. 228, of Ho Ping-ti's *The Ladder of Success in Imperial China*, the bannermen rank well ahead of Fukien and Anhwei in the Shun-chih reign.

131. *PCTC* (1795), ch. 102, pp. 2–14, and *HTSL*, ch. 348 and 350, on the various changes within the Banner exam structure, which were much more complex that this outline shows. Banner licentiates and certain *chien-sheng* and *sheng-yüan* skilled at martial arts were examined at the Shun-t'ien provincial examinations, the Banner quota being added to the normal Shun-t'ien quota.

Manchu and Chinese bondservants were regularly granted *chü-jen* degrees from 1696 onward, and *chin-shih* degrees from 1700. Their ratio between the two exams was much less favorable than that for ordinary bannermen, since in the K'ang-hsi reign bondservants had fifty-seven *chü-jen* degrees and only nine *chin-shih*. (The Manchu ratios were 301 : 95, and Chinese bannermen 150 : 47.) By 1733 it had become necessary to insist that *pao-i*, being of Chinese origin, must only be examined in the Chinese quotas and not block the Manchu quotas. The order was sternly repeated in 1738.

Banner students were also troublemakers. From 1705 onward, because of past disturbances, several senior military officers had to attend all examinations in which bannermen participated, and be responsible for the discipline of Banner candidates.

132. To give two examples: the Bordered White bondservant Chao Shih-hsün, *chü-jen* of 1705 (*PCTC* [1795], ch. 105, p. 20) must have had close ties with his captain Lei Shih-chün (ibid., and *PCST*, ch. 74, p. 4), as with the prince in whose household he initially served. Chao Shih-hsün became a prefect (*PCST*, ch. 76, p. 15) so might have been in a strong position to defend his superior's interests. So-chu, Plain Yellow Banner bondservant, also *chü-jen* of 1705 (*PCTC* [1795], ch. 105, p. 19b), was in the same bondservant company as Sun Wen-ch'eng, a close friend of Ts'ao Yin's and long-time Hangchow textile commissioner. Since So-chu became a *nei-kuan-ling* in the Imperial Household (*PCST*, ch. 75, p. 3), to which Sun Wen-ch'eng and Ts'ao Yin regularly sent their silk quotas, there is again ground for speculation.

Thus there were clearly certain complexities in the local administration of the K'ang-hsi reign which suggest that it might fall outside the generally accepted pattern of Ch'ing administration: there must have been considerable tension between Banner elite and the Chinese official elite at certain times, and the lines of bureaucratic advancement must have seemed blurred. Such factors obviously have relevance in discussing the society in which Ts'ao Yin was living and working, and it is worth examining some of the descriptions of that society made at the time.

One of the key terms in describing the structure of this local society is *hsiang-shen* (and also the related terms *shen-shih* and *shen-chin*). Definition and translation of these terms are a matter of debate among modern scholars; because of the complexity of the subject their arguments do not make for easy condensation, but it may be said very generally that Ho Ping-ti defines these terms with reference to the class of officials and potential officials,[133] Ch'ü T'ung-tsu with reference to a local elite composed of official-gentry and scholar-gentry,[134] Chang Chung-li with reference to gentry divided into upper and lower on the basis of degrees obtained,[135] and Robert Marsh with reference to a local elite of degree holders.[136] All of them at least agree that tight definitions are possible, on a basis of office and degrees.

If we concentrate on the term *hsiang-shen*, and let Ts'ao Yin and his brother-in-law Li Hsü make their own analysis, the term slips away quickly from our grasp. Admittedly, on one occasion Li Hsü did give a precise listing: he named twenty-one men as being *hsiang-shen*, and of these twenty-one two were returned Hanlin bachelors, ten were retired officials of the fourth to seventh ranks, one was an expectant official, six were *chin-shih*, and two were *chü-jen*.[137] But on other occasions he and Ts'ao Yin used the term *hsiang-shen* in different ways, as can be seen from a group of memorials that they sent in 1712 in which the term *hsiang-shen* crops up regularly; these memorials were dealing with the examination-hall scandal of 1711 and gifts of impe-

---

133. Ho Ping-ti, *The Ladder of Success in Imperial China*, p. 38.
134. Ch'ü T'ung-tsu, *Local Government in China under the Ch'ing*, p. 172.
135. Chang Chung-li, *The Chinese Gentry*, pp. 3, 7.
136. Robert Marsh, *The Mandarins*, pp. 54–55.
137. *Li Hsü Memorials*, p. 95, appendix 2 to memorial dated 57/7/16. An almost identical list appears in ibid., p. 99, appendix 1 to memorial dated 57/9/25.

rial calligraphy, and both men were intent on describing local reactions to these events. They would thus have been conscious of social groupings, yet have had no reason for lying about them. Furthermore both men must have known the local society well: Ts'ao Yin had been in Nanking, and Li Hsü in Soochow, for twenty years.[138]

In one of these memorials, written in the summer of 1712, Ts'ao Yin gave thanks to the Emperor for the present of imperial calligraphy. The news had spread fast, Ts'ao Yin wrote, and "the *chin-shih, chü-jen, hsiang-shen,* and scholar-commoners (*shih-shu*) of the whole city got to know about it." Clearly, then, the *hsiang-shen* were distinguished from the holders of the two senior degrees and from the scholar-commoners. The lower status of these latter was reiterated in the next line when Ts'ao Yin wrote that officials from the Hanlin Academy "led in all the scholar-commoners (*shih-shu*)," and again, two lines later: "the *hsiang-shen* and *shih-shu* are together checking various areas and selecting stone for the tablet." These "scholar-commoners" were clearly the lowest group worthy of mention, and must have included those with some education but no advance degrees—perhaps those students (*t'ung-sheng*) who had received a certificate of merit from their local magistrate entitling them to take the examination for the licentiate's degree. At the end of the memorial Ts'ao Yin added that he would take the imperial calligraphy to show to the "*shen-chin*" of Yangchow; but since the phrase appears by itself, it has little value in aiding definition. From this memorial of Ts'ao Yin's, therefore, it is still not clear whether or not *hsiang-shen* could include officials, or whether *shen-chin* were equivalent to *hsiang-shen*.[139]

However Li Hsü, in a memorial written two months before, referred clearly to "*shen-chin* and scholar-commoners (*shu-min*)" as being two distinct groups with vocal opinions in the matter of the examination-hall scandal. *Shen-chin* apparently was a term used rather loosely, that could include any local degree holders.[140]

138. The memorials are cited below. The K'ang-hsi Emperor had sent each man a present of calligraphy, possibly as a reward for their careful memorials on the examination-hall case. This case is discussed in detail in chapter 6, below. For their appointments, cf. *CNTC,* ch. 105, pp. 9–10, and chapter 3, below.

139. *Ts'ao Yin Memorials,* p. 26, dated 51/6/3.

140. *Li Hsü Memorials,* p. 29, dated 51/5/22. A description of the 1684 Southern Tour further distinguished "senior and junior civil and military officials" from the "local *chin-shen* and scholar-commoners" (*Shih-lu,* ch. 117, p. 19).

Hsiang-shen on the other hand was further restricted as a term by Li Hsü. In a memorial concerning the present of calligraphy, Li Hsü wrote first that "the local officials (*ti-fang kuan-yüan*) and the *hsiang-shen* begged to see it" and a little later that "the local civil and military officials, the *hsiang-shen* and the licentiates (*sheng-yüan*) wanted to see it." [141] Combining the listings of Ts'ao Yin and Li Hsü, we get a definition of *hsiang-shen* as being some local group excluding civil and military officials, and also excluding holders of the three examination degrees (*chin-shih, chü-jen,* and *sheng-yüan*) as well as all scholar-commoners (*shih-shu* and *shih-min*).

It is most unlikely that, following these listings to a logical conclusion, Ts'ao Yin and Li Hsü had meant *hsiang-shen* to include solely senior licentiates (*kung-sheng*) and students of the Imperial Academy (*chien-sheng*), which seem to be the only major degree categories that they had not specifically excluded, especially since *hsiang-shen were* in fact distinguished from both *kung-sheng* and *chien-sheng* in other official and private writings at this time.[142] Yet if this were not so, whom exactly did they mean to describe by this term *hsiang-shen* apart from a few retired officials? The most probable answer is that they meant nothing definite, but simply used the term as a general description relating to people of influence in the area, though at times they singled out more precise groups of degree holders when such degree holders acted in concert on a formal occasion. In other words, for two busy officials in the late K'ang-hsi reign, *hsiang-shen* were not always clearly defined in terms of specific ranks or literary degrees.

One passage that supports such a conclusion was written by Ts'ao Yin with reference to the examination-hall scandal. Commenting on public reactions to the case, and on the relative support that might be counted on by the feuding governor-general and governor, Ts'ao Yin concluded that "the *hsiang-shen* and the well-known people in the area are divided on the two sides." [143] "The well-known people in the area" (*ti-fang yu-ming-che*) were linked to the *hsiang-shen* by the conjunction *chi* in Ts'ao Yin's memorial, and the passage thus has a

141. *Li Hsü Memorials,* p. 31, dated 51/5/26.
142. For instance in *Sheng-tsu wu-hsing,* p. 7, and Yü Ch'eng-lung's memorial in Ho Ch'ang-ling, ed., *Huang-ch'ao ching-shih wen-pien* [Writings on Statecraft in the Ch'ing Dynasty] (Shanghai, 1887), ch. 74, p. 25b. Yü Ch'eng-lung's memorial is cited in Hsiao Kung-chuan, *Rural China, Imperial Control in the Nineteenth Century* (Seattle, University of Washington Press, 1960), pp. 68–69.
143. *Ts'ao Yin Memorials,* p. 5b, dated ?51/4/30.

more general flavor than the others quoted above in which he and Li
Hsü put their various categories in sequence, using no conjunctions. It
may be hazarded that these *hsiang-shen* and "well-known people"
comprised all those men of local influence in whose opinion Ts'ao Yin
thought that the Emperor might be interested; and that he did not
bother to specify degrees or ranks because they were irrelevant at this
particular time, since both he and the Emperor know whom was
meant.

Those meant were the local elite, men not in office who were nevertheless well known in the area. These were the men whose reactions
in a political conflict had to be watched. As was suggested at the beginning of this chapter, the local elite was not a class; rather, the
members of the local elite were part of the Chinese upper class, by virtue of their special relationship to the members of the other three elites
who were themselves in the same upper class. The definition of local
elite is inevitably loose; class delineations do not generally lend themselves to precise definition, and it is one of the peculiarities of the Chinese system that at least the Chinese official elite and the Banner elite
can be clearly defined in terms of function and rank. No such sharp-
ness is possible for the local elite, but the term is still offered as a sub-
stitute for "gentry," not just because there is a danger of the term
"gentry" being muddled up with the English meaning of gentry,[144]
but because the word "gentry" is intimately associated with the word
"class." It is attempts to define Chinese gentry as a class that have led
to such strictures as Maurice Freedman's, that "it was an odd kind of
society, one reflects, in which everyone, the imperial family apart, was
born a commoner and became a member of the gentry only by taking
an examination or buying an equivalence." [145]

"Local elite" is not an exact translation of *hsiang-shen*, whether
hsiang-shen be taken in Li Hsü's most precise, or in Ts'ao Yin's
vaguest, sense. All that the varied usages of *hsiang-shen* in their 1712
memorials show is that the term was neither rigidly defined, nor could
be totally dispensed with. As I have defined it, the local elite was composed of some but not necessarily all the retired and expectant officials

144. Dangers summarized by Ho Ping-ti, *Ladder of Success*, p. 40, and Ch'ü T'ung-tsu,
Local Government, pp. 169–70.

145. Maurice Freedman, review of Chang Chung-li's *The Chinese Gentry*, in *Pacific
Affairs*, 29 (1956), 79.

and degree holders, and of some merchants and scholar-commoners, and of the families of these, as of the families of some incumbent officials. On occasion Ts'ao Yin seems to have used *hsiang-shen* in this wide sense, at others he specifically excluded degree holders or scholar-commoners. In view of this ambiguity it seems legitimate to translate *hsiang-shen* as "local elite"; if it has a narrower meaning, this will usually be clear from the context in which it appears.[146]

As far as Ts'ao Yin was concerned, it was members of the local elite in its broadest sense whom he had known in Peking, had persuaded to contribute to his commemorative albums, and had grown friendly with in Soochow. Even if some members of this local elite refused to join the Chinese official elite under a Manchu Emperor, or were frustrated in their hopes of promotion because key posts were already occupied by members of the Banner elite, or were overawed by a member of the imperial elite, this still did not mean that they would not drink together; despite their differences they were all members of the upper class.

146. For similar reasons *chin-shen* and *shen-chin* are also translated as "local elite," since at least in the memorials of Ts'ao Yin and Li Hsü they seem to have been used in as vague a way as *hsiang-shen*. But in all cases in which "local elite" is used as a translation of a Chinese term, the romanization of the Chinese should be given as well.

CHAPTER 3

Ts'ao Yin as Textile Commissioner

Ts'ao Yin was appointed Soochow textile commissioner in 1690, and two years later was transferred to be textile commissioner in Nanking, the office that his father, Ts'ao Hsi, had held for so long before him. Now for the first time Ts'ao Yin was on his own; having served his apprenticeship in the Imperial Household in Peking, he was to be proved in the provinces.

The Office of Textile Commissioner

There were in all three textile commissioners (*chih-tsao*),[1] based in the cities of Nanking, Soochow, and Hangchow. They were in charge of managing the imperial textile factories in those cities, and sending quotas of silk for imperial and official use to Peking.[2] After the Yung-cheng period they were paid the large salary of 10,000 taels[3] a year,

1. *BH* 845. The practice of following Brunnert and Hagelstrom's translations of official terms is abandoned in this instance, since their rendering of *chih-tsao* as "Superintendents of the Imperial Manufacturies" is too cumbersome for recurrent use, and has the additional disadvantage that it suggests both other manufacturies (e.g. porcelain, which were also imperial manufacturies yet quite unrelated to the *chih-tsao*) as well as the kind of regular checking in the factory suggested by the word "superintendent." In this work, *chih-tsao* is translated "textile commissioner" throughout.

2. The outline of the *chih-tsao* organization is given in *HTSL*, pp. 16,539–41 (ch. 940, pp. 15–18) and *HTSL*, pp. 18,954–59 (ch. 1190, pp. 12b–22).

3. The tael, Chinese *liang*, meaning ounce (of silver), was the basic unit of currency in Ch'ing China. The subdivisions of the tael were as follows: 1,000 *li* made one tael; 100 *fen* made one tael; 10 *ch'ien* made one tael. Examples of the purchasing power of the tael will emerge from the text, but it is worth noting some foreigners' assessments of its worth. For Father Le Comte in about 1695 the tael was equivalent to 4 livres, 2 sels, 2 deniers. (Cf. Father Louis Le Comte, *Nouveaux mémoires sur l'état présent de la Chine* [Paris, 1696], pp. 110–11.) For Father Pelisson, writing from Canton in December 1700, the tael was worth exactly 5 livres. (Cf. *Lettres édifiantes et curieuses*, 16, 411.) An interesting list of the prices of various commodities and notes on the Chinese currency written by Lord Macartney during his embassy of 1793–94 is in J. L. Cranmer-Byng, ed., *An Embassy to China* (London, 1962), pp. 242–45. Macartney gave 6s. 8d. sterling as being equal to one

which shows that they were considered (financially at least) in the same category as governors and financial commissioners,[4] the key figures in provincial administration. But unlike these provincial officials, the textile commissioners had no fixed ranks and took up their posts after special appointment (*t'e-chien*) by the Emperor;[5] they remained outside the provincial bureaucracy, and should be thought of as members of the imperial elite, bound in their own system of mutual responsibility and surveillance. As the K'ang-hsi Emperor wrote in 1706:

> The textile commissioners in the three localities are linked in one body, and there must be a harmonious relationship between them. If the conduct of one of the three men is unsuitable, and the other two tell him and he repents of his behavior, then that's all right. But if he doesn't repent completely, he should be exposed to the Emperor.[6]

During the Ming dynasty, only eunuchs had been appointed as textile commissioners.[7] The Manchus ceased appointing eunuchs to these posts shortly after they came to power, as part of the general reaction against eunuchs, who were considered responsible for the corruption and decadence at the end of the Ming dynasty.[8] The first textile commissioners of the new regime, appointed at Hangchow in 1645, at Soochow in 1646, and at Nanking in 1648, were either Manchus, or Chinese who had joined the Manchus before the conquest. Apart from one eunuch who held the post of Soochow textile commissioner from

---

tael, and estimated that a Chinese peasant could live on 50 *li* a day, or about eighteen taels a year.

4. *HTSL*, p. 8563 (ch. 263, p. 2). After the Yung-cheng reign governors received 12,000 taels and financial commissioners 9,000.

5. *HT*, p. 0909 (ch. 89, p. 10b).

6. *Ts'ao Yin Memorials*, pp. 14b–15. The rescript was delivered orally by Sun Wen-ch'eng, and Ts'ao Yin quoted it in his memorial dated 45/7/1. From Ts'ao Yin's subsequent comment in this memorial, it seems probable that he and Li Hsü were responsible for the dismissal of Ao-fu-ho from the Hangchow office, and that the appointment of Sun Wen-ch'eng was made to please them, since the three were already friends.

7. *CNTC*, ch. 105, p. 9. The work gives no date for the beginning of this practice, ascribing it to the dynasty in general.

8. *HTSL*, pp. 19,192–97 (ch. 1216, pp. 1–11), for regulations against eunuchs. This question was dealt with in chapter 1 above. For a recent assessment of the Ming eunuchs, cf. Robert B. Crawford, "Eunuch Power in the Ming Dynasty," *T'oung Pao, 49* (1961), 115–48.

1656 to 1661, all the commissioners during the Shun-chih and K'ang-hsi reigns belonged to these same groups.[9]

The textile factories at Soochow and Hangchow, which had fallen into decay in the late Ming dynasty, were put in working order again by the Ch'ing official Ch'en Yu-ming.[10] This forgotten official [11] must have been typical of many administrators who strove energetically to transform the corrupt bureaucracy of the late Ming into the efficient machine of the early Ch'ing. Between 1646 and 1648 he wrote at least four lengthy memorials on the problems facing the textile commissioners, but he also included statements of work already accomplished, and it is interesting to see how much initiative an official could display in these early years of a new dynasty. In Hangchow, where the buildings were in ruins, the whole factory system was reorganized by concentrating the workers in one area instead of allowing them to work in their own homes. So that this work could be started at once, Ch'en Yu-ming borrowed 3,000 taels from the financial commissioner's office.[12] All patterns and prices of ceremonial silks were standardized.[13] He organized a system of escorts to accompany the textile boats, and chose two capable military officers to be in command of them.[14] By 1647 he had rebuilt ninety-five factory buildings (*chi-fang*) for the Hangchow looms and built 2,450 feet of surrounding wall, while in Soochow he took over and converted a 110-room house that had formerly belonged to one Chou K'uei into a factory for the looms.[15] At the same time he was juggling with provincial funds, tak-

9. *CNTC*, ch. 105, pp. 9–10, lists the Soochow and Nanking commissioners and gives brief biographical information. This information is missing from the listings of Hangchow commissioners in *Che-chiang t'ung-chih*, ch. 121, p. 9, but of the first three incumbents, Ch'en Yu-ming was a Feng-t'ien *jen* and Chou T'ien-ch'eng a *Man-chou*. The eunuch was Teng Ping-chung. All others with information appended were listed either as Manchus, men of Feng-t'ien, or bannermen.

10. The restoration of the textile factories is described at the beginning of the very useful article by P'eng Che-i, "Ch'ing-tai ch'ien-ch'i Chiang-nan chih-tsao ti yen-chiu" [A Study of the Chiang-nan Textile Offices in the Early Ch'ing], *Li-shih yen-chiu*, 82 (1963, no. 4), 91–116. I am grateful to Silas Wu for bringing this article to my attention.

11. He is not listed in the *Index to Thirty-three Collections of Ch'ing Dynasty Biographies*, though he does receive notice in *CNTC*.

12. *Ming-Ch'ing shih-liao*, series 3, 3, 286.

13. Ibid., p. 286b.

14. Ibid., p. 291.

15. Ibid., p. 295.

ing over a Chekiang surplus to meet a Kiangsu deficit.[16] By 1648 the refurbished factories had produced 1,340 of the complex woven patent scrolls (*kao-chu*), an impressive number although there were complaints about their poor quality.[17]

It was this kind of painstaking reconstruction that lay behind the working system which Ts'ao Hsi took over. Ts'ao Hsi, the father of Ts'ao Yin, was made Nanking textile commissioner in 1663, and his appointment marked the beginning of the Ts'ao family's control of this office. It was a control without precedent; nor indeed did officials later in the Ch'ing dynasty have comparable control over this or any other group of offices. Ts'ao Hsi was Nanking textile commissioner from 1663 until his death in 1684, his son Ts'ao Yin was Nanking textile commissioner from 1692 to 1712, Ts'ao Yin's son Ts'ao Yung held the same office from 1712 until his early death in 1715, when the office passed to Ts'ao Yin's adopted son Ts'ao Fu who held it until 1728.[18] Thus a member of the Ts'ao family held the office for fifty-seven out of a span of sixty-five years.

Furthermore, Ts'ao Yin had been Soochow textile commissioner from 1690 to 1693,[19] and he was followed by his brother-in-law Li Hsü, who kept the office until 1723.[20] The Hangchow textile commissioner from 1706 to 1728 was Sun Wen-ch'eng, who was recommended for the post by Ts'ao Yin and was possibly related to him.[21] It is also probable that Ts'ao Yin's sister was married to Chin Yü-chih, who was Hangchow textile commissioner from 1669 to 1692.[22] For the second half of the K'ang-hsi reign the three offices of the textile commissioners may be seen as virtually a family concern.

16. Ibid., p. 294.

17. Ibid., p. 297. Some of these references are quotations from Ch'en Yu-ming's memorials by his superiors. Further details of his work are given in *Su-chou fu-chih* [The Gazetteer of Soochow] (1748), ch. 14, p. 6, and in P'eng Che-i, "Chiang-nan chih-tsao," pp. 93–98.

18. *CNTC*, ch. 105, p. 9.

19. For the year 1692–93 he was concurrently Nanking and Soochow textile commissioner.

20. *CNTC*, ch. 105, p. 10.

21. *Che-chiang t'ung-chih*, ch. 121, p. 9. *Ts'ao Yin Memorials*, p. 15, dated 45/7/1. *HLMHC*, p. 91. Hypothesis by Chou Ju-ch'ang, based on the fact that Ts'ao Yin's mother, née Sun, was from a bondservant company in the Upper Three Banners, as was Sun Wen-ch'eng.

22. *Che-chiang t'ung-chih*, ch. 121, p. 9. *HLMHC*, p. 91, hypothesis by Chou Ju-ch'ang, on the grounds that Ts'ao Yin's sister married a man named Chin.

As already pointed out, the ascendancy of the Ts'ao family was largely due to the Manchu reaction against employing eunuchs in any important positions. The K'ang-hsi Emperor had no intention of making special offices like those of the textile commissioners a part of the ordinary provincial bureaucracy, yet he distrusted eunuchs, who were traditionally the confidential servants of Emperors and had become unusually powerful during the Ming dynasty. So he appointed his own men—the bondservants from the Upper Three Banners (*shang-san-ch'i pao-i*)—to hold these posts. The Ts'ao family and Li Hsü were bondservants in the Plain White Banner; [23] Sun Wen-ch'eng, the Hangchow commissioner, was a bondservant in the Plain Yellow Banner.[24] Nor were these bondservant appointments confined to one family group. Besides the four members of the Ts'ao family, five other Chinese bondservants from the Upper Three Banners were appointed as Nanking textile commissioners between 1656 and 1733.[25] In Soochow, besides Ts'ao Yin and Li Hsü, there were four bondservants from the Upper Three Banners as commissioners; [26] in addition there was one bondservant from the Bordered White Banner who, like Ts'ao Yin, had served in the Judicial Department of the Imperial Household,[27] and in the Yung-cheng reign one from the Plain Blue Banner.[28] In Hangchow, there were five Upper Three Banner bondservants as commissioners in addition to Sun Wen-ch'eng.[29] All these men

23. For the Ts'ao family, cf. *PCST*, ch. 74, pp. 8b–9. For Li Hsü, cf. *HLMHC*, pp. 99–100.

24. *PCTC*, ch. 4, pp. 35 and 38b.

25. The Nanking bondservant commissioners were: Chang Chia-mo, 1656, Bordered Yellow Banner (*PCTC*, 3/36b as a *ch'i-ku* captain; and *PCST*, 75/12b with last character written "mou," but identical Banner and stated captaincy as *PCTC*; clearly the same man); Chou T'ien-ch'eng, 1656–63, Bordered Yellow (*PCST*, 74/5); Sang-ko, 1684–92 (because seven with the identical name are listed in *PCTC* and twenty-four in *PCST*, the exact man cannot be located); Hsü Meng-hung, 1731–32, Plain White (*PCST*, 77/4 has last character of his name as "chung" but states he was a *lang-chung*; and *CNTC*, 105/9b describes him as a *nei-wu-fu lang-chung*); Kao Pin, Bordered Yellow, 1733 (*PCTC*, 3/36b and *PCST*, 74/3b).

26. Chang Chia-mo, Chou T'ien-ch'eng, and Kao Pin were all in Soochow before being appointed to Nanking. Ma P'ien-o, 1656, 1658–60, 1663–64, Plain White (*PCST*, 74/8).

27. Lei Hsien-sheng, 1666–76 (*PCST*, 74/3b).

28. Li Ping-chung, 1728–30 (*PCST*, 75/11b). He later became judicial commissioner of Honan.

29. Chou T'ien-ch'eng came to Hangchow from Soochow, and Hsü Meng-hung served in Hangchow before Nanking. There was another Sang-ko, twenty years before the one in Nanking, so he was probably a different man. Li Ch'ang-ch'un, 1658–59, Plain Yellow (*PCST*, 75/8), later Fukien financial commissioner. Ch'en Ping-cheng, Bordered Yellow (*PCTC*, 3/37b and *PCST*, 74/4b).

were listed in the Manchu genealogy as being from Chinese families captured and enslaved before the conquest in 1644. The concentration of so many men of identical background in this one group of textile offices was obviously no coincidence; it is an example of the early Manchu Emperors' decision to use men closely bound to the Imperial Household, but also able to live comfortably with the Chinese, as the representatives of the imperial elite in the provinces.

The edict of 1663 by which Ts'ao Hsi was appointed—"Cease appointing Board of Works personnel as Nanking, Soochow, and Hangchow textile commissioners. Select Imperial Household officials, one for each area, to be commissioners on long-tenure appointment" [30] —marked an important administrative change. Previously these appointments had been limited to three years,[31] and though this rule had not always been strictly adhered to, no man had held the office for a very long period, and certainly nobody had settled in as the Ts'ao family were to. The change from Board of Works personnel to members of the Imperial Household was also significant, since direction of the commissioners was now shifted formally from the regular bureaucracy to the Emperor. And again, though bondservants had been appointed as early as 1652,[32] the offices had never been staffed solely by bondservants.

By the time that Ts'ao Hsi was appointed as Nanking textile commissioner, the smallest details of the work that he was to produce had been settled. Regulations dating from 1651 determined the exact amounts of the different types of silks that should be woven, the exact colors and threads to be used in the various patents of nobility (kaoming), as well as the appropriate places for using the Manchu or Chinese language on those patents, and the type of rollers suitable for mounting the scrolls of different grades.[33] An edict of 1651 also abol-

30. *Shih-lu,* ch. 8, p. 7.

31. *HTSL,* p. 18,954 (ch. 1190, p. 12b), edict of 1644. An edict of 1661 limited appointments to one year only, but was replaced by the 1663 ruling.

32. Chang Chia-mo was appointed in this year to be concurrently Soochow and Hangchow *chih-tsao.*

33. *Kao-ming,* BH 945. *HTSL,* p. 16,539 (ch. 940, p. 15). For a detailed description of the patents of nobility, cf. Wolfgang Franke, "Patents for Hereditary Ranks and Honorary Titles during the Ch'ing Dynasty," *Monumenta Serica,* 7 (1942), 38–67.

It was in 1652 that the Manchus made definitive regulations about court formal dress; cf. Schuyler Cammann, "The Development of the Mandarin Square," *Harvard Journal of Asiatic Studies,* 8 (1944–45), 81. This article has fine illustrations of Ch'ing weaving.

ished the old system under which selected wealthy local families had
been made responsible for filling part of the weaving quotas. These assignments (ch'ien-p'ai) had meant that the designated families (chi-
hu or t'ang-ch'ang) ended up paying half the weaving costs out of
their own pockets, and had led to all kinds of corrupt practices;
henceforth the textile commissioners were to "buy the silk thread and
hire artisans" (mai-ssu chao-chiang) with government funds, and to
pay fair rates for the silk and good wages to the artisans.[34]

The only administrative changes that occurred during Ts'ao Hsi's
period in office were minor ones dealing with the quotas to be sent in;
since there was overproduction in some categories, it was decided that
the commissioners should await special orders from the Board of
Works before manufacturing certain items. There were also alterations
in transport regulations; the new ruling was that silks for the Emperor should be sent by the land route to Peking, and silks for the
officials by the cheaper but more hazardous water route.[35] Some of
these changes were made in response to recommendations made in
memorials, so it is possible that Ts'ao Hsi was behind them; but nothing definite is known of his administration.

The official regulations give an impressive picture of administrative
completeness, and there seems to have been little that Ts'ao Hsi or his
successors had to do; but in the crucial field of finance the record is
misleading. In analyzing the financial structure of the textile commissioner's offices in the 1640s, Ch'en Yu-ming had described a state of
affairs that was intrinsically chaotic, not merely warped as a result of
eunuch excesses. Besides the money from the financial commissioner
and the transfers of provincial funds mentioned above, he had to
make up his required funds from the following sources: 2,000 taels
from a surplus in shipbuilding funds, 3,511 taels from the reserve
funds of various local prefectures, 200 taels from a customs inspec-
tor;[36] other income had been drawn from sales of ranks and the
chien-sheng degree, a tax on sampans, salt revenues, and several small
local funds.[37] Ten prefectures in Chekiang were meant to contribute
154,000 taels per annum for silk manufacture at Hangchow, while

34. P'eng Che-i, "Chiang-nan chih-tsao," pp. 93–95.

35. HTSL, p. 16,540 (ch. 940, p. 17). Ts'ao Yin's handling of a similar order is described in the next section of this chapter. Ibid., p. 18,954 (ch. 1190, p. 12b), dated 1667.

36. Ming-Ch'ing shih-liao, series 3, 3, 295.

37. Ibid., p. 286.

seven Kiangsu prefectures provided 53,000 taels for Soochow weaving.[38] But these sums were difficult to collect. As Ch'en Yu-ming wrote: "I have deluged them with stern instructions, but all these prefectures are contemptuous and do not reply." [39]

The statutes record that in 1644 it was decided that all financial requirements of the three textile commissioners' offices would be met by the Board of Revenue; that this was altered in 1651 when the three offices were attached to the Board of Works; and that finally in 1664 a compromise was arrived at by which the Board of Works dealt with the materials while the Board of Revenue handled the revenue.[40] Just as Ch'en Yu-ming's struggles from 1646 to 1648 show how misleading it is to think of all financial requirements being handled by the Board of Revenue, as the statutes say they were, so for the administration of Ts'ao Yin and Li Hsü the apparent perfection of the paper administration must be forgotten. For to be textile commissioner was to be constantly innovating and grappling with contradictory laws. If it was a post in which great profits could be made, it was equally a post at which giant deficits could be accumulated; and in these crises it was native wit rather than the statutes that had to be relied on.

Ts'ao Yin as Textile Commissioner

Ts'ao Yin left Soochow in December 1692 to take up his new post as Nanking textile commissioner.[41] This Nanking office was the most important of the three although it had the fewest looms, and commissioners often served an apprenticeship in either Hangchow or Soochow before being posted there.[42]

In Nanking, Ts'ao Yin was responsible for three separate factories.

38. Ibid.

39. Ibid., p. 294. The "contemptuous" prefectures were some of the Kiangsu ones which delivered the money straight to the *chih-tsao*. The Chekiang prefectures had to pay the money in to the financial commissioner, and were on time. This neatly illustrates the weakness of the *chih-tsao* power in the local administration compared with the regular officials.

40. *HTSL*, p. 7482 (ch. 182, p. 23).

41. *HLMHC*, p. 269. The dating is from a poem by Yu T'ung.

42. For example, Chang Chia-mo had been concurrently Soochow and Hangchow *chih-tsao* before being appointed to Nanking in 1656. Chou T'ien-ch'eng was Soochow *chih-tsao* in 1653, Hangchow *chih-tsao* in 1656, and Nanking *chih-tsao* in 1658, where he remained until Ts'ao Hsi's appointment in 1663. *CNTC*, ch. 105, pp. 9–10. *Che-chiang t'ung-chih*, ch. 121, p. 9. For comparative loom figures cf. P'eng Che-i, "Chiang-nan chih-tsao," p. 99.

The first of these, at the Hsi-hua gate in the commandeered house of a Ming prince, contained 550 looms for the making of thin silk, satin, and various forms of ceremonial robes; the second, at the bridge in Ch'ang-fu street, had 46 looms for velvets and plain satins; the third had 68 looms which were used to make *kao-ming*, the imperial patent scrolls that were given as rewards to civil and military officials, and the *shen-pai*, or sacred silk, which was for use in the ancestral temples of the imperial family. Perhaps because of the costliness of the materials used, or because of the absolute need to prevent the theft of such important pieces, these looms were housed inside the Tartar City of Nanking (the former Ming imperial city) near the Pei-an gate.[43]

Taking care of the thousands of artisans involved in the weaving was a major problem. The Statutes laid down quite clearly that with the exception of those employed in the Imperial Household, all artisans were to be paid by the Board of Works, and the exact wages for all artisans and apprentices, both in summer and winter, were fixed.[44] But various memorials from local officials show, at least in the Yungcheng reign, that money had on occasion to be parceled out from the funds for provincial granaries or sent in by the financial commissioner to feed the artisans.[45] A memorial from the Soochow textile commissioner, written in 1723, reported that there were about twenty thousand persons employed by cloth traders, in the dyers' shops, as artisans, or just hanging around in the hope of employment, and that none of them had anywhere to live.[46]

According to the official listings, there were about 2,500 artisans under Ts'ao Yin's care. Of these, some 2,000 worked on the regular silk looms, 200 on the satin looms and 300 on the looms for patent scrolls. Within these three broad groups there were many specific clas-

43. *HLMHC*, p. 212, citing *Hsü-tsuan Chiang-ning fu-chih*, ch. 11, p. 13, and *HLMHC*, p. 158, citing the *Shang-Chiang liang-hsien chih*, ch. 13, p. 9. There is no guarantee that all these looms were operating at the same time in the same places throughout Ts'ao Yin's administration, but the foregoing should be a fairly accurate description of the scope of the government silk industry in Nanking. P'eng Che-i, "Chiang-nan chih-tsao," p. 99, gives slightly different figures that show a gradual increase in Nanking looms from 538 in 1645 to 600 in 1745. He shows that Nanking was the only city in which loom numbers increased. There was a steady decline in both Soochow and Hangchow.

44. *HTSL*, p. 16,640 (ch. 952, p. 4b).

45. *YCCPYC*, *ts'e* 40, p. 58, memorial from Chekiang governor Li Wei dated Yung-cheng 5/2/17, and ibid., *ts'e* 53, p. 7b, memorial from Chekiang financial commissioner Hsü Jung, dated Yung-cheng 5/3/13.

46. Ibid., *ts'e* 48, p. 101b. Memorial from Hu Feng-hui, dated Yung-cheng 1/4/5.

sifications that show how specialized the weaving labor had become: there were men to draw the threads, brush, cut or color the silk, and others who specialized in certain designs on certain fabrics or had enough experience to exercise certain supervisory functions (*kao-shou*). In addition to these weavers and artisans there were all the servants of a large yamen: secretaries and storekeepers, sedan-chair carriers and umbrella holders, coachmen, runners, and guards. Lastly, there were the children serving an apprenticeship; generally these were the sons of weavers already employed in the government factories.[47]

The wages for the various groups of artisans and servants were also split into different categories. Men might receive either living allowances (*k'ou-liang*) or cash wages (*kung-chia, kung-yin*), or both, and they might be paid by the day, the month, or the year. The wages for a skilled weaver were about 1.4 taels a month, and he also received a monthly allowance of four pecks (*tou*) of rice. We can calculate from this that Ts'ao Yin's better-trained artisans could earn around 22 taels a year. Those with less skill, however, could only have earned about 10 taels a year even if they worked every day, and since we know that there were seasonal lay-offs for the unskilled, they must have lived in great poverty.[48]

Besides checking the looms and artisans, Ts'ao Yin had a variety of routine tasks as Nanking textile commissioner. Once every three years he had to supervise the dispatch of the finished silks from the factories to Peking, a task that he performed in rotation with the commissioners of Hangchow and Soochow.[49] The factories had to be maintained

47. P'eng Che-i, "Chiang-nan chih-tsao," pp. 100 and 103–04. Precise figures for Ts'ao Yin's artisans are not known; 2,500 is the lowest probable number, 3,000 the highest, since in 1738 there were 2,936 artisans, and in 1745 there were 2,550. Cf. also *Hu-pu tse-li*, ch. 78, p. 83.

48. P'eng Che-i, "Chiang-nan chih-tsao," pp. 97 and 105–08. On the basis of Ts'ao Yin's 1708 memorial (to be discussed below) P'eng Che-i estimates that a poor artisan's average wage was 7.3 taels per annum, plus the living allowance that was given only during specific work periods; ibid., p. 109. For the purpose of finding a cash equivalent for the rice allowance I am pricing a picul of rice in this period at one tael, and assuming a straightforward ratio of ten pecks (*tou*) to one picul (*shih*). (For rice prices in the K'ang-hsi reign cf. appendix B below.) Four pecks a month were therefore equivalent to about five taels a year.

49. *Li Hsü Memorials*, p. 66, dated 54/9/10: "This autumn it was my duty to go with the dragon robes . . . to Peking" shows that the *chih-tsao* did this in person. Ch'en Yu-ming had sent deputies; cf. *Ming-Ch'ing shih-liao*, series 3, 3, 291, dated Shun-chih 4/7/–

and repaired, and sometimes expanded onto wasteland or land given by the Emperor.[50] The boats used to carry the bulk of the silks to Peking were the responsibility of the commissioners and had to be kept in good repair.[51] The most complex work lay in the area of the quotas of the different types of silk that had to be woven each year. The Boards naturally gave precise instructions about what should and should not be woven; but these were not always practicable, as can be seen from a memorial that Ts'ao Yin wrote in 1708. Since 1704 Ts'ao Yin and Li Hsü had been alternating in the lucrative office of Lianghuai salt censor [52] and had applied some of the surplus funds from the salt revenues to help with the weaving.[53] Having discussed textile problems with the Emperor in an audience,[54] Ts'ao Yin was told to check quotas and quantities with the Board of Works. When he received their answer, he sent an open memorial (*t'i-pen*) to the Emperor, since he felt a palace memorial was unwarranted.[55] Because this is the only one of his memorials on textile questions that has survived, it is cited here at some length.

Ts'ao Yin began by quoting the Board's instructions:

(August 1647). In the Ming dynasty this duty had of course been performed by eunuchs. Ricci went from Nanking to Peking with a eunuch in charge of silk boats; cf. George Dunne, S.J., *Generation of Giants* (London, 1962), p. 71 and p. 84 note 1.

50. *Li Hsü Memorials*, p. 7, dated 40/3/–, and p. 8, dated 40/8/–, give details of such repairs. Abuses arose when the *chih-tsao* used such construction jobs as an excuse to take money from local officials; cf. YCCPYC, *ts'e* 13, p. 46.

51. In *Li Hsü Memorials*, p. 23, dated 47/6/–, Ts'ao Yin mentions this as one of the topics he had discussed with the Emperor.

52. To be discussed below in chapter 5.

53. YFTC, ch. 51, p. 8b, mentions that salt revenues were first applied to weaving in 1704. *Ts'ao Yin Memorials*, p. 9b, dated 43/10/13, shows that up to 300,000 taels of surplus money from the salt revenues had been paid in by other salt censors in the past to help the textile commissioners with their expenses.

54. *Li Hsü Memorials*, p. 3, dated 47/6/–. Ts'ao Yin says that he had discussed *chih-tsao* problems with the Emperor and cleared most of them up; he would now deal with the remainder.

55. Though this memorial (*Li Hsü Memorials*, pp. 23–24b, dated 47/6/–), was written by Ts'ao Yin and Li Hsü in collaboration, Ts'ao Yin discusses his own audience with the Emperor and writes as *ch'en* Yin (your servant Ts'ao Yin) without reference to Li Hsü, so he was apparently the dominating partner on this occasion. From a memorial in *Ts'ao Yin Archives*, no. 2792, dated 47/6/16, in which Ts'ao Yin wrote, "I have now received the Board's communication and am discussing it with Li Hsü. We are sending a *t'i-pen* containing our requests, so I do not dare to send a separate memorial [*tsou*]," we know that this long memorial was an open memorial (*pen*), although it is printed together with other palace memorials (*tsou-che*). For *tsou-che* analysis cf. chapter 6 below.

"We have in storage 262½ bolts of embroidered crimson silk, which is enough for ten or more years' use, and ten bolts of yellow embroidered silk, enough for two years' use. You should therefore temporarily stop weaving these two items. When the silk in storage has been used up, we will send separate orders to recommence weaving. Though there are still 582 pieces of regulation silk in storage, this is only just enough for one year's use, so the weaving should not be stopped. . . . On the matter of official patent scrolls, all those receiving the imperial favor are dealt with by the Board of Civil Office and the Board of War; they list the number of scrolls that those officials should receive and send a communication to this Board, and then we send out orders to get them woven. It is a question of sending out orders as the need arises. At present there are not as many patent scrolls as are needed, so we order the commissioners to continue weaving and despatching the scrolls in accordance with the lists that we send to them. The amounts needed each year are hard to calculate in advance." [56]

Ts'ao Yin did not openly criticize these recommendations, but he showed clearly that he found them impractical, since the textile organization could not be run efficiently if it was constantly stopping and starting at the Board's whim. He suggested instead that thirty-three looms with an annual allotment of 3,000 taels be kept running permanently, ready to switch as needed from regulation to embroidered silks, while thirty-five looms be kept working on the patent scrolls with an annual allotment of 5,000 taels. If there were few orders, then the unused money could be accumulated at the textile commissioner's office, ready to be used on any big order that came through from the Boards.

These comments Ts'ao Yin made in the interests of business efficiency. He then developed a similar argument on the basis of compassion for the artisans:

The two buildings containing the looms for the ceremonial silk and the government patents have been operating since 1645 according to the rules laid down by the Grand Secretary Hung

56. *Li Hsü Memorials*, p. 23b.

Ch'eng-ch'ou.[57] Apart from colored threads and other materials that are bought up at current prices, there is the question of the artisans' wages. Since the weaving started, these have always been economized on, so that the wages fixed are extremely low; they only get 20 or 30 percent of the wages paid to the weavers of ordinary satin and *wo* satin.[58] All these artisans, though they are listed as receiving regular pay, are in fact just common people chosen at random and hired to do the work needed in the factories. During the last sixty or more years, successive commissioners have had no extra revenue to draw from, so they could only follow the old precedents. Now if we suddenly forbid these practices, the poor artisans will be scattered around hunting for other jobs, for they cannot just tighten their belts while waiting for work to come up.[59]

"The old precedents" that generations of textile commissioners had been following were clearly some form of the old assignment system that had nominally been abolished in 1651. Presumably the artisans had only received a living wage because of outside "contributions." Simply to forbid this practice would not solve anything. Ts'ao Yin accordingly requested that he be allowed to draw more of the surplus money from the salt revenues in order to maintain their wages at a reasonable level. He added that weavers must be supported even if no orders were coming in from the Boards.

In conclusion, Ts'ao Yin stated that there were 370 weavers of patent scrolls and special silks whose upkeep cost 2,700 taels a year,[60] and estimated that in all he needed 12,620 taels a year for these skilled weavers' wages and materials. This sum would in future be drawn from the salt revenue surplus, as would further sums of 1,000 taels for

57. 1593–1665, one of the key officials at the time of the Ming-Ch'ing transition; biography in *Eminent Chinese*, pp. 358–60.

58. *Wo-tuan* is translated as "Japanese Satin" by Schuyler Cammann, *China's Dragon Robes* (New York, Ronald Press, 1952). Satin weavers themselves only got allowances of seven pecks of rice per month; these poor artisans therefore had received under one *sheng* a day, and total wages of four or five taels a year. *Hu-pu tse-li*, ch. 78, p. 83.

59. *Li Hsü Memorials*, p. 24.

60. The complete absence of growth in this branch of the imperially managed textile factories is shown by comparing figures one and a half centuries apart. Ts'ao Yin in 1708 estimated 370 weavers needing 2,700 taels; the *Hu-pu tse-li* of 1874, ch. 78, p. 83b, lists 361 men needing 2,634 taels.

the upkeep of the factories in Nanking and Soochow, and 2,000 taels
for transportation boats.

Though it is clear that the survival of such a memorial enables a historian to get past the Statutes into the details of finance, it still tells
only part of the story. The K'ang-hsi Emperor accepted the proposals
of his commissioners, and from 1708 onward salt funds were used to
pay for the weaving.[61] But the sum mentioned by Ts'ao Yin in this
memorial—a number of small items totaling some 20,000 taels for
Soochow and Nanking—was only for certain supplementary expenses.
Another memorial [62] shows that the amounts furnished by the salt
censors to the two textile commissioners' offices were the entire basic
payments of 105,000 taels to each city (which in the seventeenth century had been supplied initially by the provincial treasuries and then
by the Boards of Works and Revenue [63]), in addition to the 20,000
taels. In other words, the cost of running the two textile offices in this
period was about 230,000 taels per annum, and after 1708 the *entire*
sum came from the salt revenues.

The surviving records relating to Ts'ao Yin's handling of his specific duties as textile commissioner show that much of the business was
purely routine, but also that improvisation was necessary. The financial problems were only satisfactorily solved when Ts'ao Yin could call
on the extra incomes that he commanded as salt censor. This was
clearly satisfactory to the Emperor, but it proves that there were flaws
in the financial appropriations for the textile commissioners' offices
even in the early years of the Manchu dynasty, when the irregularities
of the Ming dynasty were supposed to have been abolished, and the
new machinery put in motion.

Despite the financial difficulties there is little doubt that Ts'ao Yin
was an efficient administrator. The dragon robes woven under his di-

61. *Li Hsü Memorials*, p. 113, dated 61/3/8, gives Li Hsü the credit for this solution
"when I received the favor of being Liang-huai salt censor," i.e. 1705. The Salt Gazetteer
dates the change from 1704. Ts'ao Yin states that it was completed by 1708. It is probable
that the salt censors had been increasingly using their revenues for the weaving from 1704
onward (Ts'ao Yin's first year as censor), but that this only applied to all aspects of the
weaving operations after 1708.

62. *Ts'ao Yung Memorials*, pp. 28b–29, supplement to Ts'ao Yung's memorial dated
52/11/13 dealing with Li Hsü's handling of the family financial problems.

63. *Ming-Ch'ing shih-liao*, series 3, 3, 294. P'eng Che-i, "Chiang-nan chih-tsao," p. 100,
shows that in the 1660's these two Boards had paid over an annual 225,992 taels to Soochow and Nanking.

rection were of a fine quality—showing "strength rather than com-
plexity, with simple patterns strongly woven in bright colors." [64]
There is also little doubt that he was a popular administrator. Chang
Po-hsing,[65] the friend who wrote his funeral eulogy, described Ts'ao
Yin's administration in flattering terms, but his comments also show
that he had an accurate knowledge of Ts'ao Yin's 1708 reforms:

> As soon as he arrived in Soochow, he cleaned up corruption and
> checked wastage. He was compassionate both to the artisans and
> the common people, and his reputation as a leader and as a benev-
> olent man spread far and wide. Next he was sent to Nanking,
> where he stopped the enforced subsidies (*pang-t'ieh*) to aid the
> people, and reduced his own salary so that the artisans might
> have better livelihood.[66] He stored up supplies and planned
> things so that both private and public good resulted; he displayed
> mercy and affection without partiality.[67]

In Ts'ao Yin's case, the conventional image of the good administrator seems to have fitted the facts. For when he left Soochow, a temple
was erected in his honor at the nearby resort area of Hu-ch'iu.[68] The
inscription for this temple, written in 1693 by another of Ts'ao Yin's
friends, Yu T'ung, provides a charming record of Ts'ao Yin's life at
that time. Inevitably, the description of Ts'ao Yin's character and
duties is judiciously blended with clichés about the perfect official;
but since it is the best essay of its kind surviving, it is worth quoting.

> Ts'ao Yin was in office here in Soochow from May 1690 until
> December 1692, when he received orders to move to Nanking, a
> total of two years and eight months, not a very long time. More-
> over, his official duty was to supervise the manufacture of impe-

64. Schuyler Cammann, *China's Dragon Robes*, p. 181. This passage does not deal specifically with Ts'ao Yin, but with "early Ch'ing" weaving as contrasted with that of the
Ch'ien-lung reign. Ts'ao Yin and Li Hsü were both presumably ultimately responsible for
the weaving standards in their cities. In this passage Cammann neatly discusses the rise
and fall of the Ch'ing dynasty in terms of weaving standards, providing an interesting
supplement to normal treatments of the dynastic cycle.

65. An earlier section of his eulogy was cited in chapter 1 above.

66. These are clearly references to Ts'ao Yin's actions in finally ending the assignment
system and transferring salt funds to meet the weaving payments, discussed above with
reference to his 1708 memorial.

67. *HLMHC*, p. 388.

68. *HLMHC*, p. 301.

rial garments. He was not like a governor-general, governor, a judicial or financial commmissioner, a prefect or magistrate, who by day are in charge of financial accounts and by night hold trials at law, so that every day they have dealings with the common people.

Anyone he met by chance he treated with great courtesy, but how can we say that he has an awe-inspiring reputation or abundantly benefited the people? Yet when he came here, everyone was happy and welcomed him; while he lived here the people were all happy and at peace with him; when he left, all wept and wanted him to stay. When he could not be made to stay, everyone composed ballads in memory of him. And as they did not stop thinking of him, they then got together and made a temple with his image in it, so that now people offer sacrifices to him.

How did Ts'ao Yin obtain such recognition from the people at Soochow? I know his character. He was a man who was sincere in his dealings with others. Whenever he spoke a word, whenever he performed an action, he did it from the heart. He was not one to be hypocritical or to delight in his power. He treated his subordinates leniently, and in all their dealings with public affairs they did not need to use the naked whip, and yet things were done properly. He spent plenty of money [on his duties] and yet he always had some left over, thus the public treasury and the people benefited. But he was strict in self-discipline and used no bribery to request interviews in the yamens of the senior provincial officials. Within his jurisdiction even the yamen runners did not dare cross over to the shops in the market and demand wine or food.

Our class of petty men lived nearby under his protection yet though he worked from dawn till late into the night, we knew of his reputation without there being any clamor; it was almost as if there were no such office at all. And so every house was influenced by his virtue and the people were sheltered by his teaching; they were happy at his coming as at the coming of the new year, and they grieved at his departure as one grieves at the death of one's parents.

Though high in office, he moved his subordinates by his sincerity, and therefore his subordinates responded sincerely. There is no one who is unmoved by sincerity. To show the abundance of his knowledge and the profundity of his thinking, the above can serve. Ts'ao Yin was moved to Nanking because the Emperor knew that his father had served in that place for over twenty years, his achievements being manifest to all people, and therefore made Yin his successor, that the son might complete what the father had started. I know that in Nanking Yin governs as he virtuously governed in Soochow, they bathe in his light and their time is taken up in singing songs of praise to him. But do they know the extent to which the people of Soochow still think of him and will continue thus, never forgetting?

Now, following the requests of the local people, we have established this temple to the living Ts'ao Yin at Hu-ch'iu; in Hu-ch'iu there is already a tower in honor of the Emperor, so it is fitting that Yin as the Emperor's servant should have one there too. Also this is the place where for three years past he and our group, on fine days in spring and autumn, drank and sang together. Is it then a place that Yin remembers, and will be unable to forget? [69]

There is hyperbole enough in this piece, which was after all written by a close friend of Ts'ao Yin's as an inscription for a temple. But it does show clearly the textile commissioner's position, one of power and influence, on the edge of the official provincial organization. Ts'ao Yin's friend Yeh Hsieh described it as a position that "made one intimate with the Emperor yet not too busy, respectable, yet with plenty of leisure." [70]

During the early Ch'ing dynasty, textile commissioners were often highly cultured men. For instance, two friends of the eighteenth-century poet Yüan Mei held the office. Yüan Mei reported approvingly on the wit and poetic ability of the Nanking commissioner Liu Fang,[71] and was deeply impressed by the culture of T'o-yung, another Nanking commissioner.[72] It may well have been in remembrance of these friendships that Yüan Mei wrote of Ts'ao Yin:

69. Yu T'ung, Ken-chai ch'üan-kao wen-chi, ch. 10, pp. 2–3. The essay is also quoted in full in HLMHC, pp. 303–04.

70. HLMHC, p. 248, in an essay written for Ts'ao Yin.

71. Yüan Mei, Sui-yüan shih-hua, p. 430, on his poetic ability, which Yüan Mei used as evidence in his favor when Liu Fang was arrested for debt, and p. 519, on his wit.

72. Their meetings are described in Arthur Waley, Yuan Mei, pp. 89–90.

In the K'ang-hsi reign, Ts'ao Yin was Nanking textile commissioner. Each time he went out, he took with him eight attendants. And he would always bring a book along, so that he could read and enjoy it without stopping. Someone asked him: "Why are you so fond of studying?" He replied: "It's not that. I am not a local official, and when the common people see me and have to stand up, I get uneasy. Therefore I just use reading as a pretext to screen my eyes." [73]

But though Ts'ao Yin may even have encouraged such a precious image of himself during his lifetime, he also dealt energetically with the problems of his new office. There is no doubt that he was appointed because of imperial favor, either to "inherit" his father's office as his friend the poet Singde guessed, since Ts'ao Hsi had been efficient and the son showed the same promise; [74] or because he had proved himself as a young man in the Judicial Department of the Imperial Household (the office that was a stepping-stone in the career of the great statesman O-er-t'ai); [75] or because his mother had been the Emperor's nurse and promotion to textile commissioner was sometimes given as a reward for the sons of such nurses; [76] or simply because the Emperor knew and liked him. He was appointed by imperial favor, but the appointment was not a sinecure. As well as an ability to cope with the difficulties of normal administration, it called for financial acumen, and paid extra dividends to those who had it.

Subsidiary Income of the Textile Commissioners

Ts'ao Yin had started using salt funds for weaving expenses in 1704 and this process was completed by 1708, but it may be assumed that during his first twelve years as Nanking textile commissioner—from 1692 to 1704—he had run the office in the normal way, with money

73. Yüan Mei, *Sui-yüan shih-hua*, p. 42.

74. Singde's eulogy on the death of Ts'ao Hsi, cited *HLMHC*, p. 234, and previously discussed in chapter 2.

75. 1680–1745, great statesman of the Yung-cheng reign; his biography is in *Eminent Chinese*, pp. 601–03. For evidence that he had served in the *shen-hsing-ssu*, BH 81, cf. *Yung-hsien lu*, p. 115.

76. As it was in the case of Hai-pao, who was the son of an imperial *pao-mu* and was appointed Soochow *chih-tsao* in 1730 (though he committed suicide that year by taking poison); cf. *Yung-hsien lu*, p. 266, and *CNTC*, ch. 105, p. 10.

from the Board of Revenue and the Board of Works.[77] In this earlier
period the accounting must have been a good deal stricter than it was
after 1704—when he and Li Hsü as concurrent salt censors and textile
commissioners were in a sense making appropriations to themselves—
but in either period there were clearly several ways in which Ts'ao Yin
could have made a fortune from the textile office without resorting to
the grosser forms of corruption.

One of these ways was in the skillful manipulation of the purchase
appropriations for the raw materials of silk weaving—the "colored
threads and other materials that are bought up at current prices" to
which Ts'ao Yin referred in his 1708 memorial. It was these silken
threads, made from the raw silk in the homes of local families, that
were bought up by the commissioners and then woven into silk cloth
on the government looms.[78] The "current prices" of course fluctuated
sharply, though the purchase appropriations remained the same. Some
of the prices that Li Hsü reported during his administration were: in
1712, 8.4 *fen* for each ounce of highest grade silk thread; in 1713, 8.9
fen; in 1721, 7.2 *fen*; in 1722, 7.9 *fen*. Figures for low-grade silk in
the same years were 7.5, 7.8, 5.8, and 6.3 *fen*.[79] In years when the
price was cheap, there were chances of making a considerable profit,
either by spending only a part of the appropriation in order to meet
the government quota, and then keeping the rest of the money; or by
making more silk than the quota called for, and then selling it on the
side. The very calculation of the going price depended on the commissioner, who had to collate the reports of his underlings—though of
course these underlings might cheat him as he cheated the Emperor, or
they might abuse the workers on their own initiative. Ts'ao Yin mentioned how hard it was to stop the workers being squeezed by the
yamen clerks.[80] But large-scale manipulation by textile commissioners
must have been limited by the fact that during the first century of

77. Though the textile commissioners had apparently been receiving some money from the
salt censors in the late seventeenth century, as much as 300,000 taels being taken on occasion
from the salt merchants, allegedly to help with weaving expenses (*Ts'ao Yin Memorials*, p.
9b, dated 43/10/13).

78. Ts'ao Yin did not report these silk prices (at least no memorials in which he did so
have survived), but Li Hsü reported the current price each year in either the fifth or the
sixth month, cf. note following.

79. *Li Hsü Memorials*, pp. 29b, 44, 111, and 114. For detailed silk prices in these and
other years, cf. appendix A. below.

80. *Li Hsü Memorials*, p. 24.

the Ch'ing dynasty, silk prices seem to have remained remarkably stable. (They began rising in the mid-eighteenth century and had trebled by the late nineteenth.) [81]

Besides profiting from the broad trends of silk prices over the years, the commissioners could also make money by buying shrewdly at the right time within the year. Li Hsü revealed one such method in a memorial of 1695, only three years after he and Ts'ao Yin had taken up their new appointments. In explaining these manipulations to the Emperor, Li Hsü was not being garrulous or overgenerous, any more than Ts'ao Yin was in 1708. Both were proving their ability to the Emperor. In each case they offered to save the government money.

The point made by Li Hsü in this memorial of 1695, after he had received an order from the Board of Revenue to buy up 300,000 bolts of blue cotton cloth, was that the weaving should be done when the people were otherwise unemployed, as this would force prices down. He wrote:

> This kind of cotton cloth comes from one *hsien*, Shanghai. The weaving is done by the people in their houses after the autumn harvest has been gathered in. They rely on this occupation to pay their taxes to the government and to care for their families. If we prepare the wages and give them out during the year, then the common people will be happy and have some capital. The price will be several *fen* lower than if we made provisional purchases.[82]

The point was, he went on, that purchases were usually made in the spring, summer, or autumn, when people demanded higher prices to make up for the time they lost from farming. This way they would have the money when they needed it, to tide them over the winter, and the work would be done before farming recommenced. Also, Li Hsü added, this would stop the local authorities making haphazard purchases, and would eliminate the commission agents and brokers. By this means he could save just over 6 *fen* on each bolt, amounting to 20,000 taels on the order of 300,000 bolts.

---

81. *HTSL*, pp. 18,955–59 (ch. 1190, pp. 14b–22). The prices in 1745 were: high grade, 8.2 *fen* per ounce; low grade, 7.5 *fen* per ounce. In 1755: 10.3 and 8.2 *fen* per ounce. In 1886: 26.5 and 23.3 *fen* per ounce.

82. *Li Hsü Memorials*, p. 3, dated 34/9/–.

The exactness of the 6 *fen* is curious. It suggests that Li Hsü had already tried this method successfully on his own.

Such manipulations could bring great profits, but the risks were high. In following Ts'ao Yin's later career it will be essential to remember that he had in a way mortgaged 230,000 taels a year of surplus salt revenues in order to pay for the upkeep of the textile commissioner's office from which he drew further profit. This was a highly speculative venture, and it was also dangerously dependent on the continuing maintenance of the status quo. During his life, Ts'ao Yin was able to keep things going successfully; but when he died suddenly in the summer of 1712, the textile commissioner's payments had been made, but the surplus revenues from his term as salt censor had not been received. The result was that he bequeathed his son a debt to the government of over 373,000 taels.[83]

Li Hsü's scheme collapsed in 1705. He had been receiving 160,000 taels every year from the financial commissioner's office for the purpose of buying blue cottons, and he had been paying this out in advance to the weavers each year, as he had advocated. The weavers themselves had apparently either speculated in the prices of raw cotton, or else had been caught by local shortages which had forced prices up; anyway they had fallen into arrears, and had been borrowing the *following* year's wages from Li Hsü in order to buy the raw cotton needed to meet his requirements of woven cloth. In 1705, because there was a surplus of blue cotton in the imperial storehouses, the Board of Revenue ordered that no more be woven until the surplus was exhausted. But Li Hsü had already given out the advance wages and was unable to recall them. He could not buy the cloth that would enable the weavers to pay off their debts to him. This mishap probably cost Li Hsü nearly 200,000 taels.[84]

Li Hsü's scheme, and Ts'ao Yin's plan of 1708, which probably meant that he used the textile revenues for his own purposes when no silk was ordered, represented what might be called semiofficial specula-

83. Ibid., p. 68, dated 55/2/3 on debts. This problem is discussed at length in chapter 7 below.

84. *Li Hsü Memorials*, p. 64, dated 54/6/15. Here Li Hsü gave details of the whole complex transaction, and plaintively requested that a new government order for blue cotton be placed, since surely the surplus must be finally exhausted, after ten years! The Emperor wrote in his rescript that he would have to think it over, since it was a complex matter.

tion; the textile commissioners manipulated the official funds at their disposal with at least tacit imperial consent, provided that they saved the treasury money in return.

The government also acted as an official usurer, to enable provincial officials to indulge in private speculation. Ts'ao Yin was lent the sum of 33,333 [85] taels by the treasury of the Imperial Household in 1701, and repaid it eight years later in full, though apparently without interest.[86] In 1700 Li Hsü was lent the enormous sum of 100,000 taels by the Imperial Household treasury for his personal expenses, which sum he was to pay back at the rate of 11,000 taels a year for ten years —that is, at exactly 10 percent interest. But the Emperor took no personal interest in such transactions, since Li Hsü's request for information as to whether he should pay back the money to the Imperial Household or to the Kiangsu treasury received this tart endorsement from the Emperor, in Manchu:

> On matters concerning the directors of the Imperial Household you must communicate with the directors of the Imperial Household. This applies to the three of you.[87]

The "three of you" were presumably the three textile commissioners of Soochow, Nanking, and Hangchow.

Customs Houses

Another source of revenue granted to the textile commissioners was the management or part management of some of the great customs houses on the Yangtze River and the Grand Canal. The directorships of these customs houses were often given to the Chinese bondservants in the Upper Three Banners by the K'ang-hsi Emperor, who thus assured himself of control over these key financial posts and guaran-

85. The rather curious amount of 33,333 taels might in fact mean that he borrowed 30,000 taels at 10 percent interest, and added an odd 333 for the sake of literary elegance. It is also possible that the figure 33,333 does not mean anything more than "a large sum of money," being one of the "pseudo numbers" which are discussed in Lien-sheng Yang, *Studies in Chinese Institutional History* (Cambridge, Harvard University Press, 1961), p. 77.

86. *Ts'ao Yin Memorials*, p. 20b, dated 48/2/28.

87. *Li Hsü Memorials*, p. 6, dated 39/4/–. The Manchu rescript was translated into Chinese by the editors of *Wen-hsien ts'ung-pien*.

teed a flow of money into the treasury of the Imperial Household.[88] Many of the first Canton Hoppos were also Chinese bondservants, among them Ts'ao Yin's friend Sun Wen-ch'eng.[89]

One of the richest of the customs houses was at Hu-shu, near Soochow. It yielded an annual tax quota of 191,151 taels.[90] This office became a perquisite of the Soochow textile commissioners during the Yung-cheng reign, and the two offices were held concurrently by three consecutive commissioners, Hu Feng-hui, Kao Pin, and Li Ping-

88. Examples of Chinese Upper Three Banner bondservants as directors of the Hu-shu customs are: Tung Tien-pang in 1695, Plain Yellow bannerman and *ch'i-ku tso-ling* (*PCST*, 74/5b and *PCTC*, 4/40b); Li Yen-hsi in 1706, Plain White bannerman and later *nei-wu-fu tsung-kuan* (*PCST*, 74/2b and *PCTC*, 5/42); Hua-shan in 1709, Plain White bannerman and third-class *shih-wei* (*PCST*, 78/3b), Liu Wu in 1711, Plain Yellow bannerman and later magistrate (*PCST*, 76/2). Liu Wu was probably a Hu-shu customs director; though described as first-generation bondservant, the nature of the family listing suggests they had been made bondservants late in the reign. A definite answer can only be obtained if his name appears with the date of his magistracy in a local gazetteer, and the two dates roughly coincide.

Earlier examples at the Lung-chiang customs of Chinese bondservant directors are: Ma Erh-han in 1681, Plain White (*PCST*, 75/15 and *PCTC*, 5/40b) or *Plain Yellow* (*PCST*, 76/17 and *PCTC*, 4/34b); Shang Chih-chieh, Plain White, *lang-chung*, *tso-ling* and later acting *nei-wu-fu tsung-kuan* (*PCST*, 74/7b and *PCTC*, 5/41 and 5/42); T'a Chin-t'ai, in ?1685 was a Plain Blue bannerman (*PCST*, 80/9b). After him, no dates or other information are given for incumbents in *CNTC*.

In general, however, more Manchus seem to have been appointed as these customs directors than Chinese. Correlation of listings of directors in *CNTC*, 105/11–14, with those of bondservant captains and *kuan-ling* in *PCTC*, ch. 3–10, yields many identical names (names not included in *PCST* Chinese listings) which support the general theory that senior Manchu bondservants held the bulk of the customs directorships. But the Manchu names are often so common and recur so frequently that a definitive statement cannot be made.

89. *Kuang-tung t'ung-chih*, ch. 44, pp. 1–3, under *Yüeh-hai kuan chien-tu*, BH, 833A. Sun Wen-ch'eng served as the Hoppo in 1703. Between 1687 and 1712 there were twelve Hoppos whose names also appear among the Chinese bondservants in *PCST* and *PCTC*. Besides Sun Wen-ch'eng, there was Sa-ha-lien, 1700 Hoppo, *PCTC* 5/38 and *PCST* 75/1b, Plain White Banner; 1704 Hoppo An-t'ai, *PCST* 77/18b (later financial commissioner of Kiangsu); 1710 Hoppo Li Kuo-p'ing, *PCST* 74/2b, Plain White Banner; 1722 Hoppo Sa-k'o-su, *PCST* 77/20. Despite their Manchu names, all were from Chinese families; bondservants often took Manchu names, presumably because it better fitted their new status. The other Hoppos—in 1687, 1689, 1693, 1699, 1701, 1717, and 1721—have common names that appear frequently in *PCST* and *PCTC* Chinese bondservant sections, too frequently to make definite correlations possible.

H. B. Morse noted that Hoppos were always Manchus who were also "Boyi, the hereditary bondsmen of the imperial family"; *The International Relations of the Chinese Empire* (3 vols., London, 1910–18), 2, 4. At least for the K'ang-hsi reign this can be modified to "Manchu and Chinese bondservants."

90. *HTSL*, pp. 8203–04 (ch. 234, pp. 9b–11b).

chung.[91] Kao Pin raised a surplus of 120,188 taels in 1726, for which he was praised by the Emperor, and in 1729 Li Ping-chung raised a surplus of 168,398 taels, despite the fact that for two months the water level had been so low that no boats could get through.[92] Besides these declared surpluses there must have been considerable undeclared ones, and the directorship was highly coveted.[93] Li Hsü tried to get his hands on it three times. His first attempt in 1716 was to merge the staffs of the two offices, since they were so near to each other. The chief clerks (*wu-lin-ta*) from the textile commissioner's office, he wrote, had offered to take over from the clerks (*pi-t'ieh-shih*) of the customs office. They would manage the dues for ten years, and would use the surplus money from the customs to pay the weavers an allowance in silver, instead of an allowance of government grain which they had drawn previously. "The weavers will be pleased with their monthly allowance," wrote Li Hsü, "and each year the Court will be saved 9,000 piculs of government rice." Unfortunately, Li Hsü had got his facts wrong. As the Emperor K'ang-hsi put it succinctly in his rescript: "Since the post of clerk (*pi-t'ieh-shih*) in all customs houses has been abolished, this discussion is pointless." [94] Li Hsü made a further attempt in 1720, offering to send the full quota of 190,000 taels every year, plus as large a surplus as possible. Rather surprisingly the Emperor stalled, saying merely that the present director still had several commissions to undertake, and that Li Hsü should recuperate after his recent illness and not undertake new responsibilities.[95] He was not given the directorship when it fell vacant in the autumn; instead, he was ordered to transmit memorials for the new director dealing with customs matters,[96] which must have rubbed salt in the wound. In 1722 Li Hsü tried again, saying that if he was granted the

---

91. Kao Pin styled himself "*chih-tsao* of Soochow and concurrently Hu-shu kuan director," YCCPYC, *ts'e* 50, p. 65. For the others, cf. YCCPYC, *ts'e* 47, p. 39b, and *ts'e* 48, p. 104.

92. Ibid., *ts'e* 50, p. 65, and *ts'e* 47, pp. 39–40.

93. As Friar Domingo Navarrete wrote in 1665: "Two Tartars were [at a Grand Canal customs house], who, as our officers told us, got 500 ducats a day each, in presents passengers made them. We argued against it, believing it was too much; but they gave convincing reasons for what they said." *The Travels and Controversies of Friar Domingo Navarrete, 1618–1686*, ed. J. S. Cummins (2 vols. Cambridge, 1962), p. 207.

94. *Li Hsü Memorials*, p. 70, dated 55/intercalary 3/12.

95. Ibid., pp. 106b–107, dated 59/4/15 and endorsement on same.

96. Ibid., p. 109b, dated 59/11/4.

directorship he would staff the lower echelons of the customs with men from the textile commissioner's office, and would send the Emperor 50,000 taels surplus every year, as well as paying off the textile commissioner's deficits.[97] The K'ang-hsi Emperor did not comment on this request, which was not granted.[98]

Ts'ao Yin, however, was more fortunate. As he described it:

> In 1701 I sent a memorial offering to manage the copper allotment of various customs houses, so as to save money for the Emperor as a humble subject should. I received the Emperor's favor, and was granted the management of copper purchasing for the five customs houses of Lung-chiang, Huai-an, Lin-ch'ing, Kankuan, and Nan-hsin, totaling over 10,100 piculs.[99]

Since the price of copper at this period was between 10 and 12½ taels per picul (approximately 133 pounds),[100] this meant that Ts'ao Yin would be handling about another 125,000 taels of government money each year, in order to buy one quarter of the total annual copper requirement of the mints in Peking.[101]

The five customs houses he mentioned were all among the fourteen major customs houses of eastern China.[102] Lung-chiang had an annual assessment of 46,838 taels,[103] and was sometimes managed by the Nanking textile commissioner.[104] Huai-an had a fixed assessment

97. Ibid., p. 113, dated 61/3/8.

98. Li Hsü is not listed among the Hu-shu kuan directors in *CNTC*, ch. 105, pp. 12–14.

99. *Ts'ao Yin Memorials*, p. 20b, dated 48/2/28.

100. *HTSL*, p. 7945 (ch. 214, p. 19), gives a copper price of one *ch'ien* per *chin* in 1684. *Ts'ao Fu Archives*, no. 2850, dated 58/6/11, gives the current price of copper as 1.25 *ch'ien* per *chin*, and says that transport fees added another 5 *fen* to this price before the copper reached Peking. Ts'ao Fu was probably exaggerating this price a little, since he was trying to get the job for himself by undercutting the competition; cf. chapter 7, below. At this time the Japanese at Nagasaki were selling copper of very high quality for 11.5 taels per picul (1.15 *ch'ien* per *chin*), cf. John Hall, "Notes on the Early Ch'ing Copper Trade with Japan," *HJAS*, 12 (1949), 454 note 33. I am also indebted to this article for leads into the copper sections of *Huang-ch'ao wen-hsien t'ung-k'ao*, cited below as *T'ung-k'ao*.

101. *T'ung-k'ao*, p. 4979a, gives the annual requirement of the mints in 1716 as 4,435,200 *chin*.

102. Ibid., p. 4976c. Sixteen customs houses are listed, but Lung-chiang paired with Hsi-hsin and Pei-hsin with Nan-hsin to make fourteen.

103. *HTSL*, pp. 16,544–45 (ch. 941, pp. 7–8).

104. As by Kao Pin in 1733–34. *YCCPYC*, ts'e 50, p. 86.

of 245,479 taels and an added assessed surplus of 121,000 in the middle of the Ch'ing period; it was expected to provide 3,076.9 piculs of copper each year.[105] Lin-ch'ing was assessed at 37,376 taels;[106] its location in Shantung must have made it difficult for Ts'ao Yin to reach, but he presumably passed through it at intervals when escorting the silk boats up the Grand Canal to the Capital.[107] Kan-kuan was assessed at 46,471 taels,[108] and Nan-hsin, which later in the Ch'ing was a concurrent post of the Hangchow textile commissioner,[109] was assessed at 30,247 taels, with a copper purchase quota of 3076.9 taels.[110] Their assessments were based on the numbers of all boats passing the customs houses, which paid on varying scales according to width of crossbeam, length of boat, weight and nature of cargo, and direction of travel.

Ts'ao Yin was not the director of any of the five customs houses, so he did not have to play any part in raising their quota taxation, which amounted to some 400,000 taels. He was in effect the purchasing agent for the government, using the resources and facilities of the customs houses to help him in collecting the copper. The Chinese government was in constant need of copper for the minting of coinage, and a growing shortage of copper in the first years of the Ch'ing dynasty had reached crisis proportions by 1700.[111] Early Ch'ing statutes had granted certain customs houses the right to use 10,000 taels a year from their own revenues for the purpose of buying up copper which was to be sent to the Board of Revenue. Since these sums proved inadequate, an extra 164,510 taels were added in 1664 from the taxes on

105. HTSL, p. 8204 (ch. 234, pp. 11b–13). Changes in the assessed surplus are given from the Chia-ch'ing period onward. Therefore the 121,000-tael surplus applies to the late eighteenth century, and possibly back to the K'ang-hsi reign. T'ung-k'ao, p. 4976c.

106. HTSL, pp. 8201–02 (ch. 234, pp. 5b–7). Lin-ch'ing was one of these customs houses that had special categories for salt and grain boats; cf. HTSL, p. 16,544 (ch. 941, p. 7).

107. The textile commissioners traveled by land or water, and often had an audience when they reached the Capital. Li Hsü Memorials, p. 66, dated 54/9/10, quoted above on silk escorts, continues: "as the water was dried in the canal . . . I am now setting off to accompany them by the land route to the Capital, and then I will have an audience with the Emperor."

108. HTSL, p. 8215 (ch. 235, pp. 9–10).

109. Ibid., p. 18,958 (ch. 1190, p. 20).

110. Ibid., p. 16,547 (ch. 941, p. 12b). T'ung-k'ao, p. 4976c.

111. John Hall, "Early Ch'ing Copper Trade," p. 446.

reed beds, and in 1679 a further 65,000 taels were provided from the salt revenues.[112]

By the time that Ts'ao Yin took over copper purchases, despite an enormous increase in copper imports from Japan,[113] continued shortages had led the Board of Revenue to give up its old standards concerning the purity of the metal, and the commissioners were allowed to send ruined old copper vessels containing up to 40 percent of lead. Finally even old printing blocks (*pan-k'uai*) were allowed to be used in making up the weight.[114] Thus Ts'ao Yin had the funds made over to him from a variety of sources, and was allowed considerable latitude in buying up his quotas. Naturally, the cheaper he bought, the more profit he made. His account of his stewardship, sent to the Emperor in 1709, was complacent:

> Besides the annual quotas, which I collected and handed over to the Board without delay, I saved 39,530 taels each year. This amount over the eight years, with one year less in Kan-kuan, I have handed over: the savings totalled 312,070 taels. Also for the years 1706, 1707, and 1708, following an edict that the money for the purchase of copper at each customs house should thereafter be received from the treasury of the financial commissioner, I passed on total savings in transportation costs of 8,470 taels. All this has already been paid into the Imperial Household Treasury.[115]

By "savings" Ts'ao Yin meant that he had bought up and forwarded the full quota of copper for a sum well below the full appropriation. It was this balance that he was returning to the Emperor. There is no way of knowing how much he kept for himself. The Emperor may have been satisfied with this record, but when, in the same memorial, Ts'ao Yin rather tentatively requested a further eight-year appointment, it was not granted.

---

112. *HTSL*, pp. 7944–45 (ch. 214, pp. 18–19). The salt payments were stopped in 1681. For the taxes on reed beds, cf. *HTSL*, p. 8297 (ch. 242, p. 1). These reed-bed taxes yielded a surprising amount of money: 153,200 taels per annum in Kiangsu, 50,347 taels p.a. in Anhwei, 6,053 taels p.a. in Kiangsi.

113. John Hall, "Early Ch'ing Copper Trade," pp. 452–54.

114. *HTSL*, p. 7945 (ch. 214, p. 19). The use of printing blocks was finally permitted in 1684.

115. *Ts'ao Yin Memorials*, p. 20b, dated 48/2/28.

This episode shows the remarkable extent of the K'ang-hsi Emperor's hold over provincial finances. A statute of 1699 had given the rights of copper purchasing to the merchants from the Imperial Household, instead of leaving these rights in the hands of private merchants, and it has been rightly said that this was "apparently for the purpose of putting the copper procurement under closer government control." [116] But the surprising thing is that these purchase rights were not just granted to merchants under the control of the Imperial Household; they were granted also to the textile commissioner of Nanking who was one of the Emperor's trusted bondservants.

Stabilization of Rice Prices

The textile commissioners of the K'ang-hsi reign were bondservants, the Emperor's men rather than ordinary bureaucrats. Also, it was almost certainly because he was a bondservant that Ts'ao Yin had been granted the copper purchasing rights at the five customs houses. Once the K'ang-hsi Emperor had lodged his bondservants in responsible and lucrative positions in the provinces, it is not surprising that he used them to carry out a number of subsidiary tasks which had little apparent connection with their ostensible official duties.

The most important and time-consuming of the extra duties that Ts'ao Yin performed while Nanking textile commissioner was the checking and the stabilization of rice prices. In this, he was acting both as the personal agent of the Emperor and also in cooperation with the provincial bureaucracy, as his memorials show.

The basic national plan for granaries had been fixed by statute in 1660. Rice was to be bought up during the autumn and winter, and to be sold at controlled prices during the spring and summer when supplies were low. This was both a humanitarian and a lucrative venture; as the Statutes said: "Making a profit with a view to helping the people." But in times of famine, rice was to be distributed to all starving people. These statutes were expanded in 1691, and this was the version under which Ts'ao Yin was operating. Each large *hsien* was to store 5,000 piculs, each small *hsien* 3,000. All surpluses remaining in the third and fourth months—the end of spring and early summer— were to be sold off at current market prices; then in the ninth month

116. John Hall, "Early Ch'ing Copper Trade," p. 454. (There is one digit missing in note 35 on this page; the reference to the 1699 statute is *T'ung-k'ao*, p. 4976b, not 497b.)

the *hsien* officials bought up new grain and returned it to the granaries.[117]

These operations were carried out by the provincial officials under the direction of the Board of Revenue.[118] But the Statutes present a misleadingly simple and lucid picture. In fact, the Imperial Household and the Emperor's agents played a considerable part in keeping this complex system in running order.

One basic duty of the textile commissioners was to keep the Emperor informed of the current rice prices at all times, and they submitted these prices nearly every month in their memorials.[119] The reports clearly enabled the Emperor to check personally on the veracity of the similar reports sent through normal channels by the provincial governors. Though governors were not made definitely responsible for sending in rice prices until the year 1736,[120] the K'ang-hsi Emperor often urged individual governors to send in rice prices and weather reports.[121] Weather reports were also submitted every month by the commissioners.[122]

117. *HTSL*, p. 8746 (ch. 275, p. 1).

118. At least all price stabilization was concentrated under this Board, as in *HTSL*, ch. 275 above.

119. Ts'ao Yin was rather casual about this, often writing merely that rice prices were "normal" or "as usual." But some of his short memorials are preserved in the archives; in these he greets the Emperor briefly and then notes the exact rice prices. Cf. *Ts'ao Yin Archives*, nos. 2797 and 2798; dates of 48/8/3 and 48/9/2. Li Hsü sent the prices intermittently up to 1712; from then on he reported them almost every single month until the end of the K'ang-hsi reign (*Li Hsü Memorials*, pp. 38 ff.). For the rice prices, cf. appendix B, below.

120. *HTSL*, pp. 7423–24 (ch. 177, pp. 18b–19). By the statute of 1736, the Kiangsu and Anhwei governors were to report the summer harvests in the sixth month and the autumn harvests in the tenth. This was after the introduction of the new varieties of early-ripening rice; cf. chapter 7, below.

121. K'ang-hsi rescript to Kiangsi governor, T'ung Kuo-jang (governor from 1712–17), undated memorial in National Palace Museum archives, Taichung, Taiwan, crate 76, package 91, no. 2600: "After this, write and send all memorials in your own hand. You must write out the weather conditions and the rice prices clearly." Ibid., crate 77, package 88, rescript to memorial by Honan governor Lu Yu, dated 49/8/20: "Include rice prices in all future memorials."

122. For a sequence of weather reports, cf. *Li Hsü Memorials*, for the fifty-second year of the K'ang-hsi reign (1713); p. 45b, sixth month; p. 46, seventh month; p. 47, eighth month; p. 48, ninth month; p. 48b, tenth month. It is not certain whether Ts'ao Yin was more casual, or his memorials have been lost. *Ts'ao Yin Memorials*, p. 20, dated 48/2/8, states that Ts'ao Yin is sending with it the weather report for the first month, and has

Besides sending reports, Ts'ao Yin as textile commissioner also played an active part in the distribution of rice relief. Thus in 1697, during a winter of unusually bad weather, he received orders from the ministers of the Imperial Household to take 4,000 piculs of rice then in storage down to Huai-an, and to hand it over personally to the director-general of grain transport, Sang-ko.[123] After he and Sang-ko had calculated the extent of the area hit by natural calamities, Tsa'o Yin wrote in his memorial, they proceeded with the rice distribution:

> Then Sang-ko selected industrious and honest officials, and I hired local boats to effect the deliveries to the various areas. Sang-ko gave strict orders that when the rice reached these areas, only small amounts might be sold at random to the poor. He refused all requests that the rice be sold speedily, or wholesale, for this might stir up corrupt practices in the sales and obstruct the Emperor's benevolence.

Since many people could not even afford the current price of 8 *ch'ien* per picul, Ts'ao Yin fixed the price of the emergency rice at 4.85 *ch'ien*. As he noted, this was exceptionally cheap, and the people were correspondingly grateful.[124]

The Emperor allowed Ts'ao Yin considerable initiative in these matters of purchase and distribution. In December 1699 Ts'ao Yin received an edict to buy up rice; but since there had been heavy rain and snow in Nanking, and the rice boats had been unable to get through from Kiangsi and Hu-kuang, he memorialized that he was

---

this rescript: "Noted. If anyone is coming to Peking with a memorial, enter the Chiang-nan rice prices in it." This suggests that the Emperor only expected Ts'ao Yin to report rice prices when he was reporting some other matter anyway.

123. *Ts'ao-yün tsung-tu*, BH 834. This is probably yet another Sang-ko from the two *chih-tsao* of the same name mentioned above, since his office was one of the most senior in the bureaucracy and it is most unlikely that a *chih-tsao* would ever hold it.

124. *Ts'ao Yin Memorials*, p. 8, dated 36/10/22. He added that he was sending a detailed report separately to the Imperial Household. Also that the governor, Sung Lao, was on the way with further stores of rice and money. The price of 4.85 *ch'ien* (0.485 taels) was about half the normal winter price. Ordinarily, the commissioners were happy to report winter prices as low as 8 *ch'ien* for hulled and 7 *ch'ien* for unhulled rice. Presumably on this occasion, not only was rice in short supply, but the people were also at the end of their resources.

going to wait until the weather cleared and prices came down before making any purchases.[125]

In April 1704 he received an order from the Imperial Household to buy up cheap rice in Hu-kuang and Kiangsi; he was to work in conjunction with the governor-general, Asan, using 10,000 taels taken from the textile commissioner's treasury to make the purchases. But, Ts'ao Yin reported to the Emperor the following month, though it was true that the rice had been cheap in the two areas mentioned, the good news had spread too fast; numerous buyers had come down from Shantung province, and prices had already climbed back to 9.2 *ch'ien* per picul. Therefore he would hold off until after the next harvest. The Emperor's rescript on this memorial is typical of the friendly colloquial style he used with Ts'ao Yin, in which questions were asked, comments passed, and further instructions given. It ran:

> Noted. What's the wheat harvest going to be like this year? Send a report on this as quickly as possible. In Peking the spring has been excellent, but there's a lot of sickness about.[126]

After the harvest, Ts'ao Yin reported back as promised. He had sent men to Hankow, who bought rice at 6.3 *ch'ien*; thus with his 10,000 taels, he pointed out with some pride, he had bought 15,800 piculs. (Had he bought in April, as ordered, he could only have got about 11,000 piculs.) The use to which this purchase should be put remained a matter for private discussion between the Emperor and his agent. At the end of his memorial, Ts'ao Yin asked what he should do with the rice he had just bought. "The rice was originally intended for use in Shantung," the Emperor answered, "but there have been such good harvests in the eastern provinces that there is nowhere to put it to use. Send another memorial about this in the spring." [127]

On the surface, the episode shows Ts'ao Yin using his business acumen and knowledge of local prices to make a profit for the Emperor with the Emperor's money. But it is only necessary to look just below the surface to see how such operations might bring profit to the textile commissioners themselves. In the above example, Ts'ao Yin had

125. *Ts'ao Yin Archives*, no. 2711, dated 38/12/12, quoting edict of 38/11/6.
126. Ibid., no. 2739, dated 43/4/1, quoting orders received on 43/3/20.
127. Ibid., no. 2740, dated 43/9/16.

an extra 10,000 taels in his charge during the months between sowing
and harvest; this was the time when the people were short of food and
money, and handsome profits could be realized on short-term loans.
There was also the possibility of simple dishonesty. On at least one
occasion Li Hsü stole rice purchase money, as was proved by investigations conducted in 1723. The examining official reported:

> In 1693 Li Hsü received a communication from the Imperial
> Household, telling him to use 2,000 taels of reserve funds to buy
> up some 4,100 piculs of rice. For this item, the revenue needed
> was entered in the accounts as having been received, but the pur-
> chased rice was never stored up. Clearly this was his deficit, and it
> is fitting that I report it.[128]

Such corruption was easy if supervision was lax and the textile commissioners were left on their own.

In times of major crisis, however, Ts'ao Yin lost his independent
role and acted as a coordinator and liaison man between the provincial
officials and the special stabilization officials sent down from the Capital by the Board of Revenue. Such was the case in 1708. The previous
year there had been a serious drought in Kiangsu, and rice prices
climbed steadily.[129] By December 1707 they had reached 17 ch'ien
per picul,[130] over twice the normal price. In March 1708 Ts'ao Yin
returned from Peking, accompanied by six price stabilization officials.
The news that prices were to be officially stabilized spread alarm in the
shops of the rice merchants, Ts'ao Yin reported, and all those who had
been hoarding rice and speculating on a continued rise in prices tried
to sell at once. Ts'ao Yin also had orders to confer with Sang-ko, the
director-general of grain transport, about the nonarrival of some rice

128. YCCPYC, ts'e 48, p. 101, dated Yung-cheng 1/3/22. The memorial was sent by the
newly appointed Soochow chih-tsao, Hu Feng-hui.

129. Ch'ing pai lei-ch'ao, section 87, p. 10, has a discussion of this drought and its general effect on rice prices in the following years, giving some useful facts for a comparative study of rice prices. Prices were as high as 2.4 taels per picul in 1707, and were still at
1.7 taels in 1709. The average should have been about 7 ch'ien. The average during the
Yung-cheng and Ch'ien-lung reigns was about 1 tael. In the early nineteenth century the
average price was about 1.5 taels, though they hit 3.5 during a locust plague in 1815. The
average in the middle nineteenth century was between 2.7 and 3.5 taels; by the end of the
century the average was 8 or 9 taels.

130. Li Hsü Memorials, p. 18, dated 46/12/–.

shipments, and to pass on instructions from the Emperor to the governor-general, Shao-mu-pu.[131]

Thereafter, Ts'ao Yin sent one of the heaviest concentrations of memorials in his career, as he described the various attempts to end the crisis. On April 6 he reported that Sang-ko had decided to hold the tribute rice in reserve, that rice boats would soon be coming through from Kiangsi and Hu-kuang, and that the six stabilization officials were looking into local conditions.[132] A week later, Sang-ko was holding 100,000 piculs of rice in the ports, and Ts'ao Yin was waiting for some definite decision on prices before selling the rice still stored in the textile commissioner's granaries. Apparently wary of what might happen, the Emperor told Ts'ao Yin to send him a secret memorial as soon as any of the price stabilization officers made a major decision.[133] On May 2, Ts'ao Yin sold his rice reserves, on his own initiative, at 8 *ch'ien* per picul, 20 percent below the prevailing price. Two weeks later the governor-general fixed rice prices at 9 *ch'ien;* Ts'ao Yin reported some abuses and dishonesty among the stabilization officers, though he added generously that it did not seem to be a serious matter. Yet more memorials followed: on June 1 to report prices down to 8 *ch'ien,* on June 4 to report that his rice reserves were now exhausted, on July 5 to report that all the stabilization rice had been sold and that since several ports in Kiangsi and Hu-kuang had forbidden the export of any more rice to Kiangsu, prices were already climbing again. In this July memorial he also pointed out that his position was an awkward one:

> I do not have a provincial appointment, and can only send repeated instructions to the *chou* and *hsien* officials, or communications to the governor-general and governor, that on the one hand they should issue proclamations to the traveling merchants, and on the other write to Kiangsi and Hu-kuang to have the prohibition lifted. Then naturally this matter would be settled and our anxiety ended.[134]

131. *Ts'ao Yin Memorials,* p. 16b, dated 47/3/1.
132. *Ts'ao Yin Archives,* no. 2771, dated 47/3/16.
133. Ibid., no. 2772, dated 47/3/21, for memorial and rescript.
134. This sequence of five memorials is in *Ts'ao Yin Archives,* no. 2774, dated 47/intercalary 3/12; no. 2770, dated 47/4/1; no. 2786, dated 47/4/13; no. 2775, dated 47/4/16; no. 2776, dated 47/5/18.

Pressure was apparently brought to bear on the officials of Kiangsi and Hu-kuang, for on July 12 Ts'ao Yin was able to report that this prohibition had been lifted, that over two hundred merchants' boats had already come through, and that the governor-general and governor had already sent their orders to start buying up rice for the following year.[135]

So the cycle started again, but it had clearly been a close call, proving that the combined resources of provincial, textile commissioner, and tribute reserves could not support Kiangsu province for more than a year. But Ts'ao Yin's efficiency had not gone unnoticed. In an imperial command (ch'ih) issued on October 23, 1708, he was ordered to supervise personally the transport of rice from Yangchow, Huai-an, and three other cities to the Capital. What had started as a casual commission to check price stabilization was made a permanent appointment to guarantee government revenue. The bondservants were proving their uses as adjuncts of the provincial bureaucracy.[136]

Such extra appointments brought prestige and the chance for gain, but also much extra work and the possibilities of catastrophe. As if anticipating the dangers, Ts'ao Yin had already hedged his bets by calling on the local salt merchants:

> Li Hsü, the salt controller Li Ssu-ch'üan, and I, discussed the matter of getting funds for buying rice, which could then be sent out as needed to stabilize prices. The Liang-huai merchants are also deeply grateful for the Emperor's favor, and are willing to sell salt in Kiangsi and Hu-kuang and then buy rice and bring it back to stabilize rice prices.[137]

It is apparent from this that discussion by officials preceded the salt merchants' willingness to turn rice dealers; but the collaboration brought good results the following year when heavy rains again sent prices in Kiangsu up to 14 ch'ien. For this time the reserves held out, the winds changed and the boats came through, and finally there was a good harvest.[138]

There were no more such crises in the K'ang-hsi reign. But for a

135. Ts'ao Yin Memorials, p. 18, dated 47/5/25.
136. Ts'ao Yin Ch'ih. For full reference, cf. bibliography below. I am grateful to Mr. Lawrence Kessler for sending me a copy of this document.
137. Ts'ao Yin Memorials, p. 18b, dated 47/5/25.
138. Ibid., p. 2, dated 48/3/16.

time the situation had been dangerous, and that there was no famine or wide-scale suffering was certainly due to the adaptable and generally competent planning of the textile commissioner, the provincial officials, the stabilization officers, and the director-general of grain transport, operating more or less together under the watchful eyes of their Emperor. The Emperor had acted rapidly and publicly as the protector of the people; but he could only act thus when he was given accurate information and when his orders were promptly obeyed.

The Execution of Imperial Commissions

As textile commissioner, agent for copper purchase, and assistant in the distribution of rice, Ts'ao Yin worked personally for the Emperor, although the work also involved him with the ordinary bureaucracy and the business of day-to-day provincial government. But, in addition, he and the other commissioners were used by the Emperor to carry out many personal commissions which had nothing at all to do with the workings of the provincial government.

One of these sidelines was the procuring of rare objects for the Emperor. Li Hsü sent many such objects to the Court: boxes, trays, and brush-holders in lacquer from foreign lands; caskets inlaid with gold and silver; a mixed assortment of lemons, lichees, papaya, cassia oil, and attar of roses; the tender new shoots of early spring or winter vegetables; lavishly embroidered peony-style collars and cuffs; crystallized fruits; rare books.[139] On one occasion the Emperor cautioned him about his extravagance, on another gave him special praise because of the excellence of the objects.[140]

Sometimes the Emperor took a special interest in these activities. For

139. References to these items, in the above order, are: a. *Li Hsü Memorials*, p. 2b, dated 32/12/–. The character translated as "foreign" is *yang* meaning "sea," or, as in this context, "from overseas," here referring probably to Japan. b. Ibid., p. 1b, dated 32/10/–. c. Ibid., p. 5, dated 37/10/–. This particular melange of fruit and flowers were probably for the making of fermented liquor of great delicacy. The list closely parallels that of ingredients used by Mao Hsiang's concubine to make special drinks for him in the 1640s; cf. Pan Tze-yen, trans., *The Reminiscences of Tung Hsiao-wan* (Shanghai, 1931), pp. 61–63. d. *Li Hsü Memorials*, p. 12, dated 45/2/–; p. 13b, dated 45/12/13; p. 17, dated 46/10/10. e. Ibid., p. 110, dated 60/4/11. In this particular case Li Hsü was returning from Peking when he met his own servant on the road, bringing the embroidered collars to the Capital; so he stopped him and rechecked the quality before letting him proceed. f. Ibid., p. 14, dated 46/6/–. g. Ibid., p. 63, dated 54/5/6.

140. Ibid., p. 46b, endorsement to memorial dated 52/8/21, and ibid., p. 84, rescript quoted in memorial dated 56/6/22.

example, in 1693 Li Hsü was "getting together a troupe of girl actresses, and was going to send them to the Emperor to amuse him." Hearing of this, the K'ang-hsi Emperor sent down the famous voice instructor Yeh Kuo-chen from the Court to complete the girls' training.[141] At other times the Emperor himself gave the instructions in minute detail, as when he told Li Hsü and Ts'ao Yin's son Ts'ao Yung:

> I am short of instrument makers and good bamboo for making musical instruments. Send to Soochow for the skilled trader named Chou, an old man. In his home there are men who can make musical instruments. And choose several of the various kinds of good bamboo and send them in.
>
> Also ask him if he knows how to regulate pitches, or if he has someone, to send him along too. But he is an old man, and if he cannot come in person and picks out the best man to come, then that will be all right.

Li Hsü replied that he had tracked down the man, who was called Chou Ch'i-lan. Too old to travel, he had recommended two men, who were now being escorted to Peking. The perfect bamboo came from Chekiang, and had to be cut in winter if it was to be at its best. The year's stocks were already exhausted, but he would buy from the new crop as soon as it was cut.[142]

On one occasion the Emperor ordered the three textile commissioners to pick out a suitable man and send him to investigate conditions in Japan. They picked the chief clerk (*wu-lin-ta*) from the commissioner's office in Hangchow, a Chinese bondservant named Mo-erh-sen,[143] whom the Franciscan della Chiesa later described, perhaps too flatteringly, as a "sagace esploratore." [144] When they reported that all was ready, they received an acknowledgment and the rescript:

141. Ibid., p. 2, dated 32/12/–. Yeh, who was a specialist in *i* opera, reached Soochow on 32/12/16. Li Hsü added that he had been trying to get a good *i* instructor for a long time, but had failed. This made the imperial gesture especially welcome. The incident is discussed in *HLMHC*, pp. 301 and 304.

142. *Li Hsü Memorials*, p. 47b, dated 52/9/18, quoting orders received 52/8/8. Li Hsü bought 2,000 lengths of bamboo in the twelfth month and sent them off to Peking; cf. ibid., p. 50, dated 52/12/24.

143. *PCST*, ch. 75, p. 6b; he was a member of the Bordered Blue Banner, and became a sixth-rank official.

144. *Sinica Franciscana*, 5, 441.

"Absolute secrecy is essential." [145] Mo-erh-sen sailed from Shanghai, in secret and disguised as a merchant, on July 9, 1701. He returned to Ningpo in November, and left almost immediately for Peking, to report to the Emperor.[146] The Yung-cheng Emperor recalled Mo-erh-sen's mission twenty-seven years later. Mo-erh-sen's report contained many fabrications, and mistakenly claimed that the Japanese were "weak and obedient," wrote the Emperor; nevertheless his mission had extended Chinese knowledge of foreign parts. It is clear from the Emperor's comments that Mo-erh-sen had been sent to check on Japanese naval and trade activities.[147]

Apart from one ink-stick, so exquisitely made that it was kept as a treasure, which Ts'ao Yin sent to the Court in 1695,[148] there is no record of his gifts to the Emperor. But from the numerous accounts of Western objects to be found in the *Dream of the Red Chamber* (the famous novel by Ts'ao Yin's grandson Ts'ao Chan), historians have inferred that Ts'ao Yin probably had regular contacts with Western traders, and may have been commissioned to supply the Court with unusual Western objects.[149] Objects used in this fictional household ranged from the large clock that so startled a visiting farmer's wife [150] to an elaborate snuffbox decorated with a "nude blonde with two flesh wings on her back." [151]

That Ts'ao Yin did act as general purchasing agent of exotica for the Emperor is suggested by a passage in the *Dream of the Red Chamber*. Though it is dangerous to assume that everything Ts'ao Chan wrote in his novel refers to specific moments of Ts'ao family history,[152] an exception can be made with regard to this particular pas-

145. *Li Hsü Memorials*, p. 7, dated 40/3/–, quoting orders received 39/11/–. The discussion between the three *chih-tsao*, Li Hsü, Ts'ao Yin, and Ao-fu-ho, took place on 40/1/–.
146. Ibid., p. 7b, dated 40/6/–, and p. 8b, dated 40/10/–.
147. YCCPYC, *ts'e* 41, p. 61, endorsement to memorial of Li Wei dated Yung-cheng 6/8/8. The Emperor wrote an incorrect homophone for the Mo of Mo-erh-sen's name. The second and third characters are identical in both versions.
148. For this ink-stick, 7.3 centimeters long, made in imitation of a Han stone tablet, with beautifully inscribed *k'ai-shu* writing on the faces, filled in with gold, the ink of the deepest, finest black, cf. HLMHC, pp. 307–08.
149. HLMHC, p. 241, where Chou Ju-ch'ang also discusses the writings of Fang Hao on this problem. Wu Shih-ch'ang, *On the Red Chamber Dream*, p. 355.
150. *Hung-lou meng*, trans. Joly, I, 97–98.
151. Quoted in Wu Shih-ch'ang, p. 355.
152. As Chou Ju-ch'ang does throughout HLMHC, giving both character equivalents and a chronological table to prove the accuracy of Ts'ao Chan as a novelist. Chou Ju-chang's

sage. For here Ts'ao Chan says that the Chen family acted as host to the Emperor on four occasions, which is a definite reference to the fact that Ts'ao Yin received the K'ang-hsi Emperor on four of his Southern Tours; [153] furthermore, references to the Chen family occur only rarely in the novel, at moments of the greatest importance to the plot. Chih-yen, the most knowledgeable of Ts'ao Chan's contemporary commentators, wrote that reference to the Chen family represented the "true facts" of the novel,[154] and remarked about the passage quoted below that it was accurate and of the greatest importance.[155] Here, the old family nurse Chao is speaking:

> Furthermore, there is the present Chen family of Chiang-nan. Ai ya ya, what a scale they lived on! That one family alone received the Emperor four times. If we hadn't seen it with our own eyes we would never have believed it, no matter who told us. Without speaking of the silver treated like mud, no matter what thing there is on earth, there it was piled up like mountains or the waters of the sea. . . .

Wang Hsi-feng answered that she too had heard this, but had never been able to understand how the Chen family achieved such opulence.

> I can tell you that in one sentence, answered nurse Chao. There was no more to it than taking money from the Emperor's household and then using it all on the Emperor's person. What family has so much money that they can buy all those pretentious curiosities? [156]

---

work is of such subtlety and meticulous scholarship that it is hard to fault, and the material that he has collected is invaluable. It is only in some of the more exact parallelisms that our doubts are roused: for example when, to fit the chronology of Ts'ao Chan's life, Chou Ju-ch'ang states that Pao-yü's first erotic dream, followed by an affair with his maid, occurred when Pao-yü was seven years old (8 *sui*) (*HLMHC*, p. 176). The language in *Hung-lou meng pa-shih-hui chiao-pen*, p. 59, is quite unambiguous with regard to the physical details of this incident. One is tempted to say that it is more likely that Pao-yü was about twelve or thirteen, and that either Ts'ao Chan was born earlier than Chou Ju-ch'ang says he was, or that the novel is not a meticulous record of Ts'ao Chan's life.

153. In 1699, 1703, 1705, 1707. Cf. chapter 4, below.

154. For the "true facts," cf. commentary by Chih-yen quoted and discussed in Wu Shih-ch'ang, *On the Red Chamber Dream*, p. 198.

155. *Chih-yen chai hung-lou meng chi-p'ing*, p. 199. The interlinear commentary by Chih-yen opposite the characters for "the present Chen family of Chiang-nan" reads: "This Chen family is truly the key to all the really important things, this is not just idle chatter."

156. *Hung-lou meng pa-shih-hui chiao pen*, p. 156.

"The pretentious curiosities" were certainly Western objects. Just before the above passage, the same two characters had this dialogue, also talking about Southern Tours. Wang Hsi-feng speaks first:

> Our Wang family also made the preparations on one occasion. At that time my grandfather was in sole charge of all matters concerning foreign offerings to the Court. All the foreigners who came were looked after by our family, and all the foreign goods brought by sea that are now in Kwangtung, Fukien, Yunnan, and Chekiang came originally from our house.

Nurse Chao replied:

> Who doesn't know that? There's still a saying that goes: "In the Eastern Seas they were short of a white jade bed, so the Dragon King came to ask the Wangs of Chiang-nan for one." That saying refers to your family.

There are four further pieces of evidence that suggest Ts'ao Yin may have had considerable contacts with Europeans, and thus been intermediary between them and the Emperor. Firstly, the Nanking textile commissioner's yamen was next to one of the Christian churches in that city.[157] Secondly, on at least two of his Southern Tours the K'ang-hsi Emperor summoned missionaries to attend him in the textile commissioner's yamen, which he was using as a temporary palace while in Nanking.[158] Thirdly, the K'ang-hsi Emperor had specially ordered that bondservants should be used to accompany Westerners,[159] and textile commissioners were called in on conferences dealing with Westerners.[160] Fourthly, there was a considerable traffic of gifts, mainly of wine, from missionaries in the Kiangsi area,[161] and similar practices presumably prevailed in Kiangsu.

157. Joseph Dehergne, S.J., "La Chine centrale vers 1700. I. L'évêché de Nankin, étude de géographie missionaire," *Archivum Historicum Societatis Iesu, 28* (1959), 309. There is a misprint of radical 149 for radical 120 in the character *chih* of *chih-tsao,* but it is obviously this office that is meant.

158. See below, chapter 4.

159. As his son, the Yung-cheng Emperor, recalled in the endorsement to a memorial from the Kiangsu governor Ch'en Shih-hsia, dated Yung-cheng 5/11/24. YCCPYC, *ts'e* 5, p. 107b.

160. As in the visit of the Portuguese ambassador Metello in 1727. YCCPYC, *ts'e* 40, p. 86, memorial by Li Wei, dated Yung-cheng 5/9/19.

161. *Lang T'ing-chi Memorials,* pp. 40b–42.

Ts'ao Yin's memorials, however, mention nothing of Westerners. The only unusual commissions he is definitely known to have undertaken were the distribution of imperial gifts to Buddhist temples. Sometimes all three of the textile commissioners worked together on these occasions, as when the Emperor sent the gift of a Buddha to the monastery of P'u-t'o shan, in 1708. Li Hsü and Ts'ao Yin took delivery in Yangchow, and then Ts'ao Yin personally accompanied it to Hangchow, where he handed it over to Sun Wen-ch'eng. After discussion, Sun Wen-ch'eng went ahead to P'u-t'o shan to arrange for its arrival, while Ts'ao Yin's youngest brother Ts'ao I took the Buddha on the sea crossing to the island temple.[162]

More usually Ts'ao Yin took care of the arrangements himself. The bulk of the Emperor's gifts which he handled were for the two great temples near Yangchow, for both of which the Emperor had some special affection, and which were used as temporary palaces during his Southern Tours.[163] These were the temple at Chin-shan, on an island near Chen-chiang-fu, with dwellings clustered round the shore and giant terraces rising behind them to the ten-story pagoda,[164] and the Kao-min temple, 15 li south of Yangchow, built out on a wooded promontory over the water, with its temple to the Buddha of the three ages, and a special new temple for the golden Buddha presented by K'ang-hsi.[165] Gifts for the T'ien-ning temple to the northwest of the city, where the Buddha of the western regions was worshiped in an area famous for its flower markets and tea shops,[166] were usually handled by Li Hsü, who also raised a "contribution" of 14,000 taels from the local merchants to repair the fabric of the temple.[167]

Ts'ao Yin took gifts of imperial calligraphy to the Chin-shan tem-

162. There are two complementary memorials on the delivery of this Buddha: *Ts'ao Yin Memorials*, p. 18, dated 47/4/13, and *Li Hsü Memorials*, p. 22b, dated 47/3/29.

163. *Yang-chou hua-fang lu*, p. 102. The same work, p. 24, lists the T'ien-ning and the Kao-min (though not the Chin-shan) temples as being among the "eight great temples" of Yangchow.

164. *Nan-hsün sheng-tien*, ch. 98, p. 2, has an illustration and a brief description of the temple.

165. *Yang-chou hua-fang lu*, pp. 161–62, and *Nan-hsün sheng-tien*, ch. 97, p. 21.

166. *Yang-chou hua-fang lu*, pp. 82–86.

167. *Li Hsü Memorials*, p. 112, dated 60/10/14. Li Hsü took imperial gifts to the T'ien-ning temple in 1707 (ibid., p. 15, dated 46/9/–) and 1717 (ibid., p. 86b, dated 56/7/27). He also engaged the monks there to chant for one week to aid the Empress Dowager during her serious illness (ibid., p. 89, dated 56/11/7).

ple in 1703 and 1704.[168] These gifts cost the Emperor merely the
time and paper of writing—if indeed he wrote them himself. The cost
to Ts'ao Yin was considerable, however. The calligraphy was first
copied onto a tablet so that it could be hung in the temple for the people to see, then carved onto a perfect piece of stone and displayed in
the open.[169] Gifts of imperial calligraphy came for the Kao-min temple in 1704 and 1705;[170] in the case of the 1704 calligraphy, the
Emperor gave special orders to Ts'ao Yin to send him rubbings as soon
as the carving was finished,[171] presumably so that he could check on
the standard of the work.

These and the relaying of other presents from the Emperor to their
destination[172] were mainly routine. It was an exceptional case when
Ts'ao Yin had to penetrate the mountains and bring back an obstinate
recluse, as he did in the winter of 1704 when the K'ang-hsi Emperor
presented a golden Buddha to the Kao-min temple. Ts'ao Yin memorialized:

> But in the temple there was no monk worthy of the task of look-
> ing after it. . . . I learned that there was a Buddhist monk
> called Chi Yin living on Mount Ma-chi, a recluse who was puri-
> fying his conduct, who would be equal to the duties of the post.
> Li Hsü and I led the civil and military officials of Yangchow, and
> the merchants and people, and invited the monk Chi Yin. But he
> repeatedly and firmly refused us. Then we sincerely told him that
> the Kao-min temple was a place visited by the Emperor, that this
> gift of a golden Buddha was something of prime importance,
> that someone must be found to look after it, and that this was a
> fitting time for him to repay the Emperor's favor. Thereupon the
> monk Chi Yin happily accompanied us.

168. *Ts'ao Yin Archives*, no. 2814, dated 42/7/3. The calligraphy was brought from the
Court by Kao Shih-ch'i. Ts'ao Yin "led the monks in praising the Emperor, and added it
to the temple treasures." *Ts'ao Yin Memorials*, p. 9, dated 43/2/15.

169. This was the procedure followed in 1704, when he was aided by the Tartar general
Ma San-ch'i.

170. *Ts'ao Yin Memorials*, p. 11b, dated 43/12/2, and pp. 13b–14, dated 44/10/22.

171. Ibid., p. 9, endorsement to memorial dated 43/10/13.

172. As with Ts'ao Yin's handling of a batch of sacred trees (*p'u-t'i tzu*) sent south by
the Emperor, which he distributed between his own yamen and the Kao-min, T'ien-ning,
Chin-shan, and other temples. *Ts'ao Yin Archives*, no. 2713, dated 50/3/1.

All should now have been well, "while in the morning the bells rang out and at night the drums sounded," and Ts'ao Yin either thanked the Emperor on the monks' behalf, or received orders from the Emperor for the monks to send their thanks in person.[173] But the monk took matters into his own hands:

> Now the monk Chi Yin is sending a palace memorial thanking the Emperor for his favor, saying that in the past he saw the Emperor on one of his journeys, and received permission to send palace memorials. I do not dare to hide this from the Emperor.[174]

It is not surprising that Ts'ao Yin was upset. It must have been distinctly unnerving to learn that a recluse living in the mountains above Yangchow had, with imperial permission, quite possibly been sending secret reports about him. Within four years, however, the balance was restored; for Ts'ao Yin received orders to send secret palace memorials about other people. In the meantime, Ts'ao Yin had acted as host to the Emperor on his Southern Tours and been made a salt censor, increasing steadily in prestige and wealth.

173. As happened in 1717 when Li Hsü relayed the thanks of the monk Kuang Ming for an imperial present and received the endorsement: "Noted. Why doesn't Kuang Ming send a memorial?" The following month Li Hsü reported the dispatch of such a memorial. *Li Hsü Memorials*, p. 86b, endorsement to memorial dated 56/7/27, and ibid., p. 87, dated 56/9/9.

174. The whole incident of the golden Buddha and the monk Chi Yin is in *Ts'ao Yin Memorials*, p. 12, dated 43/12/10.

CHAPTER 4

The Southern Tours

The K'ang-hsi Emperor made six Southern Tours (*nan-hsün*), in 1684, 1689, 1699, 1703, 1705, and 1707.[1] On the last four of these tours, Ts'ao Yin, as Nanking textile commissioner, acted as host to the Emperor. From various accounts such as a private diary of the 1705 tour and his grandson's novel, the *Dream of the Red Chamber*, it is possible to recreate a fairly clear picture of the rewards and burdens that such a duty brought Ts'ao Yin. We can thus supplement a general description of the tours with a specific case study.

The K'ang-hsi Emperor's Six Southern Tours

In official histories these Southern Tours are presented primarily as river inspections, and most of the space is given to debates and edicts on problems of river conservancy. Provincial officials arrive regularly to greet the Emperor, who holds elevating conversations with them or famous local scholars. The common people only appear on the scene to "cheer like thunder" or to implore the Emperor to stay longer among them. Foreign observers in the seventeenth century, however, ignored the administrative side of the tours and concentrated on the benevolent aspects; for them, the tours were arranged so that the Emperor could speak in person to the poor people of China, hearing their grievances and dealing out swift justice to any mandarins accused of extortion.[2] Both these views must be combined in describing the tours. Though inevitably much of the Emperor's dealings were with the members of the bureaucracy, the tours gave him a chance to check on

1. *Shih-lu,* ch. 116, p. 30b; ch. 139, p. 3b; ch. 192, p. 7; ch. 211, p. 3b; ch. 219, p. 7; ch. 228, p. 4b.

2. Cf. Father J. Bouvet, *Histoire de l'empereur de la Chine* (La Haye, 1699), p. 52; and Father Louis Le Comte, *Nouveaux mémoires sur l'état présent de la Chine* (Paris, 1696), pp. 36–37. For a good critical appraisal of Bouvet's work, cf. J. J. Heeren, "Father Bouvet's Picture of Emperor K'ang-hsi," *Asia Major,* 1st series, 7 (1932), 556–72.

them personally; and it is probable, as will be shown later, that he did sometimes meet the common people.

The first of the Southern Tours was one section of a general tour of inspection that the K'ang-hsi Emperor made in the years following the final suppression of the rebellion of the Three Feudatories in 1681. As a later Chinese popularizer put it, during the early part of his reign when the kingdom was troubled the Emperor stayed deep in his palace, but when nothing was happening he went out to inspect it.[3] In 1683, the Emperor and Empress Dowager went on a tour to Shansi, and this was the first of his Western Tours.[4] In 1684 he went on a Northern Tour, from which he returned on September 9.[5] He then announced an Eastern Tour, so it is probable that he was planning a series of four tours, one for each of the cardinal points; but presumably a tour just to Shantung seemed impractical, so it was included in the longer journey called a Southern Tour, and the term Eastern Tour was abandoned.[6]

Before the 1684 Southern Tour began, various edicts were issued in an attempt to keep serious abuses from arising. All supplies were to be bought up in advance, the Board of Revenue taking care of fodder for the animals, the Board of Works laying in charcoal, and the Banqueting Court [7] getting the necessary food. Local officials were forbidden to take these items from the people. All amounts were to be calculated in advance and bought at current prices.[8] The composition of the retinue (*hu-ts'ung*) was decided: escorting the Emperor were princes and imperial clansmen, chamberlains, guards officers, armorers, men from the Imperial Stud and Equipage Department, troops from the Peking divisions of the Banners; following them were the civil retinue (*ya-men hu-ts'ung kuan*), about ninety men drawn from among the grand secretaries, Hanlin academicians, Board presidents, department directors, censors, doctors, diarists, all these in turn being accompanied

3. *K'ang-hsi nan-hsün pi-chi*, p. 1. In the context, the irony seems to be unconscious.

4. HTSL, pp. 9261–62 (ch. 311, pp. 16b–18b). The other Western Tours were in 1698, 1702, 1703, and 1710.

5. *Shih-lu*, ch. 116, p. 12.

6. HTSL, p. 9234 (ch. 310, p. 6b), lists this as the first of the Southern Tours, but on p. 9253 (ch. 311, p. 1) refers to the Emperor's return from the south via Shantung as comprising an Eastern Tour. This is the only Eastern Tour listed. *Shih-lu*, ch. 116, p. 30b, calls the 1684 tour in general an Eastern Tour.

7. *kuang-lu-ssu*, BH 934.

8. *Shih-lu*, ch. 116, pp. 23b–24.

by the necessary secretaries and clerks.[9] The total must have been about one thousand persons, and it is quite possible that Ts'ao Yin was one of them.[10]

It is not surprising that vast crowds of officials and people greeted the Emperor wherever he went. Statutes of 1675 had laid down that whenever the Emperor traveled through an area, all officials living within one hundred *li* must come and welcome him; those failing to do so were to forfeit one year's salary for the first offence, on the second offence they were to be lowered two grades and transferred.[11] These statutes were enforced in 1684 by officials from the Court of State Cermonial, who rode out ahead of the cortege ordering all officials within a hundred *li* to assemble the local elite (*hsiang-shen*) and scholar-commoners (*shih-min*) in their area to kneel and greet the Emperor on his arrival and departure. Military commanders did the same with their troops.[12]

On November 5, 1684, the Emperor and his retinue left Peking and traveled due south by land, passing through Yung-ch'ing-hsien, Jen-ch'iu-hsien, and Hsien-hsien, and crossing the Grand Canal at Fu-ch'eng-hsien on November 10. The following day he was formally welcomed by the officials of Shantung province at Te-chou. The Emperor continued to the sacred mountain of T'ai-shan, which he climbed, presenting calligraphy to a summit temple, but rejecting the sycophantic suggestion of an official that he use the fact that 1684 was an auspicious *chia-tzu* year (the first of the sexagenary cycle) to proclaim his reign as the beginning of a new era.[13] He moved south again through Hsin-t'ai-hsien and I-chou, rejoining the Grand Canal at Su-ch'ien-hsien on November 24. The next day he embarked at T'ao-yüan-hsien and traveled down the Grand Canal and across the Yangtze to Soochow, which he reached on December 2. From December 7 to 9 he was in Nanking, whence he returned by water to T'ao-

9. *HTSL*, p. 9234 (ch. 310, pp. 7–8).

10. At this time he was serving in the Imperial Household in Peking, cf. chapter 1 above. We know Singde was on this tour; cf. *HLMHC*, p. 227, and Singde's own enthusiastic poems on Chiang-nan in *Na-lan tz'u* [The *tz'u* of Singde] (Hong Kong, 1960), pp. 106–07.

11. *HTSL*, p. 9233 (ch. 310, p. 6b).

12. Ibid., p. 9234 (ch. 310, p. 8). The Court of State Ceremonial is the *hung-lu-ssu*, BH 935.

13. On the K'ang-hsi Emperor's visit to T'ai-shan, cf. Edouard Chevannes, *Le T'ai Chan, essai de monographie d'un culte chinois* (Paris, 1910), especially pp. 59 and 392–93. (I am indebted to Professor Arthur Wright for this reference).

yüan-hsien, by land to Te-chou, and so north to Peking by the former route, returning to the palace on January 3, 1685, after sixty days of travel.[14]

There is little doubt that on this tour the K'ang-hsi Emperor was sizing up the attitudes of the central provinces toward the Manchu regime, and that he proceeded very cautiously. For instance he by-passed Yangchow, the scene of the terrible massacre by Manchu troops of the Chinese inhabitants in 1645,[15] and did not move south of Soochow to the area of the bitter fighting around Hangchow, where the implacable Ming loyalist Mao Hsiang (still living at this time) had seen all his servants killed and his possessions seized by marauding Manchu troops.[16] In Nanking, which had strong associations with the former Ming dynasty, having been once the Ming capital and later the center of Ming-loyalist resistance, the Emperor was meticulous in his attention to local susceptibilities. On December 7 he first sent a chancellor from the Grand Secretariat to sacrifice at the tomb of Ming T'ai-tsu, but then decided to pour a libation in person.[17] The Nanking prefect Yü Ch'eng-lung was singled out for special praise because of his excellent administration; this praise redounded to the credit of the city, but it was also convenient that Yü Ch'eng-lung was a bannerman and that he brought credit to the Manchu system.[18] The Emperor made a particular point of his Chinese studies, and told the scholar Kao Shih-ch'i [19] that although he had ascended the throne at eight *sui*, he had persevered with his reading in the Classics and was

14. *Shih-lu*, ch. 116, p. 30b through ch. 117, p. 33.

15. Ibid., ch. 117, p. 9b, passed by Yangchow; ch. 117, p. 20, on return journey goes straight from I-chen to Chiang-tu-hsien. For translations that have been made of Wang Hsiu-ch'u's eye-witness account of the Yangchow massacre, *Yang-chou shih-jih chi*, cf. *Eminent Chinese*, p. 652, in the bibliography for the biography of the Ming general Shih K'o-fa.

16. For Mao Hsiang's sufferings during this fighting, cf. Pan Tze-yen, trans., *The Reminiscences of Tung Hsiao-wan* (Shanghai, 1931), pp. 66–83. Mao Hsiang's biography is in *Eminent Chinese*, pp. 566–67.

17. *Shih-lu*, ch. 117, pp. 13–15b. Resumption of these sacrifices had been ordered four days before (ibid., p. 11).

18. Ibid., p. 18b. Biography of Yü Ch'eng-lung in *Eminent Chinese*, pp. 938–39. The Emperor promoted him at the end of the tour to Anhwei judicial commissioner (*Shih-lu*, ch. 117, p. 25). The governor-general at this time had an identical name, which makes confusion easy.

19. For Kao Shih-ch'i, a famous scholar and confidant of the K'ang-hsi Emperor, cf. *Eminent Chinese*, pp. 413–15.

at the present time reading the *Book of History* every night into the small hours.[20] In Chü-jung-hsien, just outside Nanking, he stopped the cortege to ask the local magistrate how the harvest had been, and to urge him to love the people as his children.[21] Such questions created a fine imperial image; this incident was popularly transformed into the Emperor galloping into the magistrate's yamen, abruptly reining in his horse, and gently asking after the people's well-being.[22] He even praised the excellence of the local boats.[23] But for all these well-aimed attempts to gain popularity, the Emperor was still cautious and practical, staying with the Tartar general in the closed Manchu city of Nanking. It was only on later tours that he ventured out into the city proper to stay in the yamen of the textile commissioner.[24]

This first tour had been something of a scouting expedition, and though the Emperor had given attention to river works,[25] it was not until the second Southern Tour, in 1689, that he tackled this problem seriously. An edict before the second tour announced that it was being undertaken because of requests that the Emperor inspect the river works in person. He repeated orders that there must be no extra levies from the people on account of the tour, that all supplies must be bought in advance at current market prices, that local officials must not make presents to members of the retinue.[26] The fact that these same orders were issued again and again before each tour strongly suggests that the poeple were subject to ceaseless harassments by their officials, who were more frightened of failing to create a good impression than of being caught out in minor financial irregularities.

Leaving Peking on January 28, 1689, accompanied by his eldest son Yin-t'i and Yü Ch'eng-lung (who had gained his favor in 1684 and was now Chihli governor), the Emperor traveled due south on land to Su-ch'ien-hsien. This was the area of the key junction between the Yellow River and the Grand Canal. Here he began the business of inspecting the river works in earnest; "he got off his horse and sat on the dike, and taking out a map of the river pointed things out to his offi-

20. *Shih-lu*, ch. 117, p. 19b.
21. Ibid., p. 13.
22. *Ch'ing pai lei-ch'ao*, section 11, p. 1.
23. *Shih-lu*, ch. 117, p. 10.
24. *Shang-Chiang liang-hsien chih* (1874), *shou-chüan* 1, p. 1.
25. *Shih-lu*, ch. 117, pp. 6–7, 21, 22b.
26. Ibid., ch. 139, pp. 2 and 3b. *HTSL*, pp. 9234–36 (ch. 310, pp. 8b–11b).

cials" the Veritable Records state,[27] clearly shaken into informality of language by the informality of the Emperor's action. Long discussions on river works followed, and the Emperor inspected the Ch'ing-ho-hsien area by boat.[28] Proceeding down the Grand Canal he crossed the Yangtze, and after spending two days in Soochow, reached Hangchow at the end of the Grand Canal on February 28.[29]

The Emperor had wanted to move further south to inspect river works, but when he reached Hsiao-shan-hsien, some miles southeast of Hangchow, he received a report that the water level was too low for boats to pass and that the land route was extremely difficult. Whether this was a true report or a fabrication by officials anxious to stop him from seeing too much, the Emperor accepted it, and after spending two more days in Hangchow, headed north once more.[30] From March 16 to 21 he was in Nanking, on March 23 and 24 in Yangchow. Then he returned rapidly up the Grand Canal, pausing only for two days of further river inspection, and reached Tientsin on April 7. As it was his birthday, the heir apparent (Yin-jeng), and the other princes, and all the senior officials from the Capital came to greet him and escort him back to the palace.[31] The second tour had taken seventy days.

This tour was clearly more informal than the first. The enormous retinue of the first tour had been drastically cut back to about three hundred persons,[32] and less insignia were displayed. The unofficial welcome, however, was less restrained. Gay festoons and banners were hung in the streets, and colored lanterns shone at night.[33] For the first time crowds assembled around the temporary palaces imploring the Emperor to stay longer; [34] this later became customary, but in 1689 may well have reflected the genuine pleasure of the people at having the Emperor in their cities, despite the hardships that such visits entailed. In 1684 the Emperor had appeared as serious-minded scholar but now he encouraged the image of the sensitive aesthete as he gazed at an exquisite plum tree in early spring bloom and stroked it with hi

27. *Shih-lu*, ch. 139, p. 10.
28. Ibid., pp. 10b–13.
29. Ibid., p. 17.
30. Ibid., pp. 20–23.
31. Ibid., ch. 140, p. 10b.
32. Ibid., ch. 139, p. 14. *HTSL*, p. 9235 (ch. 310, p. 9b).
33. *Ch'ing pai lei-ch'ao*, section 11, p. 1. *HTSL*, p. 9235 (ch. 310, p. 9b).
34. *Shih-lu*, ch. 139, p. 25b, in Soochow.

hands.[35] Taxes were remitted and minor criminals pardoned.[36] Even the merchants were encouraged, since the Emperor, on passing certain customs houses, had learned that merchants were often detained after they had paid their full dues; he ordered that they must be passed through as soon as they had paid.[37]

The third Southern Tour in 1699 was a sprawling affair, in which the Emperor took along not only the Empress Dowager but also no less than seven of his sons: the first, third, fifth, seventh, eighth, thirteenth, and fourteenth.[38] They left Peking on March 4, but progressed so slowly that the Emperor left the cortege and went on ahead to inspect the river works, rejoining his family on March 31, when he accompanied the Empress Dowager across the Yellow River. Then he left the party again, taking a small boat and making a detailed examination of some of the dikes (after this trip he gave the most detailed instructions on the water levels that should be maintained), before resuming his leisurely progress.[39] The party spent six days in Soochow, one week in Hangchow, and one week in Nanking, before returning as slowly as they had come, reaching Peking on June 14, having spent one hundred and two days on the tour.

On this tour the Emperor was more confidently Manchu, and references to the Classics and aesthetic posturings were dropped. The dominating image of the tour is the Emperor as horseman. On previous tours the Emperor had held archery tests and sometimes shot arrows himself,[40] but in 1699 he gave for the first time an exhibition of his skill that must have been aimed primarily at the military men, though it also clearly impressed the civil officials. The Emperor was in Hangchow on April 26, and after he, the princes, and the best archers from the Imperial Bodyguard had done some shooting, he led them in shooting from horseback. After his first arrow had hit the target, he

35. *Ch'ing pai lei-ch'ao,* section 11, p. 1.

36. *Shih-lu,* ch. 139, p. 13. *HTSL,* p. 9235 (ch. 310, pp. 9b–10b).

37. *HTSL,* p. 9236 (ch. 310, p. 11).

38. These seven included neither the heir apparent Yin-jeng nor the future Yung-cheng Emperor Yin-chen (*Shih-lu,* ch. 192, p. 7). The K'ang-hsi Emperor took his thirteenth son, Yin-hsiang, on the 1699, 1702, 1703, 1705, and 1707 tours; no other son was ordered to accompany him so often. This may lead us to modify the view that "Yin-hsiang seems to have received but little favor from his imperial father," *Eminent Chinese,* p. 923.

39. *Shih-lu,* ch. 192, p. 12, leaves the Empress Dowager; ch. 192, p. 13b, rejoins her; ch. 192, p. 17, leaves in small boat; ch. 192, p. 19, speaks on water levels.

40. Ibid., ch. 117, p. 16; ch. 139, pp. 23 and 31b.

moved on to something harder: he dropped the reins and rode straight toward the target, but just as he was about to shoot the horse shied sharply away to the left; quickly the Emperor changed his grip on the bow and shot, the arrow hitting the target as the horse galloped past.[41] The treatment given to this episode in the Veritable Records, which is quite unlike the normal brief mentions that "the Emperor also shot and all his arrows hit the target," shows that the feat was regarded as unusual. On this occasion the Emperor had clearly been out to impress, but in addition he won extra fame by turning a near accident into a triumph.

This 1699 tour also gives some evidence that the Emperor did in fact occasionally leave his retinue and go off almost alone to talk to the people. On April 30 and May 1 the Emperor was in Soochow, and on May 5 he was at Wang-t'ing. But for the period of three days, May 2, 3, and 4, there is no reference of any kind in the Veritable Records, the very dates are not even mentioned.[42] The only record that fills this hiatus is one in a popular account, which states that on May 2 the Emperor left Soochow, and after meeting with some fishermen and himself catching some fish, he went on alone with the governor Sung Lao in two small wooden boats. The two then went ashore and talked to various groups of country people about the crops and local problems, the Emperor remarking that "one should see everything for oneself." [43] This passage might be pure invention, built around the stereotype of the benevolent Emperor, the popularizer using the total blank in the official records to support his contention that the Emperor went off on a side trip. But the blank could be explained by the fact that no diarist was in attendance, and that Court historiographers were quite content to ignore an example of imperial fraternization in which the bureaucracy played no part, whereas the popularizer made the most of such an occasion.

In 1702 the Emperor started off on a fourth tour, leaving Peking on November 14 with the heir apparent Yin-jeng, Yin-chen (the future Yung-cheng Emperor), and Yin-hsiang (the thirteenth son). But when the party reached Te-chou on the Grand Canal the heir apparent fell seriously ill. The Emperor waited in the city for him to re-

41. Ibid., ch. 192, pp. 29b–30.
42. Ibid., ch. 193, pp. 1b–3.
43. *Ch'ing pai lei-ch'ao*, section 11, pp. 2–3.

cover, passing the time in calligraphy and archery, and dealing with administrative problems as they came up. The prince was ill for over two weeks, and when he had recovered the Emperor decided to abandon the tour and return to Peking.[44] The Emperor clearly enjoyed the role of fond father; as he wrote to Li Hsü, who had been patiently waiting his arrival: "The heir apparent unexpectedly caught a bad chill and became seriously ill; fortunately I was careful in every way and he was cured and recovered completely." [45]

The interrupted fourth tour was completed the following year, when the Emperor and the same three princes left Peking on March 3. They made a rapid tour of only fifty-eight days, traveling by land to T'ao-yüan-hsien, then by water to Yangchow, Soochow, Hangchow, Nanking, and back north to Tientsin. Nothing is preserved in the records of this trip except for minor points—the Emperor sends his bodyguard to put out a fire in a poor village; a few short edicts on river work are issued; some girls are sent off as concubines to the Korean King. The fact that this tour receives only cursory treatment in the Veritable Records may possibly be due to the fact that the future Yung-cheng Emperor was present; for reasons now unknown, he may have erased from the past all references to his contacts with officials and others on the tour, leaving nothing but this bare outline.[46]

The last two Southern Tours, in 1705 and 1707, were both leisurely, taking one hundred and eight and one hundred and seventeen days respectively.[47] On both tours the Emperor traveled by water, on the Grand Canal and the southern rivers, since he had decided that this was the most economical means of transport.[48] The

44. *Shih-lu*, ch. 209, p. 23 through ch. 210, p. 7.

45. *Li Hsü Memorials*, p. 10, endorsement to memorial dated 41/10/–.

46. The fourth tour is in *Shih-lu*, ch. 211, pp. 3b–21. This tour, which lasted fifty-eight days, is covered in a mere eighteen pages of the *Shih-lu*. The 1684 tour of sixty days has thirty-four pages; the 1689 tour of seventy days has forty-one pages. The long tours of 1699, 1705, and 1707, have thirty-seven, thirty-eight, and thirty-seven pages respectively. But though this means that they have about the same ratio of pages to days as the 1703 tour, the circumstances are very different, since naturally on the slow tours many days were spent in rest and recreation, and no record is placed in the *Shih-lu*, whereas for the working days there is always a full record. The only tour (besides the abortive one of 1702) that Yin-chen went on was the 1703 tour, and this is unique in the sparseness of information furnished.

47. *Shih-lu*, ch. 219, p. 7 through ch. 220, p. 20 (March 3–June 19, 1705), and ch. 228, p. 4b through ch. 229, p. 17 (February 24–June 21, 1707).

48. *HSTL*, p. 9237 (ch. 310, p. 14).

first four tours had set the precedents for the routes to be followed
and the places visited, and the Emperor seems to have shown no interest in further innovation. He met with the local officials, inspected the
dikes, discoursed on local conditions, talked to retired scholars, remitted taxes, pardoned criminals, tested archery, held extra examinations,
rewarded his retinue and the local troops, and usually agreed to stay
on another day when the people begged him to, which they nearly always did. But since the image of the benevolent Emperor steals on the
reader so rapidly, it is worth lingering on one episode that shows the
Emperor in a different light.

On March 23, 1707, the Emperor inspected the site of a canal
which Chang P'eng-ko, the director-general of river conservancy, had
recommended opening in order to lower the level of lakes bordering
on the Yellow River and the Grand Canal. The Emperor was dissatis-
fied, and after his inspection he ordered all the members of his retinue,
all civil and military officials in attendance, the local officials of all
ranks, and Chang P'eng-ko with his staff of river officials, to kneel in
rows in front of his temporary palace. He then asked Chang P'eng-
ko on what grounds he had proposed opening up the canal. Chang
P'eng-ko did not give a direct answer, but replied: "My Emperor
loves his subjects as his children, he does not grudge ten million taels
from his treasury to save his people from danger, and all praise his
great mercies." On hearing this, the Emperor launched into a blister-
ing attack on Chang P'eng-ko, reminding him that the writing of
fancy essays and the handling of practical administration were very
different things, and ending: "River works are your special responsibility. If you are careless on this matter, when will you ever be careful?" Chang P'eng-ko made no reply and prostrated himself.[49]

Two days later the Emperor returned to the charge. All the officials
were ordered to kneel in a line along the river bank, while the Emperor addressed them from his boat. He blasted Chang P'eng-ko again
for incompetence and ordered him to speak out in his own defence if
he could: "Now officials of all ranks are assembled here; if you have
anything to say, you can say it plainly before them all." Chang P'eng-
ko doffed his hat and begged for punishment. Still the Emperor did
not spare him, but made a long speech in which he mocked Chang

49. *Shih-lu*, ch. 228, pp. 10–11b. The incident is briefly described in *Eminent Chinese*,
p. 50.

P'eng-ko's literary language, and then proposed his own solutions. He ended: "Let Chang P'eng-ko take *capable* river officials, and make a *factual* survey, and confer with them and memorialize." [50] From the Veritable Records we know that Ts'ao Yin was present at this scene; [51] it must have been an effective reminder that the Emperor expected accurate information at all times.

These Southern Tours were clearly a part of the K'ang-hsi Emperor's system of personal government; as with his use of bondservants and palace memorials, they enabled him both to check on, and to bypass, the regular bureaucracy. But the tours were time-consuming and tiring. The K'ang-hsi Emperor traveled back very slowly after the last tour in 1707, stopping frequently for rests. He was now fifty-three, and clearly found the heat in the south oppressive; [52] so it may well be that Ts'ao Yin's sending of important secret memorials from 1708 onward (to be examined below) arose from the Emperor's realization that he would not again be making a Southern Tour in person. It therefore became all the more necessary to receive information from trusted sources.

Jesuits and the Southern Tours

That the Southern Tours were a part of the K'ang-hsi Emperor's system of personal government can be clearly seen in one use he made of the tours—to keep in touch with the Catholic missionaries in the central provinces. Despite the large number of missionaries in China by the late seventeenth century, there was no settled institutional means of dealing with them. By seeing the missionaries at regular intervals, the Emperor could keep relations at an informal level, which made formal recognition of their status unnecessary. The missionaries in turn were flattered by this attention, and these tours were an important factor in creating the highly favorable picture of the K'ang-hsi Emperor which the missionaries transmitted to Europe.

In 1684, the Emperor summoned the two Jesuit fathers Valat and Gabiani to an audience while he was in Nanking. He received them "sitting cross-legged on his throne in the Tartar fashion," and asked

50. *Shih-lu*, ch. 228, pp. 17–21.

51. Ibid., p. 9, says that the Nanking *chih-tsao* Ts'ao Yin greeted the Emperor at T'eng-hsien on March 16 (46/2/13).

52. He refers to excessive heat in *Shih-lu*, ch. 229, pp. 3 and 10, and took sixteen days to get from T'eng-hsien to Peking (*Shih-lu*, ch. 229, pp. 16–17).

them their names and ages, how long they had been in China, whether they had studied any philosophy or not, and if they could name a new star that had recently appeared. They were given a glass of wine that had been made for the Emperor by Jesuit fathers in Peking, which they drank kneeling in his presence, and presents of cloth and gold. The missionaries showed the Emperor a crucifix, in which he expressed polite interest. On another occasion an official was sent to Valat's house to inquire after him (he was prostrated with a headache), and later when the Emperor was passing through the streets of Nanking he stopped and talked to Valat who had "set up a little table, after the manner of the country, on the route along which the Emperor would pass, on which some incense was burning." [53] At other points on his route the Emperor inquired after various churches. Besides the Jesuits, of course, there were both Franciscans and Dominicans in the city; the Franciscans acknowledged the kindness of Jesuits, who introduced them to the Emperor.[54]

The Jesuit de Fontaney has left an account of the 1689 tour in Nanking, which shows that the Jesuits greeted the Emperor on his tours in the same manner as the local officials did. On March 15, the day before the Emperor reached Nanking, de Fontaney and Gabiani went out two leagues beyond the city to await his coming.

> The next day we saw the Emperor pass; he had the goodness to stop and to speak to us in the most obliging way in the world. He was on horseback, followed by his bodyguard and two or three thousand horsemen. The whole town came out to receive him with standards, silken flags, daises, umbrellas, and other ornaments without number. Every twenty paces, triumphal arches

53. Letter from Father J. Valat, dated 19 May 1685, printed in *Der Neue Welt-Bott mit Allerhand Nachrichten deren Missionarien Soc. Iesu (1642–1726)*, Joseph Stöcklein, ed. (corrected edition, Augsburg and Gratz, 1728), pp. 48–49. Cf. also Pfister, *Notices*, p. 317. For biographical information on Valat, cf. Pfister, *Notices*, no. 96; for Gabiani, ibid., no. 118. Details concerning the episode of the wine, and other favors conferred by the Emperor to Jesuits during this Southern Tour, can be found in H. Josson and L. Willaert, *Correspondence de Ferdinand Verbiest de la compagnie de Jésus (1623–1688), directeur de l'observatoire de Pékin* (Brussels, Palais des Académies, 1938), p. 499. This letter has been translated by H. Bosmans in pp. 424–33 of his excellent and still not superseded study of Verbiest: "Ferdinand Verbiest, directeur de l'observatoire de Peking (1623–1688)," *Revue des questions scientifiques*, 71 (Brussels, 1912), 195–273 and 375–464.

54. *Sinica Franciscana*, 5, 397–98, della Chiesa letter dated August 1699. Gaillard, *Nankin*, pp. 243–44, lists Dominicans as well as Franciscans in Nanking at the time.

were raised in the roads, covered with brocade, and ornamented with streamers, ribbons, and bows of silk, beneath which he passed. There were an infinite number of people in the road, but they had such great respect and were in such a profound silence that one could not hear the slightest noise.[55]

According to Gabiani, they visited the Emperor every day in his temporary palace, and it was on their recommendation that he went at dusk to the old observatory to view the star Canopus. The Emperor sent officials to their house, and they presented him with a thermometer and a barometer.[56] The missionaries saw him off in due fashion:

He left Nanking on March 22 to return to Peking. As our duty obliged us to be part of his cortege for several days, we followed him for about thirty leagues, after which we awaited him by the bank of the river [while the Emperor visited the temple at Chinshan]. He saw us and had the kindness to make our little boat draw near, and his vessel towed it for over two leagues. He was sitting on a platform, and first read our *tsou-pen*, that is our written expression of thanks, following the Chinese custom. . . . He asked us how we had crossed the Yangtze, and if he would find any of our churches on his route. He himself showed us some books he had with him, and in our presence gave various orders to mandarins whom he summoned; and after having had put into our little boat some bread from his table and quantities of other provisions, he sent us off loaded with honor.[57]

This was the pattern of contact between the Emperor and the Jesuits that became customary. In 1699, when Bouvet returned to China from France, he went straight from Canton to Yangchow where the Emperor was on his third Southern Tour. There, Bouvet and Gerbillon introduced the new missionaries who presented various curios, and were in turn invited to draw near the imperial boat and exchange a few words with the Emperor, after which they were given delicacies from the Emperor's table and some money. Bouvet was granted two audiences, and ordered to accompany the Emperor for the remainder

55. *Lettres édifiantes et curieuses*, 17, 273–74, For de Fontaney, cf, Pfister, *Notices*, no. 170.
56. Gaillard, *Nankin*, pp. 244–45. *Lettres édifiantes et curieuses*, 17, 275. Du Halde, *History of China*, 4, 343–53.
57. *Lettres édifiantes et curieuses*, 17, 275–76.

of the tour, before returning to Peking.[58] The Jesuits naturally made all they could out of these meetings in the letters they sent to Europe, but there is absolutely no doubt that such casual encounters did take place. For example, a diary of the Emperor's fifth Southern Tour, kept by a Chinese member of the retinue, mentions one such episode that occurred in Nanking on May 18, 1705:

> As the Emperor was passing by the Pei-t'ing lane, a Christian missionary offered up a book in Western letters and presented a statement of his antecedents in a yellow memorial. The Emperor stopped his carriage and talked to him for a long time, and tried out some of the Western words he had learned. The Emperor seemed delighted, and told the eunuch Li to bring the missionary along to the temporary palace.[59]

The missionaries valued these meetings because they were public expressions of imperial benevolence. As de Fontaney put it:

> These imperial kindnesses gave us much honor, because he manifested them to us in the view of the whole Court and the mandarins of the neighboring provinces, who upon returning to their appointments were influenced in favor of our holy law and of the missionaries who preached it.[60]

At the same time, the K'ang-hsi Emperor was keeping a rather closer eye on the missionaries during his tours than they may have realized. Though he remained of the opinion that the Westerners were basically of good character [61] and out to please him—"As long as I shall reign, there is nothing to fear from them; I treat them well, they love and admire me, and seek to cause me pleasure" [62]—he remained on his guard. On the fourth Southern Tour in 1703 the Emperor came across many groups of missionaries whose existence he had not suspected, and was extremely angry, both because he feared that

---

58. Ibid., 16, 384–89. For Bouvet, cf. Pfister, Notices, no. 171; for Gerbillion, cf. ibid., no. 173.

59. Sheng-tsu wu-hsing, p. 39.

60. Lettres édifiantes et curieuses, 17, 275.

61. Chao Hung-hsieh Memorials, p. 37b, memorial dated 54/4/2 quoting endorsement.

62. From a manuscript left by Father Gaubil, who attended an audience in which the Yung-cheng Emperor read out some of his father's maxims on government. Printed in Etudes de théologie de philosophie et d'histoire, 2 (Paris, 1857) 493–94.

some political activity was brewing, and because they had been moving around the country at will (*luan-luan-ti, mao-mao-ti*). The senior missionary, Grimaldi, could only placate him by agreeing to catalog all Jesuit personnel and possessions, and standing guaranty for the missionaries of other orders.[63] Again, on his last tour in 1707 the Emperor was careful to check if the missionaries in Nanking had registered and received the *p'iao*, certificates in which they promised to follow the practices of Ricci; those who refused were expelled from China.[64]

In the K'ang-hsi Emperor's dealings with the Jesuits, we can see the same factors that appeared in the general description of the tours—an extreme affability coupled with shrewdness, and an apparent casualness that was stripped away as soon as there was any threat, either real or imagined, to the imperial authority.

Ts'ao Yin and the Southern Tours

It can have been no easy task to be responsible for the Emperor's well-being on the Southern Tours, but this was the task that Ts'ao Yin had to perform in Nanking on the last four of them. In fact he had encountered the Emperor even earlier in Nanking, for his father Ts'ao Hsi, who had been textile commissioner there since 1663, died in office in July 1684. As we saw above, when the emperor reached Nanking in December, he visited the Ts'ao residence in person to console the bereaved family, and also sent a chamberlain of the Imperial Bodyguard to offer libations to the deceased and present the family with some imperial calligraphy.[65] Ts'ao Yin, as the eldest son in charge of the funeral arrangements, presumably received the Emperor on this occasion.

Fifteen years later Ts'ao Yin was official host to the Emperor on the third Southern Tour. Ts'ao Yin was Nanking textile commissioner, and it was his official yamen and residence that was used as the Emperor's temporary palace. The Emperor had first stayed there in 1689,

63. Francis A. Rouleau, S.J., "Maillard de Tournon, Papal Legate at the Court of Peking," *Archivum Historicum Societatis Iesu,* 31 (1962), 296–97.

64. Antonio Sisto Rosso, O.F.M., *Apostolic Legations to China of the Eighteenth Century* (South Pasadena, California, 1948), pp. 171–76.

65. *HLMHC*, pp. 227–31, using as the main source a commemorative essay written for Ts'ao Hsi by Hsiung Tz'u-li. For the Emperor's arrival in Nanking, cf. *Shih-lu*, ch. 117, p. 13. Chamberlain of the Imperial Bodyguard, *nei-ta-ch'en, BH* 98.

when Sang-ko was commissioner, and it became his Nanking palace for all subsequent Southern Tours.[66] In 1699 the Emperor spent a week in Nanking.[67] It was on this tour that he summoned Ts'ao Yin's widowed mother to an audience, talked cheerfully with her, and then wrote the three characters "hall of celebrations for a distinguished mother" and presented them to her. Ts'ao Yin's contemporaries recorded this as an exceptional favor; elderly mothers were often called into audience and praised by the Emperor, even given presents of silk; but for characters from the imperial brush to be presented to the elderly mother was an act of extraordinary grace. The Empress Dowager also exchanged a few words with her, increasing the honor.[68]

On this same visit the Emperor gave Ts'ao Yin a special commission. An edict of May 14, 1699, stated that on his visit to the tomb of Ming T'ai-tsu the Emperor had noticed that it was in bad repair; the Kiangsu governor Sung Lao and Ts'ao Yin were ordered to restore it. The Emperor also wrote four large characters saying "the rule of Ming T'ai-tsu surpassed that of T'ang and Sung times," and ordered Ts'ao Yin to have them carved in stone.[69] In a memorial on June 23, Ts'ao

66. HLMHC, pp. 157–59 studies the location in detail and ends the confusion that previously prevented distinction between the three chih-tsao chü (the factories where the fabrics were made) and the chih-tsao shu (the office and residence of Ts'ao Yin as chih-tsao). The chih-tsao shu, with its surrounding gardens, formed the Emperor's hsing-kung. In 1751 it was made into a permanent palace for the Ch'ien-lung Emperor, and the chih-tsao was without an office until more land was bought in 1768.

67. Shih-lu, ch. 193, pp. 4–6b, from 38/4/10 to 38/4/16.

68. Ch'ing pai lei-ch'ao, section 10, p. 11. HLMHC, pp. 316–19, gives the records of this incident left by Yin's contemporaries. Ibid., p. 205, discusses the Empress Dowager's speech.

69. Shih-lu, ch. 193, p. 6 gives a summary of the edict. A much fuller version was recorded by the scholar Chang Yü-shu and is cited in HLMHC, p. 316. Chang Yü-shu's version of the edict includes two mentions of Ts'ao Yin's name, which is not mentioned at all in the Shih-lu version.

It is interesting that the K'ang-hsi Emperor should thus single out Ming T'ai-tsu for special recognition and homage. This man—the Hung-wu Emperor (r. 1368–99), whose personal name was Chu Yüan-chang—was a ruthless and efficient despot who brought Chinese absolutism to its peak. Cf. F. W. Mote, "The Growth of Chinese Despotism," Oriens Extremus, 8 (1961), 1–41, where he is described as "the harshest and the most unreasonable tyrant in all of Chinese history" (p. 20). However, it is most likely that the K'ang-hsi Emperor was simply making what he felt to be a placatory gesture to the shades of the Ming and their few remaining vocal supporters, rather than some specific acknowledgment of the genius of a character so unlike his own; though it must be admitted that both men had an aggressive hardiness and a lack of advanced education that placed them in a curious relationship to their more refined officials.

Yin reported that he, the acting governor-general T'ao-tai, Sung Lao, and other local officials had inspected the area of the tomb on foot and had arrived at an estimate of the labor and materials that would be needed. An assistant prefect named Ting I had been appointed to supervise the work, and it had been decided that the work be paid for with funds from the category of official salaries and wages (*kuan-li feng-kung*). But since it rained so much in the summer months, they would wait until the cool of the autumn before starting. The Emperor's calligraphy would be carved in stone after the repairs were completed.[70] Ts'ao Yin had in fact got out of the whole business very neatly by delegating the responsibility to another official and having the work paid for from public funds.

After the tour, Ts'ao Yin sent two memorials; in one he thanked the Emperor for the happiness he had brought the people on the tour, in the other he gave specific thanks on behalf of his mother, writing that "even if she were to become a Buddhist nun it would be hard for her to repay the Emperor." [71] The Emperor passed no special comment on these memorials, but before the fourth Southern Tour in 1703 he sent this message:

> On November 14 I shall be coming by the land route to inspect the river works. You three [textile commissioners] must under no circumstances make the kind of preparations that you made last time. Any of you disobeying this edict will be severely punished.[72]

So we know that the 1699 tour had been lavishly prepared for by Ts'ao Yin. The Emperor's disapproval of his extravagance, written in a secret edict that was not a bid for popular approval, may well have

70. *Ts'ao Yin Memorials*, p. 8b, dated 38/5/26. He added that as he was the Emperor's household servant it was fitting that he report on the deliberations in a palace memorial (*che*) before the formal memorial (*hung-pen*) was despatched by the senior officials. The wording of this passage implies that the *hung-pen* had not yet been sent, and that *hung-pen* were not necessarily memorials that had already been seen by the Emperor.

T'ao-tai was acting governor-general of Liang-chiang because the actual governor-general, Chang P'eng-ko, had been ordered to accompany the Emperor for the whole of the tour. Cf. *Ch'ing-shih*, pp. 2877–78.

For "official salaries and wages" cf. the slightly different phrase in Sun, *Ch'ing Administrative Terms*, no. 423.

71. *Ts'ao Yin Archives*, nos. 2787 and 2809, both dated 38/5/26.

72. *Li Hsü Memorials*, p. 9b, endorsement to memorial dated 41/8/–. Also discussed in HLMHC, p. 325.

been genuine. Certainly the 1699 tour had been lavish—"ten times better than that of 1684." [73]

By the 1705 tour however, Ts'ao Yin appeared as an important official in his own right, having been made salt censor of Liang-huai, and his lavish hospitality was gratefully accepted by the K'ang-hsi Emperor, who had clearly developed a taste for luxury. This tour can be studied in extra detail because an anonymous diarist, clearly either a member of the retinue or an unusually well-informed observer, has left a record of it.[74] If this record is supplemented by the recollections of Chang Ying, a celebrated grand secretary who had gone on the 1689 tour and left an amusing account of his tribulations,[75] a fairly detailed picture of Ts'ao Yin's activities in 1705 may be drawn.

The Emperor had left Peking on March 3, 1705, and reached Yü-t'ai-hsien, on the Grand Canal in southern Shantung, on March 25.[76] Here he was greeted by the civil and military officials of Chiang-nan. Among them was Ts'ao Yin, who had traveled over 250 miles from Nanking to greet the Emperor. He and the other Chiang-nan officials apparently traveled this enormous distance on every tour, and their expenses must have been high; in addition, they had to arrive well before the Emperor—they had been waiting ten days in Yü-t'ai-hsien before the Emperor finally appeared.[77] Once they had formally greeted the Emperor, they swelled the ranks of the already sizable retinue and followed the Emperor south. Considerable confusion en-

73. *Ch'ing pai lei-ch'ao*, section 11, p. 2.

74. *Sheng-tsu wu-hsing Chiang-nan ch'üan-lu* [A Complete Record of the K'ang-hsi Emperor's Fifth Southern Tour], anon., printed in *Chen-ch'i t'ang ts'ung-shu*, 1st series. Cited hereafter as *Sheng-tsu wu-hsing*.

75. Chang Ying, *Nan-hsün hu-ts'ung chi-lüeh* [Records from the Retinue on the Southern Tour of 1689], printed in *Chao-tai ts'ung-shu*, collection 5.

76. *Shih-lu*, ch. 219, pp. 7 and 12b. *Sheng-tsu wu-hsing*, p. 5, uses the name Nan-yang, presumably referring to the area of Nan-yang lake, east of Yü-t'ai-hsien. cf. *Ch'in-ting ta-Ch'ing hui-tien t'u* (1899, Taiwan 1963 reprint), p. 3187.

77. *Sheng-tsu wu-hsing*, p. 5. Ts'ao Yin is not mentioned by name, but as *"yen-yüan,"* the salt official, referring to the fact that he was the newly appointed salt censor of Liang-huai. Further evidence that the *chih-tsao* regularly traveled 250 miles to greet the Emperor is in *Li Hsü Memorials*, p. 9b, dated 41/10/–, where Li Hsü discusses the abortive 1702 tour and writes "I reached Su-ch'ien-hsien on 10/11 but [because the heir apparent was ill] I dared proceed no further," i.e. further north. Again, *Shih-lu*, ch. 228, p. 9, lists Ts'ao Yin, Li Hsü, and Sun Wen-ch'eng among the officials who met the Emperor in 1707 at T'eng-hsien in southern Shantung, across the Grand Canal from Yü-t'ai-hsien. *Sheng-tsu wu-hsing*, p. 5, the Emperor asked Asan how long he had been in Nan-yang and Asan replied, "ten days or more."

sued. This is how Chang Ying described the problem of getting a night's sleep on one of the K'ang-hsi Emperor's Southern Tours:

> The day before I had sent off my baggage, servants, and tent, to wait for me at the stopping place. By this time it was quite dark, and when I saw my servant coming to greet me, I was delighted that at last I was going to have somewhere to rest. I asked him for directions, but he was completely confused and could not remember where he had come from; for there were thousands of tents of the same color, and more tents were going up all the time on any piece of clear ground, it was really difficult to get one's bearings.
>
> The military regulations forbid one to shout loudly, and these are even more strictly enforced at night, so I had to ask people for directions in whispers. After a while one of my servants heard me in the distance and came rushing up. By now I had passed dozens of tents; he hurried up to me, but just by turning around he too got totally lost. I was now desperately hungry, and longing for the rest that I could not obtain. When a good deal later I at last reached my tent, it was past the time of the third drum.[78]

This incident occurred at the beginning of a tour, and Chang Ying had no prior experience of life on the road. Ts'ao Yin may never have had such a harrowing time, but many of the tour regulations must have been irksome to him also. Those following the retinue had their own carts in which they carried their tents, bedding, and eating utensils, but none of these carts could leave the camp until the imperial baggage had gone. As a result, the carts never arrived until well after sundown, while the retinue sat around growing hungrier and hungrier. Even when the carts arrived their troubles were not over; all the wells and springs within ten *li* were reserved for the Emperor and his entourage, so the others had to travel considerable distances to water their horses and cook rice. They had to wait respectfully until the Emperor had gone to bed before retiring, and had to be at his temporary palace well before dawn, with their tents and equipment already packed away.[79]

78. Chang Ying, *Nan-hsün*, p. 1.
79. Ibid., pp. 1b–2b.

In late March 1705 Ts'ao Yin and his Emperor moved slowly south, in heavy rain and wind that made the crossing of the Yellow River impossible and held up the entourage so much that the Emperor had to issue extra food from his own stores.[80] On March 30 he entered Chiang-nan, where he was welcomed by the local elite (*shen-chin*) and local troops; [81] they presumably followed along with the rest. On April 1 the retinue crossed the Yellow River.[82] This simple sentence covers a complex event; here is Chang Ying's version of his own crossing of the Yellow River in 1689, and Ts'ao Yin must have faced similar problems.

> We set off from Su-ch'ien at the fifth drum, and went along the bank for forty or fifty *li*, till we heard that the Emperor had already embarked. So four or five of us also embarked, but our boat traveled rather slowly, and after we had gone fifty or sixty *li* we learned that the Emperor had landed. So we also landed and got to Ch'ing-ho by sundown. We had covered two hundred *li* during the day. My eight servants had not arrived, and only one servant caught up with me, bringing an extra horse. I ordered him to lead the way, and followed on behind. At first I traveled with Chang Yü-shu, Li Kuang-ti, and Chang P'eng-ko,[83] but I fell off my horse and soaked my clothes. The other worthies had all galloped ahead, and though I pressed on I didn't catch up with them.
>
> At Ch'ing-ho I had learned that the Emperor had crossed the Yellow River, and moreover had ordered all his retinue to cross on the same day. So I took the one servant with me, and our three horses, and reached the river bank. It was quite dark. Just when I was at a total loss, a clerk from the Board of Rites appeared at this point, waiting for me. I accompanied him across the river, leaving my servant and the three horses among the mud flats, to wait for the latecomers.

80. *Sheng-tsu wu-hsing*, p. 5b.
81. *Shih-lu*, ch. 219, p. 13b.
82. *Sheng-tsu wu-hsing*, p. 5b; *Shih-lu*, ch. 219, p. 14.
83. All three were famous K'ang-hsi officials; their biographies are in *Eminent Chinese*, pp. 65–66, 473–475, 49–51. Chang Ying called them respectively Ching-chiang (the home of Chang Yü-shu), Hou-an (the *hao* of Li Kuang-ti), and Yün-ch'ing (the *tzu* of Chang P'eng-ko).

Chang Ying's troubles were not over. The clerk sent a servant off to find another boat, and the servant got lost. So the clerk went off to find his servant and got lost himself. Finally Chang Ying stomped off alone into the darkness to find his Emperor.[84]

Ts'ao Yin must have followed along behind the Emperor in these days of late March and early April 1705; since he had no definite rank in the regular bureaucracy and was outside his own territory, his position in the retinue may well have been an insignificant one. It is unlikely that Ts'ao Yin played any prominent part in the glittering scene on April 2 when the Emperor, in response to a request by Sangko, the director-general of grain transport, that he enter Huai-an, sent ahead the Imperial Bodyguard to clear the streets and then followed with his palace women in a procession of over thirty sedan chairs, each one carried by eunuchs.[85] Yet only two days later Ts'ao Yin began to rank with the most senior officials, for the Emperor was entering the area in which Ts'ao Yin held his special offices: in Yangchow as salt censor, in Nanking as textile commissioner.

When the Emperor landed near Yangchow on the night of April 4, he was greeted not by officials but by the local salt merchants who offered him presents of antiques, curios, books, and paintings, which the Emperor accepted.[86] The next day Ts'ao Yin, as salt censor, requested the Emperor to visit a temporary palace in a flower garden which had been specially prepared by the salt merchants. The Emperor not only agreed, but brought along the heir apparent, his thirteenth son, and the palace women. The whole party relaxed there while operas were performed and a banquet given.[87] Almost certainly the expenses of this interlude, which the Emperor calculated at several thousand taels,[88] had been met by the salt merchants alone, not by Ts'ao Yin.

Ts'ao Yin's first large expense came on April 7, when he combined with two other officials to give a banquet for one hundred persons and the Emperor. Strangely enough, the three officials who gave this banquet represented among themselves the three sections of the ruling

84. Chang Ying, *Nan-hsün*, pp. 4–5b.

85. *Sheng-tsu wu-hsing*, p. 6b.

86. Ibid., p. 7, where this, the eleventh day of the third month, is misprinted as the sixteenth day.

87. Ibid., p. 7b.

88. Ibid., p. 8, on 3/13.

group—Banner elite, Chinese official elite, and the imperial elite—for one was Ma San-ch'i, the Tartar general of Ching-k'ou, one was the grand secretary Chang Yü-shu, and one was Ts'ao Yin. They also offered presents to the Emperor, who accepted a set of old books, two cups in foreign lacquer, and a basket of carp from Ma San-ch'i; one jade bowl and one white jade parrot from Ts'ao Yin; and some books from Chang Yü-shu.[89] The pattern on these tours was that the officials offered a large variety of presents to the Emperor, who then selected a few items and returned the rest. But salt merchants were treated rather differently. When, after Ts'ao Yin and the others had offered their gifts, the salt merchants of Yangchow offered sixty antiques to the Emperor, and forty to the heir apparent, *all* were gratefully accepted.[90] The merchants of course got nothing in return; Ts'ao Yin and the officials were given lines from poems (presumably written by the Emperor) and other small presents.[91]

On April 10 the Emperor arrived at Soochow; for miles outside the city stages had been set up on which plays were performed, and as the Emperor rode into the city in a parade of eight carriages, followed by all his women in sedan chairs, he was greeted by the sight of an incense table before each door and of multicolored awnings and strings of colored lanterns hung across the streets. His temporary palace was in the yamen of the textile commissioner Li Hsü, and it was Li Hsü who, together with the Kiangsu governor Sung Lao, had formally invited the Emperor to enter the city. After officials from Chiang-nan, Shantung, and Fukien had paid their respects, and a monk from P'u-t'o shan had been received in audience, Li Hsü gave a banquet for the Emperor and staged several well-known plays.[92]

The next day was even more festive, since it was the Emperor's birthday, the eighteenth day of the third month (April 11). All military and civil officials from the adjacent provinces, retired officials, the local elite (*hsiang-shen*), scholars, and monks came to congratulate the Emperor and bring him presents. The Emperor refused many presents on the grounds that his needs had been supplied long in advance by the Imperial Household, and himself gave a banquet for the senior

89. Ibid., p. 8b.
90. Ibid., p. 9.
91. Ibid.
92. Ibid., pp. 9b–10. *Shih-lu*, ch. 219, p. 17b.

provincial officials. He also gave out presents—sums of money from 1,000 taels downward, fans, bamboo, silk, and cakes. Ts'ao Yin was presented with two lines of verse and objects of glass, ink-sticks, and mutton for a feast. The unfortunate Li Hsü, who had presumably paid for the senior officials' banquet, apparently received nothing on this occasion.[93]

While the Emperor was in Soochow at this time, he gave public commissions to Li Hsü and Ts'ao Yin. Li Hsü was ordered to collect money from local officials to pay for the education of the two sons of the retired brigade general Yen Hung, who was sick and impoverished and unable to support them. When the children grew up, they were to report to the Boards and receive employment.[94] Ts'ao Yin received orders to assemble and print the complete poems of the T'ang dynasty. He wrote later that he had received these orders on April 12,[95] but the official records for that day and even the full diary of the tour do not mention any such edict. It is possible that the order was given informally at first, since this was an unusual commission for a bond-servant and textile commissioner. The Emperor waited to see if the venture would prove a success before making any public pronouncement.

From Soochow, the Emperor moved on to Sung-chiang-fu, where he stayed from April 18 to April 22.[96] Again Ts'ao Yin accompanied him, and was made a member of a three-man commission that the Emperor appointed to check the presents given to Chang Yün-i. Chang Yün-i was the provincial commander in chief [97] stationed in Sung-chiang-fu, and he had lavishly entertained the Emperor during his stay there with banquets and operas and archery displays, while maintaining his reputation as a man of intelligence and integrity. Ts'ao Yin and his two colleagues reported the full list of presents, and

93. *Sheng-tsu wu-hsing*, pp. 10–11b. *Shih-lu*, ch. 219, pp. 18–22. The Emperor got through a good deal of administrative work on this day as well, and had a lengthy discussion of river conservancy problems. For more details on the possible nature of Ts'ao Yin's presents, cf. *Sheng-tsu wu-hsing*, p. 18, where the basic categories of glass, ink, and mutton are subdivided in the list of presents given to Asan on 3/28.

94. *Shih-lu*, ch. 219, p. 23. *Sheng-tsu wu-hsing*, p. 14.

95. Ts'ao Yin, in the preface to the *Ch'üan T'ang shih*, says he received the orders on 44/3/19.

96. *Shih-lu*, ch. 219, pp. 23–25.

97. *Chiang-nan t'i-tu*, BH 750. Chang Yün-i was from Shensi; he held this office from 1696–1709. Cf. *CNTC*, ch. 111, p. 17, and reference in *Eminent Chinese*, p. 788.

noted that all the items of clothing, both robes and hats, had been
worn by the Emperor himself and thus represented special recognition
of Chang Yün-i's services. (A few days before Chang Yün-i had been
given a horse the Emperor had ridden. He was the most highly rewarded official on the 1705 tour.) [98] As well as making sure that
none of the Emperor's gifts fell into the wrong hands, the appointment of Ts'ao Yin and the others to inventory the presents ensured
that the Emperor's benevolence would be widely known.

On April 23 the Emperor left Sung-chiang and traveled to Hangchow, where he spent a week; he left Hangchow on May 2 and then
spent a further week in Soochow.[99] During this period there is no
mention of Ts'ao Yin, and it is probable that after he had finished his
task of making an inventory of Chang Yün-i's presents, he returned
to Nanking to put the finishing touches to the arrangements for the
Emperor's reception in that city.

When the Emperor reached Nanking on May 14, Ts'ao Yin became
his official host. The Emperor passed through the Hsi-hua gate at
noon, having ordered his Imperial Bodyguard not to clear away the
common people but to let them have a good look at the retinue, and
proceeded to the textile commissioner's yamen. Here he was greeted
by the local civil and military officials, and as soon as these formalities
were over, Ts'ao Yin gave him a banquet. After the banquet, the Emperor accepted presents from the military officials of the area, and attended another banquet given by the governor-general, Asan. After
this second banquet, all officials were received at a special night audience.

Ts'ao Yin, who seems to have had a knack of giving presents that
particularly pleased the Emperor, presented him with some cherries.
The Emperor was delighted, and declared that before he tasted them
he would send some to the Empress Dowager in Peking. Accordingly,
officials were chosen to ride to the palace with some of the cherries,
which they accomplished in the amazingly short time of under forty-
eight hours. (The cherries, presumably carried by a succession of
riders changing horses at the post stations, thus covered the 2,300 *li* to
Peking at an average speed of sixteen miles per hour, which was dou-

98. The three men were commissioned on 3/19 and sent back a preliminary report the
same day. *Sheng-tsu wu-hsing*, p. 18, and p. 16b for the gift of the Emperor's own horse.
99. *Sheng-tsu wu-hsing*, pp. 19–31. *Shih-lu*, ch. 220, pp. 1b–7b.

ble the maximum speed stipulated for the transmission of urgent despatches at this time.) Here the Manchu delight in hard riding, and
the Chinese respect for open manifestations of filial piety, were both
catered to by the Emperor's flamboyant gesture. Later that night,
Ts'ao Yin gave a second banquet, followed by a performance of
scenes from well-known operas.[100]

The next day, May 15, after a dawn audience for senior officials, the
Emperor sent the president of the Board of Revenue, Hsü Ch'ao,[101]
to offer sacrifices at the tomb of Ming T'ai-tsu. Asan, the governor-
general, offered the Emperor splendid presents consisting of a hundred
and sixty bolts of different silks and satin, thirty antique curiosities,
and thirty-four horses, as well as twenty antiques to the heir apparent,
and sachets, toilet articles, and scent to the concubines. In exception
to the general rule, all of these presents were accepted. Local officials
and scholars brought presents of paintings and books, which the
Kiangsu governor Sung Lao was ordered to examine. A projected
archery test was abandoned because the wind was gusty and
rain threatening. The military officials brought further presents of
antiques and horses. In the evening Ts'ao Yin gave a banquet and
opera performances.[102]

This generally leisurely rhythm was followed throughout the Emperor's 1705 visit to Nanking. Thus on May 16, the Emperor spent the
morning in the temporary palace because it was drizzling, and summoned various local officials and scholars to come and write poetry; in
the afternoon he took the heir apparent and the palace women to
watch the weavers at work in one of the textile commissioner's factories. That night Ts'ao Yin again gave a banquet and opera performances.[103] On May 17 the streets were cleared and the imperial party
went to the Pao-en temple; after the monks had been ordered to withdraw, the Emperor worshiped the Buddha in the main temple. The
monks had prepared a temporary palace, where the Emperor relaxed
and looked at the view. On returning to the textile commissioner's
yamen, he was given yet another banquet by Ts'ao Yin, who also

100. *Shih-lu*, ch. 220, p. 7b for arrival. Details of the day are in *Sheng-tsu wu-hsing*,
p. 31b. The official rode to Peking within twenty-four Chinese hours (*shih-ch'en*), which
equal forty-eight Western hours. For speed of despatches, cf. Fairbank and Teng, *Ch'ing
Administration, Three Studies*, p. 10.
101. *Ch'ing-shih*, p. 2589. Reference in *Eminent Chinese*, p. 602.
102. *Sheng-tsu wu-hsing*, p. 32.
103. Ibid., pp. 33–36.

brought some of the Nanking salt merchants into the palace to pay their respects to the Emperor.[104]

During the Emperor's stay in his yamen, Ts'ao Yin performed one of those actions that won him the praise of local Chinese officials and scholars, as his conspicuous filial piety and his exemplary administration in Soochow had done in the past.[105] At this time the prefect of Nanking, Ch'en P'eng-nien, had been accused by governor-general Asan of corruption and violation of the rites, and had been sentenced to death for these offences. One day the Emperor was crossing one of the courtyards of the temporary palace, when he came across Ts'ao Yin's son Ts'ao Lien-sheng (later called Ts'ao Yung) playing there, and asked him if he knew of any especially good officials in the area. Ts'ao Lien-sheng replied that he knew of one, the prefect Ch'en P'eng-nien. The significance of this reply was of course that it proved that Ts'ao Yin must have disagreed with the verdict finding against Ch'en P'eng-nien, and Ts'ao Yin subsequently begged the Emperor to spare Ch'en P'eng-nien's life. As a result of his entreaties, Ch'en P'eng-nien was pardoned. Contemporaries found this incident particularly impressive because Ts'ao Yin and Ch'en P'eng-nien had never been close friends, and Ts'ao Yin apparently risked his whole career to see justice done.[106]

Ts'ao Yin had a short respite after the Emperor left Nanking, but as soon as the Emperor reached Yangchow, Ts'ao Yin was once again responsible for his well-being. The retinue reached Yangchow on May 23, and Ts'ao Yin and the leading salt merchants requested the Emperor to lodge in the temporary palace at San-ch'a ho. Their request was granted, and the Emperor disembarked and inspected the palace set in a flower garden; the merchants had spent an enormous amount of money on the palace, and set up ingenious mechanical devices and antique objects which so delighted the Emperor that he summoned his women and the retinue to come and examine them.[107] This was obviously something of a personal triumph for Ts'ao Yin, especially since the Emperor had been angered by the low standard of workmanship and comfort at the Lung-t'an temporary palace on the voyage south,

104. Ibid., pp. 36–37b.
105. Cf. chapters 2 and 3 above.
106. HLMHC, pp. 332, 335–337. Yüan Mei, Sui-yüan shih-hua, p. 42. Eminent Chinese, p. 96. It is possible that the lavish presents given to the Emperor by Asan on May 15 were partly to deflect the Emperor's wrath at his false accusation of Ch'en P'eng-nien.
107. Sheng-tsu wu-hsing, p. 44b.

and had refused to visit it again on the return journey despite the repeated pleas of the governor-general.[108] Though previously the Emperor had told Ts'ao Yin that he need not build a special temporary palace in Yangchow,[109] he clearly expected the highest standards in entertainment and comfort, and Ts'ao Yin was not expected to take his continued admonitions about economy too literally.

On the evening of May 23 the salt merchants gave a banquet and operas. The next day Ts'ao Yin did the same, in his capacity as salt censor. On May 25 the Emperor visited another temporary palace, probably built by the salt merchants and Ts'ao Yin in concert; here they had erected a high artificial mound in the center of the garden, and the Emperor climbed it and could gaze out at the scenery in all directions. Again he expressed his pleasure, and was treated to another banquet and operatic performances. On May 26 he ordered the Imperial Bodyguard to bring the salt merchants to his temporary palace, presumably to express his appreciation; that night they put on a special show of colored lantern boats which the Emperor watched from the edge of a lake covered with lilies. This entertainment was followed by a banquet and operas. So for a whole day, the climax of three days of festivities, the Emperor passed his time with Ts'ao Yin and the salt merchants; not surprisingly this day is a complete blank in the Veritable Records.[110] The Emperor was due to return north, but stayed on at the request of the salt merchants, and May 27 and 28 were passed in banquets, operas, and the presenting of gifts. He left finally on May 29.[111]

Later that day the Emperor rested at Pao-ying-hsien, and the following edict was issued:

> Because the textile commissioners of Kiangsu took great pains in preparing the temporary palaces, and behaved reverently, let the

108. Ibid., pp. 36, 41b. The Emperor gave rainy weather as his nominal excuse for not returning.

109. Ts'ao Yin Memorials, p. 11b, interlinear rescript to memorial dated 43/12/2, reading "you can build a temporary palace, but it's not essential."

110. Sheng-tsu wu-hsing, pp. 44b–45b. May 26, 1705, (44/intercalary 4/4) is left blank in Shih-lu, ch. 220, p. 14.

111. Sheng-tsu wu-hsing, p. 46, states that he left Yangchow on intercalary 4/7, Shih-lu, ch. 220, p. 15, that he left one day earlier. The Shih-lu date refers to the departure from the temporary palace at Pao-t'a wan, while the author of Sheng-tsu wu-hsing was probably thinking more loosely of the Yangchow area in general.

textile commissioner of Nanking Ts'ao Yin be given the higher-ranking title of commissioner of the Transmission Office, and the textile commissioner of Soochow Li Hsü the higher-ranking title of director of the Court of Judicature and Revision.[112]

Then, as the diarist of this tour wrote, "both men thanked the Emperor for his favors, and returned ahead of the others." This was the highest point in Ts'ao Yin's career, and it is not hard to imagine his feelings as he rode back at the head of the column of officials, a man immensely rich, publicly rewarded by his Emperor, with a new title of the third rank and orders to compile a prestigious literary collection. These were the crucial goals of all those pursuing careers in the traditional Chinese bureaucracy; and Ts'ao Yin had attained every one of them without ever being a member of that bureaucracy.

Southern Tours in the Dream of the Red Chamber

Official and private histories alike give no more than Ts'ao Yin's public involvement with the Southern Tours. To learn anything of the personal impact of these tours would be impossible were it not for the novel the *Dream of the Red Chamber*, written by Ts'ao Yin's grandson Ts'ao Chan. The eighteenth chapter of the novel describes the visit of the imperial consort Yüan-ch'un to the house of her parents, the Chia. The chapter has the most meticulous details of this visit; the lavishness of the preparations made by the family, and the brilliance of Yüan-ch'un's entourage, suggest that this visit is no less than an imperial tour transposed into fictional form.

The splendor of the Chia house accurately reflects what is known of the Ts'ao establishment that gave the K'ang-hsi Emperor his lavish banquets and opera performances day after day.[113] Though the novelist never says exactly how the Chia family made their money, the gap may be filled from what is known about Ts'ao Yin's activities as an imperial commissioner who dealt with silk and copper and

---

112. *Sheng-tsu wu-hsing*, p. 46. The titles are *t'ung-cheng-shih ssu*, BH 928, and *kuang-lu-ssu-ch'ing*, BH 934. This latter title is actually an error, for Li Hsü was awarded the title of *ta-li-ssu*, BH 215; cf. his memorial of thanks in *Li Hsü Memorials*, p. 11, dated 44/5/–. The correct title has been substituted in my translation of the edict. For Ts'ao Yin's memorial of thanks, cf. *Ts'ao Yin Archives*, no. 2812, dated 44/5/1. For the history of Ts'ao Yin's new title, cf. *HTSL*, p. 5300 (ch. 18, p. 32b). It was third rank after 1670.

113. *Sheng-tsu wu-hsing*, pp. 31–37b.

rice.[114] Though there was no imperial consort in the Ts'ao family, both of Ts'ao Yin's daughters married princes,[115] and the Emperor had taken a personal interest in those marriages, ordering a bondservant captain in the Plain White Banner to supervise the wedding arrangements of the elder daughter,[116] and giving an imperial feast to the wedding party.[117] So the Ts'ao family was socially on the rise, rich, and personally known to the Emperor.

Such things must have been family lore to Ts'ao Yin's grandson Ts'ao Chan, who drew on all these past glories for his novel. At the same time, of course, he drew on the family events that he had himself shared in, and it is quite possible that his aunt, who had married Prince Nersu of the Bordered Red Banner and borne him a male heir,[118] visited the Ts'ao family in some considerable style while Ts'ao Chan was a child.[119] Sometimes, too, Ts'ao Chan has precise statements that exactly mirror past events, and show that besides family lore and personal experience he could draw on the historical record. For instance, just before the fifth Southern Tour, Ts'ao Yin wrote in a memorial, "Li Hsü and I are constructing the boats for the Yangtze, and for the small rivers, and expect to have the work ready [before the Emperor's arrival]"; [120] Ts'ao Chan has a character describe a South-

114. Cf. Chapter 3 above.

115. *Yung-hsien lu*, p. 390. *HLMHC*, pp. 93–96 on the elder daughter, pp. 96–97 on the younger.

116. *Ts'ao Yin Memorials*, p. 15, dated 45/8/4, states that Yin had received the imperial favor when Shang Chih-chieh was ordered to ensure that all preparations for the wedding were properly carried out. Shang Chih-chieh is listed in *PCTC*, 5/41 and 5/42, as being a *ch'i-ku tso-ling* in the Plain White Banner, and in *PCST*, 74/7b, as acting *nei-wu-fu tsung-kuan*. There is a difference in the second character "chih" of his name in the two sources, but it seems probable that the same man is referred to. This man had also been Lung-chiang customs director; cf. the section on customs houses in chapter 3 above.

117. *Ts'ao Yin Memorials*, p. 16, dated 45/12/5, "then on the same day we were again given a feast by the Emperor, and both our families shared this kindness." Ibid., pp. 19b–20, dated 48/2/8, shows that the Emperor was also following the arrangements for the marriage of Ts'ao Yin's second daughter to a *shih-wei*.

118. Ibid., p. 19b, dated 47/7/15.

119. While Ts'ao Fu was Nanking *chih-tsao*. Wu Shih-ch'ang, *On the Red Chamber Dream*, pp. 88–90, discusses this telescoping of two events.

The simple statement that this visit occurred in Nanking "while Ts'ao Chan was a child" is, in the context of present-day studies of the *Dream of the Red Chamber*, an extremely controversial one; though I cannot here go into the incredibly complex area of exegesis of Ts'ao Chan's novel, the background reasoning behind the statement is summarized in appendix D below.

120. *Ts'ao Yin Memorials*, p. 12b, dated 43/12/12.

ern Tour thus: "at that time our Chia family was supervising the construction of ships on the stretch of river between Ku-su and Yangchow." [121] If the following descriptions be seen as a combination of historical fact, family lore, and later personal experience, and subject to either the exaggeration or understatement that a novelist might employ as he chose, they may be useful as a kind of generic summary of the impact of a Southern Tour on the Ts'ao family. As a further cautionary measure, the visit will be discussed as it was written by Ts'ao Chan, in terms of Yüan-ch'un's visit to the Chia family, rather than as the historian may see it, as a visit by the K'ang-hsi Emperor to the Ts'ao family.

When the Chia family received definite news that Yüan-ch'un was to visit them, they selected an area from the gardens of their two adjoining mansions about 3½ *li* (a little over one mile) in circumference, and commissioned an architect to draw up plans for a suitable residence to be built there. At the same time someone was sent off to hire singing girls and their instructors, and the necessary musical instruments and theatrical properties; [122] 30,000 taels of the family's money was to be used for this, and a further 20,000 taels for the purchase of colored lanterns, banners, curtains, and streamers.[123] (The novelist suggests that there was considerable dishonesty among the family members deputed to make these purchases.)

From this time onward, steady streams of workmen and masons entered the Chia family mansions, bringing all the required materials from gold and silver to timber, bricks, and tiles. Walls, towers, and a complete wing of servants' quarters were demolished to make way for the new construction; luckily there was already a stream on the site and it was not necessary to divert one. Such items as small trees and shrubs, ornamental rocks, railings, and pavilions were transported from other parts of the grounds; by carefully utilizing the resources already to hand, it proved possible to carry out the alterations moderately cheaply.[124] Many of the walls and pavilions were made from polished brick, and white marble was used for some of the steps and terraces; some of the marble was decorated with Western designs.[125]

121. *Hung-lou meng pa-shih-hui chiao-pen,* p. 156.

122. *Hung-lou meng,* trans. Joly, p. 235.

123. Ibid., p. 236.

124. Ibid., p. 238.

125. Ibid., pp. 243–44. Ts'ao Chan clearly considered this in execrable taste, and said so.

The interiors of the buildings were finished in luxurious style, with scented woods carved with fretted designs of clouds and flowers and birds, and further inlaid with gold or precious stones.[126] One of the characters neatly summed up the justification for so much display: "The imperial consort has, it is true, an exalted preference for economy and frugality, but her present honorable position requires the observance of such courtesies, so that finery is no fault." [127]

Work continued through the summer and autumn. By the tenth month things were under control: twelve young singing girls had been selected and were undergoing instruction in some twenty plays, and twelve young girls—novice Taoist and Buddhist nuns—had been obtained and were being taught to intone the required prayers.[128] This took care of the 30,000 tael allotment; the 20,000 tael fabric fund was used to obtain one hundred and twenty sets of curtains of stiff silk embroidered with dragons, hundreds of door hangings of lacquered bamboo and rattan, or of netting, and over a thousand sets of table and bed covers, and cushions.[129] Curios and writing materials were all assembled, scrolls hung at scenic spots, and birds and animals to delight the eye and the palate had been bought. After a final inspection, the head of the house, Chia Cheng, sent a routine memorial (*t'i-pen*) announcing that the preparations were complete.[130] He received an edict that Yüan-ch'un would visit the house on the fifteenth day of the first month.[131]

A week before Yüan-ch'un's arrival, eunuchs from the palace came to inspect the arrangements and all the different rooms in which she would change her clothes, rest, eat, and receive the greetings of the family. Other eunuchs came to patrol the grounds and make sure that they were properly protected, and to screen off all prohibited areas. Still others gave the members of the Chia family the most detailed instructions concerning the etiquette to be observed. Outside the mansion, officials from the Board of Works, and the local police magis-

126. Ibid., p. 260.
127. Ibid., p. 257.
128. Ibid., pp. 264 and 266.
129. Ibid., p. 249.
130. Ibid., p. 266.
131. This was about the time the Emperor normally left on his tours; the last five commenced in 28/1/8, 38/2/3, 42/1/16, 44/2/9, and 46/1/22. Cf. *Shih-lu* references in the section above devoted to the tours in general.

trates,[132] saw that the streets were completely clean and free from vagrants.[133]

At dawn on the fifteenth day, after a sleepless night, the whole Chia family assembled at the gate of the mansion in their official full dress, where they waited in complete silence. After various false alarms, ten eunuchs galloped up to announce the arrival of the imperial consort. They were followed after a time by pairs of eunuchs riding at a dignified pace, and behind these came Yüan-ch'un's entourage, with dragon banners and phoenix fans, with golden incense burners and a state umbrella, and with the luxurious articles for her personal toilette. Then came several marching companies of eunuchs, and at last Yüan-ch'un herself, in an imperial sedan chair of golden yellow carried by eight eunuchs.[134]

After Yüan-ch'un had changed, she was carried in her chair to view the garden. Since it was already dusk, it was ablaze with thousands of colored lanterns. The trees, normally quite bare in this season, were covered with blossoms made of silk and paper attached to the branches; and on the waters of the pond, that would otherwise have been empty, floated lotus plants and ducks made by hand from shells and feathers.[135] After the formal greetings were over, she talked with her family and was given a banquet, followed by a poetry-writing contest among the members of the family; the festivities ended with the performance of four scenes from opera, and the exchange of lavish presents.[136]

The most important part of this *Dream of the Red Chamber* account of an imperial consort's visit to the Chia family is probably the description of the arrangements that had to be made in advance.

132. *wu-ch'eng ping-ma-ssu, BH* 796A. This is in fact a Peking office.

133. *Hung-lou meng,* trans. Joly, p. 266.

134. Ibid., p. 268. Kao E's emendations on this passage are discussed by Wu Shih-ch'ang, *On the Red Chamber Dream,* p. 239. Lin Yutang, "P'ing-hsin lun Kao E" (Re-opening the Question of Authorship of "Red Chamber Dream"), *Bulletin of the Institute of History and Philology Academia Sinica,* 29 (1958), 327–87, denies Kao E's role as author of the last forty chapters, which he attributes to Ts'ao Chan. If Lin Yutang's arguments held water, they would complicate the question of such emendations even further, since if Ts'ao Chan wrote the whole novel we would have to find new explanations for the many inconsistencies in the last forty chapters. But his views have been brusquely and convincingly rejected by Wu Shih-ch'ang, *On the Red Chamber Dream,* pp. 355–58.

135. *Hung-lou meng,* trans. Joly, p. 269.

136. Ibid., pp. 269–82.

For a careful examination of details leads to an apparently unlikely conclusion: the Southern Tours were expensive to Ts'ao Yin, but almost certainly not disastrously so, as some writers have claimed.[137] The novel mentions the figure of 50,000 taels as covering special expenses; though this was meant to seem enormously high to the novel's readers, examination of Ts'ao Yin's resources shows that such a sum was comfortably within his means.[138] Ts'ao Chan also pointed out how much could be done by merely rearranging objects that were already in the possession of the family, and the labor for this came from the servants who were already in the family's employ. Again, the expense of preparing the palace only had to be met once; after it was built, it only needed to be refurbished at intervals. Since the Emperor had already stayed at the Nanking textile commissioner's yamen in 1689, before Ts'ao Yin was appointed to the post, the basic costs had probably already been met by Ts'ao Yin's predecessor, Sang-ko. In any case, many of the costs of the Southern Tours were met by borrowings from public funds, although the Emperor protested the practice.[139] As to the costs of the curios and luxury items, these may well have been met, as a character in the novel observed in a slightly different connection, by "taking money from the Emperor's household and then using it all on the Emperor's person." [140] Lastly, there is the incident mentioned by Ts'ao Chan after Yüan-ch'un had returned to the palace and told the Emperor how well the family had received her. The Emperor was delighted, and gave orders for presents of satin, gold, and silk to be sent to the Chia family from the imperial storehouse.[141] Such presents amounted to straightforward cash awards. The K'ang-hsi Emperor may well have rewarded Ts'ao Yin in such a way; these payments for services rendered would not have been common knowledge, and were quite different from the rewards of a horse,

137. Wu Shih-ch'ang, On the Red Chamber Dream, p. 115, writes that the Ts'ao family had "previously exhausted its coffers while acting as host of the Emperor and his entourage several times during the Royal Southern Excursions." This is not to deny the general excellence of Wu Shih-ch'ang's analysis of the novel.

138. Cf. chapter 3 above and chapter 5 below. Tu Lien-che noted the ease with which Ts'ao Yin met the expenses of the Southern Tours in her biography of Ts'ao Yin in Eminent Chinese, p. 741.

139. K'ang-hsi nan-hsün pi-chi, pp. 121–22. Also cited in HLMHC, pp. 415–16.

140. Hung-lou meng pa-shih-hui chiao-pen, p. 156. Also cited in chapter 3 above.

141. Hung-lou meng, trans. Joly, p. 283.

a line of poetry, a fan, or an ink-stick which appear in the records of the tours.

Ts'ao Yin and the Complete T'ang Poems

It was on the fifth Southern Tour, April 12, 1705, that Ts'ao Yin received the edict to print the *Complete T'ang Poems* (*Ch'üan T'ang shih*).[142] The K'ang-hsi Emperor thus inaugurated the first of those great literary projects for which the Ch'ing dynasty is justly famous; this was a measure of his feelings of confidence and stability: having been *"wu,"* the military conqueror of Wu San-kuei and Galdan, he would now also assure his reputation as *"wen,"* the literary Emperor, proving his appreciation of the Chinese poetic tradition despite his non-Chinese ancestry. The choice of Ts'ao Yin rather than some really famous Confucian literatus or official was also significant, however; Ts'ao Yin crossed the zones in just the right way—he was both a Manchu bondservant on special appointment to the provinces, and a Chinese literary figure and patron of some standing. That such a man was the choice to head the project shows that even after forty years of rule, the K'ang-hsi Emperor stuck to those he could truly call his own.

As Soochow textile commissioner, Ts'ao Yin had belonged to a literary circle that included several eminent Chinese scholars,[143] and his literary life continued unabated after his transfer to the more important post in Nanking.[144] He wrote numerous poems and essays [145] and also played his part in leaving behind those solid proofs of benevolence that were considered a part of the Confucian scholar's duties: he repaired the school in Nanking, restored temples, wrote tablets on request, and even paid for the repair of a local sluice gate.[146]

Prior to the 1705 edict he had not undertaken any major printing

142. *Ch'üan T'ang shih*, preface, p. 1. The date is 44/3/19.

143. Cf. chapter 2 above.

144. For extremely thorough documentation on all the figures with whom he was in contact during this period, cf. the *nien-p'u* section of HLMHC, pp. 268–384, covering the years 1692–1712.

145. His poems in *Ts'ao Yin Shih* can mostly be dated after 1692, and the dated essays in *Ts'ao Yin Wen* are mostly after 1700.

146. *Ts'ao Yin Wen*, pp. 6, 10, and 27. The essay which he wrote on repairing the sluice gate was included in the collection of writings by bannermen entitled *Pa-ch'i wen-ching*, ed. Sheng-yü (printed by Chang Chih-tung in 1902), ch. 36, p. 13. The repairing of the Nanking school is recorded in the local history, and cited in HLMHC, p. 358.

projects, but he had gained some experience in helping Ku Ch'ang assemble and print the works of his father Ku Ching-hsing,[147] and had worked closely with Shih Li who was compiling the works of his grandfather, the famous poet Shih Jun-chang.[148] Ts'ao Yin threw himself into the new work with apparent enthusiasm, and through his surviving memorials it is possible to trace the evolution of the massive *Complete T'ang Poems* from its earliest beginnings to the appearance of the completed work.

At the same time that Ts'ao Yin was ordered to supervise the printing, nine Hanlin scholars were appointed to take care of collating the poems. They were headed by P'eng Ting-ch'iu, a subexpositor [149] of the Hanlin Academy, who had edited the edicts of the early Manchu Emperors, been a Court diarist, and recommended the translation of the Classic of Filial Piety into Manchu; the edict recalled him to duty after he had spent eleven years in voluntary retirement.[150] The other eight men were second-class compilers from the Hanlin Academy.[151] Since Ts'ao Yin had been awarded his new rank of commissioner of the Transmission Office on May 29,[152] he was comfortably senior to all these men, and appears to have been in sole charge of the printing.

Ts'ao Yin's first memorial on the project was sent on June 21, 1705. Using his new title for the first time, he humbly acknowledged the Emperor's edict that he print the *Complete T'ang Poems*, but added that there was little to report as yet;

> I sent a message [to the Hanlin officials] fixing today June 21 for the opening of the poetry office in the T'ien-ning temple, but so far none of them has arrived in Yangchow. When they arrive to help with the printing, I will memorialize.[153]

The T'ien-ning temple, outside the Kung-chen gate of Yangchow, was an elaborate structure with woods and ornamental gardens that

147. *HLMHC*, pp. 324–27. The work was finished in 1704. For Ku Ching-hsing, cf. chapter 2, above.

148. *HLMHC*, pp. 358 and 362. The work took some years and was finished in 1707. For Shih Jun-chang, cf. *Eminent Chinese*, p. 651.

149. *han-lin-yüan shih-chiang*, BH 197. Rank 5B.

150. *Eminent Chinese*, pp. 616–17.

151. *han-lin-yüan pien-hsiu*, BH 200B. Rank 7A.

152. See above, pp. 150–51.

153. *Ts'ao Yin Memorials*, p. 12b, dated 44/5/1.

was used as a temporary palace on the Southern Tours.[154] Since it had
its own wharf, it must have been particularly convenient for assembling the materials needed for a project of this size; the actual printing work may well have taken place in areas that could no longer be
used as dwellings by the monks because the Emperor himself had
lodged in them.

Though the appointed scholars had not arrived, Ts'ao Yin continued, a certain Hanlin bachelor [155] named Yü Mei had appeared, saying that he had received special orders to assist with the collation since
he lived nearby. Ts'ao Yin was clearly not happy about this, and requested an edict of confirmation. He ended his June 21 memorial
thus:

> I sent a communication to the Kiangsu governor Sung Lao, ask-
> ing him to send a communication to the Board of Civil Office
> and the Hanlin Academy. When the printing is finished, those
> offices will also send a memorial.

This illustrates the difficulty that Ts'ao Yin so often had to face: because of the fact that his appointments were in the form of special
commissions received from the Emperor, there was often no proper
channel through which he could communicate with the normal bureaucracy.

By the time Ts'ao Yin sent his next memorial on August 19, all the
Hanlin scholars but one had arrived, and with the poetry before them
"were all happy and excited, diligently correcting the drafts." One of
his friends, however, gave a rather different picture of the operation in
a poem he wrote at this time:

> Ts'ao Yin's poetry office is a regular nest of books,
> He's started to loathe collation, with misprints
> wherever he looks.[156]

Fortunately, Ts'ao Yin did not have to bother too much with such details. His responsibility was for the blocks, and in this he showed himself to be a true perfectionist:

154. *Nan-hsün sheng-tien*, ch. 97, p. 7.
155. *han-lin-yüan shu-chi-shih, BH* 201.
156. Ma Yü-t'ang, quoted in *HLMHC*, p. 372.

Apart from one or two details and the explanatory notes, which I am discussing with the Hanlin scholars and about which I will send a separate memorial, I have been directing my attention to the arrangements concerning the calligraphers. It was very hard to get men with the same calligraphic style, and I had to be content with choosing men whose style was similar. But I ordered them to practice and perfect a common style, and then to start their copying. Because of this delay, I'm afraid that it will not be possible to finish the work within the year. There are still the poems of the middle and the late T'ang to be done, and poems that are missing. I have sent men in all directions to look for these, and they will be added to the collection and collated. Because of my salt duties I have to keep moving between I-chen and Yangchow. But as I am in charge of the printing, I shall have the collated parts copied out immediately, for I dare not be idle.[157]

This memorial shows clearly how the compilation was done. The Hanlin scholars had brought with them various existing editions of T'ang poems, which they checked against each other in an attempt to find a true version. In the meantime, Ts'ao Yin sent round to private collections to make up any gaps. He also trained his calligraphers in a common style so that they could copy out all the versions collated by the Hanlin scholars in a uniform manner, prior to having this calligraphy carved onto wood blocks by skilled artisans for the actual printing. The calligraphy that Ts'ao Yin evolved for this work was light and elegant, and the books printed under his direction are regarded as masterpieces of xylography.[158] It is thus all the more astonishing that Ts'ao Yin could have dreamed of finishing the whole enormous work within the year. But he had apparently done so, and felt it necessary to apologize for delays less than two months after work had commenced. The whole project was carried out under great pressure, and was clearly a prestige venture rather than a purely scholarly undertaking.

A memorial of October 2 reported that work was progressing smoothly, and gratefully acknowledged the endorsement in vermilion

157. *Ts'ao Yin Memorials,* p. 13, dated 44/7/1.
158. By Tu Lien-che in *Eminent Chinese,* p. 741.

ink with which the Emperor had graced the memorial sending him the first sample: "The explanatory notes are very good." [159] Only a month later, Ts'ao Yin sent off to the Emperor two proof copies containing the works of T'ang T'ai-tsung, Kao Shih, Ch'en Shen, Wang Wei, and Meng Chiao; he added that the works of several dozen more poets were being bound, and that he would bring them to Peking in person when he came to report on his year's salt administration.[160] Work apparently proceeded smoothly in his absence, and when he returned to the south on April 1, 1706, he was able to report that work would be finished within the year.[161]

His next memorial on August 8 was to report that this deadline would be beaten, and that the work should be finished within a month since there were only about five hundred leaves left to be printed. Two cases (*t'ao*) had been sent off in the spring, and six more were almost ready. The total work would consist of twelve cases. The mention of the size of the work at this late stage suggests that Ts'ao Yin had not initially had any idea what size it would be, and had simply ploughed ahead, printing each section as it was finished, in order to meet his self-imposed deadline. The incredible pace at which this earliest of the great literary projects of the Ch'ing dynasty was undertaken is graphically shown by the sentences with which Ts'ao Yin closed this memorial:

> Those Hanlin scholars who fell ill and requested leave of absence were all permitted to return to their homes. Those unaffected are all in Yangchow, collating the works. The second-class compiler Wang I frequently suffered from hemorrhages, and this old disease broke out again while he was at the poetry office, so I let him return home to be looked after. But he died in June. I took care of the funeral and his family. Those at present in Yangchow working on the collating are P'eng Ting-ch'iu, Yang Chung-na, Wang Shih-hung, Hsü Shu-pen, and Yü Mei, five in all.[162]

That is to say, of the ten officials originally appointed to manage the collation, only half had lasted the course. These survivors may have

159. *Ts'ao Yin Memorials*, p. 13, dated 44/8/15.
160. Ibid., pp. 13b–14, dated 44/10/22.
161. Ibid., p. 14, dated 45/2/18.
162. Ibid., p. 14b, dated 45/7/1.

been cheered by the Emperor's endorsement: "The volumes printed are very good. Wait until I have read them through carefully, and when the preface is finished I'll send it to you." But the story of the compilation shows that to be a literary man was by no means necessarily to have a life of leisure.

By October 21, 1706, the proofs of cases nine and ten were checked and sent off to the Emperor, and the blocks of the remaining two cases had all been carved.[163] Various minor problems still arose, but after a spell of unusually fine weather in the spring of 1707, which presumably allowed the printed sheets to be dried in the open air, Ts'ao Yin reported on June 14 that he had ordered the last of the Hanlin scholars to return to Peking and report to the Board of Civil Office.[164] Under Ts'ao Yin's direction, the collation and the carving of an entire set of new blocks of excellent quality for the *Complete T'ang Poems*, 900 *chüan* containing 48,900 poems by over 2,200 authors,[165] had been completed in slightly under two years.

Ts'ao Yin had had some literary reputation before he received the edict to print the *Complete T'ang Poems*. Naturally enough, once he had carried the work through so successfully, his stock rose enormously. He achieved fame as a printer, and in the nineteenth century bibliophiles were still hunting for the blocks with which he had printed certain rare Sung editions;[166] it was said that he "exhausted his strength on the matter of printing."[167] His best-known works are the two collections of rare Sung works called *Lien-t'ing wu chung* and *Lien-t'ing shih-erh chung*, named from his studio name of Lien-t'ing.

Examination of these works shows that they need not have been such a drain on his finances and his time as might be supposed. They are exquisitely printed, the *Shih-erh chung* on the thinnest paper with a double interleaf of fine white paper, the *Wu chung* with transparent overleaf title pages, in the elegant type of his own design, but the end of each *ts'e* has the distinctive narrow seal of the Yangchow poetry office. It is certain that Ts'ao Yin utilized the resources available in

163. Ibid., p. 15b, dated 45/9/15.

164. *Ts'ao Yin Archives*, no. 2790, dated 46/5/15.

165. The figures are from *Ssu-k'u ch'üan-shu tsung-mu t'i-yao* (Shanghai, 1933 ed.), p. 4217.

166. Yü Sung-nien so hunted; cf. *Ch'ing pai lei-ch'ao*, section 72, p. 120.

167. Ibid., section 72, p. 51.

Yangchow for printing the *Complete T'ang Poems,* and it is by no means unlikely that he "borrowed" some of the paper and labor available there for his private projects. All three works seem to have been conceived about 1705, and finished a year or so later.[168] At the end of the fourth part of the *Wu chung,* thirty-two men are listed as being "fellow collators" (*t'ung-chiao*). Those who can be traced seem to have been minor literary figures who may have done the work either for the prestige involved, or for money. At the end of the whole work, two men are listed as being "chief collators" (*ch'üan-chiao*).[169]

Besides the printing material to hand in Yangchow, and the help of local scholars, Ts'ao Yin had the constant help of one of the most famous scholars of his time, Chu I-tsun.[170] Chu I-tsun wrote a short epilogue for part four of the *Wu chung,* discussed problems arising from the *Complete T'ang Poems* with Ts'ao Yin,[171] was commissioned by him to write a history of the Liang-huai salt area (which was never printed, though the bibliography for it was well known),[172] and was to have his prose works printed by Ts'ao Yin, who died before he could complete it.[173] The two exchanged poems regularly, and were close friends.[174] With such help, Ts'ao Yin could not go far wrong on matters of scholarship.

This is not to deny the nature of his achievement in bringing out the *Complete T'ang Poems.* The Emperor may well have realized how hard this task had been, because when the great phrase dictionary, the *P'ei-wen yün-fu,* was compiled, all three textile commissioners were ordered to see to the printing of it in the Yangchow printing office.

---

168. The tall seal in *Shih-erh chung* has the date 1706 (*ping-hsü*). The edition has eleven columns to the page and twenty-one characters to the column. The rarer *Wu chung* has a colophon after section 4 by Chu I-tsun that is also dated 1706. The edition I used from the Research Institute for Humanistic Studies in Kyoto has the missing third section made up (*pu-k'an*) by the scholar Ku Kuang-ch'i (cf. *Eminent Chinese,* pp. 417–19), and he added the date 1814 to the title page of this section. This edition has the same long seal bearing the date 1706 as the *Shih-erh chung,* but has only eight columns to the page and sixteen characters to the column.

169. One was Yü Yang-chih, the other Ts'ao Yüeh-ying. (Only the latter's *ming* is given, but comparison with the list after part 4 makes it almost certain that the Ts'ao Yüeh-ying there is the Yüeh-ying at the end of the volume. He was no known relation of Ts'ao Yin's.)

170. *Eminent Chinese,* pp. 182–85.

171. *Ch'en-feng-ko ts'ung-shu,* 1909, "Ch'ien-ts'ai t'ang shu-mu," part 4, section 1.

172. Ibid., section 3.

173. *Eminent Chinese,* p. 184.

174. *Ts'ao Yin Shih,* passim.

Ts'ao Yin selected over a hundred craftsmen to work on it, while Sun Wen-ch'eng was put in charge of procuring the paper, and Li Hsü checked printing.[175] None of them had to worry about assembling the material of the dictionary, which had been in the hands of the grand secretary, Chang Yü-shu, and compiled over an eight-year period.[176]

Ts'ao Yin had sent off the last proofs of the *Complete T'ang Poems,* and dismissed the academicians, in June 1707. It was not until 1711 that he at last received a communication from the Hanlin Academy, in which they transmitted to him the edict in which the definitive form of official titles and the order of precedence for those who had worked on the compilation were given by the Emperor. On April 27, Ts'ao Yin wrote thus in his memorial of thanks:

> Obedient to your edict, I have added our names to the book. Who am I that I should be on this list of names? This is an eternal favor that will never fade. I cannot overcome my emotions and am ashamed. I do not know what happiness could ever compare with this.[177]

It was a kind gesture by the Emperor, and for once Ts'ao Yin may have written the hyperbole of thanks with total conviction. For here he had been granted that special immortality which the Chinese literary tradition was able to bestow. Though he was a bondservant, and

175. *Ts'ao Yin Memorials,* p. 25b, dated 51/4/3. *Li Hsü Memorials,* p. 47, dated 52/9/10, which received the vermilion endorsement, "This book is extraordinarily well printed." Here Li Hsü had been working from Ts'ao Yin's blocks and design. When he tried on his own to print an edition of imperial poems, the result was near disaster, for after he had sent the first two *chüan* he received the endorsement: "I've looked carefully at the collected imperial poems you've been printing this year; the pages are not of uniform length, the characters are different sizes, the collation is not uniform, this is extremely careless, the work is useless. Speedily put it in order, make it all standard, then send it and I'll look at it again" (*Li Hsü Memorials,* p. 63b, dated 54/6/6). Li Hsü in a panic had all the work redone (ibid., p. 65, dated 54/8/20) and after having them checked in the *Nan-shu-fang* (ibid., p. 71b, dated 55/5/25), sent them in to the Emperor and won the endorsement, "The poems are well-printed" (ibid., p. 78, dated 55/11/8). So the Emperor got tough if the work was shoddy.

176. *Eminent Chinese,* pp. 66 and 741.

177. *Ts'ao Yin Memorials,* p. 20, dated 50/3/10. Though Ts'ao Yin's name was printed first in the *Complete T'ang Poems* itself, he did not win similar recognition in the *Ssu-k'u ch'üan-shu tsung-mu t'i-yao,* p. 4217, where the *Poems* are mentioned simply as an imperial compilation (*yü-ting*).

had been no more than the supervisor and printer of the project (as he reminded the Emperor in his memorial of thanks), Ts'ao Yin was now listed first in the introductory section of the *Complete T'ang Poems*, first among all those responsible for editing the poems that were themselves one of the foremost glories of that tradition.

CHAPTER 5

Liang-huai Salt Administration

Ts'ao Yin was appointed salt censor of Liang-huai in 1704, and was reappointed in 1706, 1708, and 1710. Since the salt administration area of Liang-huai covered a major part of central China, and yielded a total income of around two and a half million taels a year in this period, it was an important and complex office. The salt censors were responsible for issuing the government salt certificates (*yin*) to the salt merchants; these certificates authorized the merchants to sell a given amount of salt in a given area, in return for which privilege they paid the various taxes that constituted the bulk of the government's salt revenue. This meant that unless the merchants were prosperous, the salt censors were unlikely to be able to meet their tax quotas, and unless the common people were prosperous enough to buy salt at a good price, the merchants were unlikely to realize a high profit. At the same time the wealth of the merchants tempted the salt officials to demand numerous extra fees, and corruption was widespread.

In addition to legal taxation and the illegal exaction of extra fees, there was a third category of payments, which yielded the so-called "surplus-money" (*yü-yin*); these were officially sanctioned payments made by the merchants to the salt censors over and above their ordinary taxation, in return for the right to sell extra salt. This surplus amounted to about half a million taels a year, and the uses to which this large sum should be put were often decided personally by the Emperor. The K'ang-hsi Emperor used his two bondservants Ts'ao Yin and Li Hsü as salt censors of Liang-huai since they had proved their ability and loyalty as textile commissioners, knew the Yangtze valley area, and could be relied on to get the maximum surplus possible and use it both for running the textile works and for executing the Emperor's public and private commissions—from printing the *Complete T'ang Poems* to buying bamboo pitch pipes.

The opportunities for corruption were enormous, and there is no way of telling how honestly Ts'ao Yin collected or distributed the surplus money. His memorials show that initially he was full of zeal to reform the system, but the Emperor discouraged him from precipitate action; Ts'ao Yin gave up any attempts to change things as he became more conscious of the complexities of the office. His reports of giant deficits in his second and third terms of administration were probably exaggerated, since it was in his personal interest to collect as much money as possible and hand as little over to the Emperor as could be done without arousing suspicion. By his fourth term the Emperor *was* suspicious, and Ts'ao Yin accordingly paid over large sums to the treasury.

At the same time, Ts'ao Yin did have genuine difficulties. He had inherited a corrupt system and a sizable deficit. In 1707 and 1708 there were serious droughts; rice prices rose alarmingly and the economy was disrupted. Merchants and salt officials were caught by the system that demanded unchanging tax revenues regardless of local conditions. The shifts to which Ts'ao Yin and the salt merchants were reduced show that behind the mid-eighteenth-century heyday of the Liang-huai salt area [1] lay at least a few years of doubt and experimentation.

The Liang-huai Salt Taxes

The area that for the purposes of salt administration was known as Liang-huai included large sections of the provinces of Kiangsu, Anhwei, Kiangsi, Hupei, and Hunan, and parts of Honan. It was considerably richer than the other major salt areas into which China was divided, such as Ch'ang-lu, which consisted of the Peking metropolitan area and the provinces of Chihli and much of Honan, or Liang-

1. This heyday is described in the now famous article by Ho Ping-ti, "The Salt Merchants of Yang-chou: A Study of Commercial Capitalism in Eighteenth-Century China," *HJAS*, 17 (1954), 130–68. (Cited hereafter as Ho Ping-ti, "Salt Merchants.") Cf. also Ho Ping-ti, *The Ladder of Success in Imperial China*, pp. 81–85 and 158–59. A useful introduction in English to the salt systems of successive Chinese dynasties has been written by Esson M. Gale and Ch'en Sung-ch'iao and appears in the Korean periodical *Journal of Asiatic Studies* (*Asea Yon'gu*), 1:1 (1958), 137–217; 1:2 (1958), 193–216; 2:1 (1959), 273–316. (I am grateful to Silas Wu for bringing this article to my attention.)

kuang, which included Kwangtung and Kwangsi, Kweichow, and parts of Fukien, Hunan, and Kiangsi. There were further salt areas that usually coincided with the boundaries of single provinces and were insignificant in comparison.[2]

From 1705 to 1720, during most of which period either Ts'ao Yin or Li Hsü was salt censor, the annual yield of the various Liang-huai salt taxes was 2,500,000 taels,[3] 1,950,000 taels being standard tax revenue and 550,000 being surplus.[4] (Naturally in poor years the yield fell below this total.) At this time a standard Liang-huai yield was 52 percent of the money that the government received from all salt areas, and about 6½ percent of the revenue that the government received from salt and land taxes combined.[5]

The salt of Liang-huai was sea salt, the sea water usually being boiled to bring salt by evaporation, though this was just one of the current production methods; in the area of Sung-chiang in Chekiang it was evaporated on boards (*pan-shai*), and north of the Huai River it was evaporated by the sun on the foreshore (*t'an-shai*).[6] Sea salt

2. *HTSL*, p. 8060 (ch. 223, p. 1). *YFTC*, ch. 6. Ho Ping-ti, "Salt Merchants," p. 131, says the Liang-huai area "easily outstripped all other areas in production, sale and revenue." This Liang-huai dominance is clearly shown by the charts in Saeki Tomi, *Shin-dai ensei no kenkyū*, pp. 15, 19.

3. *Ts'ao Yin Memorials*, p. 23, dated 50/3/9, states that regular and miscellaneous revenue (*ch'ien-liang cheng-tsa*) was 2,380,000 taels. *Li Hsü Memorials*, p. 40, dated 51/11/22, says revenue (*ch'ien-liang*) was 2,400,000 taels. In 1732 the salt censor Kao Pin estimated that the Liang-huai salt merchants paid over 2,500,000 taels for their salt certificates every year, in standard and miscellaneous taxes. Expenses at the distribution points, and for packing, were extra (*YCCPYC*, *ts'e* 50, p. 82, memorial dated Yung-cheng 10/3/16). By the year 1812 the standard tax yielded 2,993,614 taels, though this was described as exceptional; the 1811 yield had been 2,552,550. Cf. *Shih-liao hsün-k'an*, no. 27, p. 999 (p. 535 in continuous pagination edition).

4. *Li Hsü Memorials*, pp. 80b–81, dated 56/2/24 (1717) states that year's salt tax quota (*e-cheng ch'ien-liang*) to be 1,950,000 taels—i.e. without the surplus. Some declared surpluses in this period were: 1713, 586,000 taels; 1714, 550,000 to 560,000 taels as annual average; 1716, 527,000 taels. Cf, *Li Hsü Memorials*, pp. 48b, 54b, 77b.

5. *Ch'ing Shih-lu ching-chi tzu-liao chi-yao* [Selection of the Economic Materials in the Ch'ing Shih-lu] (Shanghai, 1959), pp. 9–35, gives revenue figures for the years 1644–1734. Saeki, *Shin-dai ensei*, p. 15, shows Liang-huai salt taxes in 1685 yielding 52 percent of all salt revenues, and in 1726, 45 percent. The 1711 figures were: total salt tax, 3,729,228 taels, land tax 29,904,000.

6. *YFTC*, ch. 33, p. 3. The Liang-huai salt fields, grouped mainly around T'ung-chou and T'ai-chou, are conveniently tabulated in Saeki, *Shin-dai ensei*, pp. 76–77. For the many other methods of salt production, cf. Gale and Ch'en, "China's Salt Administration," 2:1, 273–316.

was considered superior to the lake or well salt from inland regions, and sea salt evaporated on the foreshore was favored over that evaporated on boards, or by boiling.[7]

Salt production was controlled by some thirty factories (*ch'ang*); these factories collected the salt from a varying number of subsidiary salterns, which were often owned or managed by independent salt masters (*tsao-hu*), and from the smaller depots (*yüan*) where the salt was stored immediately after manufacture. The factory merchants (*ch'ang-shang*) were the only men connected with salt production who could expect to make really large profits; similarly, they were the only ones who faced really heavy losses if the salt could not be sold, since their salt might spoil in vast quantities.[8]

The unit for salt taxation was the certificate called the *yin*.[9] Possession of a *yin* certificate gave a merchant the right to transport salt to a specified area and sell it; the *yin* were issued every year to the transport merchants (*yün-shang*) by the salt officials in Yangchow. To transport salt when not in possession of a *yin* certificate was to risk being sentenced as a smuggler; the merchant had to travel with his salt and his certificates. After the salt was sold, the old certificates had to be returned to the authorities. Those using old certificates with intent to deceive would be punished on the same scale as salt smugglers. Those forging salt certificates could be beheaded.[10]

The word *yin* meant both the certificate itself and the standard weight of salt officially prescribed for each certificate;[11] there were three variables that must be considered in any attempt to discuss the *yin* system: first, the number of *yin* that the government issued in any one year; second, the price at which each *yin* was assessed; third, the weight of salt that could be transported on each *yin* certificate.

The number of *yin* that should be issued every year in Liang-huai was set at 1,410,360 in 1645. A further 92,697 were added in 1653,

7. *YFTC*, ch. 38, p. 3.

8. Ho Ping-ti, "Salt Merchants," pp. 131–35. Ho estimates that there were thirty factory merchants.

9. *YFTC*, ch. 43, p. 1, which also gives the terms current in other salt areas.

10. Ibid., ch. 53, pp. 19b–20, from a sample certificate as issued by the Board of Revenue.

11. Sun, *Ch'ing Administrative Terms*, no. 1034. (The issuing of certificates by the Board of Revenue directly to the head merchants described there was a later eighteenth-century practice.)

and 160,000 in 1656. In 1660, on the advice of the expert salt censor Li Tsang-yüan, who felt that the new total of almost 1.7 million *yin* was far too high and led to absconding and defaulting, the two additions were canceled, and the 1645 quota was restored.[12] In the following half century only small increases were made, and during the salt-administration terms of Ts'ao Yin and Li Hsü the basic number of *yin* issued each year in Liang-huai was 1,425,949.[13] The total rose again in the mid-eighteenth century until once again it was almost 1.7 million.[14]

The same edict that fixed the 1645 *yin* quota also set the regular tax (*k'o-yin*) on each *yin* at 0.675 taels. This gave the government a salt-tax revenue of 951,992 taels from Liang-huai. The additions of 252,697 to the *yin* quota in 1653 and 1656 brought in a further 170,570 taels of revenue. These additions were abolished in 1660 as explained above; but the government was reluctant to lose this extra revenue, and accordingly reapportioned (*t'an-na*) the new revenue to the old quota. That is, by adding 0.121 taels to each *yin* of the 1645 quota, they brought in a further 170,653 taels and thus kept the revenue constant at its new height of 1,122,645 taels per annum. But of course each *yin* now cost the merchant 0.796 taels instead of the 0.675 taels he had paid previously.[15] Further increases in tax assessment followed shortly. In 1667, following reapportionment from other areas, 0.0682 taels was added to each *yin*, making the tax 0.864 taels. An increase of 0.1159 taels in 1669 brought the tax to 0.98 taels. Two further increases, of 0.25 taels in 1677, and of 0.125 taels in 1694, had brought the tax on each *yin* up to 1.35 taels by the time Ts'ao Yin and Li Hsü became Liang-huai salt censors.[16] Though the average tax on a salt *yin* throughout the whole of China was only about 0.72 taels in 1712,[17] Liang-huai was nearly twice as high, presumably because the area was prosperous enough to stand far higher taxation.

This was the official quota revenue that was forwarded on to the

---

12. *HTSL*, p. 8061 (ch. 223, pp. 2b–3). *YFTC*, ch. 45, pp. 24–26 and ch. 72, p. 17.

13. *HTSL*, pp. 8061–62 (ch. 223, pp. 3–5): 1,285,881 were quota transport *yin* (*kang-yin*) and 140,068 were *yin* for salt consumed near the area of production (*shih-yen*).

14. Ho Ping-ti, "Salt Merchants," pp. 140 and 144, gives the eighteenth-century figure as 1,685,492. Saeki, *Shin-dai ensei*, p. 19, gives 1,692,490.

15. *HTSL*, p. 8061 (ch. 223, p. 3a), two-column summary under the year Shun-chih 17 (1660).

16. Figures drawn from *HTSL*, pp. 8061–62 and *YFTC*, ch. 72, p. 17.

17. The *Shih-lu* for 1712 gives a total sale of 5,093,608 *yin*, yielding 3,729,898 taels in taxes.

Board of Revenue in the Capital. But in fact the *yin* in the late K'ang-hsi reign cost about 1.6 taels each, since an extra 0.25 taels had been added to each *yin* in 1704 to bring in an extra 300,000 taels per annum, which was to be used for the expenses of the imperial textile factories, purchases of copper, and river repairs. This extra money was handled by the salt censors and the textile commissioners, and does not seem to have been sent in to the Board of Revenue as a part of the fixed quota of imperial revenue.[18]

The weight of salt that might be transported per *yin* certificate had been set at 200 catties in 1645; this was a major change, since by the end of the Ming dynasty the official weight of each *yin* had varied from 430 to 450 catties.[19] (By halving the weight and doubling the number of *yin*, the salt officials hoped to make the system more manageable.) In 1677 each *yin* was raised to 225 catties. This meant that upon receiving their *yin* certificates the merchants could sell 225 catties of salt instead of 200 catties, and made it possible for them to meet the price increases of the same year, since they would now earn more from sales. In 1704, when *yin* taxes were raised 300,000 taels per annum to pay for textile and other expenses, the weight of each *yin* was officially increased by 42 catties, bringing it up to 267. In the Yung-cheng reign increases of 50 catties were made in 1723 and again in 1725, so that in some Liang-huai areas a peak of 367 catties was reached. In 1732 the Liang-huai *yin* was standardized at 344 catties, though later in the century it rose again to 364 catties.[20]

In summary, then, the following figures should be reasonably accurate for the Liang-huai area during Ts'ao Yin's administration in the late K'ang-hsi reign: annual taxes on quota and surplus *yin* paid by the merchants, 2,500,000 taels; annual quota of *yin* issued by the salt officials to the salt merchants, 1,400,000; tax that the salt merchants paid on transport quota *yin* (*kang-yin*), 1.6 taels per *yin*. The discrepancies in the figures are due to the fact that the surplus revenue to make up the 2,500,000-tael total came from the sale of surplus *yin* at a different rate.[21]

18. *HTSL*, p. 8062. *YFTC*, ch. 72, p. 17. Saeki, *Shin-dai ensei*, pp. 212, 217–22. The surplus at least does not seem to have been sent in to the Board of Revenue while Ts'ao Yin and Li Hsü held the concurrent offices of salt censor and textile commissioner.

19. *YFTC*, ch. 45, p. 24. Gale and Ch'en, "China's Salt Administration," 2:1, 295.

20. *YFTC*, ch. 51, pp. 8b–9. Saeki, *Shin-dai ensei*, p. 19.

21. Also the 140,068 *shih-yin* were only assessed at 1.025 taels each. The maximum *yin* (quota and surplus) issued in one year seems to have been 1,700,000; cf. *Li Hsü Memorials*,

The statutes and salt gazetteers show that there were five basic ways (including the Liang-huai adjustments already discussed) in which the ratios between *yin* weight, *yin* price, and total income might be adjusted, and these are also worth summarizing briefly. First, existing *yin* quotas might be moved to different localities within the Liang-huai area. This was a question of production and demand, and did not affect revenue or prices. Second, the number of catties within a *yin* might be raised, while the cost of the *yin* remained unchanged. This benefited the merchants, who obtained the right to sell more salt without paying any more taxation. Third, the number of *yin* might be increased at the prevailing rate. Doing so increased government revenue, but also meant that merchants had a chance to sell more and

---

p. 40, dated 51/11/22. Of the 300,000 taels extra assessment made for the imperial textile factories, copper purchase, and river repairs, 210,000 taels went each year to the textile commissioners who described this money within the salt category of "surplus" (*yü-yin*); cf. ibid., pp. 49, 54b, 77b. The remaining sum of 90,000 taels that was paid over to the provincial authorities for copper purchase and river repairs, however, was never mentioned in the salt censors' reports as being "surplus," and it seems to have been considered quota revenue. Bearing these facts in mind, we get the following income picture for Liang-huai at this time:

Tax on 1,285,881 *kang-yin* @ 1.35 taels	1,735,939 taels
Tax on 140,068 *shih-yin* @ 1.025 taels	143,569
90,000 taels of 1704 extra 300,000 assessment	90,000
Total	1,969,508 taels

The figures tally with Li Hsü's statement of 1717 that the tax quota revenue (*e-cheng ch'ien-liang*) was 1,950,000 taels (*Li Hsü Memorials*, pp. 80b–81, dated 56/2/24).

To the sum of 1,969,508 should be added the 210,000 taels that the textile commissioners got from the 1704 assessment but still described as surplus, which gives a revenue total of 2,179,508 taels. (This was a modified quota revenue and may be compared with the mid-K'ang-hsi figures given in Saeki, *Shin-dai ensei*, p. 15, of 2,039,285 taels as the 1685 Liang-huai revenue.)

Ts'ao Yin and Li Hsü declared surpluses of around 550,000 taels; *Li Hsü Memorials*, p. 54b, dated 53/7/1, says that the figure was an "average annual" (*mei-nien*) figure. Since 210,000 of that amount was always *chih-tsao* funds, and has been counted in above, we need only add the remaining 340,000 taels, which brings a grand total for all Liang-huai revenues of 2,519,508. Kao Pin, salt censor in 1732, estimated total Liang-huai revenues at over 2,500,000, while Ts'ao Yin and Li Hsü announced total yields of 2,380,000 and 2,400,000 (cf. references in note 2 above).

The above calculations are still tentative and are drawn mainly from the salt censors' memorials and the rather abbreviated presentation in the Ch'ing Statutes (*Hui-tien shih-li*). A completely reliable picture can only be drawn after a full study has been made of the Liang-huai tax structure, which I have not attempted. Such a study of the Liang-huai administration in the late eighteenth century is now being made by Thomas Metzger at Harvard University.

increase their profits. Fourth, the number of catties in a *yin* could be increased at the same time as the tax on each *yin* was raised. The government again got more revenue; the merchants got more salt, but also had to pay more in taxes. Fifth, the government could retrench if it cut back the total number of *yin* but left the revenue unchanged by increasing the tax on the remaining *yin*. This hit the merchants hard, as they had to pay the same as before but received less salt for their payment. All these effects had to be kept in mind by the salt censors who directed the Liang-huai area.

The Liang-huai Salt Censors

The salt censor [22] of Liang-huai was in charge of all aspects of salt administration in the Liang-huai area; because of the difficulties of the office, or perhaps because the chances for corruption were so great, an edict of 1651 ordered that in future the salt censors should be changed every year. In 1653 the office was abolished altogether, and the duties were taken over by the salt controller; [23] yet the job proved too much for one man, and in 1655 the Board of Revenue requested the Emperor to order the Censorate to appoint an honest and capable censor to supervise the salt administration of Liang-huai.[24] It is obvious that the salt censors continued to be either inefficient or corrupt, for in 1672 the office was abolished yet again, and the duties were taken over by the governor of Anhwei. This new experiment only lasted one year, as the governor could not handle the extra work. The edict of 1673 restoring the office of salt censor introduced rigid controls concerning the yamen servants' freedom of movement, and the numbers that might be employed by the censor, and the salt censor himself was forbidden to fraternize with officials or personal friends passing through his area.[25]

These regulations must have been successful, for in 1691 two new salt censors were appointed at Liang-kuang and Fukien; with the salt censors already working in Liang-huai, Liang-che, Ch'ang-lu, and Ho-tung, this brought the total up to six. The late K'ang-hsi reign was thus the peak point for the office, but it was short-lived. In 1720 the

22. *hsün-yen yü-shih*, BH 835B.
23. *yen-yün-shih*, BH 835.
24. YFTC, ch. 14, p. 5b.
25. HTSL, pp. 17,370–72 (ch. 1028, pp. 1–4). YFTC, ch. 15, p. 6b.

Liang-kuang office was abolished, in 1723 that of Fukien; both were to be managed in the future by the governors-general of the respective provinces. The Liang-che office was abolished in 1726, and was taken over by the governor. The Liang-huai office proved the most enduring, probably because the vast size of the area made it impossible for some other official to handle it concurrently; but finally it too was abolished in 1830, and its duties passed to the Liang-chiang governor-general.[26]

Considerable changes took place in the kind of men appointed to be Liang-huai salt censors. During the Shun-chih reign they were Chinese, normally with a *chin-shih* degree, appointed for one, or at most two or three, years. After 1668, when the K'ang-hsi Emperor began to rule in person, one Manchu was appointed to hold the office concurrently with one Chinese *chin-shih*. Both men were changed every year. From 1672 onward, the Emperor began to alternate Manchus and Chinese *chin-shih*, only appointing one man each year, and following him with a man from the other category. Still no man was appointed twice. Gradually more Manchus were appointed than Chinese; the last Chinese *chin-shih* was Liang-huai salt censor in 1687, and from 1688 until 1714 only "Manchus" were appointed.[27]

However, the term "Manchu" (*Man-chou jen*) used in the official listings referred both to Manchus and to Chinese bondservants in Manchu Banners such as Ts'ao Yin and Li Hsü. It is not easy to know at exactly which date the K'ang-hsi Emperor began to use bondservants from the Upper Three Banners as salt censors, but it may be assumed that he did this as deliberately as he had gradually substituted Manchus for Chinese in the same office. Certainly from 1691 onward bondservants from the Emperor's three Banners were being appointed Liang-huai salt censors, and this office can thus be seen as yet one more part of the K'ang-hsi Emperor's growing personal bureaucracy. The salt censors in 1691, 1692, 1694, and 1695 were all Upper Three Banner bondservant captains.[28] As yet the Emperor did not keep the same man in office for more than a year, but even that regulation was abandoned for all practical purposes when Ts'ao Yin and Li Hsü were

26. References as in note 25 above.

27. *CNTC*, ch. 105, pp. 7–8.

28. K'o-pai, *PCTC*, 5/40b; Kuan-yin Pu, *PCTC*, 3/34; Ch'ang Shou, *PCTC*, 3/39; Ya-t'u, *PCTC*, 3/33.

appointed to be salt censors in alternate years from 1704 to 1713.[29]

It was only in Liang-huai that the Emperor made use of Chinese bondservants as salt censors. In Ho-tung and Liang-che after 1688 the Emperor ceased appointing Chinese holders of advanced degrees to the office and used only Manchus until the end of his reign. In the thirty years, from the 1690s to the 1720s, in which salt censors were appointed to Fukien and Liang-kuang, all but one man were Manchus. In Ch'ang-lu some Chinese degree holders were appointed until 1702, but thereafter only Manchus were used.[30] This strongly suggests that the late 1680s may be regarded as the time at which the K'ang-hsi Emperor first began to have absolute confidence in the stability of his regime; also the Manchus were becoming more fluent in the Chinese language, and presumably competing for lucrative offices now that the dynasty was peacefully settled. The Liang-huai area was an exception because it was much the largest and most complex, much the richest, and still, at least around Nanking and Yangchow, an area in which it was advisable to appoint Chinese for political reasons. By appointing Chinese bondservants the Emperor was both playing it safe and assuring his own control.

The duties of the salt censors were officially summed up as: "Being in charge of the salt administration, investigating subordinate officials,

29. *Liang-huai yen-fa chih*, ch. 8, p. 38, though the number of years that they were to serve was not specified; but cf. *Li Hsü Memorials*, p. 54b, dated 53/7/1: "I and Ts'ao Yin received the imperial favor in being appointed to manage Huai salt an unprecedented number of times. Now our ten years are up."

30. *Ho-tung yen-fa chih* (12 *chüan*, 1730), ch. 6, pp. 12–20. In 1719 the only Chinese bondservant traceable was appointed (Wang Kuo-pi, Bordered White Banner, *PCST*, ch. 77, p. 14), and in 1720 a Mongol was appointed. *Liang-che yen-fa chih* (30 *chüan*, 1801), ch. 22, pp. 1–5. *Fu-chien yen-fa chih* (22 *chüan*, 1830), ch. 6, pp. 20–23. *Kuang-tung t'ung-chih* (334 *chüan*, 1822), ch. 43, p. 16. *Ch'ang-lu yen-fa chih* (20 *chüan*, 1805), ch. 14, pp. 5–15.

Apart from one or two men who served for two years successively, none was ever appointed for more than one year as salt censor. Thus the use made of Ts'ao Yin and Li Hsü was unique. From the Yung-cheng reign onward, men were appointed for much longer terms.

There are several names of the Manchu incumbents that also appear in *PCST* as Chinese bondservants, but they are all such common names that it is impossible to say definitely whether such men were from Chinese families or not. (There were few such ambiguities with the textile commissioners or customs directors.) The *Liang-che yen-fa chih*, which gives the most detailed information on incumbents, shows that many of them were Manchu circuit censors (*tao chien-ch'a yü-shih*, BH 213); others were from the Imperial Household, and many of these were probably Manchu bondservants, as the office is listed in the Banner gazetteer (*PCTC* [1795], ch. 48, p. 18b).

keeping those who fail to obey the laws up to the mark, checking on
the prices at intervals and adjusting them, reporting to the Emperor
on the collection of salt taxes, and revising the salt laws if necessary." [31] In practice their time was mainly occupied in three fields:
collecting the taxes on their full quota of *yin* certificates, auditing the
accounts, and checking salt smuggling.

Once the salt censor had received an edict appointing him, or in the
case of Li Hsü and Ts'ao Yin seen notice of their reappointment in the
Peking Gazette (*ti-ch'ao*) where it was always printed,[32] he received
his seal of office and the *yin* certificates for the coming year. The seal
was brought to him by an official in the Censorate,[33] but he had to
collect the newly printed certificates from the Board of Revenue. In
1696 fourteen plates were cast for printing the Liang-huai *yin;* after
1703 it was decided that the salt censor would himself collect the
plates during the winter and see that the *yin* certificates were printed
by the following summer.[34]

The reason for this curious timing is that the salt censors were always appointed in the tenth month of the year and held their
appointment until the tenth month of the following year.[35] They
had to make most of their preparations in advance, since the salt was
generally sold to the transport merchants in the sixth month. As Li
Hsü described the process:

> At all the salt factories of the Huai River and Yangchow, the salt
> masters work away at boiling the salt during the long summer
> days of the fifth month, so as to make up the merchants' quotas.
> During the sixth month, the salt is taken successively from the
> factories to I-chen, where the salt officials weigh and check it.
> This is the customary practice.[36]

31. YFTC, ch. 14, p. 5b.

32. Both men always acknowledged their reappointments "after reading the Peking
Gazette." Cf. *Ts'ao Yin Memorials*, pp. 15 dated 45/8/4 and p. 22 dated 49/9/2, and
Ts'ao Yin Archives, no. 2811, dated 47/9/1. *Li Hsü Memorials*, p. 14b dated 46/9/–,
p. 25 dated 48/8/21, p. 46b dated 52/8/21.

33. *Ts'ao Yin Memorials*, p. 9, dated 43/10/13.

34. YFTC, ch. 52, p. 7. There is a version of this procedure applying to a period later in
the dynasty in Sun, *Ch'ing Administrative Terms*, no. 1034, when these *yin* were handed
over directly to the head merchants by the Board of Revenue.

35. *Ts'ao Yin* and *Li Hsü* Memorials, passim.

36. *Li Hsü Memorials*, p. 44, dated 52/intercalary 5/23. The name I-chen was later changed
to I-cheng.

Then the transport merchants, who had bought the salt at the factories, paid their taxes to the salt officials and were issued their *yin* certificates. The system had two disadvantages. Firstly, as Li Hsü pointed out, if the weather was consistently bad during the early summer it was impossible for the factory merchants to boil out enough salt; the transport merchants consequently had no chance to bale up the salt and take it to I-chen by the sixth month. Secondly, as Li Hsü wrote on another occasion, the fact that the transport merchants had to pay taxes in the sixth month before they had sold a grain of salt meant that they had to have an extremely large capital fund, and had a very difficult time when business was bad.[37]

Li Hsü was not the first to point out this problem, which was fundamental to the merchants' convenience, if not to their fortunes as a whole. In 1670 the salt censor had contrasted an old ideal time, in which the salt was sold in the spring and summer and taxes collected in autumn and winter, with the present in which levies started in the fifth month before any salt had been sold. "The merchants have no way to whistle up this money," he wrote, "but have to run up debts and mortgages." Nor did this bring any extra profit to the government, he continued, which still got its one unit of cash while the merchants had to pay several units more in interest to the moneylenders. The Emperor backed the salt censor over the Board of Revenue's protests, and advanced levies were officially discontinued;[38] however, they had clearly crept back by Li Hsü's time.

Li Hsü's first attempt to give the merchants permission to pay their taxes in the tenth month, once they had sold their salt, was a failure. But in 1710 he was given imperial permission to make this change, and in 1722 another salt censor delayed the *yin* payments until the first month of the *following* year.[39] This gave the merchants seven months to pay, since they still collected their salt in the sixth month. The earlier regulation that tax payments must be made in advance was returned to in 1734, and once again merchants had to have large capital to enter the salt trade. But it is interesting to reflect that had Li Hsü's system been adhered to, the state of affairs that perpetuated a

37. Ibid., p. 12b, dated 45/5/–.
38. *Huang-ch'ao wen-hsien t'ung-k'ao*, p. 5100a.
39. YCCPYC, *ts'e* 50, p. 93, memorial by salt censor Kao Pin dated Yung-cheng 12/9/15.

few vastly wealthy merchant families in the Ch'ien-lung reign might never have existed. Though the great merchant families would of course still have been in an advantageous position, and it would have remained in the government's interest to control the number of merchants for reasons of administrative convenience and discipline, there would have been at least a chance of the emergence of a more diffuse and energetic merchant stratum, composed of a large body of men all possessed of moderate fortunes. The presence of such men would have had a profound effect on the social composition and attitudes of the Yangtze valley area.

The problems of auditing arose directly from the nature of the *yin* certificate system. The basic regulation was that at the end of his appointment the salt censor had to send records of all levied salt taxes to the Board of Revenue; the Board then examined the records in collaboration with officials from the Censorate, before they sent a memorial on their findings. The salt censors made out their records on the basis of the many reports sent in by the salt controller, the salt intendants, the officials at the salt treasury, and the various inspectors at the salt factories.[40] Salt censors were penalized in direct proportion to the amount of quota taxes they failed to pay in, and similar penalties of loss of pay, lowering of official grades, and dismissal, were meted out to their subordinates.[41] In addition to the ceaseless problems of just selling the *yin* certificates, and collecting the money from the merchants, which Ts'ao Yin and Li Hsü had to face, there were problems of overlapping authority that caused further trouble. For instance, in 1702 and 1703 the Kiangsu financial commissioner borrowed 11,490 taels from the salt treasury and never returned it. Since this was not discovered until 1726, the accounting methods cannot have been of the strictest.[42] It was presumably to keep a closer eye on things that the K'ang-hsi Emperor made Ts'ao Yin and Li Hsü report to him privately in palace memorials (*tsou-che*) on their salt problems, and report to him in person at the end of each year in office. This meant that his bondservant salt censors had even less chance of concealing irregularities than ordinary salt censors who merely sent in routine memori-

40. HTSL, p. 17,299 (ch. 1020, p. 11b) and ibid., p. 7492 (ch. 183, p. 15).
41. Ibid., pp. 6459–61 (ch. 105, pp. 1–5).
42. YCCPYC, ts'e 15, p. 69, memorial by salt controller Chang T'an-lin dated Yung-cheng 4/6/26.

als (*t'i-pen*) to accompany the accounts submitted to the financial section of the Censorate (*hu-k'o*).[43] When a salt censor in 1723 reported to the Yung-cheng Emperor that the previous salt censor had failed to sell 139,605 *yin* of his quota, the Emperor wrote: "How on earth can I be expected to know all the details? It's up to the memorialist to point out specific problems." [44] But it had been in these very details that the K'ang-hsi Emperor took such a close interest.

The last basic area of salt censor activity, the checking of salt smuggling, needs little comment, since obviously the whole *yin* system depended on keeping smuggling to a minimum; this was in the interests of both the government and the merchants. The salt censors were held responsible for checking both the illegal sale and the illegal manufacture of salt; [45] in addition to specific laws that prohibited smuggling and laid down severe punishments for offenders, they could invoke a statute of 1670 binding communities in mutual responsibility. Neighbors of those receiving smuggled salt could be flogged if they failed to report the matter to the authorities, and the headman (*tsung-chia*) given thirty strokes of the flat bamboo if any of his villagers received smuggled salt. Even those who lent horses that were used to smuggle salt were heavily punished. Since the salt censor had little force with which to back up his attempt, this too was taken care of: the officers of local military units that failed to move rapidly to apprehend smugglers were to be fined double the normal amount for such laxity; their sergeants were to be beaten with eighty strokes; and the garrison commanders who had sent out the troops would also be heavily fined. These measures, it was hoped, would "settle one aspect of the salt smuggling problem." [46]

The Liang-huai Salt Merchants

During the K'ang-hsi reign the Liang-huai salt merchants were an integral part of the complex salt organization, as they were to remain through the eighteenth century. Their area of sale was vast, and like the salt administration itself, amounted to what was described as "ig-

43. *HTSL*, p. 17,244 (ch. 1015, p. 23).

44. *YCCPYC*, *ts'e* 13, p. 30, vermilion endorsement to Hsieh Tz'u-li memorial dated Yung-cheng 1/3/26.

45. *HTSL*, pp. 6466–67 (ch. 105, pp. 16–17), statute of 1676; this checking was also extended to bannermen.

46. *YFTC*, ch. 22, p. 16.

noring the administrative boundaries and assigning independent jurisdiction." [47] This was not a situation that appealed to the ordinary
Chinese official, and the anomaly had already struck a Western observer in the sixteenth century, who described "the seven cities of the
salt makers" as being virtually independent.[48]

It has been estimated that there were about 230 transport merchants (*yün-shang*) at this time. These were the men who had either
purchased the right to sell salt (*ken-wo*) from the government, or
who held leases on other merchants' *ken-wo*: that is to say had
bought the right to sell salt for a limited time from other merchants
who preferred to speculate in *ken-wo* rather than to run the greater
risks attendant upon open participation in the salt trade. Both the
owners of *ken-wo*, and those who had leased *ken-wo*, could then obtain the *yin* certificates from the government salt officials, transport
the salt inland to the authorized areas of sale, and try to make their
profit. Thirty of the richest transport merchants were chosen by the
salt officials to be head merchants (*tsung-shang*), and were held responsible for arrears in tax payments by the group as a whole. The
richest of this group of head merchants were known as the merchant
chiefs (*ta-tsung*), and dominated the remainder.[49]

Despite the apparent stability and permanence suggested by such a
system, the merchants were almost totally dependent on the salt officials for their prosperity, since during the K'ang-hsi reign their
margin of profit does not seem to have been as high as it was during
the Ch'ien-lung reign.[50] The memorials of Ts'ao Yin and Li Hsü
show that the merchants were constantly falling behind on their tax
payments. The Yung-cheng Emperor's generalization that provincial
officials were partial to the people while high salt officials were partial
to the merchants [51] did not always apply to the K'ang-hsi reign any
more than to his own. The *yin* quota changes outlined in the Liang-
huai section above show that many salt censors agreed with Li Tsang-

47. Ibid., ch. 4, p. 1.

48. The observer was Martin de Rada, cf. C. R. Boxer, *South China in the Sixteenth
Century*, The Hakluyt Society, 2nd series, 106 (London, 1953), 269 and 276–77.

49. Ho Ping-ti, "Salt Merchants," pp. 136–41.

50. Or even the Yung-cheng reign, when their profit was estimated at 2.74 taels per *yin*.
Cf. Ho Ping-ti, "Salt Merchants," p. 146. Some evidence suggesting the lower K'ang-hsi
margin of profit is given below.

51. Cited in Ho Ping-ti, "Salt Merchants," p. 145.

yüan that one could simply raise the tax on each *yin* without increasing the number of *yin* or the weight of salt per *yin*, and that "the tax quota would be filled and neither merchants nor common people be inconvenienced." [52]

A dramatic example of what might happen came to light when investigations were made into the salt administration of the Liang-kuang area. The 1692 quota payable by the merchants was 290,000 taels, but by 1707 the salt censor and salt controller had added over 160,000 taels in illegal fees, so that the merchants had to pay about 455,000 taels every year. This was too much for their resources; in an average year only about 70 or 80 percent of the tax quota could be collected. Their accumulated deficit over the period from 1702 to 1716 was 910,000 taels. The governor-general who submitted these figures noted that the merchants had this deficit because they could not sell their salt. To make a reasonable profit after paying the rapacious officials, they had to price the salt so high that the people could not afford it; even if they dropped the price and sold more, they would not make enough to pay the tax on the following year's *yin* certificates.[53]

It was estimated above that the combined taxes paid on a *yin* by Liang-huai salt merchants were 1.6 taels in the early eighteenth century. If they had leased the *ken-wo*, right to sell salt, this added about 0.5 or 0.6 taels per *yin*.[54] The two Liang-huai salt censors who investigated grievances in 1670 listed six main categories of extra fees that the merchants had to pay before the salt could be sold. These were: Extra payments to salt officials and yamen clerks before the *yin* were issued, which amounted to about 2 *ch'ien* per *yin* (0.2 taels). An inspection held at the hatchway of the salt transport vessel to check the bulk and weight of the salt, for which they paid about seven *fen* per *yin* (0.07 taels). Payments to pass the check points in which the salt was officially entered on record and to buy tea for the examining officials, 2 *ch'ien* per *yin*. Boats traveling down the Yangtze had to obtain a water permit priced at several *fen* per *yin*, authorization for the vessel, fees for sealing and untying the certificates, and final permission to

52. YFTC, ch. 45, p. 26, salt censor's memorial of 1660.
53. YCCPYC, *ts'e* 6, pp. 87–88, memorial by Liang-kuang governor-general Yang Lin, dated Yung-cheng 1/3/3.
54. Ho Ping-ti, "Salt Merchants," p. 137.

sail based on several *ch'ien* per *yin*, the total per *yin* being perhaps 2.7 *ch'ien*. There were miscellaneous charges at all customs houses, and to salt intendants and military patrols, which cannot be assessed. Lastly, when the boats berthed at the ports (*k'ou-an*) in Kiangsi, Hunan, and Hupei, there were payments to the salt intendant of several *ch'ien*, stationary fees of several *fen*, and salt sample fees of several *li*, not to mention the general charge for examining the boats' documents, a total of perhaps 2.5 *ch'ien* per *yin*.[55] At a minimum, such general fees must have added one tael per *yin*. In addition to this, of course, the transport merchant had to pay for the salt he bought from the factory merchant; the price of this must have been about 1.2 taels per *yin* of 267 catties.[56]

If a merchant bought his salt after leasing a *ken-wo*, paid his *yin* taxes and then paid the extra charges involved in getting the salt to Kiangsi, each *yin* of 267 catties would have cost him about 4.3 taels, and would then be sold for about 5.5 taels.[57] This would have given the merchant a margin of profit of only 1.2 taels per *yin* in the late K'ang-hsi reign, whereas the profit per *yin* in the 1730s was 2.47 taels.[58]

Corroboration of the hypothesis that the Liang-huai salt merchants were less affluent during the K'ang-hsi reign than during the Ch'ien-lung reign is offered by examining the amounts contributed to the government during this period. One contribution of 35,000 taels is listed in official records for the year 1678, and no other Liang-huai contributions are recorded for the entire K'ang-hsi reign; but they become common in the Yung-cheng period and rocket upward during the Ch'ien-lung and later periods.[59] Examination of the salt memorials of Li Hsü and Ts'ao Yin enables us to narrow down this depressed period even farther. Neither man records a single gift by a salt mer-

55. YFTC, ch. 95, pp. 14–15b. Memorial by salt censors Hsi-t'e-na and Hsü Hsü-ling, dated 1670.

56. Ho Ping-ti, "Salt Merchants," p. 151, shows that gross cost of salt after conveyance to Yangchow was 1.55 taels per *yin* of 344 catties. My calculation, which is only approximate, depends on the price of salt being largely unchanged between 1700 and 1740 (ibid., note 55).

57. Again following Ho Ping-ti, "Salt Merchants," p. 146 estimating that 7.139 taels was the wholesale price of a *yin* of 344 catties weight in 1740, and assuming salt prices were stable.

58. Ibid.

59. YFTC, ch. 83, p. 1.

chant for the years 1704 to 1717; but in 1717 the salt merchants Chiang Ch'u-chi and others contributed 98,000 taels to rebuild the dikes, in 1718 they presented a contribution of 132,000 taels to the salt treasury and 240,000 taels for river works.[60] With their quota payments in 1725 they presented an extra 320,000 taels.[61] They were clearly over the hump, and felt it wise to express their gratitude to the government in tangible form.

By 1732 the Liang-huai merchants were in comfortable circumstances, partly because the weight of each *yin* had been so substantially increased over the previous ten years. In this year the newly appointed salt censor Kao Pin made a thorough investigation of malpractices at the salt factories and distribution points, and examined the standard of living of the head merchants and the transport merchants. He concluded that the merchants' style of living was so wasteful and extravagant that it could not be said that they had any valid grievances. Those who were in financial trouble needed only to practice a little economy to be in the clear; "the profits from one year's trading would still be enough to enable them to lead wanton lives." Kao Pin felt that they could comfortably be made to pay several hundred thousand a year more, to clear all the deficits that had accumulated over the previous decades. "It is not the merchants' resources that are deficient," he wrote; "it is only the management of the taxes that is difficult." [62]

For the remainder of the eighteenth century the Liang-huai salt merchants seem to have grown increasingly prosperous.[63] But from reading the salt memorials of Ts'ao Yin and Li Hsü, even though they might have been guilty of misreporting and dishonesty, it is apparent that this high prosperity lay in the future. Certainly the K'ang-hsi salt merchants were not paupers; they entertained the Emperor lavishly enough when he came to Yangchow on his Southern Tours.[64] But their situation was not stable, and their incomes were by no means

60. *Li Hsü Memorials*, p. 90, dated 56/11/27; p. 96b, dated 57/intercalary 8/2; p. 101, dated 56/11/16.

61. *Yung-hsien lu*, p. 340, quoting memorial from Ka-erh-t'ai dated Yung-cheng 5/1/–. The contributing merchant Wang Chin-te received a button of the seventh rank.

62. YCCPYC, *ts'e* 50, pp. 81b–82b, memorial by Kao Pin dated Yung-cheng 10/3/16. For Kao Pin, cf. *Eminent Chinese* pp. 412–13.

63. Ho Ping-ti, "Salt Merchants," pp. 154–68, on lives of Yangchow salt merchants.

64. Cf. chapter 4 above.

guaranteed. Nor could the salt censors bank on filling their *yin* quotas without trouble each year. Perhaps the feeling of the times was best captured by the Yung-cheng Emperor's first salt censor of Liang-huai, Hsieh Tz'u-li; after surveying the shambles of his area of jurisdiction he could only write: "Liang-huai is an important area, and its tax quotas are in great confusion." [65]

Ts'ao Yin as Liang-huai Salt Censor

Ts'ao Yin received orders from the Emperor in 1703 that he was to be prepared to alternate in the office of salt censor with Li Hsü, and these orders were confirmed in the summer of 1704. In his memorial of thanks, Ts'ao Yin expressed his amazement that the Emperor had extended such favors to a bondservant family. Then he switched abruptly to a thoroughly realistic note:

> Though salt censor is a financial appointment, at the highest level it is concerned with national policy, at the lowest with helping the people's livelihood. For several years now there has been unusual corruption; it is hard to escape the Emperor's vigilance. I planned to hurry to the palace to thank the Emperor for his favor, but fear that this might cause alarm.

He requested permission to come to an audience in Peking, so that he might receive the Emperor's instructions in person. The Emperor replied:

> I am well. There is no need for you to come. Next spring I intend to come down to the south, but the date isn't fixed. If there is anything you are doubtful about you can send a secret memorial requesting instructions. You must not let anyone else write these memorials, for if rumors spread, the consequences will be severe. Take care, take care, take care, take care.[66]

This is an astonishingly secret exchange to have taken place over such an apparently straightforward matter as the promotion of a textile commissioner to the post of salt censor. Almost certainly this secrecy

65. YCCPYC, *ts'e* 13, p. 30, dated Yung-cheng 1/3/26.
66. *Ts'ao Yin Memorials*, p. 1b, dated 43/7/29 and endorsement to same. At the beginning of the memorial Yin mentions that he received orders "last year" to be salt censor with Li Hsü, and had now "again received the imperial command."

had something to do with the K'ang-hsi Emperor's decision to appoint the two bondservants Ts'ao Yin and Li Hsü to manage the Liang-huai salt revenues for ten years.[67] This was a totally unprecedented step,[68] and the Emperor may have taken it either to stabilize the revenue of Liang-huai, or to draw more power and money into his own hands. His secrecy, and his selection of trusted bondservants, suggests the latter alternative.

On November 4 Ts'ao Yin received his new seal of office. Three days later he left his textile commissioner's office in Nanking, and on November 10 reached Yangchow and took up his new duties. That same day he sent his memorial of thanks, which revealed the new order: "Apart from the routine memorials (*pen*) that are sent according to the old precedents of the salt censor's yamen, as is fitting I first send a palace memorial (*che*) . . . written in my own hand." The same day he sent another memorial, as a complement to his memorial of thanks. This second memorial dealt with some of the problems he encountered in taking up office; and by writing it Ts'ao Yin got firmly entangled in the intricacies of Liang-huai finance and corruption. That he could write such a memorial on his first day in office shows his impetuosity and also some political naïveté. He wrote:

I have been a textile commissioner for fifteen consecutive years, first in Soochow and then in Nanking. Thus I knew that the salt censor of Liang-huai received an extra twenty catties of salt on each *yin* certificate in the annual quota, in so-called "office fees" (*yüan-fei*). Thus the salt censor and his clerks received an extra 300,000 taels. This sum was used to meet the expenses of supplies at the textile commissioners' yamens. In recent years, allegedly to pay various deputies and clerks,[69] they have illegally increased these twenty catties by a further seven catties. It is hard to conceal such irregularities from the Emperor.

Formerly I requested to send a secret memorial (*mi-tsou*) on this matter, but because I had not then taken up my duties I did

67. As revealed in *Li Hsü Memorials*, p. 54b, dated 53/7/1.

68. Except for one three-year term from 1652–54, and four two-year terms starting 1649, 1658, 1673 (this probably being a misprint), and 1677, no Liang-huai salt censor had ever been appointed more than once. Cf. *CNTC*, ch. 105, pp. 7–8.

69. ch'eng-ch'ai (Sun, *Ch'ing Administrative Terms*, no. 199) and *fa-shou* (literally "those issuing and receiving [salt]").

not dare to act out of turn. But now that I have taken up my
post, I followed up the items taken for the clerks and deputies
without authorization by the Censorate, and abolished them.
After this the merchants will have a measure of relief.

However in stopping these excess fees it is necessary to clear up
their source. They start at the top with the governor-general and
the governor, and at the bottom there are the magistrates and the
government personnel from the Capital and the provinces who
are passing through; there are still many of these people. Governor-general Asan made a nominal prohibition of these excess
fees, but he did not extend this prohibition to himself or to those
in his service. In fact he feared that I and others from the Imperial Household might send in reports to the Emperor about what
was going on. So he hit on the plan of making this prohibition
before I was appointed.

Ts'ao Yin concluded that in the blanket prohibition of excess fees
written by Asan, there were in fact one or two items that should be
kept, since the money from them was used to relieve the local poor.[70]

If Ts'ao Yin had expected an imperial accolade to greet this lucid
and courageous analysis of hypocrisy and corruption at the highest
level, he must have been rudely awakened by the K'ang-hsi Emperor's
reply:

Stirring up trouble is not as good as preventing trouble occurring; just concentrate on matters of immediate concern.
Otherwise I'm afraid that you'll get more than you bargained
for, and pile up difficulties for your successors. This sort of thing
is not practicable on a long-term basis. Consider this matter once
again, with care and in detail.[71]

Ts'ao Yin, however, was not deterred by this chilling breath of
political realism; in fact he could not afford to be deterred, because his
preliminary investigation into salt finances had revealed a state of
affairs that had to be remedied as soon as possible, or he himself would
be blamed together with the truly guilty parties. As he memorialized
on December 6, 1704:

70. Asan's memorial is printed in *Liang-huai yen-fa chih*, ch. 31, pp. 8b–10, dated the
eighth month of K'ang-hsi 43 (September, 1704). A shortened form of Asan's memorial is
in Shih-lu, ch. 215, p. 11b, with further comments in ibid., ch. 216, p. 17a.

71. *Ts'ao Yin Memorials*, pp. 9b–10, dated 43/10/13 and vermilion endorsement to same.

When I investigated the treasury of the salt controller's office, I found a deficit in the revenue of 800,000 taels. I am a household slave, how dare I act like other provincial officials and simply make excuses? I should send an impeachment memorial with all speed, and use the rigors of the law in pursuing my investigations, to frighten the officials involved.

But, Ts'ao Yin continued, this was not a realistic policy since the deficit had been accumulating over the years. Merchants in serious difficulties had been granted their certificates in advance (*yü-t'ou*) by the salt officials so that they could pay their taxes after selling their salt; if these merchants were ruined, the rich merchants refused to take any responsibility, and so the salt officials could not collect their money.

He and the new salt controller Li Ts'an had set a limit of two months in which the last two years' deficit was to be paid, he reported, but they were not very hopeful that it would be. They had found that the deficits had been slowly piling up both because of the laxity of the salt censors, and because everyone covered up for everyone else; each man wanted to complete his year in office and did not care whether the national treasury gained or lost. The more unscrupulous merchants profited from the situation by lending money to officials so that they could meet the tax requirements on a short-term basis. Since Man-p'u became salt censor in 1701 there had been an annual deficit of two or three hundred thousand taels, and such a sum of money could be made up by future salt censors. But in 1702 the salt censor Lo-chan had demanded half as much again on each *yin*, leading to salt stoppages and revenue shortages. The 1703 salt censor Ka-shih-t'u had retrenched by lowering the weight and numbers of *yin* sold, but had only been able to fill 40 percent of his tax quota. Ts'ao Yin concluded:

When I, with my mediocre talents, received this important appointment, I worried day and night; I have been striving to carry out my task of preventing the honest merchants from suffering painful losses, and to pay up the accumulated deficits.

This may be cliché official terminology, but it was a good enough summary of what had to be done. With merchant resources falling as a result of prolonged abuse, and official deficits rising because of manipulation of *yin* quotas and indiscriminate borrowing, some strong action was called for. The vermilion endorsement reading "Noted" gave the puzzled Ts'ao Yin little guidance.[72]

Two days after he had despatched this memorial summarizing the deficit problems in Liang-huai, Ts'ao Yin sent another in which he proffered a solution. This is probably his most intelligent and practical memorial dealing with financial problems; it is both concise and lucid, and can stand as an example of his ability. He titled it "A memorial on the prohibition of excess fees (*fou-fei*)."

> Since my appointment, I have been examining in detail the very large amount of excess fees in Liang-huai. In recent years the sale of salt has been slowed and the merchants have suffered; there has also been a gradually increasing deficit in the taxation revenues paid in to the Court. If an extremely severe prohibition is not issued, then revenue collection will be obstructed. I have repeatedly considered this problem, and have made detailed plans on how to abolish these excess fees. Having calculated the capital available to the merchants in any one year, I can say that even if salt prices do not rise in Kiangsi and Hu-kuang, the merchants' capital would definitely not depreciate; and if abolition of fees continued for one or two years the merchants would have such a surplus that it would be easy to increase the taxes.
>
> The thirteen points that governor-general Asan listed in his memorial were all fees that had been increased year after year by unscrupulous people. But the items I list here have all been basic fees. If this year we temporarily stop collecting these, to relieve the merchants, and if [in addition to this tax relief it happens that] Kiangsi and Hu-kuang salt prices do rise, then the items in this memorial can be made a part of the official tax structure.
>
> I respectfully set out the list of items as follows:
>
> 1. Censorate fees. At the salt censor's yamen by precedent there are fees on his birthday, at the lantern festival, for scribes, his household, his servants, totalling 86,100 taels.
>
> 2. Provincial fees. To the offices of the governor-general and governor, and all the commissioners and intendants, in Kiangsu, there are regular presents totalling 34,500 taels.

---

72. Ibid., pp. 10b–11, dated 43/11/20. Ts'ao Yin regularly uses the term *yün-tao* for salt controller, rather than the commoner *yün-shih*, BH 835. Li Ts'an was definitely salt controller; cf. *CNTC*, ch. 116, p. 14b.

3. Salt controller's office fees. These are irregular fees to the controller's yamen. The new controller Li Ts'an is a man who has been specially employed by the Emperor. Following my instructions he could reduce or abolish miscellaneous fees for couriers, yamen runners, and household servants totalling 24,600 taels, leaving 10,000 taels for the wages of different kinds of servants.

4. Miscellaneous fees. These are for various uses as entertainment allowances in Liang-huai. According to Asan's memorial, without counting the two categories of offerings and presents to passing scholars, these total some 62,500 taels.

The above four items are all paid for from the common box (*hsia*) to which all merchants contribute. Before the quota items of taxation for the Court have been paid, these fees are first paid to the officials. When I became aware of this, I could not conquer my painful feelings.

Ts'ao Yin aimed to let the merchants off some 207,700 taels a year. If prices remained stable, they would then have enough money to pay their taxes and some extra. If the areas of sale were prosperous enough to stand higher salt prices, which would increase merchant profits, then these basic fees could be incorporated in the tax structure and the merchants could pay them by buying their *yin* at a higher rate. Either way, they could retrench their position, and the basic taxes would be paid. He had cited the deficit at 800,000 taels. If his plan were implemented, and his figures accurate, the Liang-huai area would have a balanced revenue by 1708.

The Emperor made no comment on the memorial as a whole, but next to the item of 34,500 taels paid to the governor-general and governor he wrote the interlinear vermilion endorsement:

On no account should you delete this item, or you will be bound to offend the governor-general and governor. The sum involved is not large, so why make trouble for yourself? [73]

It is probable that the subsequent troubles plaguing the Liang-huai administration of Ts'ao Yin and Li Hsü spring from this casual remark of the Emperor's. For though it was true that the item was small, it must have been perfectly clear that the financial difficulties of

73. *Ts'ao Yin Memorials*, p. 10, dated 43/11/22. On the question of *hsia* fees, cf. Ho Ping-ti, "Salt Merchants," pp. 142–43, 147–48.

Liang-huai at this time were caused by the accumulation of such small items. As the minor deficits of 1701 to 1704 had developed, so might much larger ones. The Emperor had a difficult role to play in keeping his senior provincial officials contented, and getting an adequate revenue. He was content to let this matter slide. He was no more interested when Ts'ao Yin told him, in another memorial written that day, that of the sum of one million taels which had been loaned to the Liang-huai merchants in 1703 from the imperial treasury, only 800,000 taels had reached the merchants. And that furthermore many of the men who took parts of this remaining 800,000 were not in fact merchants at all, but people masquerading as merchants to get the money.[74] The K'ang-hsi Emperor had an exceptional toleration of corruption, and the lesson of these first memorials may not have been lost on Ts'ao Yin. He does not figure again as a reformer; but there is little doubt that he got steadily richer.[75]

These discussions between the Emperor and Ts'ao Yin in the winter of 1704 had been secret; but naturally Ts'ao Yin also handled the regular problems of administration through the Board of Revenue. In May 1705 he memorialized, together with Asan and the Kiangsu and Anhwei governors, concerning Liang-huai deficits. The merchants now owed 1,200,000 taels on the shipments (*kang*) for 1703 and 1704; they were to make up these arrears by paying off the sum in eight annual installments (*tai-cheng*) starting from 1705.[76] During 1705, Ts'ao Yin also concentrated on the problem of controlling salt smugglers and requested the Board to ensure that they be sternly dealt with. The Board accepted Ts'ao Yin's recommendation but added the rider that strict punishments should only be applied to those who had definitely been proved guilty. This suggests that Ts'ao Yin may have been responsible for using excessively harsh measures against all those even suspected of salt smuggling; further evidence in this direction is found in a Board ruling of this same year that salt officials must stop using instruments of torture on their own authority; were there smugglers who should be tortured in order to extract confessions, they

74. *Ts'ao Yin Memorials*, p. 11, dated 43/11/22.

75. Cf. chapter 4, above, describing the lavish Nanking and Yangchow receptions of the K'ang-hsi Emperor on his Southern Tours, and Ts'ao Yin's rapid handling of the vast *Complete T'ang Poems* printing project.

76. *Liang-huai yen-fa chih*, ch. 31, p. 10. Sun, *Ch'ing Administrative Terms*, no. 505.

should be sent for trial to the proper courts of law. Yet another ruling hit strongly at the category of very poor people who traditionally were permitted to sell small amounts of unlicensed salt in order to keep alive. These paupers were charged with having been in alliance with salt smugglers, and were to be arrested.[77] It is likely that Ts'ao Yin moved as brusquely into the maze of salt-smuggling problems as he had into the problems of excess fees.

It cannot be denied that certain inconsistencies appear in the record of Ts'ao Yin's first year as salt censor. If the K'ang-hsi Emperor appointed bondservants as salt censors for his own ulterior motives, why was he so discouraging when they presented their analyses of the wrongs of the system? Was Ts'ao Yin just meant to crack down on smuggling, a straightforward and easily punishable crime involving the common people, while he let more serious corruption at higher levels continue unchecked? One tentative answer to these and similar questions that arise later in Ts'ao Yin's administration, and in that of Li Hsü, is that the K'ang-hsi Emperor appointed his own bondservants as salt censors in order to keep a close eye on the surplus money that could be produced, and to make sure that it was spent on the Emperor's projects or else paid into the treasury of the Imperial Household.

This surplus revenue (yü-yin) was the money that could be collected over and above the official quota of taxation that was forwarded to the Board of Revenue and formed a part of the basic income of the government. The surplus arose when merchants were granted the right to transport extra salt in return for extra payments. The collection (or extortion) of surplus money had been sternly forbidden by edict in 1651, and the same edict gave special permission to the merchants to inform the Board of Revenue and the Censorate if salt censors and salt intendants continued to demand surpluses.[78] Yet naturally when times were good, the surplus was beneficial to both merchants and salt officials, and by the time of Ts'ao Yin and Li Hsü's administration the annual Liang-huai surplus obtained was 550,000 taels; salt supervisors (tu-hsiao) were instructed to check on the distribution of surplus salt as they checked on that in the regular quota

77. The chien-t'iao pei-fu, Sun, Ch'ing Administrative Terms, no. 1068. The Ts'ao Yin memorial and the two other recommendations are under the year 1705 in YFTC, ch. 22, p. 17.

78. Huang-ch'ao wen-hsien t'ung-k'ao, p. 5098a.

shipments.[79] Ts'ao Yin had been using part of the surplus since he became a textile commissioner in 1690, because one of the uses of surplus
revenue was to pay for the expenses of the Kiangsu textile factories in
Nanking and Soochow. He described this surplus to the Emperor as
having been a sum of 300,000 taels per annum, collected by adding an
extra twenty catties to each *yin* and charging the merchants propor-
tionally more.[80] What he was saying in that 1704 memorial was that
the various forms of surplus and excess fees were proving too much
for the merchants, and that the system would be self-defeating, since
merchants growing progressively poorer would contribute progressively less. The official decision made in 1704 was as follows:

> To increase the money in Liang-huai by 300,000 taels for textile
> commissioners, purchase of copper, and canal work, add forty-
> two catties to each *yin* certificate.[81]

This was the same 300,000 taels that had been collected previously on
an extra twenty catties of salt, but now it was made a part of the basic
revenue quota, and the extra amount of salt was doubled, to give the
merchants the chance to make a larger profit on each *yin*. Some time
in the summer of 1705 the merchants were given more assistance; the
actual number of issued *yin* certificates was cut back, so that salt
prices rose in Kiangsi and Hu-kuang and higher profits could be obtained.[82]

The curious thing about this surplus system is that during the administrative terms of Ts'ao Yin and Li Hsü, the surplus seems to have
been collected regularly, even though the regular tax quota could not
be met. This could only have been permitted by the Emperor in person. Ts'ao Yin was outraged in his 1704 memorial that excess fees were
collected from the merchants before the regular revenue; but soon he
too was doing the same with surplus. This highly irregular use of the
surplus system cannot have been widely publicized; even though the

79. *Li Hsü Memorials*, pp. 54b–55, dated 53/7/1. Even the poorer salt area of Liang-kuang
yielded an annual surplus of 50,000 taels between 1718 and 1721, according to the governor-general Yang Lin (*YCCPYC, ts'e 6*, p. 87b, dated Yung-cheng 1/3/3). On the checking of surplus, cf. *Ts'ao Yin Ch'ih*.

80. *Ts'ao Yin Memorials*, pp. 9b–10, dated 43/10/13.

81. *YFTC*, ch. 51, p. 8b and ch. 72, p. 17. *HTSL*, p. 8062 (ch. 213, p. 4b), in response to a *t'i-pen*.

82. *Ts'ao Yin Archives*, no. 2767, dated 44/7/1 records the merchants' gratitude to the
Emperor, because *yin* were cut back and prices rising.

raising of the 300,000 taels was listed as part of the regular taxation, there was a further 340,000 taels that the salt censors collected. An extremely well-informed historian living in the early eighteenth century quotes a Yung-cheng official as saying that exaction of surplus money began with a sum of 150,000 taels in 1695, and that it then increased to something over 320,000 taels during the terms of Li Hsü and Ts'ao Yin; when their terms were up, the regulation was fittingly abolished.[83] He seems to have thought it was a private venture, and somehow illegal. In fact the system had imperial approval and had not been abolished, for in 1723 a salt censor reported that Liang-huai merchants were still paying "several hundred thousand taels" for the textile commissioners and the other items.[84] In a sense the Liang-huai surplus constituted a private fund for the K'ang-hsi Emperor's use; he used bondservants to manage it and exact over half a million taels a year from the salt merchants.

Ts'ao Yin's first term as Liang-huai salt censor expired on November 27, 1705, and he was replaced by Li Hsü.[85] The following September he read in the Gazette that he had been reappointed, but since he had to be in Peking for the marriage of his daughter to Prince Nersu, he requested leave of absence; he asked whether he should follow precedent and hand the seal over to the governor-general, or hand it to the salt controller, or hand it to Li Hsü who had just finished his first term in office. The Emperor ordered Li Hsü to take over the seal and continue in office during Ts'ao Yin's absence; [86] despite the warnings he had given Ts'ao Yin about attacking governor-general Asan, the Emperor clearly did not feel it wise to entrust Asan with total control of the Liang-huai administration.[87] Ts'ao Yin also had to take care of his mother's funeral at this same time; [88] however he was given no leave of absence to observe a mourning period.

83. *Yung-hsien lu*, pp. 12–13, under dates 61/2/10–19, citing the memorial of salt censor Wei T'ing-chen who had been investigating a corruption charge in Liang-huai.

84. YCCPYC, *ts'e* 13, p. 31, memorial dated Yung-cheng 1/4/21.

85. *Li Hsü Memorials*, p. 11, dated 44/10/–. Li Hsü took over on 44/10/13. Ts'ao Yin's term presumably expired on 44/10/12; Li Hsü's definitely expired on 45/10/12; cf. ibid., p. 13, dated 45/11/7.

86. *Ts'ao Yin Memorials*, p. 15, dated 45/8/4, and *Li Hsü Memorials*, pp. 13 and 13b, dated 45/11/7 and 45/12/13.

87. In late December 1706 Asan was transferred to be president of the Board of Punishments. CS, pp. 2591, 2881. *Ch'ing-shih lieh-chuan*, ch. 12, p. 26.

88. *Ts'ao Yin Memorials*, p. 15, dated 45/8/4.

It was not until February 1707 that Ts'ao Yin returned to Yang-chow to manage the salt administration,[89] and there is almost no information on this second term of his. There was none of the lengthy analysis of problems that he had produced in 1704. The only surviving memorial from the period, though apparently trivial, was a grim forecast of trouble ahead. For Ts'ao Yin wrote in July that the rivers were already so shallow that the salt boats could not get from the salt factories to the administrative headquarters at I-chen, where officials weighed the salt and distributed the certificates to the transport merchants. Thus delays were inevitable. The Emperor wrote in his endorsement that this southern drought was making him very uneasy.[90] He was right to be uneasy, for the drought caused a crisis in Kiangsu, sent rice prices soaring, and caused general economic dislocation throughout 1708 and 1709.[91]

There is no evidence that at the time Ts'ao Yin was aware of this cloud on the horizon. When he traveled to Peking in the winter of 1707 to discuss the results of his second term with the Emperor, he brought up three problems which he and Li Hsü had agreed were crucial to maintaining the stability of the Liang-huai salt area. These three problems were, firstly, that there was not enough cooperation between civil and military officials in hunting down the larger gangs of salt smugglers, and that the salt censor must be given some position of authority at the local garrisons; secondly, that the merchants were still being harassed on their journeys to Kiangsi and Hu-kuang by official "inspections" that were merely private extortion, and must be prohibited; thirdly, that although southern Honan was mainly a zone for the sale of salt of the Ch'ang-lu area, the one prefecture of Ju-ning was in the Liang-huai area, and there Ch'ang-lu merchants and smugglers were pushing out the Liang-huai merchants, so the zoning regulations must be rigidly enforced.[92]

All these matters were of course peripheral to the real problems of Liang-huai salt administration, which Ts'ao Yin had described so well

89. Ibid., p. 16, dated 45/12/5, states that "I will set off for Yangchow tomorrow to manage affairs there." The journey would have taken about three weeks.

90. Ibid., p. 16, dated 46/6/20, and endorsement to same.

91. Cf. chapter 3 above, the section on stabilizing rice prices.

92. *Li Hsü Memorials*, pp. 20b–21, dated 47/3/–. At the end of the memorial Li Hsü writes that he and Ts'ao Yin had discussed these matters, and then Ts'ao Yin had presented them in audience.

in 1704 as being an interaction between adequate merchant resources for purchase and transport of salt, and reasonable official prices which would fill basic tax quotas while enabling merchants to sell salt fairly cheaply. Ts'ao Yin's initial suggestions for reform measures had been disregarded by the Emperor; a slowly worsening situation was raised to crisis proportions by the 1707 drought and the 1708 floods which followed it. By his third term, which began in the winter of 1708, Ts'ao Yin found himself in an impossible position.

He had admittedly received some official encouragement in the form of an Imperial Command (*ch'ih*) which was issued in October 1708, a month before his third term began. This Command gave him quite sweeping powers to deal with local salt officials of all grades who were guilty of embezzlement, extortion, or idleness, and empowered him to order out the local garrisons (*wei* and *so*) to hunt down salt smugglers. He was also instructed to consult with the governor-general and governor whenever the situation seemed to warrant it. But in general the means that Ts'ao Yin was to employ were left totally unspecified: he should cause his subordinates "to obey the laws and regulations respectfully," "prevent them from making trouble," and at all times bear in mind the distinctions "between legitimate gain and corruption, between profit and loss." Furthermore though he was to end salt smuggling, he must not harass the common people who smuggled a little salt because they were in straitened circumstances.[93] Admirable though such advice was, it could not solve the problem of the Liang-huai deficit.

In July 1709 Ts'ao Yin sent the memorial which he must have hoped that he would never need to send. It was a detailed description of the crisis, incorporating reports from local departments, merchants, and the salt controller. It ran:

> At the moment, north of the Yangtze, in Ning-kuo, Ch'ih-chou, T'ai-p'ing, and other prefectures, because they suffered floods last year, and the spring this year was cloudy with continuous heavy rain, the certificate salt proved hard to sell. I have repeatedly issued urgent directives about this, which are on record. Now I have received a succession of detailed reports on the situation from An-ch'ing, Ning-kuo, Ch'ih-chou, T'ai-p'ing, and

93. *Ts'ao Yin Ch'ih.*

Feng-yang, and from the various departments south of the Yangtze that are attached to the prefecture of Nanking, stating:

"Because there were repeated floods last year, the people (*min*) have no reserves. From the spring onward this year it has again rained without stopping, and in the low marshy areas wheat harvests have been bad. At the same time rice prices have risen, and there is an epidemic. The government *yin* certificates are covered with dust, unsold. At this time we have received great favors from the Emperor, taxes have been remitted and the rice tribute stopped, the homeless have been comforted. But while the stricken people are simply anxious to keep alive, how can we expect them to eat a specific amount of salt? The time to report on sales is approaching, but the salt that should have been sold really could not be got rid of. We beg to request that the date be postponed."

I received this and then ordered the salt controller and intendants to make a factual investigation, deliberate, and reply. Now I have received this report from the controller:

"The merchants have sent in a petition that in areas of sale such as An-ch'ing, T'ai-p'ing, Ch'ih-chou, and Ning-kuo, because last autumn and this spring there were heavy floods which have caused the accumulation of salt, they have over 300,000 *yin* [about eighty million catties] of salt that cannot be sold. It is estimated that in all over 800,000 or 900,000 taels of merchant capital are tied up and out of circulation. At present also all the salt fields are covered with water and submerged, and little salt is being produced. The poor salt workers have no way of planning to keep alive. We are now making requests for contributions to relieve them, for how is the new salt to be produced and prepared? We beg that in the 1708 shipments the delivery of 300,000 *yin* certificates of quota salt and salt consumed in the area of production (*kang-shih e-yen*) may be deferred. Once things are going better at the distribution points, the merchants can pay more taxes and sell more salt, thus gradually completing and restoring the full quota. We beg you to pass on these detailed statements and requests."

According to the regulations governing the taxation of merchants, they must sell according to a certain quota. Moreover

Liang-huai has already received many favors, how dare I mention these petty details which are bound to annoy you? But I am concerned for all these flooded areas, and the consequences have really been as stated. Ning-kuo and these other places are crucial to Liang-huai. If the salt is bottled up and cannot be sold, then the new salt certificates are bound to be even harder to sell. If we force more salt to be transported according to the regulations for one year's allotment, the certificates will just pile up; afterward I and others will have to round up five years' back taxes from the merchants, and I fear that this will cause trouble and loss to the merchants and the people.

Ts'ao Yin ended by saying that he and Li Hsü had discussed the matter together, and presented this plan of deferring payments on 300,000 *yin* as a purely temporary expedient; it would lead to no general lowering of the tax quota. He begged the Emperor to have the matter discussed by the Board of Revenue. The vermilion endorsement was simply "Noted." [94] The Emperor does not seem to have had any remedial action taken at the time and may have believed that Ts'ao Yin was exaggerating the crisis to avoid paying in the taxes. But in December Ts'ao Yin prepared a detailed record of the various salt problems, which he took to Peking to submit to the Emperor.[95] This time he must have convinced the Emperor of the seriousness of the problem, for when he returned south in April, he brought the merchants the welcome news that they might defer payments of one million taels on the new salt quotas, so as to make up the old deficit.[96]

Deferring the payments was of course no solution. Unless basic economic conditions improved, the deficit would continue to grow larger. The only measure that Li Hsü took during his third term in 1710—to move the date for merchant payments from the sixth month to the tenth, when salt had been sold and their financial reserves replenished[97]—was an important theoretical advance but irrelevant in the context, since the merchants were already over a year behind with their taxes.

94. *Ts'ao Yin Memorials*, p. 21, dated 48/6/1.
95. Ibid., p. 21b, dated 48/11/11.
96. Ibid., p. 22, dated 49/10/2, summarizing events of the previous spring.
97. Cf. Kao Pin's memorial in *YCCPYC*, *ts'e* 50, p. 93, dated Yung-cheng 12/9/15, which discusses the problem of these deferred payments.

So Ts'ao Yin took up his fourth term as Liang-huai salt censor, in the winter of 1710, under inauspicious circumstances. And the Emperor's bleak endorsement to his memorial of thanks for his appointment cannot have made the outlook any more promising:

> Noted. In Liang-huai there are many kinds of corrupt practices, and the deficit is very large. You must find a way of making up this deficit and bringing it to an end. During your tour of duty it is best that there be no trouble. You cannot be careless. Again and again I say take care, take care, take care, take care.[98]

Not surprisingly, the memorials from this last term of Ts'ao Yin as salt censor are rather dejected; furthermore, they show that he was running out of ideas of his own and tended to rely on his subordinate salt controllers to sort out the confusion of the Liang-huai deficits.

His first hope was the salt controller Li Ssu-ch'üan, but unfortunately he died, and Ts'ao Yin wrote: "After Li Ssu-ch'üan was retained in office, he contracted a serious illness and died. Thus the accumulated deficit was not worked on and cleared up."[99] Li Ssu-ch'üan had in fact been salt controller since 1706,[100] and had proved quite unable to handle the financial problems of Liang-huai.

The second hope was Man-tu, a grain transport official with an excellent administrative record, who had been appointed to fill the vacancy left by Li Ssu-ch'üan. Ts'ao Yin wrote of him: "He is really industrious and intelligent, and the merchants and salt workers love him and pay him especial respect. If he were temporarily kept in office to help us for one or two years, the accumulated deficit could be easily made up."[101] The Emperor refused to keep Man-tu in office, because to do so would violate the regulation that no Manchu might be appointed as salt controller.[102] But Ts'ao Yin had a chance to work with Man-tu until the new salt controller took up office. In a memorial of April 26, 1711, he reported the results of this partnership: the outstanding deficit stood at 1,900,000 taels; it had stood at 2,862,000

---

98. *Ts'ao Yin Memorials*, p. 22, endorsement to memorial dated 49/9/2.

99. Ibid., p. 24b, dated 49/10/28.

100. *CNTC*, ch. 106, p. 14b.

101. *Ts'ao Yin Memorials*, p. 24b, dated 49/10/28.

102. Emperor's endorsement to above memorial dated 49/10/28. This regulation seems to have been very closely followed. The salt controllers were often Chinese bannermen or men from Feng-t'ien, but no Manchu was appointed until 1722. Cf. *CNTC*, ch. 106, p. 14.

taels; if the whole debt was to be cleared, the merchants would have to produce the incredible sum of 5,200,000 taels.

Ts'ao Yin explained that this state of affairs had come about as follows. The Emperor's generosity in allowing Li Hsü to defer payments of one million taels (and presumably also Li Hsü's action in further deferring payments until the tenth month) meant that when Ts'ao Yin took up office he had found that the merchants owed the government 2,862,000 taels in "old and new" debts—that is, the accumulated deficits of the past few years, and the deferred quota payments from 1710. He and Man-tu had collected 900,000 of this sum so far, and they were confident of making up about 90 percent of the remainder, since "all the merchants engaged in transport have mutual guarantees, and all the merchants will take shares in making up the amount that cannot be collected." But the time when the merchants must pay for their new 1711 salt *yin* was approaching. Ts'ao Yin estimated that the present year's taxes and "standard and miscellaneous levies" would come to 2,380,000 taels. If the merchants had to pay all this and the previous debts in one year, they would need to find 5,200,000 taels, which Ts'ao Yin feared "would exhaust the merchants' resources."

He also submitted an account sheet on which he broke down the merchants' debts into six categories. First, 280,000 taels that had not yet been collected on the 1709 allotment. Second, payments of 92,000 taels that should have been made to Li Hsü. Third, 800,000 taels owed on *yin* that had been given out in advance on the *yü-t'ou* system during 1708 and 1709. Fourth, 90,000 taels in back taxes owed by the salt manufacturers. Fifth, dragging debts of merchants who had gone bankrupt, totaling 440,000 taels. All merchants would cooperate in paying off these debts. Sixth, 200,000 in regular taxation owed by bankrupt merchants. The Emperor remained unimpressed by such assiduous categorizing of the existing debts, and wary of Ts'ao Yin's guarantee that 90 percent would be collected. It is possible that he doubted the accuracy or honesty of Ts'ao Yin's figures. He wrote:

> The deficit is too large. This is a very serious matter. You must be extremely careful. I still don't know what things will be like later on. Don't treat this lightly.[103]

103. *Ts'ao Yin Memorials*, pp. 23–24, for deficit memorial dated 50/3/9, endorsement, and account sheet.

He was right to be wary, but he could not criticize Ts'ao Yin too strongly. For in the first place Ts'ao Yin had warned him quite accurately of the dangers of continuing without some systematic reforms, and in the second place the Emperor had apparently fallen back on the old Ming dynasty practice of "using the surplus salt to make up the regular tax quotas" (yü-yen pu-ch'ung cheng-k'o).[104] This meant nothing less than ordering the salt censors to use part of the surplus money, which they received each year, to pay off the merchants' debts at a rate of 230,000 taels per annum. In other words, to take the irregular exactions, which had been partly responsible for the merchants' initial difficulties, and then to use this money to help the merchants with their regular tax payments. It is not clear at exactly what time the K'ang-hsi Emperor had ordered his salt censors to adopt this remedy. Ts'ao Yin mentioned that he had received the edict in an explanatory note appended to the 1711 account sheet. Li Hsü wrote later that the use of 230,000 taels per annum to pay off merchant deficits had applied to "the 1706 shipments onwards." [105] (This probably refers to debts accumulated since 1706, rather than to the year 1706 itself, when the situation still seemed moderately stable.) He added that the deficit was finally paid off in 1714. So Ts'ao Yin had not done too badly in his last term: he passed Li Hsü a deficit of at least 690,000 taels,[106] but it must be remembered that he had started off with a deficit which he claimed was 2,862,000 taels. Even if Ts'ao Yin had been scared into action by the Emperor's strictures, or had distorted the figures in the first place, by the rough and ready standards of late K'ang-hsi salt administration he had had an exemplary final term as salt censor of Liang-huai.

Li Hsü as Liang-huai Salt Censor

Li Hsü handled the administration of Liang-huai in a way totally different from Ts'ao Yin. His memorial of thanks on his first appointment, written in November 1705, was formal and brief. He suggested no far-reaching plans of reform and gave no descriptions of corrup-

104. For the Ming precedent, cf. Gale and Ch'en, "China's Salt Administration," 1:2, 209 and 212.

105. Account Sheet in Ts'ao Yin Memorials, p. 23b, under item 2, and Li Hsü Memorials, p. 54b, dated 53/7/1.

106. Assuming from Li Hsü's figures that after 1711 only three more payments of 230,000 were needed to clear the deficits.

tion. In his endorsement, the Emperor did not even mention salt matters, but told Li Hsü to continue acting as confidential informant, on a broad basis:

> If you hear that any kind of people from Soochow are making trouble, you must investigate and memorialize. Do not be remiss. It is best for you to make regular inquiries.[107]

He used Li Hsü's couriers to carry memorials from the governor Sung Lao, and to return instructions secretly to the governor.[108] Li Hsü was also warned to carry out no favors asked of him by stupid and ignorant people in Peking, and told that "this is extremely important, you must not be careless." [109] The Emperor was clearly determined that Li Hsü should not be involved with any political factions.

The only palace memorial that Li Hsü sent to the Emperor during his first term that dealt with salt problems was one in June 1706. In this he reiterated the facts that Ts'ao Yin had mentioned as being of special value to the salt merchants—the raising of the number of catties in each *yin*, a rise in salt prices, and the treasury loan. But he added that the merchants got into difficulties because they had to pay for their salt certificates in the sixth month before they had sold any salt; he requested that the limit for *yin* payments be fixed at the tenth month, when the merchants would have an easier time in paying. The Emperor turned down the request, saying: "Last year Ts'ao Yin didn't extend the time limit. Discuss this with Ts'ao Yin, then send another memorial requesting an edict." [110] No further memorial was sent, so Li Hsü must have decided to give up this idea for the time being.

Nor was Li Hsü's second term any more productive of ideas or criticisms. There is no suggestion in his memorials that there was an economic crisis and that the salt merchants were in grave difficulties. Li Hsü wrote two palace memorials on salt problems in this year. In the first, he repeated the points that Ts'ao Yin had discussed in audience with the Emperor concerning the need for civil cooperation with the military, for the ending of illegal exactions on the waterways, and for insisting on the clear zoning of the areas in which Liang-huai salt

107. *Li Hsü Memorials,* p. 11b, endorsement to memorial dated 44/10/–.
108. Ibid., dated 44/11/–, and p. 12b, endorsement to memorial dated 45/3/–.
109. Ibid., p. 12, endorsement to memorial dated 45/2/–.
110. Ibid., pp. 12b–13, dated 45/5/– and endorsement.

might be sold.[111] The second memorial was a detailed discussion of the salt smugglers operating around Yangchow. Li Hsü had made a personal inspection of these areas on horseback in the spring, and concluded that stern orders should be issued to the governing officials and the garrisons to clear up certain well-known smugglers' lairs. The Emperor was not interested in this kind of non-financial problem. As he told Li Hsü: "These are matters arising in the ordinary course of your official duties. You should write out a routine memorial explaining them." [112] In other words, this was a Board matter, not a matter to be dealt with through the palace memorial system, demanding the Emperor's personal attention.

Apart from a short memorial thanking the Emperor for his reappointment as salt censor in 1709,[113] no palace memorials from Li Hsü's third term have survived. It cannot be said definitely whether Li Hsü wrote none, or those he wrote have been lost. The latter is more likely, since this was the catastrophic year at the end of which Li Hsü bequeathed Ts'ao Yin a Liang-huai deficit of 2,862,000 taels. It is unlikely that Li Hsü could have ignored such events altogether, in hopes that the Emperor would not get to hear about them. Furthermore, it was in this year that Li Hsü received permission to defer merchant payments until the tenth month; since the Emperor had already refused the same request once, Li Hsü must have applied to him in person. All that can be said of this third term was that the general downward trend in the Liang-huai area continued, and that Li Hsü took no effective action to stop it.[114]

This downward trend was checked during Ts'ao Yin's fourth and last term in 1711. Ts'ao Yin paid off a substantial amount of the deficit, and met a high percentage of his own quota. By this time the effects of the natural calamities and concomitant economic dislocation of the years 1707–09 were wearing off. During Li Hsü's fourth term in 1712 there were some minor crises; heavy rains coincided with some exceptionally high tides and washed out many of the salt fields along

111. Ibid., pp. 20b–21, dated 47/3/–. Also discussed in the preceding section.

112. Ibid., pp. 21b–22, dated 47/3/–, and endorsement.

113. Ibid., p. 25, dated 48/8/21. This received no endorsement.

114. There are no memorials by Li Hsü for the years 1710 and 1711 printed in *Wen-hsien ts'ung-pien*. This might mean only that the memorials for these two years were mislaid in the Palace Museum. Also see the section above on Ts'ao Yin as salt censor.

the coast,[115] and in a pitched battle between staff from Li Hsü's yamen and salt smugglers, four of his men were killed and a patrol boat burned.[116] But his memorial at the end of his term in office showed affairs in better shape than they had been for a decade.

Li Hsü memorialized that during his term ending on November 11, 1712, he had collected in full the taxes of 2,400,000 taels.[117] Of this amount he had sent 1,200,000 to the Capital, and 1,040,000 to the provincial government. The remainder was kept in the salt treasury, and would be forwarded on receipt of the Board's instruction. The merchants had paid off 220,000 taels of their deficit, and Li Hsü had paid in the required 230,000 taels that the Emperor had ordered be paid from the surplus revenue to meet the deficit every year. The number of yin sold had been 1,590,000.[118]

In the normal course of events Li Hsü would have gone to Peking in person to report to the Emperor on his tour of duty, and would not have written out these details in a palace memorial. But the Emperor had reappointed Li Hsü to be salt censor for the year 1713. By the rotation system on which Ts'ao Yin and Li Hsü had been appointed since 1704, this would of course have been Ts'ao Yin's term. But Ts'ao Yin had died in the summer of 1712, and the Emperor ordered Li Hsü to serve out Ts'ao Yin's fifth term, and use the surplus revenue to pay off the debts of the Ts'ao family.[119]

As Ts'ao Yin had relied on his salt controllers Li Ssu-ch'üan and Man-tu, so Li Hsü put his faith in his salt controller Li Ch'en-ch'ang, a holder of the *chin-shih* degree from Chekiang, who had been appointed in 1711.[120] At the beginning of Li Hsü's fifth term a crisis

---

115. *Li Hsü Memorials*, p. 36b, dated 51/8/21; p. 36b, dated 51/9/6.

116. Ibid., p. 39, dated 51/11/3. Li Hsü impeached the military officials whose laxity had led to this debacle.

117. Ibid., p. 38b, dated 51/11/3. The figure printed is actually 2,040,000, and is presumably a misprint since it contradicts the figures that Li Hsü gives immediately below, that he had sent 1,200,000 to Peking, 1,040,000 to the provinces, and kept *the rest* in the treasury. Therefore he must have collected 2,240,000 plus a sizable sum. If the character *shih* (ten) is put before *wan* (ten thousand), Li Hsü's figure becomes 2,400,000. This coincides exactly with the figure that he gave nineteen days later, ibid., p. 40, dated 51/11/22: "the salt controller's yamen receieves 2,400,000 taels."

118. Li Hsü had probably issued about 165,000 surplus *yin*.

119. Cf. chapter 7, below.

120. *CNTC*, ch. 106, p. 14b.

occurred when the Kiangsu governor appointed Li Ch'en-ch'ang to be
acting financial commissioner, while the incumbent was in mourning
for the death of his mother. Li Hsü wrote a frantic memorial in which
he pleaded the importance of the salt controller's job, and said that the
salt controller could not be away even for a day; were he to be sent to
the financial commissioner's yamen in Soochow, how could he cope
with salt affairs in Yangchow? Yet the governor had already sent the
seal; he must be ordered to appoint someone else as acting financial
commissioner. The Emperor agreed to this request.[121] This enormous
reliance on their salt controllers that both Ts'ao Yin and Li Hsü had,
may well mean that they in fact had a rather inadequate knowledge
of the complexities of their office.

In the spring of 1713 Li Hsü traveled to the Capital to greet the
Emperor on his sixtieth birthday, and a number of Liang-huai salt
merchants did the same, although the Emperor had told them not to
bother.[122] He returned to find that heavy rains had again disrupted
Liang-huai salt production, and that deliveries to I-chen, the weighing
and distribution center, were up to two months behind.[123] This of
course meant that salt could not be sent out by the transport merchants until the autumn, and they would again have trouble in making their yin payments on time. Nevertheless, at the end of the year Li
Hsü reported the collection of a record surplus of 586,000 taels.[124]

At this point the even tenor of Li Hsü's life was disrupted by a case
of corruption involving himself, a eunuch in the Capital, and some of
the salt merchants. The merchants and Li Hsü had paid considerable
sums to this eunuch, perhaps on their visit to the Capital to congratulate the Emperor on his birthday; Li Hsü was not actually accused of
corruption, but of failing to report what he knew of the case to the
relevant authorities. The Judicial Department of the Imperial Household sentenced him to be dismissed from office but retained at his
post.[125]

But Li Hsü's career did not depend on maintaining an impeccable

121. Li Hsü Memorials, p. 40, dated 51/11/22, with endorsement "So be it" (shih).
122. Ibid., pp. 42–43, dated 52/1/13, 52/2/4, 52/2/17.
123. Ibid., pp. 44–46, dated 52/intercalary 5/23, 52/6/9, 52/7/5, 52/8/6.
124. Ibid., pp. 48b–49 dated, 52/11/12. Exact details on uses to which this surplus was
put are given below, chapter 7, the section on Ts'ao Yung.
125. ko-chih liu-jen, Sun, Ch'ing Administrative Terms, nos. 119 and 128. For a description of the case without specific details, cf. Li Hsü Memorials, p. 49, dated 52/12/9.

official record; it depended on his success in retaining the imperial favor, and this he seems to have at last forfeited during 1714. The first danger signal after the corruption case came in April. Li Hsü sent a memorial saying that though the 1713 quotas were all filled, there would be difficulty in selling all of the 1,600,000 *yin* certificates during the coming year; he therefore requested that the salt controller Li Ch'en-ch'ang be retained at his post for a further three years, since he was an official of such exceptional honesty and ability. In this request the merchants joined him. The Emperor's endorsement was short and angry: "It is not your place to speak on this matter." [126]

The last straw came in August. In a concise memorial Li Hsü pointed out that his office was drawing an annual surplus of 550,000 taels a year. In the past, 210,000 of this had gone for the textile commissioners' expenses, and 230,000 to pay off the Liang-huai salt merchants' deficits. The merchants' deficits were now paid, Li Hsü wrote. If he were given a few more terms as salt censor, he would ensure that this 230,000 taels was sent to the Emperor who could use it for his various expenses; 210,000 would go to the textile commissioners as before, and Li Hsü would use the remaining 100,000 on his own commissions for the Emperor and to pay off the last deficits at the textile commissioners' yamen. The Emperor's refusal was polite, but definite:

> These matters are of the greatest importance, and can by no means be granted lightly. Moreover I have no idea how these deficits keep on arising. If I extended your appointment for three or four years, at the end of it there would be an even larger deficit.[127]

At the end of his term Li Hsü was not reappointed; instead, the Emperor appointed Li Ch'en-ch'ang, that same salt controller whom Li Hsü had praised so lavishly in the past. At this same time Li Hsü's wife died.[128] If this were a moral fable, Li Hsü might well have collapsed at this point, a bereaved man, heavily in debt, disowned by his Emperor. But Li Hsü was irrepressible, and in a short time was consolidating his hold over his successor. He requested and obtained permission for Li Ch'en-ch'ang to send palace memorials, and then lent one

126. *Li Hsü Memorials*, pp. 51b–52, dated 53/3/1 and endorsement.
127. Ibid., pp. 54b–55, dated 53/7/1, and endorsement.
128. Ibid., p. 57, dated 53/8/21. His wife, née Han, died at 63 *sui*.

of his own household servants who knew the ropes of the memorial system to accompany Li Ch'en-ch'ang's servant to Peking and show him around.[129] Perhaps touched by Li Hsü's plight, and by the generous help that he was giving his successor, the Emperor ordered the new salt censor to pay off the debts still owed by Li Hsü and the Ts'ao family.[130]

Only two years after his fall from grace, Li Hsü received the perfect chance to oust his successor, for to a memorial he had sent reporting on rice prices, the Emperor wrote this endorsement:

> Noted. It is rumored that Li Ch'en-ch'ang has greatly changed his unswerving integrity. I don't know if this is true or not.[131]

Li Hsü replied immediately that the Emperor was unfortunately quite right in his assessment. Though Li Ch'en-ch'ang was incredibly secret about his personal affairs, Li Hsü had sent someone to make inquiries at Li Ch'en-ch'ang's Chekiang home. There the family that had once been poverty-stricken now had between four and five thousand *mou* of fine fields, dozens of shops, three pawnshops, and an unknown amount of cash. Besides this, many business enterprises were being run by Li Ch'en-ch'ang under borrowed names. And he also had a painfully swollen leg, so that he was unable to get about and attend to his salt work, but sat at home instead. The Emperor warned Li Hsü that "absolutely no one must know of this memorial" and requested further information.[132] Li Hsü complied; after half a year's illness, Li Ch'en-ch'ang had died on September 12, 1716.[133]

Had Li Hsü planned everything, it could not have turned out better. At a loss after the trusted man of integrity Li Ch'en-ch'ang had turned out to be dishonest, the Emperor turned again to the one man on the spot who at least had experience of the salt censor's office; on November 9 he sent an edict to the Censorate that they were to inform Li Hsü that he was reappointed. Li Hsü replied in suitable gratitude, adding that though Li Ch'en-ch'ang had paid off most of the debts, he had left a deficit of 288,000 taels. The Emperor, rather wear-

129. Ibid., p. 58b, dated 53/10/6; and p. 59, dated 53/11/26.
130. Ibid., p. 67, dated 54/12/5.
131. Ibid., p. 70b, endorsement to memorial dated 55/4/9.
132. Ibid., pp. 71b–72, dated 55/6/12.
133. Ibid., p. 75, dated 55/8/3.

ily one feels, wrote that if Li Hsü could not get rid of the deficit in one year, he would be allowed one last chance to pay it off.[134]

Li Hsü now moved into the field with considerable energy. He discovered that Li Ch'en-ch'ang had added three totally illegal levies, making the merchants pay an extra 32,000 taels. Li Hsü abolished these. Also, because Li Ch'en-ch'ang had been perverse and stupid and ill half the year, there were "millions and millions" of units of salt still held up at the factories. Li Hsü sped up the delivery of this salt.[135] He calculated that he could raise a surplus of 527,000 taels in the year. After 288,000 had gone to pay off the deficit, and 210,000 for the textile commissioners, he would send the remaining 29,000 to the Board to help with payment of wages. He planned to add five catties to every *yin* to make up for the wastage caused by delays in transporting the salt; in return the merchants would pay an extra 5 *fen* per *yin* (0.05 taels). This sum would be negligible for the merchants north of the Huai River who "have trifling capital," and for the merchants dealing in salt sold near the area of production (*shih-yen*); but for the 1,330,000 *yin* certificates sold south of the Huai this would bring the government an extra 66,000 taels. The levy was to be outside normal revenues, for Li Hsü said that he would personally bring it to the Emperor to use for his expenses. The Emperor's response to this barrage of information and fund-raising plans was the comprehensive "So be it." [136]

In the next five months Li Hsü sent no less than nine palace memorials dealing with various aspects of salt administration. A new plan of getting the salt processed for distribution in the second month instead of the sixth was put into operation and proved successful.[137] A provincial official was transferred so that he would reside in the notorious San-chiang ying, a base of smuggling operations. The Emperor was sceptical that the governor-general, whom he described as none too honest, would be happy at this change.[138] A Board of Revenue decision to increase the *yin* quota by 18,000 *yin*, to bring in an

134. Ibid., p. 76b, dated 55/10/21, quoting date of edict from Censorate communication, and endorsement.

135. Ibid., p. 77, dated 55/11/18.

136. Ibid., pp. 77b–78, dated 55/11/18.

137. Ibid., p. 79, dated 56/2/10. In fact Li Ch'en-ch'ang had suggested this already, ibid., pp. 77b–78.

138. Ibid., p. 79b, dated 56/2/10.

extra 20,400 taels, was vigorously protested by Li Hsü, since the merchants had not entirely caught up on their back payments, and the new obligation would cause them difficulty.[139] The new year's revenue was assessed at 1,950,000 taels, of which 500,000 had already been collected; the 288,000-tael debt would be paid off in four months.[140] Official coercion of merchants was again deplored,[141] and since the merchants had paid back their 1703 loan of one million taels in full, they now requested a new loan of 1,200,000 taels, which they would pay back at 10 percent interest over ten years. The Emperor refused to authorize the loan, writing: "This loan is absolutely out of the question. Let me hear no more about it." [142]

So Li Hsü continued. He paid off the 288,000-tael debt, collected the extra 66,000 taels he had planned to, discussed bringing the surplus revenue to Peking and handing surpluses over to the Board of Revenue in the future.[143] In December 1717, shortly before the expiration of his seventh term, he received the news that he had been reappointed for an eighth; as he quite correctly remarked, "since the establishment of the salt censor's yamen, never has one person been salt censor eight times; in ten thousand ages there has been nothing like this." [144] Within three weeks Li Hsü reported all debts paid off and a further surplus collected and paid into the treasury, that the entire year's quota of salt had been produced and sent out leaving large reserves for the following year, and that the Liang-huai salt merchant Chiang Ch'u-chi and others had gratefully contributed 98,000 taels toward repairing dikes along the river.[145] In January 1718, Li Hsü was raised by the Emperor to the rank of vice-president of the Board of Revenue; [146] this appointment, which was honorary, not substantive, gave him the dignities of an official of the second rank, first class.

This was the peak of Li Hsü's career. He had reached it because of the apparently brilliant year he had spent as salt censor; the year had been brilliant because with the full cooperation of the merchants he

139. Ibid., p. 80, dated 56/2/16.
140. Ibid., p. 80b, dated 56/2/24.
141. Ibid., p. 81, dated 56/3/11.
142. Ibid., p. 82, dated 56/4/10.
143. Ibid., pp. 85b–86, dated 56/7/13 (two memorials); p. 88, dated 56/11/2.
144. Ibid., p. 88, dated 56/11/2; p. 88b, dated 56/11/2.
145. Ibid., p. 89, dated 56/11/7; p. 90, dated 56/11/15; p. 90, dated 56/11/27.
146. Ibid., p. 91, dated 56/12/17.

had filled all quotas and even built up salt reserves. But the merchants may have paid up in return for certain benefits, and it may thus be no coincidence that during his last term, in 1718, Li Hsü spent most of his time seeking various favors from the Emperor specifically for the salt merchants.

One such memorial concerned the enrollment of merchants in the prefectural schools and in taking the *chü-jen* degree. (As soon as the merchants had a really good year, they began to look to their status.) Li Hsü wrote that most of the salt merchants in Liang-huai were from Shansi and Shensi, or else from Hui-chou. Those merchants from the far-western provinces of Shansi and Shensi were permitted to send fourteen boys to be students (*t'ung-sheng*) at the Yangchow school, where they would be trained for the first literary degree. The Hui-chou merchants had no such quota, because Hui-chou was in the same province as Yangchow.[147] Yet Hui-chou was over one thousand *li* from Yangchow, and Hui-chou merchants living in Yangchow found it impossible to return to their town of registration to take the examinations. They therefore requested a quota of fourteen students in the prefectural school, following the example of the western merchants. But this was only part of the problem; neither western nor Hui-chou licentiates had any rights to take the *chü-jen* exam. Since so many "merchants' sons and nephews were determined to study and enter on an official career," they requested permission to submit a list of the names of those eligible to take the *chü-jen* examination following the regulations for Manchus, Mongols, and sons of incumbent officials (*kuan-sheng*). Li Hsü added that he had not dared send an open memorial about such a question, but had preferred to send a palace memorial requesting instructions. The Emperor was potentially encouraging:

> This business is strongly connected with your own reputation. You cannot treat it lightly, but must discuss it with the salt controller and arrive at a suitable decision. Then you may send a memorial (*t'i-pen*).[148]

147. Hui-chou is in Anhwei, but at this time Anhwei and Kiangsu were still combined for certain purposes in the one province of Chiang-nan.

148. *Li Hsü Memorials*, p. 92b, dated 57/5/17 and endorsement; ibid., p. 97b, dated 57/intercalary 8/9. Li Hsü wrote that he had discussed the matter with the salt controller and was sending a *t'i-pen*.

Other memorials followed on different points, whose only common
theme was increased benefits to merchants. Thus an edict that the
merchants making up their backlog of *yin* quotas (as opposed to their
cash deficit, which had been paid off) should speed things up, was appealed by Li Hsü on grounds that it would cause hardship to the merchants and strain their resources.[149] Definitive action was taken
against the smugglers' lairs at San-chiang ying, which must have been
continually cutting away at merchant profits.[150] Li Hsü vigorously
contested attempts being made by the Kiangsi governor to cut salt
prices so as to relieve the common people:

> When local officials take up office they always say that price in-
> creases harm the people, and strictly forbid any increase in prices.
> They do not know that among the common people, each person
> only eats three-tenths of an ounce of salt every day, so that each
> man only eats about seven catties of salt a year, that's all. Thus if
> salt prices are raised a few thousandths of a tael, I don't see that it
> harms the common people. If prices are restricted then merchant
> resources are deficient, and where can the revenue come from?
> This restricting of prices has a harmful effect on the national
> revenue.[151]

This memorial received no imperial comment, so we cannot tell the
Emperor's reaction. The memorial in which Li Hsü finally went too
far was written on September 25, 1718. In it he passed on the request
of the Liang-huai merchants for a loan of 150,000 taels from the salt
treasury. The reason they gave for wanting the money was that they
had already contributed 240,000 taels for river works, and were now
anxious to make further contributions to the army on the western
frontier; however they did not have the necessary sum to hand, and if
they received the loan they would make the contribution and then
repay the loan in five annual installments. The Emperor's endorsement
was acid and to the point:

> This memorial is completely impractical. The money needed for
> the western frontiers can be issued from the treasuries, why

149. Ibid., p. 96, dated 57/8/8.
150. Ibid., p. 98, dated 57/intercalary 8/22. YFTC, ch. 85, p. 9.
151. *Li Hsü Memorials*, p. 97, dated 57/intercalary 8/9.

bother about payments in five annual installments? This is all because dishonest merchants plan to use this pretext to pay up their
arrears.[152]

A few days after writing this endorsement, the K'ang-hsi Emperor
confided to Ts'ao Yin's son Ts'ao Fu that he had found Li Hsü's
memorial on money for the western frontiers extremely unsatisfactory, and that he feared Li Hsü had lost his grip since his recent illness, and was being swindled.[153]

Only a few months before Li Hsü had crossed the Emperor in a
stupid manner by writing in a memorial that his last greetings
memorial had received no endorsement because the Emperor was
grieving too much for the death of the Empress Dowager, and was
making himself unwell. This received the angry endorsement:

> I am at present extremely well. The words in this memorial make
> no sense. This is not a fitting memorial.[154]

So ended Li Hsü's last term, his eighth, as salt censor of Liang-huai.
It cannot be denied that he left the financial system in good order,
with most debts paid and full quota revenue and large surpluses flow-
ing in to the treasury. But it is probable that the natural buoyancy of
the Chinese economy in a time of fine harvests and expanding population was more responsible for this than was Li Hsü's administration.
Yet long after he had been relieved of his duties, Li Hsü continued to
snipe at his successor, mentioning that he was lazy about checking the
amounts produced by the salt masters at the fields, so that smuggling
was increasing, and that delays were occurring because of bad weather.[155] When the Emperor finally gave him a chance to speak his
mind, by asking in an endorsement whether or not it was true that the
salt censor Chang Ying-chao was corrupt, Li Hsü made the most of
the opportunity. The area was in chaos, he wrote, with merchants
heavily in debt and smugglers trading openly at the distribution
points, while rapacious officials groped blindly for solutions. Chang
Ying-chao was dim and bookish, with no experience of crisis, and was

152. Ibid., p. 96b, dated 57/intercalary 8/2.
153. *Ts'ao Fu Archives*, endorsement to no. 2849, dated 57/intercalary 8/1.
154. *Li Hsü Memorials*, p. 93, dated 57/6/16.
155. Ibid., p. 102b, dated 58/4/26; and p. 104b, dated 58/8/7.

becoming the butt of the merchants who joked about him in Yang-chow.[156]

The memorial received no endorsement, and one feels that this was correct at that stage of the game. The K'ang-hsi Emperor and Li Hsü knew each other too well by now to make comment necessary. The death of the Emperor the following year forced the seventy-year-old [157] Li Hsü to adjust to the harsher realities of the world around him. The Yung-cheng Emperor had no reason to be grateful to Li Hsü, or to the Ts'ao family. Under his dispassionate eye they became valueless, and even worse than valueless because they failed at the simple levels of competence and honesty. But the K'ang-hsi Emperor had had easier standards; as long as Ts'ao Yin and Li Hsü prevented total disaster and collected the surplus revenues regularly, they were left largely to their own devices in the Liang-huai area. Surveying their records as a whole, there are some grounds for believing them guilty of dishonesty, yet for the K'ang-hsi Emperor this was not a crucial issue. He had never been one to insist on a sharp distinction between duty and interest.

156. Ibid., p. 111b, dated 60/8/8, citing rescript and endorsement.

157. Ibid., p. 57, dated 53/8/21, says Li Hsü's wife Han died aged 63 sui. Li Hsü would have been ?65 sui. Ibid., p. 110, dated 59/11/6, says that Li Hsü's mother, née Wen, died aged 93 sui. Were Li Hsü born in 1650, she would have been 23 sui at the time. Li Hsü was her eldest son. The date of 1650 is therefore suggested for Li Hsü's birth.

CHAPTER 6

Ts'ao Yin as the Emperor's Secret Informant

During the K'ang-hsi period the routine memorials (*pen-chang*), in which provincial and metropolitan officials brought administrative problems to the Emperor's notice, were taken either to the Transmission Office or to the Grand Secretariat; the contents of the memorials were summarized and their format was checked before they were submitted to the Emperor for his ruling. Most memorials went through these channels, whether they dealt with public administrative matters (*t'i-pen*) or the personal concerns of the memorialist (*tsou-pen*). Such a system made secrecy almost impossible, and it was for this reason that the K'ang-hsi Emperor developed the system of "palace memorials" (*tsou-che*), memorials that were sent straight to the palace and read only by him.[1]

The Yung-cheng Emperor expanded the system of enclosing information in palace memorials and institutionalized it. So efficient did he make this system of rapid and secret communication between the Emperor and his officials that it has been seen as the prime instrument in that Emperor's attainment of "a new stage of totalitarianism." [2] But during the K'ang-hsi reign, the palace memorial system was personal

1. HTSL, pp. 17,494–95 (ch. 1042, pp. 1–5). Fairbank and Teng, *Ch'ing Administration, Three Studies*, pp. 44–48. The important distinction between the palace memorials (*tsou-che*) on the one hand, and the routine memorials (*tsou-pen* and *t'i-pen*) on the other, is studied with great thoroughness by Silas Wu (Wu Hsiu-liang) in his MS "The Memorial Systems of the Ch'ing Dynasty." I am indebted to Silas Wu for permission to read his long draft article (which will appear in the *Harvard Journal of Asiatic Studies*), and for help on this problem given in subsequent correspondence.

2. Huang P'ei, "Yung-cheng shih-tai-ti mi-tsou chih-tu" (The Secret-Report System During the Yung-cheng Period, 1723–1735), *Ch'ing-hua hsüeh-pao*, new series, 3 (1962), 17–52. The phrase cited is from the English abstract, ibid. p. 52. Huang P'ei does not discuss Ts'ao Yin and Li Hsü as being the pioneers of the system in his section on the K'ang-hsi reign (pp. 19–20), and does not distinguish institutionally between *mi-t'i* and *mi-che*; but the article gives an excellent listing of the topics covered in the *Yung-cheng chu-p'i yü-chih*.

and flexible. The first two men known to have used this system were the bondservant textile commissioners Ts'ao Yin and Li Hsü.

Ts'ao Yin's Palace Memorials

Owing to an extraordinary accident it is possible to examine the very early stages of the palace memorial system, long before it became an acknowledged part of imperial government. For on one occasion Li Hsü's household servant lost a palace memorial, and the discussion between Li Hsü and the K'ang-hsi Emperor about the mishap has been preserved.

On December 30, 1707, Li Hsü sent the K'ang-hsi Emperor a palace memorial about a series of robberies that had been taking place in the T'ai-ts'ang area of Chiang-nan.[3] Since the Emperor had specially requested information about robberies in Chiang-nan,[4] Li Hsü followed it up a few days later with another memorial. In this, he wrote that as well as sending off one palace memorial by his household servant Wang K'o-ch'eng on December 30, he had also sent a man off to study the conditions in T'ai-ts'ang. Opposite the name of Wang K'o-ch'eng the Emperor wrote this interlinear endorsement:

> I haven't yet seen this secret memorial (*mi-che*) brought here by Wang K'o-ch'eng. Check up on this and memorialize.[5]

Even before he received the endorsement,[6] Li Hsü's suspicions had been aroused. The ensuing investigation he reported to the Emperor in detail on February 10, 1708:

3. *Li Hsü Memorials*, p. 17, dated 46/12/7. As the note on p. 17b explains, this is a copy of Li Hsü's original memorial, which was resubmitted with Li Hsü's memorial of 47/1/19. The editors of *Wen-hsien ts'ung-pien* have merely replaced it in its chronological setting.

4. In a rescript received by Li Hsü in 46/8/25, brought back by his servant Wang K'o-ch'eng (*Li Hsü Memorials*, p. 15, dated 46/9/-).

5. Ibid., p. 17b, dated 46/12/-. Since it refers to 46/12/7, the memorial must be written a few days later. The Emperor made an error in the radical of the "ch'eng" in Li Hsü's servant's name, but his Chinese often contained such minor errors. Cf. the endorsement of this same memorial, when he wrote the homophone *mi-mi*, meaning "honey," instead of the almost identical *mi-mi* meaning "secretly," ibid., p. 18. Li Hsü of course requoted this endorsement with the correct characters in his memorial of 47/2/-, ibid., p. 19b.

6. The endorsement at the end of the same memorial is acknowledged in a memorial of 47/2/-, ibid., p. 19b, at least eleven days after the dispatch of his major memorial dated 47/1/19.

Last year, on December 30, having heard about the robbers at
T'ai-ts'ang, I both sent off a man to make detailed inquiries and
commissioned my household servant Wang K'o-ch'eng to take a
memorial and some bamboo without knots [as a present for the
Emperor] to Peking. On February 8 Wang K'o-ch'eng returned
to Yangchow and reported that he had handed in both the bamboo without knots and the memorial, but that the memorial had
not been sent out again.

When I heard this I was alarmed, for I knew that all memorials
that have received the imperial endorsement are sent out again,
and that even when there is no endorsement the original memorial is still sent out again. When he reported that it had not
been sent out I was concerned and uncertain, so I questioned him
repeatedly under severe torture. Only then did he make the following statement:

"The memorial was hidden in a bag as I hurried along at night,
but the bindings were not secure and I dropped the bag and lost
it on the Te-chou road and didn't know where to start looking
for it. On top of that, since the bamboo was so important, I
didn't dare delay a moment. I arrived in Peking and handed over
the bamboo willy-nilly, and made up a story about there being
no memorial. That is the real truth."

I then sent Wang K'o-ch'eng off in chains to be flogged and
await a decree about how to dispose of him. But it was because I
was wrong in my choice of employee that this mishap occurred; I
tremble and am afraid; it is a crime beyond atonement, and I beg
the Emperor to decide my punishment. Now I humbly enclose
another copy of that original memorial.

The K'ang-hsi Emperor, in his endorsement, showed that he did not
want Li Hsü to press any official charges against Wang K'o-ch'eng, as
this would bring the whole business out into the open. Li Hsü's
memorials were outside the regular system.

All these reports that you send are no more than secret memorials
about things you have heard, and are not on the same footing as
those of the local officials. So let this household servant of yours

be forgiven as well. If outsiders were to hear about this, it wouldn't be too good.[7]

Bearing this uniquely frank and informative memorial in mind, we can now address ourselves to some of the administrative and institutional problems that it raises. The first problem is the couriers, of whom the unfortunate Wang K'o-ch'eng is an example. He was clearly not an official courier of the kind employed on regular government business, managed by the Board of War and using the whole elaborate system of tallies and post stations.[8] Li Hsü described Wang K'o-ch'eng as his household servant (*chia-jen*), and this was no isolated case; many of his memorials were taken to Peking and returned by his household servants.[9] Ts'ao Yin frequently mentioned that his memorials had been returned by his household servants, or by his household slaves (*chia-nu*).[10] When Sun Wen-ch'eng was Hangchow textile commissioner and Kao Pin was Soochow textile commissioner, their memorials were carried and returned by their household servants; [11] so were those of the Soochow textile commissioner Hu Feng-hui.[12]

These *chia-jen* were not just casual servants, but were registered members of an official's household; [13] governors could have fifty, intendants thirty, magistrates and below ten each.[14] Such household servants in Banners had servile status, since statutes of 1678 forbade

7. Ibid., p. 19, dated 47/1/19, for the above memorial and endorsement. Li Hsü gratefully thanked the Emperor for this pardon to Wang K'o-ch'eng and himself in a memorial of 47/3/–, ibid., p. 21. Those losing routine memorials would be openly punished, receiving standard penalties; cf. *HTSL*, p. 6601 (ch. 114, p. 33), and pp. 14,964–65 (ch. 778, pp. 2–3).

8. As discussed in Fairbank and Teng, *Ch'ing Administration, Three Studies*, pp. 6–10.

9. Random examples are in *Li Hsü Memorials*, p. 27, dated 51/2/19; p. 36, dated 51/8/21; p. 62, dated 54/4/9.

10. *Ts'ao Yin Memorials*, p. 18b, dated 47/7/15 (this memorial is incorrectly dated on page 18b, though the correct date appears at the end of it, on p. 19b); p. 2, dated 48/3/16; p. 19b, dated 48/2/8; p. 25, dated 49/11/3.

11. *YCCPYC*, *ts'e* 47, pp. 101b and 102 for Sun Wen-ch'eng; ibid., *ts'e* 50, p. 64b for Kao Pin.

12. Ibid., *ts'e* 48, pp. 102–03.

13. *HTSL*, p. 6272 (ch. 90, p. 28b), statute dated 1724, that all ordinary bannermen must register the names of all accompanying *chia-jen* within three months of moving to a new locality. Earlier decrees fixed the numbers, though formal registration may not have been compulsory.

14. *Ch'ing pai lei-ch'ao*, section 17, p. 26, dating this decree in 1686.

the selling of household servants in Manchu or Mongol Banners into the Chinese Banners; [15] *chia-jen* in private households were commonly bought and sold.[16] It was not only the textile commissioners who used household servants as couriers: a Kiangsi governor and a Soochow financial commissioner also sent household servants with memorials.[17]

Though the use of private couriers in the provincial administration as a whole is a separate problem, it may be said definitely that the textile commissioners in the K'ang-hsi and Yung-cheng reigns did use their own couriers, and thus were not subject to any of the statutory limitations that normally applied to officials from the provinces who wished to send memorials to the Capital.[18] This was an important guarantee of their comparative freedom of action.

The second problem is the actual processing of the memorials. Wang K'o-ch'eng stated merely that he handed over the bamboo "and made up a story about there being no memorial." The bamboo without knots was a special present or commission from Li Hsü to the Emperor,[19] and if it was to be handed in at the palace together with a memorial that was known to be secret, there must have been some very direct contact between the courier and the Emperor. This is further suggested by the fact that the Emperor simply wrote "I haven't yet seen this memorial brought here by Wang K'o-ch'eng" almost as if the name of the courier might be initially used to identify a memorial rather than the content of the memorial itself.

15. *HTSL*, p. 6383 (ch. 99, p. 6b).

16. As is shown by a case discussed in *Li Hsü Memorials*, pp. 4–5, in two memorials dated 37/6/–, concerning the purchase of *chia-jen* from another family by the *wu-lin-ta* Li Yung-shou. Li Hsü mentions seeing the bill of sale.

17. *Lang T'ing-chi Memorials*, pp. 40b and 41. Lang T'ing-chi was a member of the Chinese Plain Yellow Banner. *YCCPYC, ts'e* 47, p. 82b, for Chao Hsiang-k'uei.

18. According to early Ch'ing statutes, only senior officials might send memorials without authorization; junior officials in the provinces had to have the governor's authorization, and in the Capital had to use the Transmission Office. *HTSL*, p. 17,496 (ch. 1042, p. 5b) statutes of 1644(?) and 1645. This applied to the *t'i-pen* and *tsou-pen*. *Tsou-che* passed through the Chancery of Memorials where they had to be inspected and, in the case of secret memorials, resealed. *HT*, p. 0831 (ch. 82, p. 10b). Ibid., p. 11, places *chih-tsao* with education commissioners and customs directors in a category requiring special permission to submit memorials.

19. Since this occurred in December it was probably the same type of bamboo that Li Hsü was ordered to get from Chekiang in 1713. *Li Hsü Memorials*, p. 47b dated 52/9/18 and p. 50 dated 52/12/24.

From two casual remarks made by Ts'ao Yin we can be sure that the memorials were received by the *tsou-shih-ch'u*—the Chancery of Memorials to the Emperor.[20] The first is in a memorial of 1708, when Ts'ao Yin states that his servant has just come back to the south with his memorial and with an "orally transmitted edict" issued in the *tsou-shih ts'un-chu*—which can be translated as the Storehouse of Memorials to the Emperor;[21] this could be either a casual phrase for the Chancery of Memorials or an earlier name. It is more likely that it is a casual phrase, since Ts'ao Yin's second reference is extremely colloquial: "Sha-tzu at the Chancery of Memorials (*tsou-shih*) transmitted this decree."[22] Sha-tzu literally means "dimwit." This was probably the childhood personal name of some official or eunuch in the Chancery; in the context, it is unlikely to have been simple abuse, though it certainly implies familiarity.

Had the couriers brought their memorials to the Transmission Office, they would have had to have the memorials formally submitted and checked like everyone else. But these palace memorials sent by Ts'ao Yin and Li Hsü were delivered by their own couriers to the Chancery of Memorials[23] and were handled by eunuchs known by name to the bondservants. Li Hsü wrote in 1716 that his household servant had just brought him a decree transmitted by the Chief Eunuch Wei Chu;[24] on two occasions decrees were brought to Ts'ao Yin by the eunuch Liang Chiu-kung.[25] Although eunuchs were never strong during the K'ang-hsi reign, Wei Chu and Liang Chiu-kung were famous as the two eunuchs who had served the Emperor since their childhood and enjoyed his special favor.[26] If they dealt directly with memorials from Ts'ao Yin and Li Hsü, it might be safely assumed that those memorials bypassed all normal channels, both when being submitted and returned.

20. *BH*, no. 105. The Chancery was in charge of handling *tsou-che, HT*, p. 0831 (ch. 82, p. 10); no history of the Chancery is given in *HTSL*.

21. *Ts'ao Yin Archives*, no. 2756, dated 47/10/5.

22. *Ts'ao Yin Memorials* p. 15b, dated 45/9/15. The character for *sha* used in *Wen-hsien ts'ung-pien* (and presumably by Ts'ao Yin) is a less common variant, but is listed with the common *sha* in *Kuo-yü tz'u-tien* (4 vols., Taiwan, 1961), p. 3051; both mean "stupid" or "simpleton." Sha-tzu is sometimes used as a child's name.

23. As described in Fairbank and Teng, *Ch'ing Administration, Three Studies*, p. 60.

24. *Li Hsü Memorials*, p. 74, dated 55/7/6.

25. *Ts'ao Yin Memorials*, p. 15, dated 45/8/4 and p. 19b, dated 48/2/8.

26. *Yung-hsien lu*, p. 143, in discussing the fall of Wei Chu in 1723.

A third problem is the time taken over the transmittal of the memorials. Several of Ts'ao Yin's memorials can be placed very accurately, since the date an original memorial was sent and the date on which Ts'ao Yin received it again, bearing the imperial endorsement, have sometimes both survived. This gives an exact figure of twenty-nine days for the time taken on the courier's journey from Nanking to Peking and back; [27] from Yangchow to Peking and back the figures are thirty-one days and thirty-five days.[28] Wang K'o-ch'eng's trip (described above) took forty days.[29] This was standard time for a foot courier from Yangchow to the Capital and back,[30] and Wang K'o-ch'eng's language—"I hurried along at night"—suggests foot rather than horse travel, the phrase being *kan-lu,* which is not normally applied to riding. The thirty-day journeys are awkward to classify, for that time would be rather slow for a mounted courier and rather fast for a foot courier.[31] Ts'ao Yin took twenty days for the one-way journey from Peking to Nanking,[32] and presumably he traveled at a comfortable pace. It seems most likely, then, that his couriers traveled on foot or by boat, specially since the cost of independent horse couriers would have been prohibitive.

27. *Ts'ao Yin Memorials,* p. 22; memorial dated 49/9/2 was received back by Ts'ao Yin, bearing imperial endorsement, on 49/10/1. Internal evidence, ibid., shows Ts'ao Yin was in Nanking, recovering from an illness. The dates on Ts'ao Yin's memorials are definitely the dates on which they were written; *Wen-hsien ts'ung-pien* prints the dates, which are also written clearly in the memorials in *Ts'ao Yin Archives* as integral parts of the memorial. These dates could not conceivably be additions made in the palace at time of receipt; there is plenty of internal proof of this: for example, *Ts'ao Yin Memorials,* p. 11b, dated 43/12/2, mentions events occurring the same day, 43/12/2. The only dating problem is thus the converse of the one mentioned for the later Ch'ing period in Fairbank and Teng, *Ch'ing Administration, Three Studies,* p. 1, where they state that with foreign-policy memorials the date of receipt but not the date of dispatch is known.

28. *Ts'ao Yin Memorials,* pp. 22 and 25. Memorial dated 49/10/2 is received back with endorsement on 49/11/3 (or earlier). Ibid., pp. 22b and 23, memorial dated 50/2/3 is received back on 50/3/8.

29. *Li Hsü Memorials,* p. 19, dated 47/1/19 says Wang K'o-ch'eng left on 46/12/7, returned to Yangchow on 47/1/17.

30. Fairbank and Teng, *Ch'ing Administration, Three Studies,* p. 17, and assuming Wang K'o-ch'eng spent a few days in Peking.

31. Ibid., pp. 15 and 17. Their Nanking foot-courier time may be rather slow, since it is twenty-three days as opposed to sixteen days for a foot courier from Yangchow, and the distances they give for Nanking and Yangchow to Peking, and the times for mounted couriers from Nanking and Yangchow to Peking, are virtually identical.

32. *Ts'ao Yin Memorials,* p. 14, dated 45/2/18.

Fourthly, the actual physical description of the memorials: Ts'ao Yin's memorials were all long sheets of paper, folded over in concertina fashion, so that they could either be opened out flat or folded back into a thin booklet, 20 centimeters high and 10 centimeters broad.[33] A lucky chance has preserved the actual wrappings that were used on the memorials of one of Ts'ao Yin's friends and contemporaries, the Kiangsu governor Sung Lao; since they wrote on the same topics in the same format, and used the same couriers (see below), it may be assumed that these two men and Li Hsü all used the same method. The memorials of Sung Lao were enclosed in a white paper outer wrapping; down the join of this wrapping he wrote his full title and name, with a small seal reading "Ch'en Lao" (your official, Lao), and the words "prostrating myself I humbly seal this" (*k'ou-shou chin-feng*). Inside this wrapping was a large white envelope, fastened with white paper tape; down the tape was again written his name and official title, with the same seal and phrase. Inside this was a thin white envelope, with the same seal over the top and bottom joins; over the top seal was written the character *ku* (closed), and over the bottom seal was written *feng* (sealed). On the front of the envelope were written the two characters *tsou-che*—a palace memorial. Inside this thin envelope was the actual memorial. From the present state of the joins on these inner envelopes it appears that the Emperor opened them at the top join and then put the memorial back in the same envelope after he had read it and added an endorsement in vermilion ink. The envelope was then reglued and the Emperor (or an accompanying eunuch) wrote the character *feng* (sealed) over the join, with the same vermilion ink used for the endorsement. When Sung Lao received this memorial back again, he broke open the bottom seal of the envelope, so as not to deface the imperial calligraphy.[34]

Whether these memorials, already in two sealed envelopes and a sealed wrapper, were packed even more securely cannot be known. They might have been rolled and packed in a hollow tube for addi-

33. *Ts'ao Yin Archives*. They are all identical in size.
34. The memorials of Sung Lao and the wrappings were in the National Palace Museum Archives, Taichung, Taiwan, crate 76, package 87, memorials numbered 2400–43, when I saw them in November 1963. They are slightly smaller than Ts'ao Yin's memorials, being 8 cm. wide and 18 cm. long.

tional protection, following the method described in a Ch'ing administrative compendium:

> Provincial officials who have secret memorials to send, pack and seal them in a hollow tube. After this has been sealed it is covered with a memorial case. This signifies that it is extremely secret.[35]

In any case, there was little chance of any unauthorized person being able to read them.

A fifth problem concerns the nature of the memorials. Many of them are cast in the form of *ch'ing-an tsou*, which may be translated as "greetings memorials"; whereas officials regularly sent these to the Emperor to pay their formal respects, the agents then followed the greetings with a report on local affairs.[36] This was apparently the technique recommended by the K'ang-hsi Emperor; as he wrote to Wang Hung-hsü, another of his secret informants:

> If you hear anything important in the Capital, send a secret memorial sealed inside a greetings memorial, so as to prevent people knowing. Any leakage will have serious consequences. Be careful, be careful.[37]

But the subjects to be dealt with were still limited by the form, since when Ts'ao Yin's son Ts'ao Fu mentioned the death of a salt censor in his greetings memorial, K'ang-hsi wrote angrily: "Writing about sickness and death in a greetings memorial to the Emperor is grossly improper." [38]

Ordinary officials sending secret memorials usually stated in the memorial that the memorial was secret, using the phrase *mi-tsou*—"secretly memorializes"—after their name,[39] and the Transmission

35. *Rikubu seigo chukai* (Kyoto, 1940), p. 9. This is the Japanese edition of the *Liu-pu ch'eng-yü chu-chieh*, used by E-tu Zen Sun for her work *Ch'ing Administrative Terms*, Harvard University Press, 1961. Her book does not, however, include the passage on memorials.

36. Examples are in *Ts'ao Yin Memorials*, p. 2, dated 48/3/16; p. 9, dated 43/10/13; p. 19b, dated 48/2/8. *Li Hsü Memorials*, p. 4b, dated 37/6/–; p. 10, dated 42/6/–; p. 22b, dated 47/3/29.

37. *Wang Hung-hsü Memorials*, p. 1.

38. *Ts'ao Fu Archives*, no. 2858, endorsement to memorial dated 55/8/1.

39. Examples are the memorials of Hung Ch'eng-ch'ou in *Ming-Ch'ing shih-liao*, series 3, 2, 167–68.

Office had definite instructions on how to handle such memorials.[40] But the memorials of the textile commissioners Ts'ao Yin and Li Hsü, as well as those of Sung Lao, were written in the form of ordinary memorials; it is only because of various random comments made by them and the Emperor that we know that their memorials were secret, in the special category of palace memorials.

In 1704 the K'ang-hsi Emperor wrote to Ts'ao Yin "if there is anything you are in difficulties about you can send a secret palace memorial (*mi-che*) and request a decree," [41] and in 1708 he twice told him to send secret memorials about local affairs and finance.[42] On at least four occasions, Li Hsü quotes endorsements from the Emperor written "on my secret memorials" (*mi-che*); and the memorials on which these endorsements appear are apparently plain *tsou*.[43] It seems that memorialists and Emperor did consider what they were writing as being secret memorials, even if they were not officially so.[44]

Ts'ao Yin did not adhere to the standards of the Transmission Office that there should normally be eighteen characters in each line of a memorial, with the Emperor's name being elevated two spaces to make a twenty-character column; [45] he wrote twenty characters and elevated two to make twenty-two, and even twenty-two characters with two elevated to make twenty-four. But he did adhere to the regulations about no memorial exceeding three hundred characters in length,[46] except on one occasion when he apologized for exceeding

40. Discussed in Fairbank and Teng, *Ch'ing Administration, Three Studies*, p. 46 note 16; p. 47 note 18.

41. *Ts'ao Yin Memorials*, p. 1b, endorsement to memorial dated 43/7/29.

42. *Ts'ao Yin Archives*, no. 2772, endorsement to memorial dated 47/3/21; and *Ts'ao Yin Memorials*, p. 18, endorsement to memorial dated 47/3/1.

43. These references in which Li Hsü mentions his own earlier *tsou* as being *mi-che* are as follows: *Li Hsü Memorials*, p. 17b, 46/12/- referring to 46/12/7; pp. 27 and 28b, 51/3/26 referring to 51/2/19; pp. 26 and 27, 51/2/19 referring to 51/1/16; pp. 27 and 28b, 51/3/26 referring to 51/2/24.

44. The most secretive secret memorials were those of Wang Hung-hsü, which were written on very broad low strips of paper and folded into little booklets 4 cm. wide and only 8 cm. high. They could thus be concealed in the palm of a hand and slipped to the Emperor, who could read them easily in his cupped hands. Many are still preserved in the Palace Museum, Taichung. They are usually undated. A selection are printed in *Wen-hsien ts'ung-pien*, 2 and 3.

45. HTSL, p. 17,494 (ch. 1042, pp. 1 and 2), standards set in 1651.

46. Ibid., p. 17,495 (ch. 1042, p. 3), standards set in 1644, limit abolished in 1725 for all important memorials.

the limit because he had so much of importance to report.[47] As far as formal phraseology was concerned, Ts'ao Yin considered himself Chinese enough to refer to himself as *ch'en*, your official, whereas his two sons considered themselves Manchu enough to always use the term *nu-ts'ai*, your slave.[48] Li Hsü apparently was torn between the two; he was *ch'en* until 1715, both *ch'en* and *nu-ts'ai* through 1715, until the summer of 1716, after which he was always *nu-ts'ai*.[49]

Only one of Ts'ao Yin's memorials was written in the tiny cramped characters of the formal style, and that was an early memorial sent to congratulate the Emperor after Galdan's death. This memorial had a long, beautifully written rescript, presumably written by an imperial secretary, and this also is a lone example.[50] All the rest of his memorials were in a bold, clearly legible calligraphy, obviously quite rapidly written, while the K'ang-hsi Emperor's endorsements are written in inelegant characters, sometimes of a kind of modified grass writing, with errors in the radicals used and occasionally a character angrily scrubbed over with a splash of vermilion ink.[51] It is clear that no subordinate would be allowed to get away with such errors and such calligraphy, and that the endorsements were written personally by the Emperor.

In 1715 the K'ang-hsi Emperor even issued an edict reiterating that he wrote these endorsements in person:

> All the vermilion endorsements written on all palace memorials come from my own hand. On this excursion [to Jehol] my right hand grew diseased and I cannot write with it, so I am using my left hand to grasp my brush and write endorsements; I emphasize that I have not entrusted this task to anyone else. So the contents of all [palace] memorials are known only to me and the original memorialist. If there is any leakage, it is because the original

47. *Ts'ao Yin Memorials*, p. 17b, dated 47/3/1.
48. *Ts'ao Yin Memorials, Ts'ao Yung Memorials, Ts'ao Fu Memorials*, passim.
49. *Li Hsü Memorials*, *ch'en* up to p. 60, both pp. 60–70, *nu-ts'ai*, pp. 71ff.
50. *Ts'ao Yin Archives*, no. 2736, dated 36/5/3 and rescript to same.
51. These are impressions from seeing the memorials in *Ts'ao Yin Archives*, and not the result of any scientific study of the calligraphy involved. The best description of the endorsement calligraphy is that it is like the calligraphy of a good Western student of Chinese. For an error, cf. *Ts'ao Yin Archives*, no. 2735, dated 35/6/8. The Emperor forgot the water radical in the character *sha*, "sand" (in the phrase *sha-mo*, "sandy desert") and wrote *shao*, "few."

memorialist was not discreet; my years as ruler have been many, and I have never carelessly divulged information.[52]

This, then, was the secret and informal system used by the K'ang-hsi Emperor to receive his agents' reports and to send them his instructions. In its beginnings it was so secret and informal that its origins would probably have always remained unknown, had not the Yung-cheng Emperor, in his first year as ruler, decreed that all those who had any memorials with vermilion endorsements written on them by the K'ang-hsi Emperor must return them immediately, and fixed severe punishments for those who hid or burned them; while in future every official receiving "imperially written secret decrees" (ch'in-p'i mi-chih) must return them with the next memorial they wrote. Obedient to this, Ts'ao Fu returned all the family memorials in 1723.[53] This ended the casual approach that had made the K'ang-hsi Emperor's personal system truly personal. From 1723 onward there were to be records of everything.

The K'ang-hsi Emperor found the system so efficient that on occasion he used it instead of the official transmissions system, where security was less tight. Li Hsü in 1703 was ordered to transmit the secret memorials of the Kiangsu governor Sung Lao and did so.[54] This must have proved a satisfactory arrangement, for eleven years later another Kiangsu governor, Chang Po-hsing, received this decree:

---

52. *Shih-lu*, ch. 265, pp. 14b–15, dated 54/10/4, (October 30, 1715).

53. According to the editors of *Wen-hsien ts'ung-pien*, interlinear note in *Ts'ao Yin Memorials*, p. 8, these memorials were stored in the Mao-ch'in palace, and the box bore the inscription: "In the first year of Yung-cheng the *chih-tsao* Ts'ao Fu handed over this one box of memorials." The "Fu" of Ts'ao Fu is the wrong character; this is the type of mistake which suggests clerks were dealing with a considerable number of memorials which, in accordance with the Yung-cheng Emperor's edict, were all being returned from the provinces at one time. It would only have taken a moment for a clerk to check the name against one of the memorials bearing the correct character.

The writer of *Yung-hsien lu*, p. 64, dates this decree to 61/12/3–15, that is, between January 9 and 21, 1723. The strong wooden box in which the Ts'ao family memorials are kept in the Palace Museum may well be the one in which they placed the memorials in 1723 before sending them to the Capital. It is quite possible, of course, that the then head of the Ts'ao family—Ts'ao Fu—destroyed some of his or his father's memorials.

54. *Li Hsü Memorials*, p. 10, rescript to memorial dated 42/4/–. Order acknowledged by Sung Lao in 42/6/– memorial, *Sung Lao Archives*, no. 2419. Sung Lao memorial sent by Li Hsü in 42/6/–, *Li Hsü Memorials*, p. 10.

Noted. This *che* should have been a *t'i*. In future, if you have business of importance and fear your household servant will be delayed, hand over your memorial to Li Hsü for rapid delivery.[55]

There are two inferences from this: firstly, Chang Po-hsing had been sending routine matters improperly under special cover; secondly, his special cover was not satisfactory for important business. Only a month later Li Hsü sent off a memorial for him.[56] Ts'ao Yin's couriers were also used to carry other men's memorials, though apparently only rarely.[57]

Despite the one disaster of the memorial lost on the Te-chou road by Wang K'o-ch'eng, the system was clearly extremely efficient. It had to be. For it was by means of this system that the K'ang-hsi Emperor gathered the kind of detailed information about his southern provinces that helped him to make decisions in those areas.

Officials, Rumors, and Robbers

The entire system of sending confidential information in palace memorials directly to the Emperor, which later became the standard practice of the Ch'ing dynasty, may have originated quite accidentally. In August 1693 Li Hsü sent a short palace memorial to the Emperor, in the format of the greetings memorials normally sent, only on this occasion Li Hsü added a few bits of information: the drought in Kiangsu had ended, they could now expect a harvest at least 50 or 60 percent the yield of those in good years, and rice prices were steady at about seven *ch'ien* for coarse rice and one tael for fine. Li Hsü concluded by writing that though he did not have the responsibilities of a local official and should not trouble the Emperor with reports, he had nevertheless taken the liberty of doing so in this case because he knew how much the Emperor had been worrying about the common people.[58]

---

55. *Chang Po-hsing Archives*, no. 2170, vermilion endorsement to memorial dated 53/3/4.

56. *Li Hsü Memorials*, p. 53, dated 53/4/21.

57. The only examples seem to be the memorials of rice stabilization officers in 1708. *Ts'ao Yin Archives*, nos. 2772, 2773, 2776 dated 47/3/21, 47/3/26, 47/5/18.

58. *Li Hsü Memorials*, p. 1, dated 32/7/–.

Greetings memorials were normally nothing but a line or two of formal thanks and devout wishes for the Emperor's continuing health.[59] The K'ang-hsi Emperor seems to have immediately seen the possibilities of this extended use of an existing format; he did not censure Li Hsü for departing from the norm, but wrote an encouraging endorsement:

> When people come from the south, I always questioned them to learn all the details. Your memorial has slightly eased the burdens of my imperial office. After the autumn harvest report to me again in another memorial. It is absolutely imperative that nobody should know about these memorials.[60]

In November 1693 Li Hsü, obedient to these instructions, sent back details of the Kiangsu harvest.[61] The new system was launched.

Some time in the 1690s the K'ang-hsi Emperor must have given permission to Ts'ao Yin to send information in his palace memorials; Ts'ao Yin's earliest surviving memorial is dated December 1697,[62] but he may have been sending such details as rice prices and weather reports well before this time. He was the logical person to be chosen after Li Hsü, since both were bondservant textile commissioners living in the same area. For some years, however, he and Li Hsü continued to send comparatively unimportant memorials on local weather conditions, rice prices, or minor local events; it was not until after 1700 that the Emperor seriously began to use them in the role that might be described as that of "secret informant."

Li Hsü, as we saw above in the case of Wang K'o-ch'eng, had been sending palace memorials about local robbers which he and the Emperor described as secret in 1707. But his change in role from being textile commissioner and general agent to something more secretive and important may well date as late as this endorsement, sent to him in 1710. The Emperor wrote:

59. Examples in ibid., p. 1, dated 32/6/– and p. 5, dated 37/10/–. Many of the *tsou-che* preserved in the Palace Museum Archives are simple greetings memorials, yielding no information whatsoever.

60. Ibid., p. 1b, endorsement to memorial dated 32/7/–.

61. Ibid., dated 32/10/–. In this memorial Li Hsü acknowledged the Emperor's endorsement received on his previous "*tsou-che*."

62. *Ts'ao Yin Memorials*, p. 8b, dated 36/10/22.

I have learned that at present in the south there is a good deal of gossip and fabrication concerning both important and minor matters. I cannot just commission someone to make inquiries; you have received many major favors from me, so whenever you hear something, send me a memorial about it, written out in your own hand, and that will be satisfactory. You must let absolutely no one learn of this arrangement; if anyone finds out, it will be disastrous for you.[63]

Ts'ao Yin's special duties may date from 1704 when the Emperor told him:

If there is anything you are doubtful about you can send a secret memorial requesting instructions. You must not let anyone else write these memorials, for if rumors spread, the consequences will be severe. Take care, take care, take care, take care.[64]

However, this imperial endorsement may have referred largely to Ts'ao Yin's new duties as salt censor on which he was just embarking, and it is safer to date his role as a secret informant from March 1708. In this month he returned from Peking to Nanking by a certain route at the Emperor's orders, and then sent a long memorial on what he had seen, which received the endorsement: "Noted. In future if you learn any more of these details in your area, you must send a secret memorial." [65]

From this time on, Ts'ao Yin began to send secret memorials about a wide variety of local problems. The first lesson that he had to learn was that now, more than ever before, speed was essential. As the K'ang-hsi Emperor told him in 1709: "On any matter that is worth sending a memorial about, you must get in first. There is no point in my learning of it when it's over." [66] One of Ts'ao Yin's first attempts at a secret report on a great official received the same criticism. On August 12, 1709, Ts'ao Yin sent off a memorial reporting that the Chiang-nan governor-general Shao-mu-pu had been ill during June;

63. *Li Hsü Memorials*, p. 25, quoted in memorial dated 48/12/2.

64. *Ts'ao Yin Memorials*, p. 1b, endorsement to memorial (in which Ts'ao Yin thanks the Emperor for his salt appointment) dated 43/7/29.

65. Ibid., p. 18, endorsement to memorial dated 47/3/1.

66. *Ts'ao Yin Archives*, no. 2795, endorsement to memorial dated 48/7/3.

he then contracted malarial fever and dysentery while in a weakened
state, and died on August 11. Thus Ts'ao Yin sent off his memorial
the very day after Shao-mu-pu's death. This was not good enough for
the K'ang-hsi Emperor, who wrote in endorsement:

> I have known about the governor-general's death a long time.
> This memorial was late. The time to send a memorial is when the
> illness becomes serious.[67]

At the same time, the Emperor showed the change in their relationship that had been brought about by Ts'ao Yin's assumption of the
new and possibly dangerous duty of imperial informant. This change
was expressed in his vermilion endorsements to Ts'ao Yin's memorials.
Previously these endorsements had often been friendly and casual, but
had dealt mainly with the harvest or minor local matters; now the
K'ang-hsi Emperor really began to take Ts'ao Yin into his confidence
by discussing the highest provincial officials in the frankest terms. In
June 1709 Ts'ao Yin sent a report on Chiang-nan which mentioned
that the harvest would only be about 50 percent of average, rice shipments were delayed, the river was high and several dikes broken, a
governor was ill, salt distribution was disrupted, and many jobless had
fled to the Chekiang mines of Ch'u-chou fu, Sung-yang, and Yün-ho
and caused disturbances which had had to be put down by local
troops. Apart from this, he added loyally, all was well. The memorial
received this endorsement:

> Noted. Since the new governor-general and governor took up
> their appointments, there has not been a single year with a good
> harvest. Also the Anhwei governor is sick much of the time. If
> these senior officials would clean up and consider my sincere
> wishes now, than all would be well. If they just follow their old
> habits, getting by from day to day, they must surely die
> of shame.[68]

When Ts'ao Yin became a trusted secret informant, he was already
fifty years old, and since he died at the age of fifty-four, in 1712, he

67. Ibid., no. 2796, memorial dated 48/7/7 and endorsement on same.
68. Ibid., no. 2794, memorial dated 48/5/6 and endorsement on same. The governor-
general was Shao-mu-pu; the governor of Kiangsu, Yü Chun, was dismissed at the end of the
year.

left comparatively few secret memorials. But on certain of the matters he handled enough material has survived to make a detailed study worthwhile.

The first of these cases involved Hsiung Tz'u-li, a former grand secretary, official historian, and president of the Board of Civil Office.[69] Hsiung Tz'u-li was living in retirement in Nanking, and while in audience in Peking in the spring of 1708, Ts'ao Yin was ordered to inquire after him, which he did.[70] A year later he received this endorsement: "How is Hsiung Tz'u-li these days?"[71] and replied as follows:

> I have made inquiries about Hsiung Tz'u-li. He stays at home and doesn't go out. All the officials living in the same city went to greet him, but he did not receive them. At present he is spending his time with two licentiates of Nanking, Ch'en Wu-hsün and Chang Ch'un, and some monks from the Chi-ming temple, looking at the flowers and writing poetry. He has written a book *Hsiao t'ao-yüan tsa yung,* and this is the book that he had printed and circulated. I humbly report to the Emperor that because Hsiung Tz'u-li and I are not friends I cannot know any details about him. But what I could learn I have reported accurately.[72]

The amount of information in this short passage is considerable, and it was clearly designed to answer any questions the Emperor might put concerning Hsiung Tz'u-li's contacts with local officials, his way of life and activities, and rumors that he might have been circulating subversive works. Ts'ao Yin actually enclosed a copy of the poems, which the Emperor returned.[73] "Looking at the flowers" may here be the euphemism for sexual activity that it often is in poetry, since Hsiung Tz'u-li had a son in 1708 when he was seventy-three years old, and another one in 1709 shortly before his death.[74]

69. *Eminent Chinese,* pp. 308–09.

70. *Ts'ao Yin Memorials,* p. 17b, dated 47/3/1.

71. Ibid., p. 20, endorsement to memorial dated 48/2/8.

72. Ibid., p. 2b, memorial dated 48/3/16.

73. Ibid., p. 2b, endorsement to memorial dated 48/3/16. "Noted. I send back the draft of his poems."

74. Ibid., p. 3, memorial dated 48/10/–, says that of his three sons, "one was born last year and one this year."

Ts'ao Yin's next memorial showed that he still remembered the imperial rebuke over his dilatory news of Shao-mu-pu's death, but that he was too cautious to be flustered into error:

On October 4, I established that grand secretary Hsiung Tz'u-li died in the early afternoon of October 1. I was at I-chen checking the salt quotas when I got the news on October 2, and I sent someone to make inquiries about the nature of the illness and the medicines used. He reported that Hsiung Tz'u-li caught a cold and then contracted dysentery; he lay in bed for several days and never got up again. I should have reported this immediately, but because I was afraid that the news I had received might not be accurate, I verified it and memorialize.

The Emperor showed continued interest:

Noted. Make further inquiries about the medicine used. What did he say near the end? How are his sons? You had better send some money for the ceremonies.[75]

Ts'ao Yin's answer effectively disposed of any suspicions of poison, which may have been behind the Emperor's question; he suggested instead that the main cause of death was the local medical profession:

The medicine he received came from the Nanking doctors Ou I, Tai Lin-chiao, Hu Ching-sheng, Chang Yen-ch'en, Wu Chuang, and Liu Yün-chi. Because his stomach was unsettled in his illness, and he was given the medicines at random, he later refused to take any at all.

Ts'ao Yin in the same memorial gave details of the money he gave for the funeral (240 taels), the names and ages of the surviving sons, the location of the place of burial, and said that near the end Hsiung Tz'u-li had expressed his gratitude for the Emperor's favor and written out a valedictory memorial. The Emperor's brief endorsement was: "I've heard that his family is very poor. Is this true or not?"[76]

Once again, Ts'ao Yin's reply was thorough:

I found that Hsiung Tz'u-li had an ancestral home at his native place in Hu-kuang, with land not exceeding 100 *mou* [about

75. Ibid., p. 2b, memorial dated 48/9/–, endorsement to same.
76. Ibid., p. 3, dated 48/10/–, and endorsement to same.

15 acres]. In Nanking he had two large houses and over 100 *mou* of land. The houses and land in Hupeh and Nanking are probably worth seven or eight thousand taels. I don't know if he had any savings stored at home, but he had no trade or business interests outside.

The members of his household of all grades and ages probably total one hundred. While Hsiung Tz'u-li was living, I never heard that he had any debts. He might have received gifts and assistance from his students and former associates, or presents from local officials and those passing through. He lived on a comfortable scale; when compared with other high Chinese officials his way of life was about in the middle range. He didn't seem very poor.[77]

This ended Ts'ao Yin's basic reporting on Hsiung Tz'u-li; the four short memorials prove that he was conscientious, precise, and intelligent at spotting the salient points in an inquiry. But the nature of the investigation was fairly routine; it was only in the endorsement to this last memorial that the Emperor opened up new and difficult ground:

Hsiung Tz'u-li's valedictory memorial has been altered. Can you by any chance get hold of the actual draft? If you find the real one, report to me in person.[78]

Investigation of the valedictory memorial proved that it had been tampered with by Hsiung Pen, a Hanlin compiler, who had forged an entry in the memorial in which Hsiung Tz'u-li apparently recommended Hsiung Pen for promotion on the grounds of his great merit. Hsiung Pen had gambled on the fact that as they had the same family name the request would appear quite normal. In fact, the Emperor got suspicious because the passage was out of character. The governor-general of Liang-chiang, Gali, was in charge of this case, and produced what he claimed was the original memorial. Hsiung Pen was punished.[79] A good many people, however, suspected that Gali had forged this "original" draft memorial in order to gain a reputation with the Emperor as an efficient official.[80] There is no proof that Ts'ao

77. Ibid., p. 3, dated 48/11/–.
78. Ibid., p. 3b, endorsement to memorial dated 48/11/–.
79. *Ch'ing-shih lieh-chuan*, ch. 7, p. 50 (last section of Hsiung Tz'u-li biography).
80. *Ch'ing pai lei-ch'ao*, section 58, p. 10.

Yin took any part in the conclusion of this affair; it is more likely that
the Emperor expected him to hunt around on his own and see if he
could find something.

The sending of memorials about important officials was one part of
Ts'ao Yin's duties as a secret informant. Complementing these specific
memorials he also sent general reports about topics that may be summarized as "rumors and robbers," that is, any unusual or disturbing
happenings and any outbreaks of violence.

The longest extant memorial of this type written by Ts'ao Yin is
dated March 22, 1708, and deals with "the things that I heard and
saw on my journey" from Peking to Nanking. The Emperor had apparently given precise instructions about this journey, since Ts'ao Yin
wrote: "Obedient to the Emperor's orders, I began my journey on
March 2, taking the central route through Yen-chou-fu to Nanking." [81] From places mentioned in the memorial we know that this
must have been the land route, running from Peking due south
through Chihli, across western Shantung and the northwestern tip of
Kiangsu, then cutting south and slightly east down Anhwei and crossing the Yangtze to reach Nanking.[82] Thus by ordering Ts'ao Yin to
furnish a report, the Emperor changed a routine journey into a kind
of censor's inspection of four provinces.

The memorial was in three sections. The first was a report on various rice stabilization measures, orders concerning which Ts'ao Yin relayed from the Emperor to the governor-general. He reported that the
governor-general was "delighted" with the orders to lower rice prices,
and even this detail was an integral part of his report, since the K'ang-
hsi Emperor noted the reactions of his senior provincial officials.[83]
Then he added that since the governor-general had to go to Hangchow for some time to work on the rice prices, he had chosen capable
subordinates to manage the finances of the Nanking yamen. This information would again have been gratuitous, except in so far as it con-

81. *Ts'ao Yin Memorials*, p. 16b, memorial dated 47/3/1. Yen-chou-fu is the present
Tzeyang in western Shantung.

82. Besides Yen-chou-fu, the places mentioned in the memorial are Ho-chien-fu in
Chihli (this is the modern Hokien), and Ch'u-chou in southern Anhwei, which in Ch'ing
times incorporated the modern Laian and Chuhsien. Identifications are taken from *Tz'u-hai*.

83. For instance, the Emperor's rescript to Li Hsü's memorial dated 51/2/24 during the
examination-hall case: "When Chang Po-hsing saw these circumstances, what did he say?
How is Chang P'eng-ko?" *Li Hsü Memorials*, p. 27.

stituted a judgment—and a favorable one—on the governor-general's conduct.[84]

The second, and far the largest, section of the memorial was headed by Ts'ao Yin "The condition of the common people." [85] After a brief mention that "from Shantung to Nanking all the people seemed peaceful and contented with their lot as usual," and that everyone was grateful to the Emperor for his work at lowering rice prices, Ts'ao Yin got down to the darker side of the picture—various outbreaks of lawlessness that were aspects of more general discontent.

One such incident had occurred at Liu-ho-hsien (in southern Anhwei) when a group of salt smugglers, men with northern accents, had been stirring up trouble. Five had been arrested by the local officials and the rest had escaped; the governor-general had ordered out troops to catch them. Perhaps anticipating the Emperor's lack of interest, Ts'ao Yin wrote at this point: "this is a trifling matter, but as it is concerned with the salt administration I make so bold as to report it."

The next incident was apparently even more trifling. Men had been brought from Chekiang and Soochow, either common people or perhaps minor offenders, and they gave a humble little speech of thanks to the Emperor. This was not good enough for Ts'ao Yin, who delivered a Confucian homily to them. This is the only example of Ts'ao Yin in full Confucian dress, and as he was so proud of himself that he repeated his speech in full for the Emperor's benefit, although the memorial was running over the stipulated length, it is worth a glance:

> I then said: "You have received all these favors from the Emperor, and you know that the Emperor exhausts himself on your behalf. Why do you not therefore respond joyfully, competing to pay your taxes promptly and obey the laws respectfully? On a past occasion the starving people of Shantung were grateful for the Emperor's mercy and said that they would rather starve to death than become thieves and robbers. Last year's drought was no worse than that previous one; why did you spread all sorts of rumors and disobey the laws, so that the Emperor got to hear of it and the kingdom was disturbed? If this is the way you repay

84. *Ts'ao Yin Memorials,* p. 16b.
85. *pai-hsing ch'ing-hsing.*

him, one can really say that you have forgotten your loyalty and
filial duties." Those men from Soochow and Chekiang were all
ashamed and had not a word to say.[86]

The next incident was slightly more thoroughly covered. Ts'ao Yin
had been told to find out about a band of robbers at Ssu-ming-shan
(in Chekiang), and discovered that they had contacts with another
band in Fukien. The Chekiang robbers could thus cross the provincial
borders with their loot and hide out in the mountains in perfect
safety; they had been doing this for some time. Ts'ao Yin remarked
that the local officials were entirely to blame: "They only investigate
those cases that are right in front of their eyes, and do not connect up
with the background."

In the last case he mentioned, that of the "villainous monk" I-nien,
Ts'ao Yin only briefly discussed the fact that those involved were
"just the same as mounted highwaymen, who make people swear oaths
of blood-brotherhood" before he veered off again to attack the local
officials for being "spineless and idle." He said how much he agreed
with the Emperor's last edict blaming them, and hazarded that they
only had two reasons for reporting all these trifling matters: one, to
make light of them and thus prove their efficiency; two, to have an
excuse for sending secret memorials (*mi-tsou*), so that they could
claim a close relationship with the Emperor.

The third section of this lengthy memorial dealt with a lot of miscellaneous points: it had thundered in Ho-chien-fu on March 5, the
first day of the *ching-chih* solar period; wheat was growing well in
Shantung and Chiang-nan; Hsiung Tz'u-li had gone to worship at his
native place in Hu-kuang, but would be approached on his return.

To a modern reader this memorial appears tedious, conceited,
sycophantic, and irrelevant. Just because of this it is essential to remember that it was certainly none of these things to the K'ang-hsi
Emperor; for it was on this memorial that he wrote the vermilion endorsement "Noted. In future if you learn any more of these details in
your area, you must send a secret memorial," which was the initial expression of imperial confidence that launched Ts'ao Yin as imperial informant. It may well be that it was the very randomness of the cover-

86. *Ts'ao Yin Memorials*, p. 17.

age, the casual glances at men and local government, at crops and robbers, that the Emperor found so useful.

Even before this long report of March, 1708, Ts'ao Yin had been sending memorials dealing with similar matters. The first of these was in 1707, reporting on two separate disturbances, one caused by a robber band nearly two hundred strong in Kiangsi, the other by local rowdies who had broken into wealthy homes to get food. Both disturbances had been suppressed. Like Li Hsü's memorial of 1693, Ts'ao Yin's memorial was clearly sent without clear authorization, since he concluded it: "I really am afraid that a variety of false rumors are spreading about this, and it is in order to reassure the Emperor that I have dared to memorialize." [87]

Six months later, in October 1707, Ts'ao Yin received the rescript: "This year I hear there is a drought in Chiang-nan. I am very worried by this. I hear there are many cases of robbery." [88] This was clearly a request for information, but Ts'ao Yin remained cautious, answering:

> My office is involved with silk and salt, I do not dare to report on such things. Now I have received the Emperor's orders I dare not but report as carefully as possible. [89]

In his memorial he carefully blamed no one, saying merely that the governor had been away and the local officials overcautious.

The Emperor had good reason to be concerned about robber bands, not merely because they were indicative of the general instability of the provinces, but also because there was a constant threat of the bands' being used for political ends, most especially as a rallying ground for the last remnants of support for the defeated Ming dynasty. It was almost certainly for this reason that a statute of 1675 had ordered local officials to arrest all those who claimed to be gods or buddhas, who gathered crowds, who displayed flags or beat gongs. [90] Li Hsü reported in December 1707 that a gang of robbers wearing red turbans had assembled outside the tomb of the Ming Emperor Yung-

---

87. *Ts'ao Yin Archives*, no. 2709, supplement attached to memorial dated 46/3/4.

88. Endorsement quoted in Ts'ao Yin's memorial dated 46/9/20, *Ts'ao Yin Archives*, no. 2791.

89. *Ts'ao Yin Archives*, no. 2791, dated 46/9/20.

90. *HTSL*, p. 6,838 (ch. 132, p. 4).

lo and raised the Ming standard;[91] a few days later he reported that captured members of the band had claimed that "the Buddhist monk I-nien gave out papers and deluded the people."[92]

Without regular reports from trusted agents it would have been almost impossible for the K'ang-hsi Emperor to be sure of what was going on, and the question of a Ming-loyalist insurrection was still a possibility. More information was demanded from Li Hsü[93] and the remark of Ts'ao Yin's about I-nien's people being "just the same as mounted highwaymen" was to reassure the Emperor on this same topic.

The most dangerous of these later threats was that posed by Chu San T'ai-tzu, the name given to Chu Tz'u-huan, only surviving son of the last legitimate Ming Emperor. Chu Tz'u-huan was living under an assumed name and working as a teacher in Shantung, but in 1708 various uprisings occurred in Chekiang and elsewhere invoking his name.[94] This serious case was naturally handled by the senior provincial officials of the provinces concerned,[95] but Ts'ao Yin reported at some length on local robbers who had also been using the name of Chu San T'ai-tzu and gave further details of Chu Tz'u-huan's alias and places of residence, which must have rounded out the general picture.[96] But it cannot be claimed that Ts'ao Yin acted fast enough to avert any threat to the dynasty, since his first memorial was greeted with the endorsement that Chu San T'ai-tzu was already captured, his second with the endorsement that the matters discussed had been taken care of, his third with the endorsement that the Emperor had heard it long ago.[97]

In one episode that happened just at this time, however, Ts'ao Yin did play a lone and decisive role in handling a situation that was po-

91. *Li Hsü Memorials*, p. 17, dated 46/12/7. This was the memorial lost by Wang K'o-ch'eng.

92. Ibid., p. 17b, dated 46/12/–.

93. In endorsement to Li Hsü's memorial dated 47/2/–, ibid., p. 20.

94. *Shih-liao hsün-k'an*, 2, 20, editor's introduction to memorial on Chu San T'ai-tzu. *Eminent Chinese*, p. 192.

95. A group of memorials on the case are preserved in *Shih-liao hsün-k'an*, 2, 20–22. The K'ang-hsi Emperor recalled this case in 1711 as one in which local officials' failure to act swiftly and catch one or two men led to the growth of large and dangerous bands.

96. *Ts'ao Yin Archives*, no. 2719, dated 47/intercalary 3/12.

97. Endorsements to *Ts'ao Yin Archives*, no. 2719 dated 47/intercalary 3/12; no. 2717 dated 47/4/16; no. 2716, dated 47/6/23 (giving news of the capture of I-nien).

tentially as dangerous as the forming of robber bands who linked their names with those of a Ming prince. It was a tiny incident, but since it involved the Ming tombs, any sort of wild rumor might have sprung from it. Ts'ao Yin wrote:

At the Nanking tomb of the Ming Emperor Hung-wu,[98] in the northwest corner, under a *wu-t'ung* tree, the ground has caved in. The mouth of the hole is five feet and a few inches across, and the hole is about twenty feet deep. It's like looking down a well. I know that at Hung-wu's tomb there is an imperial tablet in the care of the eunuchs. Because rumors were spreading among the people, when the tomb caved in I went and inspected it; the hole is still a little over 150 feet from the underground chamber, and does not affect it. The reason is that previously the earth was not piled up firmly, and as the days passed the rain fell and formed furrows and the water flowed past the tomb enclosure. Now the local officials in charge have ordered the men at the tombs to bank up the earth and level it off. I am afraid that wild stories will start getting around, and such rumors distort the truth and worry the Emperor.

On this memorial the Emperor wrote:

Noted. On this matter it was right to memorialize. Make further inquiries. If there is any more idle talk, send a memorial.[99]

Ts'ao Yin replied that rumors had indeed been spreading. Some people said that the cave-in was over a hundred feet deep and broad at the tomb. Some said the tomb guardians were inefficient, some that thieves had broken in, some that heaven had caused the cave-in because the destiny of the Ming was finished, some that the Ming had built it badly in the first place. Ts'ao Yin checked again and found the hole to be only twenty feet deep, that it was a long way from the tomb, and that it had been caused by rain washing away loose earth.

98. As soon as Nanking surrendered in the summer of 1645, the Manchus named two directors, both eunuchs, to guard and preserve the tomb of Hung-wu, and gave them a permanent staff of forty men and their families who were lodged nearby. This measure apparently gave the new regime excellent publicity. Gaillard, *Nankin*, p. 237.

In 1699 Ts'ao Yin had been ordered to supervise the repair of the Ming tombs at Nanking, payment to be made from public funds. *Ts'ao Yin Memorials*, pp. 8b–9, dated 38/5/26.

99. *Ts'ao Yin Memorials*, p. 18, memorial dated 47/5/25 and endorsement on same.

Then I ordered the tomb guardians to open the tomb enclosure to the public for three days, to let the common people come in and take a look, so that they might all know that the rumors were false. Since then, things have been quiet and there's been no more strange talk. The ground has been leveled off and the area swept and cleaned.[100]

It is a perfect example of a public servant acting calmly and methodically, entirely on his own initiative, to remove all cause of potential trouble at a cost to no one. It was possibly this kind of casual efficiency that the K'ang-hsi Emperor valued in Ts'ao Yin.

Had Ts'ao Yin not died in 1712, the lines along which his role as a secret informant would probably have developed can be seen in the career of Li Hsü, who continued sending secret memorials after Ts'ao Yin's death until the end of the K'ang-hsi reign in 1722. Li Hsü sent detailed reports on the movements of the 5,923 grain boats that left each year from Yangchow,[101] reports which must have made it virtually impossible for the local officials, the grain intendants and even the director-general of grain transport to indulge in the various malpractices and derelictions of duty that several K'ang-hsi statutes prohibited.[102] He sent men over 600 miles to check on the story that sea pirates had raided T'ai-chou-fu in Chekiang[103] and in a follow-up memorial described the fighting and the extortion of money from local fishermen by a brigade-general which had started the trouble.[104] He reported a break in the dike of the Grand Canal near Yangchow and took charge of repairs himself until renewed breaks led to the calling in of the director-general of river conservancy.[105] He reported on wage-stealing by another brigade-general and the ensuing

100. Ibid., pp. 18b–19, dated 47/7/15.

101. *Li Hsü Memorials*, p. 28, dated 51/3/26; p. 29, dated 51/4/22; p. 29b, dated 51/5/15; p. 31b, dated 51/5/26; p. 52b, dated 53/4/11; p. 53b, dated 53/5/7.

102. *HTSL*, p. 6423 (ch. 102, pp. 1b–2), on rewards and punishments for grain intendants based on percentages of quotas filled, fixed in 1710. Ibid., p. 6426 (ch. 102, p. 7b), fixing penalties for each month late over deadline. Ibid., p. 6433 (ch. 103, p. 1) statute of 1675 concerning reports on rotting or unrepaired boats, fixing penalties for failure both to report or repair boats by deadlines. Ibid., p. 7780 (ch. 203, p. 23b) statute of 1683 discussing obligations of director-general to supervise movements of grain boats in *person*.

103. *Li Hsü Memorials*, p. 32b, dated 51/6/22.

104. Ibid., pp. 34b–35, dated 51/8/8.

105. Ibid., p. 44b, dated 52/intercalary 5/23; p. 44b, dated 52/6/9; p. 45, dated 52/7/5.

investigation.[106] He reported on the persecution mania of the Kiangsu governor Chang Po-hsing, who thought that either pirates or avengers were trying to kill him, and consequently refused to leave the city; [107] Chang Po-hsing also arrested some harmless hat sellers from Shensi because he claimed that they were a gang of secret conspirators.[108] Li Hsü also reported on cases of local sorcery: one of name magic, in which repeated invocation of the victims' names brought death,[109] one of hand magic in which the signs made by a man caused a woman's death.[110]

On only one occasion did Li Hsü make a policy recommendation. This was in 1716, during the investigation of the wage-stealing brigade-general. Li Hsü pointed out that the general had been the only official stationed at Ch'ung-ming-hsien, an area 300 *li* from Soochow, isolated and "beyond the reach of the law." Whereas in Ch'ang-shu-hsien, only 80 *li* from Soochow and easy to control, there was a grain intendant and an assistant prefect. In future, suggested Li Hsü, the assistant prefect should be stationed in Ch'ung-ming-hsien, so that "with civil and military forces mutually aiding each other, we can protect the peace everlastingly and establish official harmony." This lucid proposal received the endorsement: "The discussion in this memorial is very satisfactory. Noted." [111]

This memorial was an exception, and there is no reason to suppose that Li Hsü was, or that Ts'ao Yin would have been, expected by the Emperor to make policy recommendations. The inference from Li Hsü's surviving memorials is that the K'ang-hsi Emperor limited his secret informants to the four topics that have been discussed: agriculture, officials, robbers, and rumors. The careers of Ts'ao Yin and Li Hsü were so parallel, they were so clearly trusted by the Emperor and used in such similar ways, that it seems safe to assume that they would have continued at the same occupations. Thus Ts'ao Yin would have

106. Ibid., p. 71, dated 55/5/12; p. 73, dated 55/7/4.

107. Ibid., p. 56, dated 53/7/17.

108. Ibid., p. 53, dated 53/5/7.

109. Ibid., p. 53, dated 53/5/7.

110. Ibid., pp. 55b–56, dated 53/7/13. On this occasion, when the woman's husband returned unexpectedly, the sorcerer made some more signs and restored her to life. The sorcerer was arrested, and though refusing to admit that he could summon the life force, he hinted darkly at the possession of magic powers. He died in prison and rumors about him stopped.

111. Ibid., p. 73b, dated 55/7/4 and endorsement to same.

sent an increasing volume of memorials, but on substantially similar subjects.[112]

The work that Ts'ao Yin and Li Hsü performed as secret informants was an integral part of the K'ang-hsi Emperor's rule. Their courier service and their memorials were alike essential to his exercise of personal government; for in order to check the public bureaucracy the Emperor needed information from purely private sources. For this purpose he chose two men who were both Manchu and Chinese, bondservants and scholars, with knowledge and background that spanned both cultures. For an economic or political historian it might appear that a great deal of Ts'ao Yin's and Li Hsü's time was occupied with trivia; but in neither the political nor economic context of the time were the subjects that they dealt with trivia. Indeed, it was the very precision of detail that kept the Emperor pressing for more and more information, reading it himself and commenting on it himself. Two *ch'ien* variation per picul of rice, a group of robber bands on a provincial border, an ailing grand secretary, the date some grain boats left Yangchow—these were not trivia, and the K'ang-hsi Emperor knew that having accurate information about such things was a part of good government. For the two *ch'ien* marked the difference between contentment and suffering, the robbers might raise the Ming standard, the grand secretary had known the great in the land, the grain boats were a crucial part of the tax payments.

As long as the Emperor could get men that he knew and trusted, the system here described was incredibly efficient and incredibly cheap. It was as a man who could be trusted completely that Ts'ao Yin had his value. And in the last memorials of his life, Ts'ao Yin was called upon to describe one of the most difficult cases of the K'ang-hsi reign—the examination-hall scandal of 1711.

The Examination-Hall Case of 1711 and the Mutual Impeachment of Gali and Chang Po-hsing

The results of the Chiang-nan provincial examination of 1711 were posted in Yangchow on October 20 and caused an immediate storm of protest. For among the names of those who had been granted the *chü-*

112. The memorials of Li Hsü as printed in *Wen-hsien ts'ung-pien* occupy 116 double pages. Of these 116, 33 cover the years from 1693 until Ts'ao Yin's death in 1712. The remaining 83 pages cover the years 1712 to 1722.

jen degree there were no less than thirteen licentiates from the one city of Soochow, many sons of rich salt merchants, and several candidates known to be of inferior literary ability who could never have passed honestly. Foremost in the protest were those licentiates, holders of the junior *hsiu-ts'ai* degree, who had just failed the same examination. They claimed that the governor-general Gali and the deputy examiner had been in league to sell *chü-jen* degrees and to bribe the junior examiners.

On November 4 over a thousand students assembled in Yangchow. Carrying on their shoulders images of the five gods of wealth, as a protest against the alleged corruption, they broke into the prefectural school and ridiculed and then locked up the director of studies who tried to placate them. They composed scurrilous songs punning on the names of Tso Pi-fan the chief examiner (*chu-k'ao*) and Chao Chin his deputy examiner (*fu-chu-k'ao*); as a last gesture they pasted pieces of paper over the tablets at the entrance to the "Provincial Examination Hall" so that the characters read "Provincial Sales Hall." So great was the disturbance that the governor-general felt he had to report the matter to the Emperor.[113]

Ts'ao Yin, who at this time was completing his fourth term as salt censor, was in Yangchow and reported on the scandal in a palace memorial. He wrote that the licentiates believed that they had been unfairly treated, that two sons of rich salt merchants had been the

113. The best concise account of the examination-hall case of 1711 is in Shang Yen-liu, *Ch'ing-tai k'o-chü k'ao-shih shu-lu*, pp. 309–10. Two other accounts, with some embroidery, are in *Ch'ing pai lei-ch'ao*, section 25, pp. 80–81, and *K'ang-hsi nan-hsün pi-chi*, pp. 91–94. Gali's memorial is not in the printed sources; Ts'ao Yin mentioned that both Gali and Chang Po-hsing had sent memorials on the case in his memorial of November 1711 (*Ts'ao Yin Memorials*, p. 3b).

Such riots after examinations were not uncommon. Six years earlier the *chü-jen* candidates of Shun-t'ien had brought pressure to bear on the officials in a similar manner, by parading through the streets with, and subsequently decapitating, two straw figures bearing the names of the chief and deputy examiners; cf. *Wang Hung-hsü Memorials*, p. 17.

The anger and frustration of the candidates, and the scale of the rioting, shows how seriously the *chü-jen* degree was taken, and justifies historians' claims that "the *chü-jen* status was a crucial one in the stratification of Ming-Ch'ing society" (Ho Ping-ti, *The Ladder of Success in Imperial China*, p. 27). Ho Ping-ti (ibid., p. 193) warns that such rioting was often motivated by frustration alone, without real justification; in the 1711 examinations, however, the investigations proved that the students had been quite right to protest. The enormous Chihli scandal of 1657 (described in Ho Ping-ti, ibid., pp. 191–92) was probably the one taken as a precedent by the K'ang-hsi Emperor in the 1711 case; cf. *Shih-lu*, ch. 250, p. 21.

first men arrested, and that many of those who had passed the examination were known to lack the requisite literary ability. He added that the deputy examiner Chao Chin was suspected of being guilty of corruption.[114]

The existence of a considerable amount of documentation on this examination-hall case makes it possible to see Ts'ao Yin in his context—as one of a number of men reporting to the Emperor on an identical matter. That same November, besides a memorial from Gali and a palace memorial from Ts'ao Yin, the Emperor got reports on the case from the Kiangsu governor Chang Po-hsing, summarizing the events to date,[115] and from the chief examiner Tso Pi-fan, who naturally reported the possibility of corruption in an examination that he had supervised with some trepidation.[116] The ordinary memorials were passed on to the Board of Rites for deliberation, but the contents of Ts'ao Yin's memorial remained known only to the Emperor and Ts'ao Yin himself. As well as having an impartial report on the case, the Emperor had learned one interesting fact from Ts'ao Yin, namely that the deputy examiner Chao Chin was believed to be behind the corruption. Other memorialists had blamed dishonest students or the minor associate examiners (fang-kuan), local magistrates called in to help run the examination; but Ts'ao Yin had pointed to a member of the metropolitan bureaucracy with a special appointment as deputy examiner. Corruption at this level was a serious matter.

Ts'ao Yin had to leave Yangchow in December and go to Peking to report on his year's administration of the Liang-huai salt revenues; but the Emperor did not lack for secret information on the examination-hall case since Li Hsü was still in Kiangsu and could take up where Ts'ao Yin had left off. Li Hsü's first palace memorial on the case was written on February 22, 1712. He wrote that two of the new chü-jen were being tried; one had been passed because he was a friend of Chao Chin's, the deputy examiner, the other because he had distributed fifteen ingots of gold among various middlemen, though the exact details of this bribery had not yet been uncovered. The four-man commission that the Emperor had appointed to try the case was

---

114. *Ts'ao Yin Memorials*, p. 3b, dated approx. 50/10/–.
115. *Shih-lu*, ch. 248, p. 12b.
116. Ibid., p. 8.

making slow progress: "Each one sticks to his own views and there is no final agreement." [117]

While this memorial was on its way to Peking, the trial of the suspected *chü-jen* candidates took a surprising turn. Two members of the commission conducting the trial impeached each other in lengthy memorials. The governor-general Gali impeached the Kiangsu governor Chang Po-hsing for dishonesty, dereliction of duty, incompetence, and disrupting the course of the trial; [118] Chang Po-hsing impeached Gali for having received 500,000 taels either by direct sale of *chü-jen* degrees or as hush money to stop him from exposing the corruption, and for torturing witnesses who crossed him. [119] A fairly straightforward examination-hall scandal had suddenly been transformed into a direct confrontation between the Manchus and the Chinese: Gali, a Manchu in the Plain Red Banner, descended from one of Nurhaci's trusted councillors, had taken no exams and risen through merit to be governor-general of Liang-chiang; [120] Chang Po-hsing, a Chinese from Honan, holder of the *chin-shih* degree, had risen to be governor of Kiangsu because of his reputation for incorruptibility. [121]

On March 10, 1712, the Emperor acted on these impeachment memorials. Gali and Chang Po-hsing were both dismissed while the charges were investigated, and acting officials were appointed in their stead. In an edict to his senior officials, the Emperor took the unusual step of giving his own views on the case before the investigation had even started.

This edict was a study in impartiality. Gali was a talented administrator, it ran, and an expert at arresting robbers, "but his unswerving integrity cannot be guaranteed." Chang Po-hsing was of unswerving integrity, "but he has still not managed to catch the thieves near his own yamen." As to the statement in Chang Po-hsing's memorial that

117. *Li Hsü Memorials*, p. 26, dated 51/1/16. The four-man commission of Chang P'eng-ko, Gali, Chang Po-hsing, and the Anhwei governor had been appointed in December by the K'ang-hsi Emperor over the heads of the Board of Rites, which had suggested that the suspect *chü-jen* be brought to Peking for reexamination (*Shih-lu*, ch. 248, p. 19).

118. *Ch'ing-shih lieh-chuan*, ch. 12, p. 29, and *Shih-lu*, ch. 249, p. 8b.

119. *Ch'ing-shih lieh-chuan*, ch. 12, p. 10, and *Shih-lu*, ch. 249, p. 8b.

120. *Eminent Chinese*, pp. 268 and 291.

121. Ibid., pp. 51–52.

Gali had received 500,000 taels—"it cannot be completely true nor can it be completely false." As to the charges made by Gali against Chang Po-hsing—"there must be two or three items that are quite true." Gali was a brave man who had had the courage to attack the pirates in his area when all the other officials had been frightened and backed out; for this reason the local officials of Chiang-nan, Fukien, and Chekiang showed envious hatred toward him. But Gali had once impeached Ch'en P'eng-nien who was known to be a good official.

But the Emperor was not just dealing with a clash between incompetent incorruptibility and corruptible competence, and the tensions arising therefrom. He was confronting something much more dangerous, the threat of an open battle between his Manchu and Chinese officials. Continuing his edict, he stated one aspect of the difficulty:

> Investigation of this case is really difficult. If I order a senior Manchu official to investigate, I think that he will protect the Manchus. If I order a senior Chinese official to investigate, I think that he will protect the Chinese.

His solution was the appointment of a two-man Sino-Manchu investigating committee, composed of the Chinese president of the Board of Revenue, Chang P'eng-ko, and a Manchu from the Plain Yellow Banner, Ho-shou, who at this time was director-general of grain transport.[122]

The K'ang-hsi Emperor had appointed a new commission to carry out the investigation, but he did not intend to accept their findings uncritically and was anxious about the effects of the mutual impeachment on public opinion. At the same time that he delivered his edict on impartiality, he sent this endorsement to Li Hsü:

> The governor-general and the governor do not get on well, this is common knowledge. The governor is an honest official who does not seek a single coin. The governor-general is astute in public affairs, diligent, and careful. What is the state of public opinion (*chung-lun*) in your southern area? Make further enquiries, memorialize clearly and speedily.[123]

122. *Shih-lu*, ch. 249, p. 9.
123. *Li Hsü Memorials*, p. 26b, endorsement to memorial dated 51/1/16.

Li Hsü replied on March 25. People believed that Chang Po-hsing had impeached Gali over the examination-hall case because of personal hatred; they thought that Gali had had nothing to do with the sale of *chü-jen* degrees, that he was not corrupt, that he "has managed affairs skillfully and intelligently, is greatly loved by the people, and has brought the area much benefit." Furthermore, in Nanking and Yang-chow the people had closed the markets to show their support of the governor-general and had repeatedly begged Li Hsü to send a memorial to the Emperor, requesting that Gali be retained in his post.[124] Li Hsü's description of the extent of popular support for the Manchu Gali is interesting in view of the caution that the Ch'ing Emperors had previously displayed in appointing Manchus to high provincial office. By the early eighteenth century Manchus were clearly acceptable to the local populace, though it is impossible to tell from surviving records whether Gali's support was genuinely popular, or derived largely from Banner troops and his own entourage.

Six days later, on March 31, Li Hsü sent another secret memorial, warning that the situation was rapidly getting out of control. Not only were the markets closed and the people vociferously supporting Gali, on March 28 they had barricaded the city gates to prevent Gali from sending his governor-general's seal to the official appointed by the Emperor to act in his stead; following this the people had offered the seal first to the Anhwei governor, who pleaded sickness, and then to Li Hsü. According to Li Hsü he himself acted at this point with a restraint and tact that dispersed the crowd. On the following day an official had managed to leave the city with the seal, and the people responded by blocking the entrances to Gali's yamen with stones and timber and allowing no one to leave or enter. Both soldiers and people were very disturbed. Chang Po-hsing's governor's seal had, however, been sent off without incident. The Emperor's rescript was short but flatteringly informal and frank: "What did Chang Po-hsing say when he saw this state of affairs? How is Chang P'eng-ko doing?"[125]

Chang Po-hsing, Li Hsü replied the following month, had protested that the common people were prejudiced in favor of the governor-general, and felt that he was being unfairly treated. Then, as Li Hsü

124. Ibid., p. 27, dated 51/2/19.
125. Ibid., dated 51/2/25.

reported it, Chang Po-hsing took immediate action to restore his rather battered public image:

> Placards appeared on the streets saying that the governor was a virtuous administrator, and there were popular ballads. A group of men went round to every yamen, taking a petition that he should be retained at his post.

Chang P'eng-ko, on the other hand, was doing almost nothing. People believed that he was being circumspect for some reason. After three months of trial he was "still vague and without a lead," and all the important provincial officials were kept hanging around Yangchow and could not take care of their administrative duties.[126] It was becoming apparent that neither of the two imperial commissioners, Manchu or Chinese, was willing to go deeply into the examination-hall case or to make a definite decision on the relative guilt of Gali and Chang Po-hsing.

Ts'ao Yin, who had returned to Yangchow from Peking, elaborated on this point in a memorial written at the beginning of May. Summarizing the progress of the examination-hall case, he noted that Chang P'eng-ko was concentrating on the two guilty *chü-jen,* Wu Pi and Ch'eng Kuang-k'uei, and was making no attempt to investigate the two examiners, Tso Pi-fan and Chao Chin, since he feared that this might lead to complications. It was commonly believed that Chang P'eng-ko was "trying to mediate out of court between the governor-general and the governor to finish the case," while the Manchu, Ho-shou, "didn't give any judgment and waited to see who would win."

Ts'ao Yin also mentioned that the popular agitation had died down. People still thought that Gali was innocent of the charge that he had sold *chü-jen* degrees and still believed that Chang Po-hsing had impeached him out of a desire for revenge, but they no longer protested about it. Support for the two men now came mainly from minor officials directed by selfish motives rather than by any genuine affection for either of them, and the common people despised both Gali and Chang Po-hsing for acting pettily and selfishly.[127]

Later in May Ts'ao Yin memorialized that the imperial commission-

---

126. Ibid., p. 28, dated 51/3/26.
127. *Ts'ao Yin Memorials*, p. 4, dated approx. 51/3/26.

ers were still not going deeply into the case despite the fact that one of
the key witnesses, the associate examiner Ch'en T'ien-li, had strangled
himself immediately after a colleague had reversed his deposition under torture. Part of Chang Po-hsing's evidence that there had been
corruption in the examinations had rested on Ch'en T'ien-li's testi-
mony, and now people thought "that he was probably threatened into
killing himself, so as to stop the secret being revealed." Nor was investigation of the two impeachments going any better: Gali and Chang
Po-hsing made statements every day in court and wrote out their own
depositions, but they were never brought face to face, and it seemed
impossible to reconcile them.

The Emperor showed his frustration, and his awareness of the frustration of others, in the endorsement he returned to Ts'ao Yin; to be
read by Ts'ao Yin alone, it was probably a true statement of his feelings at the time.

> You cannot conceal public opinion. In Peking also there is much
> random discussion and they treat this trial as a joke. This is not
> the proper way to carry out a judicial investigation. But
> throughout the province of Chiang-nan everyone is shamed by
> it. I think that the Manchu [Ho-shou] is longing to get away
> from this job, then he'd be happy. Make further inquiries and
> memorialize again.[128]

In May and June of 1712, both Ts'ao Yin and Li Hsü sent
memorials on the detailed development of the cases, including the
depositions of the various witnesses, so that long before the official
findings were reported the Emperor was in possession of all the relevant facts.

The trial had revealed, they told him, that two separate methods of
cheating had been used. Two of the *chü-jen*, Ch'eng Kuang-k'uei and
Hsi Kan, had confessed that they had smuggled test material into the
examination hall. Reexamination had proved that their own calligraphy was not the same as the calligraphy on the papers they had submitted. It was also known that Wu Pi had used a code phrase "ch'i
shih yu," a harmless phrase meaning "this is really so" which he had
introduced into his paper at a certain prearranged point, where bribed

128. Ibid., pp. 4b–5b, dated approx. 51/4/21.

associate examiners could pick it up and recommend that the paper be passed.

Li Hsü in a memorial of June 19 summarized Yangchow public opinion as being critical of the imperial commissioners for failing to find out how the senior examiners had been involved in the sale of *chü-jen* degrees; after six months they "had not brought out the real facts of the case." The Emperor agreed: "What I heard was about the same. In Peking this is talked about as a joke." Ts'ao Yin was more openly contemptuous of Chang P'eng-ko's delaying tactics in the impeachment memorial investigation and of the secrecy with which he cloaked his movements, and he gave an astute forecast of the commissioners' probable course of action: "As I see it, the intention of Chang P'eng-ko and Ho-shou is probably to accuse them both of being wrong, and then wait for the Emperor's edict to settle the case." [129]

The Emperor's endorsements show clearly that he was interested in the general tenor of public opinion and in the amount of support that Gali and Chang Po-hsing could count on in the provinces. He had sent a special edict to Chang P'eng-ko ordering him to clarify the matter of "the local elite (*shen-chin*) and scholar-commoners who want to retain the governor-general at his post." [130] Support for Gali had continued strong, and as late as June the Tartar general Ma San-ch'i had written a memorial urging Gali's retention.[131] In the same month, however, Ts'ao Yin was able to reassure the Emperor that though there was still considerable activity, it was no longer of real importance, and showed signs of dying out altogether:

> All yamens have received communications from those who want to retain the governor-general or the governor. Most are for the governor-general, a smaller proportion for the governor. The local elite (*hsiang-shen*) and the well-known local people are divided. Among those calling for retention, soldiers make up most of those for the governor-general, licentiates most of those for the governor. Either they have a bias, or they are whitewashing

129. Ibid., pp. 5b and 6, dated approx. 51/4/30 and 51/5/12; *Li Hsü Memorials*, pp. 29 and 30b, dated 51/4/22 and 51/5/16.

130. *Li Hsü Memorials*, p. 29, reports that Chang P'eng-ko had received such an edict and that Li Hsü had heard he had already replied.

131. Ts'ao Yin mentioned that he had seen Ma San-ch'i's memorial in the Peking Gazette (*Ts'ao Yin Memorials*, p. 5b).

them, or they are local officials who use the pretext of retaining him to save his face, or they are subordinate officials repaying the kindness of their superior. All are haphazard and different. At present they are silent and say nothing.[132]

On June 23 Chang P'eng-ko sent off a memorial announcing the findings reached by the commissioners and the penalties they recommended. In the impeachment case, Gali was exonerated but should be lowered one rank for proffering unjustified charges. Since Chang Po-hsing had been guilty of incompetence, and had falsely accused Gali of receiving a 500,000-tael bribe, he was to be dismissed from his posts and banished (being allowed to redeem the sentence of banishment). In the examination-hall case, one guilty *chü-jen* candidate and his go-betweens were to be strangled, the deputy examiner Chao Chin, two of the associate examiners, and one other go-between named Hsien San were to be banished to malarious districts, and the chief examiner Tso Pi-fan was to be dismissed since the cheating had occurred while he was in charge.[133]

During the trial Ts'ao Yin had been critical of Chang P'eng-ko; when he heard this decision he erupted with the angriest memorial in his career, condemning the sentences passed because they violated the principle of identical punishments for identical crimes. This was the last palace memorial on an important topic that Ts'ao Yin wrote before his death; despite his thirty years as an official, and twenty as a senior administrator, he had not lost the ability to speak with a passionate private voice:

> The chief examiners and the associate examiners, from first to last, have never been thoroughly investigated, and no depositions have been obtained about their complicity in the use of code phrases or the receiving of bribes. The earlier delays occurred because the judges wanted to exonerate the chief examiners and associate examiners from guilt. I think that because there was so much random discussion among outsiders as the trial approached, therefore the judges changed their former vagueness into a verdict of guilty.

132. Ibid., p. 5b, dated approx. 51/4/30.
133. *Shih-lu,* ch. 250, pp. 20–21. *Ch'ing-shih lieh-chuan,* ch. 12, p. 10b. Both Ts'ao Yin and Li Hsü mentioned that the memorial was dispatched on June 23 (51/5/20).

Outsiders also discuss the case in these terms: "If the chief examiners and associate examiners were really guilty of the illegal sale of degrees, they should not just have such a light punishment. If they were not guilty of illegal sales and corrupt practices it is not right that they should be punished so severely. And the same applies to Hsien San: if he has been guilty of intrigue and making illegal sales he also should receive a heavy sentence; if he was not guilty of intrigue and corruption then he should not receive any penalty. Why was it that all the cases were lumped together in this chaotic way?" One cannot avoid there being public dissatisfaction.

To put it briefly, it was Chang P'eng-ko's intention to avoid giving a clear judgment, so as to keep up appearances and to keep a chance of continuing the accusations at a later date.

The Soochow *chü-jen* Hsi Kan was tried for smuggling in test material, he lost his *chü-jen* status and was sentenced to be beaten in the cangue. Ma Shih-lung lost his *chü-jen* status but received no other punishment. The three others were allowed to sit the metropolitan examination. But Hsi Kan and Ch'eng Kuang-k'uei both confessed to smuggling in test material; one is sentenced to be banished, the other to be beaten in the cangue. The same offence and different punishments; I don't know what is the point of this.

Then there is the case of the mutual impeachment of the governor-general and the governor. Gali the governor-general is sentenced to be lowered one rank and retained in office. Chang Po-hsing the governor loses his post and is banished. Outsiders say that the two men were not treated equally, demotion and dismissal are not the same thing.

. . . Chang P'eng-ko wrapped up these cases in a careless fashion because he had spent too much time on them. The director-general of grain transport Ho-shou urged him to make one more careful investigation in an effort to get true depositions, but Chang P'eng-ko would not agree, and on June 23 sent off his memorial and went to Fukien to conduct a trial there.

In such a way they have spent half a year trying an important case, and have settled it with the two words "We think." This time in Chiang-nan Chang P'eng-ko's reputation has been badly tarnished. People say that he was a fool and motivated by personal considerations.[134]

The Emperor's two-character endorsement to this memorial—that the trial was *k'o-hsiao*, "laughable"—may not have been much consolation to Ts'ao Yin, but the public action that the Emperor took on receipt of the imperial commissioners' findings was an open proclamation of everything that Ts'ao Yin and Li Hsü had urged in secret. For in two edicts issued on July 8, 1712, the Emperor totally rejected Chang P'eng-ko's memorials. In words very similar to Ts'ao Yin's, he charged Chang P'eng-ko with failing to get to the bottom of the impeachment case, of "mediating between the two sides and carelessly finishing it off"; and he rejected the verdict on the examination-hall case because it had not got to the bottom of Chao Chin's role in the affair and had applied haphazard punishments to the other offenders.[135]

Had the palace memorials of Ts'ao Yin and Li Hsü not survived, nothing could have appeared more arbitrary and despotic than the K'ang-hsi Emperor's treatment of these two cases. From the surviving official sources the historian would have known only that the Emperor appointed two commissioners to investigate the cases in March 1712, that these commissioners spent four months carefully investigating the cases, only to have their findings summarily rejected by the Emperor who had appointed them. In fact, as the memorials of Ts'ao Yin and Li Hsü show, the investigation was carelessly carried out and brought to a muddled conclusion. Because of the reports that he had received in secret from his informants, the Emperor was able to reject the verdicts on grounds that the commissioners must have known were valid.

After rejecting Chang P'eng-ko's findings, the Emperor appointed two more commissioners, Chang T'ing-shu and Mu-ho-lun, to retry the cases.[136] The evidence in the examination case was examined afresh, the examiners and *chü-jen* were questioned under torture, the tangled threads linking students, go-betweens, and corrupt examiners were unraveled, and stern and impartial punishments were meted

---

134. *Ts'ao Yin Memorials*, pp. 6b–7, dated approx. 51/5/22.
135. *Shih-lu*, ch. 250, pp. 20–21.
136. Ibid., ch. 250, p. 23b.

out.[137] After the evidence had been reviewed and some of the penalties made even stiffer (six men were condemned to death), the Emperor approved the verdicts and the examination-hall case was over.[138]

The new commissioners, however, were unable to decide the impeachment case to the Emperor's satisfaction; like the first commissioners, they exonerated Gali and condemned Chang Po-hsing. The Emperor rejected this verdict because, like the first, it had failed to get to the bottom of the case.[139] He ordered the Board of Civil Office to consider the evidence for a third time. Only a week after they had received this order, the Board reported back on the case: Chang Po-hsing and Gali had both disgraced their offices and should be dismissed. But, they added carefully, the country must have honest and upright officials, and "as to whether or not Chang Po-hsing be dismissed from office but retained at his post, we request the imperial decision." The Emperor's edict was short: "Gali is dismissed from office. Chang Po-hsing is dismissed from office and retained at his post." [140]

As in the examination-hall case, the K'ang-hsi Emperor had stuck to the tried forms of ministerial debate and response, but this time he left his ministers little choice in the matter. What were his motives in

137. *Li Hsü Memorials*, p. 35, dated 51/8/8; pp. 35b–36, dated 51/8/21; p. 37b, dated 51/9/6; pp. 37b–38, dated 51/10/4. Li Hsü summarized the commissioner's findings as follows: deputy examiner Chao Chin had agreed to pass Wu Pi on the urging of Ch'en T'ien-li, and associate examiner Fang Ming had passed Ch'eng Kuang-k'uei because of personal friendship and in the hopes that Ch'eng Kuang-k'uei, after passing, would have enough money to pay off Fang Ming's debts (ibid., p. 37b). Wu Pi had invested the large sum of 8,000 taels in bribes to get the *chü-jen* degree; as well as Chao Chin and Ch'en T'ien-li, Wu Pi's case also involved three more middlemen and possibly the former Anhwei governor Yeh Chiu-ssu. Wu Pi's papers were sent, perhaps by accident, to an associate examiner not in the plot; this examiner was persuaded to recommend Wu Pi by Ch'en T'ien-li, who claimed he was acting on instructions received from Chao Chin. Cf. Shang Yen-liu, *Ch'ing-tai k'o-chü k'ao-shih shu-lu*, pp. 309–10.

138. *Shih-lu*, ch. 253, pp. 6–7. The deputy examiner Chao Chin, who may be considered the prime villain of the case, managed to escape with his life. While he was in a Yangchow prison he was visited by a friend named Wang Shih-tan who helped him to escape. Ironically enough the connection between the two men was that they had passed first and second in the palace examination of 1703; cf. Shang Yen-liu, *Ch'ing-tai k'o-chü k'ao-shih shu-lu*, p. 311, and *Ch'ing pai lei-ch'ao*, section 25, p. 81. In 1716 the Emperor asked his grand secretaries whether Chao Chin was dead or alive, and they answered that nobody knew (*Tung-hua lu*, K'ang-hsi, ch. 97, p. 2).

139. *Shih-lu*, ch. 251, pp. 14b–16.

140. Ibid., ch. 251, p. 20.

pressing so hard for Chang Po-hsing, and bearing down so hard on Gali? Was he posing here as Sage Emperor for the edification of his Chinese subjects? Or with brilliant subtlety, consolidating the imperial position by elevating the honest but naïve scholar, the perfect prototype of the submissive official? Not the first, surely, for in the context the pose was too undignified; the case was a farce, as the Emperor had written to Ts'ao Yin, adding that the Manchus were already uneasy enough. And surely not the second either, for the government interactions were too complex and too important to allow for prolonged incompetence at the provincial level. Nor will an explanation of pure whim stand; irresponsible despotism would not have tolerated such blatant opposition from its nominated judges, nor subsequently promoted them to crucial office.[141]

The Emperor acted as he did, I suggest, because as well as being the final judicial arbiter—the role he had filled in the examination-hall case—he was also a mediator, "mediator" being used here in the precise sense of this definition:

> The mediator's function is primarily to eliminate tension which merely seeks release so that realistic contentions can be dealt with without interference. In addition he may suggest various ways to conduct the conflict, pointing out the relative advantages and costs of each.[142]

In the impeachment case, the K'ang-hsi Emperor was the mediator between the Manchus and the Chinese, and he was compelled to take a long view of the struggle between Gali and Chang Po-hsing. He warned the Manchus clearly enough that he was Emperor of China as well as a Manchu:

> I have been reigning for over fifty years, and all Manchu and Chinese ministers should know my inner feelings: that Manchus and Chinese are all my officials and that I look on them alike and make no distinctions. Those who do not understand this ask how it can be that I do not secretly help Gali. I am lord of all under

141. Of the four imperial commissioners whose verdicts the Emperor rejected, Ho-shou followed Gali as governor-general of Liang-chiang, Chang P'eng-ko became president of the Board of Civil Office, Chang T'ing-shu was reinstated as president of the Board of Punishment, and Mu-ho-lun remained president of the Board of Revenue. *CS*, pp. 2595–2600 and 2884.

142. Lewis Coser, *The Functions of Social Conflict* (London, 1956), p. 59.

heaven and should do all things in accordance with the right. How can I shelter a Manchu alone? [143]

And he had attempted to forestall criticism by preaching unity:

Manchu officials shall not say that I am partial to the Chinese. My heart is directed to public, not selfish, considerations.[144]

At this level the K'ang-hsi Emperor had to speak as one beyond all law, as one who simply knew, by virtue of his office:

I have reigned for over fifty years and am well versed in all matters; never have I made any distinctions between the Manchus, the Mongols, the Chinese bannermen, and the the Chinese people. . . . In what has been discussed, right and wrong have been confounded.[145]

But in ordinary affairs, the Emperor played his hand carefully. To get the information he needed, he used a Ts'ao Yin and may even, after reflection, have based his decisions on Ts'ao Yin's memorials. He picked his informants cautiously and repaid them for their information with his confidence.

In Ts'ao Yin's curious career, these short years as secret informant may have been the most rewarding to him; he was in direct and surprisingly personal contact with the Son of Heaven. The K'ang-hsi Emperor had a knack of getting frank responses to his casually put questions, of stripping some of the awe and distance from the relationship between Emperor and subject. If this was policy rather than knack, then he was a highly intelligent ruler. Ts'ao Yin could feel that he was acceding to a request rather than yielding to coercion, and the result was a more sincere response and a more genuine loyalty.

143. *Shih-lu*, ch. 251, pp. 15b–16.
144. Ibid., p. 18b.
145. Ibid., p. 15b.

CHAPTER 7

The Fall of the House of Ts'ao

The fall of the Ts'ao family, in 1728, was a long time in coming. The sudden death of Ts'ao Yin in 1712 led to no immediate deterioration of the family's fortunes. On the contrary, though Ts'ao Yin was heavily in debt and had been rebuked over the deficits in the salt administration, his death was the signal for the Emperor to bestow exceptional favors upon the family. It is not easy to prove anything as simple as the existence of affection between Emperor and subject; but the K'ang-hsi Emperor's behavior to Ts'ao Yin, his friendly advice and gifts of the rare medicine quinine which he sent by special messenger to treat Ts'ao Yin's malaria, his solicitude for Ts'ao Yin's son, all point to the fact that there was a strong bond between the two men.

Ts'ao Yin's Illness and Death

During the year 1709 Ts'ao Yin grew increasingly weak and rundown. He tried to bolster his strength by taking restoratives, especially ginseng of which he ate dangerously large quantities.[1] The ginseng root was widely regarded as being a life-prolonging medicine, and even the Jesuits found it beneficial; as Father Jartoux wrote at this time after taking some: "I felt my pulse fuller and brisker, I had a good appetite, found myself more sprightly, and was much more dispos'd to endure any toil than I had been before."[2] The best ginseng, which grew wild in Manchuria, was reserved for the Emperor's use,

---

1. Cf. the K'ang-hsi Emperor's endorsement to *Li Hsü Memorials*, p. 33b, dated 51/7/18.
2. *The Travels of Certain Learned Missioners of the Society of Jesus into Divers Parts of the Archipelago, India, China, and America* (London, 1714), p. 216, letter dated Peking, April 12, 1711. Ibid., p. 169, has a letter from Father d'Entrecolles saying that Brother Rhodes had further built up the Emperor's strength by giving him Canary wine, which the missionaries had sent on from Manila for their masses. This may explain the considerable traffic in wine mentioned on p. 120 above.

and if it came on the market cost several thousand taels per picul.[3] It is possible that Ts'ao Yin asked the Emperor for some of this ginseng when he came to Peking in the winter of 1709, to report on his third tour of duty as salt censor.[4] Certainly the state of his health and his penchant for dosing himself with restoratives was a matter of concern to the Emperor, as is shown by the memorials and endorsements they exchanged in the following year.

In the spring of 1710, after returning to Kiangsu, Ts'ao Yin contracted a disease of the eyes. He reported to the Emperor on May 2, assuring him that his eyes were now getting better, and that he was able to write memorials in his own hand again. To this memorial, written with rather thick strokes in the blackest of ink, the Emperor added a concerned endorsement:

> You have been living a long time in the south, and have grown emaciated and weak. Now on top of this you have had an eye disease. It is absolutely imperative that you stop taking restoratives. The best thing for you to drink is a soup with six parts of *ti-huang* (Rehmannia glutinosa);[5] these proportions should not be changed. If you take plenty of this it will certainly be efficacious.[6]

The K'ang-hsi Emperor clearly had a practical approach to medicine, perferring the homely *ti-huang* to the expensive and coveted ginseng.

A month later the Emperor sent Ts'ao Yin a cheerful endorsement concerning the good prospects for the coming year, adding that he "made a special point of telling you this so that you won't go on worrying." [7]

3. For Chinese medicinal plants, cf. E. Bretschneider, *Botanicon Sinicum*, pt. 3, "Botanical investigations into the Materia Medica of the Ancient Chinese," *Journal of the North China Branch of the Royal Asiatic Society*, new series, 29 (1894–99), 1–623. Ginseng is described in ibid., pp. 23–24.

4. *Ts'ao Yin Memorials*, p. 21b, dated 48/11/11, shows that he left Yanchow to see the Emperor in December 1709.

5. Cf. Bernard E. Read, "Chinese Medicinal Plants from the Pen Ts'ao Kang Mu, A.D. 1596," *Peking Natural History Bulletin*, 1936, item no. 107. (For full bibliographical information on this and other works by Read, cf. Joseph Needham, *Chinese Science*, 1, 289–90.) Fr. Hübotter, *Die Chinesische Medizin zu Beginn des XX Jahrhunderts und Ihr Historischer Entwicklungs-gang* (Leipzig, 1929), p. 286, defines *ti-huang* as "Rehmannia Lutea Maxim." The plant is further discussed in Bretschneider, *Botanicon*, pp. 183–85, and in *Pen-ts'ao kang-mu*, XVI.1.

6. *Ts'ao Yin Archives*, no. 2801, dated 49/4/4 and endorsement.

7. Ibid., no. 2802, endorsement to memorial dated 49/5/2.

Before the Emperor's warning and advice had arrived, however, Ts'ao Yin fell sick again and once more tried to cure himself with ginseng.[8] Only at the end of June, after he had taken *ti-huang* as the Emperor recommended, did he write that he was recovering.[9] During the summer and autumn Ts'ao Yin grew steadily stronger, but the Emperor continued to be solicitous, and Ts'ao Yin took his anxious enquiries at their face value. As he wrote in a memorial on December 22, 1710:

> When my household slave returned to the south with my memorial, I found this imperial endorsement: 'Noted. How is your illness now, compared with before?' When I knelt and read this, I could not overcome my feelings and wept. . . . This year I accidentally caught a chill, and because I made the mistake of taking ginseng, I later contracted a painful skin disease (*chieh*), and was ill in bed for over two months. I was fortunate to receive the Emperor's favor, ordering me to take *ti-huang* in soup. After taking it I recovered completely. Now I am taking *ti-huang* pills, and compared with before am in excellent health.

The Emperor's endorsement was equally clinical:

> Noted. But for this kind of skin disease, you shouldn't take drugs. If the poison entered the system, I fear that it might afterward become leprosy. Apart from cleansing with salt water, no other prescription will help you. Take care, take care. You can substitute *t'u-fu-ling* (Smilax sinensis) [10] for tea. Drinking this often is beneficial.[11]

The Emperor's straightforward advice may have had the effect of keeping Ts'ao Yin away from dangerous restoratives. At least through the following year of 1711 he was in good health, and was able to supervise the salt administration. That winter Ts'ao Yin went to Peking as usual to report on his term of office. He wrote poems de-

8. *Ts'ao Yin Memorials*, p. 22, dated 49/10/2, says this was after the third month, when he returned to Nanking from Yangchow.

9. *Ts'ao Yin Archives*, no. 2803, dated 49/6/1.

10. Hübotter, *Chinesische Medizin*, p. 292. Bretschneider, *Botanicon*, pp. 320–23, gives "China Root." Read, *Medicinal Plants*, no. 680, gives Heterosmilax Japonica, Kth. *Pen-ts'ao kang-mu*, XVIII.14.

11. *Ts'ao Yin Memorials*, p. 25, dated 49/11/3 and endorsement.

scribing his short trip in the imperial retinue to the Shih-ju Palace, and noted the Ölöd princes riding by to pay homage to the Emperor; he also pointed out with pride that he was received in audience on one occasion with four Manchu military governors and generals (*chiang-chün*). Leaving Peking on March 16, 1712, he spent sixteen days on the journey to Yangchow, writing poems busily along the way; a stormy crossing of the Yellow River reminded him that once he had hunted in these areas.[12] In Yangchow, he discussed problems in the printing of the *P'ei-wen yün-fu* with the two other textile commissioners Li Hsü and Sun Wen-ch'eng. He had also received orders to confer with the director-general of grain transport Ho-shou, who was one of the judges examining the examination-hall case, but reported that it had "not proved convenient for us to meet face to face."[13] Presumably they needed to meet in private.

During April, May, and June, Ts'ao Yin was busy reporting on the examination-hall case, which he did in a number of detailed and heartfelt memorials,[14] and in pressing on with the *P'ei-wen yün-fu*. He selected over one hundred craftsmen but found that "it's hard to get men as good as they used to be"[15]—that is, in the days when the *Complete T'ang Poems* were compiled. There was also a plague of locusts, he noted, which the acting governor-general had well in hand. In any case, since this was the rainy season the locusts would not grow large, and there was no need to worry.[16]

Leaving Yangchow, Ts'ao Yin returned to Nanking to check on affairs at the textile commissioner's yamen. While there he received a present of calligraphy written by the Emperor, and his last memorial, written on July 6, 1712, was to thank the Emperor for this gift. He wrote that news of the gift had spread abroad, and degree holders, the local elite, and the scholar-commoners clamored to be allowed to see it. So he had had the calligraphy printed from wooden blocks and cir-

12. *Ts'ao Yin Shih*, ch. 8, pp. 2b–3b for Peking visit, pp. 3b–5b for the return journey. The Manchu *chiang-chün* were from Chekiang, Heilungkiang, Sian, and Mukden (the translation of "*chiang-chün*" varies according to locality, BH 744, 802).

13. *Ts'ao Yin Archives*, no. 2825, dated 51/2/2. This date is an error for 51/3/2. Ts'ao Yin mentioned that he left Peking on 51/2/12, also that he was sending the weather reports for the first and *second* months. This, then, was the third month. Arrival in Yangchow on 51/2/26 is corroborated in *Ts'ao Yin Memorials*, p. 4, dated (?)51/3/26.

14. Cf. chapter 6 above; *Ts'ao Yin Memorials*, pp. 4–7.

15. Ibid., p. 25b, dated 51/4/3.

16. *Ts'ao Yin Archives*, no. 2827, dated 51/5/22.

culated, since otherwise "rumors might spread far and near." But now the people wanted a more permanent record of the occasion, so they had gone to select a fitting stone on which to have the Emperor's words engraved. The Emperor's endorsement was practical: "I am well. Noted. There's no need to get it carved on stone." [17]

On July 19, Ts'ao Yin returned to Yangchow, and spent a few happy days with scholars visiting the printing office there. But on August 2 he caught a chill and retired to bed. He dismissed this as a slight illness, and wrote in a poem how a slight sickness could bring its consolations of rest and solitude:

> Just as I drew back the long curtains the dew began to spar-
> kle on the eaves,
> Starting to take off my linen shirt I felt a light chill in the
> air.
> Happily I thought over the clear night when no one had
> much to say
> And I listened peacefully to the sounds of footsteps on the
> west porch.[18]

The chill did not pass; instead, while Ts'ao Yin was in a weakened state, it developed into a bout of malaria. In his last poem, he seems to have realized that this time he was seriously ill; though grateful for the visits of the young members of the family who sought to cheer him up, his thoughts turned somberly to the unknown future facing them all.[19]

When Li Hsü, who was in I-chen checking salt quotas, heard the news of Ts'ao Yin's serious illness, he hurried to Yangchow to be with him, arriving on August 16. Ts'ao Yin was by now too ill to write, so Li Hsü relayed the following message to the Emperor for him:

> Ts'ao Yin said to me: "My sickness comes and goes. The medi-
> cine used by my doctors is of no use; I must get the Emperor's
> own medicine if I am to be cured. But my son is young, and if I
> now send him off to ask the Emperor, there will be no one at my
> side to look after me. Please send a memorial for me, as I would
> do myself. If I am given the medicine, then I may still evade

17. *Ts'ao Yin Memorials*, p. 26, dated 51/6/3, and endorsement.
18. *Ts'ao Yin Shih*, ch. 8, p. 14.
19. Ibid., p. 14b.

death and return to life; I will really have received the Emperor's favor, and be born again."

I am now in Yangchow, to watch his treatment, but his illness has now grown extremely serious. I dare not report anything but the truth.

The Emperor's endorsement was concerned, but also offered practical advice and help:

You memorialized well. Now I wish to make a present of the medicine to cure malarial fever, but I fear it might be delayed, so I am allowing the use of horses from the couriers' office so your servant can rush on, day and night. If the malarial fever has not been complicated by diarrhea, there is no harm in taking the medicine, but if complications have occurred you should not use it. In the south there are so many doctors who all offer some "special tonic" that one can't count them all; you must be careful. Ts'ao Yin was very eager to eat ginseng and now he has caught this disease; it was caused by ginseng.

Quinine alone cures malarial fever. Use two-tenths of an ounce, powdered, mix with wine and swallow. If the fever abates, take one more dose, and then you must stop. Afterward change to doses of one-tenth of an ounce, or eight *fen* [0.08 ozs.], and repeat this twice; this will remove the root of the illness. If he does not have malaria, this medicine must not be used. You must be very thorough, I urge you, I urge you, I urge you.[20]

Ts'ao Yin's request and the Emperor's answer show how completely the positive sides of Western medicine could be accepted in China, and how openly the Chinese could adopt a new technique. The K'ang-hsi Emperor had been offered quinine by the Jesuits Visdelou and de Fontaney, when he was seriously ill with malaria in 1693. The Jesuits themselves had only just been sent the quinine by a fellow Jesuit in Pondicherry, and ran some risks in offering it to the Emperor. The medicine was initially tried out on three men with malarial fever, all of whom recovered. Then four members of the imperial family took small doses of a mixture of quinine and wine prepared by the heir ap-

20. *Li Hsü Memorials*, p. 33, dated 51/7/18, and endorsement on p. 33b.

parent. None of them suffered any ill effects. Finally the Emperor himself took some, and was cured.[21] The K'ang-hsi Emperor had mentioned this cure in the endorsement he added to the first memorial that Li Hsü ever sent him,[22] and this providential intervention by the missionaries was the main reason why they were given a large house near one of the Emperor's inner palaces, to use as a church.[23]

Ts'ao Yin himself had been present on one occasion when the Emperor made a present of quinine. This was during the fifth Southern Tour, in 1705, when the Emperor was being entertained by the brigade general Chang Yün-i. Noting that Chang Yün-i was much thinner than he had been, the Emperor asked the reason, and learned that Chang had been ill nine times with malarial fever. The Emperor then made a present of quinine to Chang, the gift being accompanied by this edict: "This quinine has cured the Emperor himself, and is excellent. These ten ounces are given to Chang." [24] But it required considerable courage to ask the Emperor for a gift of his own medicine, and Ts'ao Yin did not have the nerve to do so until his illness was well advanced. This hesitancy cost him his life. Five days after he had relayed Ts'ao Yin's appeal, Li Hsü sent this memorial:

> On August 2, Ts'ao Yin caught a chill, which developed into malarial fever. Finally it became an incurable illness, and on August 24, at 7 A.M., he died. Lying back on his pillow he sighed with remorse that this sudden departure from the world would mean that he would be unable to repay the Emperor for his favors. He said to me: "At the Nanking textile commissioner's yamen revenue deficits have accumulated over the years and are more than 90,000 taels; and in accordance with the edict received last year that the deficit accumulated by the Liang-huai salt merchants should be paid off by officials and merchants together, I should have paid off 230,000 taels. Yet I have no posses-

21. *Lettres édifiantes et curieuses*, 17, 306–10.

22. *Li Hsü Memorials*, p. 1, endorsement to greetings memorial dated 32/6/–.

23. *Lettres édifiantes et curieuses*, 17, 311. *Sinica Franciscana*, 5, 283.

24. *Sheng-tsu wu-hsing*, p. 16, on day 44/3/28. For further details on quinine in China, cf. Fang Hao, *Chung-Hsi chiao-t'ung shih* [A History of Contacts Between China and the West] (5 vols., Taipei, 1959), 4, 136–37. Quinine is listed by Chao Hsüeh-min, *Pen-ts'ao kang-mu shih-i* [a supplement to the *Pen-ts'ao kang-mu*, preface dated 1765] (Shanghai, 1954 ed.), p. 237. He added that quinine was also used by the Chinese to cure hangovers.

sion I can sell, no resources that I can convert. Though my body may die, my eyes shall remain open." So Ts'ao Yin spoke to me near the end.

Ts'ao Yin's widow and orphans could never pay such sums, Li Hsü continued. It was for this reason that he risked death to ask that he be made salt censor for the 1713 term that would have been Ts'ao Yin's had he not died; with this money Li Hsü would pay off the Ts'ao family debts, and thus at the moment of his death Ts'ao Yin would receive one last imperial favor.

It was a businesslike memorial, but the financial details were rather hazy; the K'ang-hsi Emperor showed his suspicions, though he granted the favor:

> Ts'ao Yin and you were as one person working at the same business, so what you memorialize here is definitely to the point. My only fear is that, as the days pass, you might change, and be concerned only about yourself. If so, you will be even less than my dog or horse.[25]

About three weeks after Li Hsü had written this memorial, his household slave returned with the first memorial warning of Ts'ao Yin's illness, which bore the Emperor's kindly endorsement and advice. The courier with the medicine had arrived some days before, but Ts'ao Yin of course was dead.[26]

More generous, and less concerned with mundane matters of finance, was the epitaph written by Ts'ao Yin's friend Chang Po-hsing. This man, a famous Confucian scholar and governor of Kiangsu, was fighting for survival against the Manchu governor-general Gali in the protracted examination-hall case,[27] but his affection for Ts'ao Yin was clearly not marred by any considerations that Ts'ao Yin as a bondservant was tied to Manchu causes; rather he wrote of Ts'ao Yin in the classical terms of deep affection between Chinese scholars:

> Alas! Who would have thought that his end would come at this time? His collection of the Classics and Histories filled ten

25. *Li Hsü Memorials*, pp. 33b–34, dated 51/7/23, and endorsement.
26. Ibid., p. 36, dated 51/8/21.
27. Cf. chapter 6 above.

thousand *chüan;* whose hand will open them now, whose heart delight in them? And the great officials and talented gentlemen with whom he met each day and delighted in writing and capping verses, whom will they follow, who could possibly have the sprightliness of his character?

In the old days when I held the judge's seal [1706] we were close friends and helped each other; he would talk without any reserve and with absolute sincerity though I was then more superficial. Later I was rushed off to the mountains of Fukien [in 1707] and regretted each day of separation. At night, when the cocks crowed in the rainy wind, it served as a connecting thread for both our thoughts. Little did I expect to return as governor of Kiangsu and sit once more at his table. For three years we were together and I drew from his vast resources; we were one heart as if united, with all the potential strength of a close and inseparable friendship.

Oh what unhappiness! How long it is already since his voice and face were with us; there is no one to take his place. Opposite me the stringed instruments and wine jars are mourning too, the very writing shows honesty and weeps. As these writings are offered all stained with wine, may my heartfelt sincerity be accepted by him.[28]

Chang Po-hsing's tasteful eulogy may serve as the public expression of regret at Ts'ao Yin's death; that regret was deep enough to win Ts'ao Yin a place in the Nanking temple of famous officials.[29] But behind the public presentation of Ts'ao Yin's virtues as friend and scholar lay the private reality of confusion and debts. It was this less attractive matter that Li Hsü had to handle.

Ts'ao Yin's Son Ts'ao Yung

When Ts'ao Yin died on August 24, 1712, his family were left in a desperate situation. They were hundreds of thousands of taels in debt, and without official positions of any kind. Ts'ao Yin's mother, née Sun, who was a favored former nurse of the K'ang-hsi Emperor, had died in 1706, aged seventy-four.[30] Ts'ao Yin's only son Ts'ao Lien-

28. Quoted *HLMHC*, pp. 388–89.
29. Ibid., p. 391.
30. *Ts'ao Yin Memorials*, p. 15, dated 45/8/4. *HLMHC*, p. 350.

sheng (his name was later changed to Ts'ao Yung) was about nineteen years old; he had worked for a short time as a bondservant in
Peking and then been granted permission by the Emperor to return to
Nanking and live with his father.[31] But he had no administrative experience and his prospects must have seemed dim.

Li Hsü had acted fast, sending the memorial in which he requested
to be made salt censor and pay Ts'ao Yin's debts on the very day that
Ts'ao Yin died.[32] The Emperor's acceptance of this request meant
that the Ts'ao family could clear themselves of debt; but it still did
nothing to assure the family's future.

Help for the family came from an apparently unlikely source—the
official Lang T'ing-chi. Lang T'ing-chi was the governor of Kiangsi,
who was at this time also acting governor-general of Liang-chiang.[33]
He and Ts'ao Yin had become friends in 1712, and Ts'ao Yin wrote a
postscript to a short collection of Lang T'ing-chi's poems.[34] Though
they seem only to have known each other for a few months, on September 27, 1712, Lang T'ing-chi sent a memorial that was to have
great importance to the family. He wrote that there had been many
people around his yamen, all begging him to send a memorial requesting that Ts'ao Yin's son Ts'ao Yung be appointed to the office of
Nanking textile commissioner, since Ts'ao Yin's administration had
been so excellent. Lang T'ing-chi gave the names and occupations of
many of the petitioners. It was not a list of names collected for the
purposes of prestige, but must have made the point that those requesting Ts'ao Yung's appointment were sound men who knew the silk
business. The petitioners were factory managers, transport supervisors,
artisans, weavers, and silk merchants. After forwarding their request,
Lang T'ing-chi added the generous comment:

31. *Ts'ao Yin Memorials*, pp. 19b–20, dated 48/2/8 on sending his son to Peking; *Ts'ao
Yung Memorials*, p. 27, dated 51/9/4, mentions the Emperor's special grace in allowing him
to return to his father. HLMHC, p. 305, estimates that Ts'ao Yung's birth was in 1695, making him ten when he talked to the Emperor on the 1705 Southern Tour (cf. p. 149 above),
and fourteen when he was sent off to work in the Imperial Household. I would place his birth
in 1693; he had probably married in 1713, about a year before his death.

32. *Li Hsü Memorials*, pp. 33b–34, dated 51/7/23.

33. Governor-general Gali at this time being under trial for corruption, cf. chapter 6 above.
There is a biography of Lang T'ing-chi in *Eminent Chinese*, pp. 441–42. For his acting
appointment, cf. *Ts'ao Yin Memorials*, p. 25b, dated 51/3/27, and CS, p. 2884.

34. *Ts'ao Yin Wen*, p. 17.

Because I was in the area I was able personally to observe these popular feelings, and can verify adequately the fact that while he was alive Ts'ao Yin managed affairs with all sincerity, both for the Emperor above and the common people below.[35]

Ts'ao Yung must have known that these demonstrations were going on, but he was not rash enough to request the Emperor to give him his late father's office. His first memorial, written on October 3, was one of thanks to the Emperor on three counts. Firstly, the Emperor had given him presents of money that had enabled Ts'ao Yung to get a suitable coffin and take care of all the funeral arrangements. Secondly, the Emperor had responded generously to Ts'ao Yin's pleas, and sent him his own special medicine; it had been an unlucky chance that "my father died unexpectedly before the medicine arrived, negating the Emperor's favor." Thirdly, Ts'ao Yung's elder cousin Ts'ao Ch'i had just arrived from the Capital bearing an edict that he had received from the eunuch Liang Chiu-kung; the edict directed that Li Hsü be made salt censor for a further year in order to pay off Ts'ao Yin's debts, and that Ts'ao Yung was to send a memorial if Li Hsü acted in an unauthorized fashion—in other words, tried to cheat him. Ts'ao Yung praised the Emperor for saving his father's name and allowing the family to live, but ended with a justification of his own behavior which shows clearly the insecurity of the position he was still in:

I am a worthless bondservant, and I ask myself who I am that I dare to act without authority and send a palace memorial? The reason is that I have received the Emperor's edict, which was an unusual bestowal of favor; an insect's feelings of private gratitude cannot be made known in any other way, so I respectfully risk death in writing out this memorial, to thank the Emperor humbly for his favor.[36]

Ts'ao Yung had started off this memorial with these words: "Ts'ao Yin's son Lien-sheng humbly memorializes." He had no title and no office, and could merely claim to be his father's son. But his second

35. *Lang T'ing-chi Memorials*, p. 42b, dated 51/8/27. It received the bare endorsement "Noted."

36. *Ts'ao Yung Memorials*, p. 27, dated 51/9/4.

memorial written on January 28, 1713, led off with the words "The
Nanking textile commissioner and secretary (*chu-shih*) in the Imperial Household Ts'ao Yung humbly memorializes" and proceeded to
relate how the change had come about:

> I am your slave and worthless bondservant, I am young and ig-
> norant, and have gratefully received everlasting and boundless
> special favors, having by special order been made Nanking textile
> commissioner, to continue my father's office. I have also received
> the imperial favor by being given the rank of a secretary in the
> Imperial Household. And yet again I received a special edict giv-
> ing me the adult name of Ts'ao Yung. All these various and great
> favors, repeated without end, are totally without precedent.[37]

As the Emperor had responded to Lang T'ing-chi's request that
Ts'ao Yung be given the office of textile commissioner, so he responded to Li Hsü's plan to save the Ts'ao family from its crippling
load of debts. The 320,000-tael debt that Ts'ao Yin on his deathbed
had confessed he owed and was quite unable to pay, consisted of a
90,000-tael deficit on the Nanking textiles and a 230,000-tael deficit
from the salt administration. So, at least, Li Hsü had reported, and on
the basis of this report the Emperor granted him permission to be salt
censor of Liang-huai for one more year, in order that he might pay off
Ts'ao Yin's debts.[38]

At the end of this extra year as salt censor, in December 1713, Li
Hsü reported that he had collected a total surplus of 586,000 taels.
This sum had been brought to Ts'ao Yung by Li Hsü and the Liang-
huai salt merchants together, to avoid any suspicions of dishonesty.[39]
To a memorial of thanks sent to the Emperor on December 30, Ts'ao
Yung appended a financial statement showing exactly how this money
had been used: 210,000 taels had gone for the basic annual expenses at
the textile commissioners' yamens in Nanking and Soochow; 12,620
had gone to pay for sacrificial silks, official patents, and artisans' wages

37. Ibid., pp. 27b–28, dated 52/1/3, with the misprint of date in arrival in Nanking as
2/2. This should be 1/2 (January 27). Lang T'ing-chi used, in his 51/8/27 memorial, the
name Ts'ao Yung. Yet Ts'ao Yung signed himself Ts'ao Lien-sheng in his 51/9/4 memorial.
This suggests that though his adult name was generally known, he himself did not feel free
to use it until specially permitted to.

38. *Li Hsü Memorials*, pp. 33b–34. Cf. page 262 above.

39. Ibid., pp. 48b–49, dated 52/11/12.

in Nanking, where Ts'ao Yung was now textile commissioner in succession to his father; 5,000 had gone on the purchase of materials, transport, and factory maintenance at Soochow and Nanking; 230,000 had been paid into the salt controller's treasury to meet the salt deficit; and 92,000 used to meet the Nanking textile deficit remaining from Ts'ao Yin's administration. These various sums totaled 549,620 taels, which still left 36,400 remaining from the total surplus.[40]

It was difficult for Ts'ao Yung to know exactly how he might use this outstanding surplus of over 36,000 taels, and in February 1714 he took the safest course of sending it off to the Emperor as a contribution toward the moneys needed at the imperial stables. The Emperor, however, knew that the Ts'ao family were still financially pressed and returned 30,000 taels with this friendly endorsement:

> In the days when Ts'ao Yin was alive, his only fear was that this deficit could not be made up. Now that he is no longer here, it has been settled. This will bring happiness to your mother's household. You must be careful with this surplus money; besides, the expenses of a textile commissioner are not small, and I think that your household still has some private debts. I only want 6,000 taels for the stables.[41]

This endorsement shows that the K'ang-hsi Emperor did follow the affairs of the Ts'ao family with close attention. By this time it was almost three years since Ts'ao Yin had mentioned, in one of his memorials on salt administration, that he had contracted considerable debts through raising private loans. The Emperor was not solely concerned with official finance, but also with personal problems.[42]

Thanks to friends' appeals and the Emperor's sympathy, Ts'ao Yung was now a textile commissioner and his family freed from pressing debts. But in none of the seventeen palace memorials that he sent

40. *Ts'ao Yung Memorials*, pp. 28–29, dated 52/11/13. These figures show that Ts'ao Yin's declared debts at this time totaled 322,000 taels. The remaining 227,620 taels were spent on the normal annual expenses of the *chih-tsao* offices. Thus Ts'ao Yin's debts were not 549,620 taels as mentioned in *Eminent Chinese*, p. 742, although the final sum of his debts was probably in excess of this figure.

41. *Ts'ao Yung Memorials*, p. 29, dated 52/12/25, and endorsement.

42. *Ts'ao Yin Memorials*, p. 23, dated 50/3/9. Of course it is more than probable that these private debts had been contracted while carrying out the Emperor's commissions, as Ts'ao Yin suggested.

during his short career did he mention textile matters, except to say that the money received from Li Hsü had been used to pay off the Nanking deficits and to meet current expenses.[43] His memorials were nearly all brief, listing the rice prices in his locality and enclosing weather reports. What had been an occasional matter for Ts'ao Yin was now apparently strict routine for his son. On nearly every occasion he received the simple endorsement "Noted." When the Emperor wrote something extra, as he did to an August 1714 memorial reporting on prices after a drought—"When this memorial returns to you at Nanking, memorialize speedily on the rain situation" [44]—Ts'ao Yung responded immediately by sending a special memorial, although he had just sent one nine days previously reporting that all was well.[45] He acted in a similar spirit when he sent back to the Emperor all of the 36,000 taels remaining when the deficit left by his father was paid off.[46] So even from the straightforward administrative reports which are all that survive from Ts'ao Yung's life, a picture of the man emerges: he took his slightest duties very seriously, was extremely cautious, and desperately anxious to please his Emperor.

It is unlikely, therefore, that he knew that Li Hsü had taken the amazing step of trying to get him appointed salt censor in the autumn of 1714. Even Li Hsü did not have the nerve to request outright that Ts'ao Yung, twenty-one years old by this time, with eighteen months of experience as a textile commissioner, be given this important and complex post. Instead, he sent a report to the Censorate, presenting them with the facts regarding Ts'ao Yung's name and ranks; since the information came from the incumbent salt censor of Liang-huai, its intention was plain, and on September 20, 1714, the Censorate in turn memorialized that it had received this information from Li Hsü.[47] It is clear enough what Li Hsü was trying to do. He and Ts'ao Yin had alternated as Liang-huai salt censors over a ten-year period, from 1704 to 1714. Now if Ts'ao Yung, the new textile commissioner of Nanking, were made salt censor, there was a chance that he and Li Hsü might alternate in the profitable office for a further long period.

43. *Ts'ao Yung Memorials*, pp. 28b–29, dated 52/11/13.

44. *Ts'ao Yung Archives*, no. 2835, dated 53/7/2.

45. Ibid., no. 2837, dated 53/8/11, and no. 2836, dated 53/8/2.

46. *Ts'ao Yung Memorials*, p. 29, dated 52/12/15.

47. *Tung-hua lu*, K'ang-hsi, ch. 94, p. 2, dated 53/8/12, gives an incorrect homophone for the Yung of Ts'ao Yung's name. The name is correct in *Shih-lu*, ch. 260, p. 3.

Li Hsü's suggestion was not followed up. In his edict responding to the memorial, the Emperor pointed out that there had been a deficit of 1,800,000 taels which had been cleared up by the salt controller Li Ch'en-ch'ang; since this was a clear proof of his ability, Li Ch'en-ch'ang should be the new salt censor and a man of his caliber be recommended to succeed him as salt controller.

This decision was a rebuff to Li Hsü, but it did not affect the Ts'ao family's newly regained prosperity. Ts'ao Yung continued to work as textile commissioner in Nanking, and in the winter of 1714 he traveled to Peking, probably to escort a shipment of silk for the Emperor. There can have been nothing to prepare the family for the next blow: the sudden death in Peking of the twenty-one-year-old Ts'ao Yung.[48] He had been Ts'ao Yin's only surviving son.[49] Now Ts'ao Yin's widow was truly helpless, and the family line threatened with extinction.

Once again, the family was saved by the personal intervention of the K'ang-hsi Emperor. In February 1715 he ordered that Ts'ao Yin's nephew Ts'ao Fu be posthumously adopted as Ts'ao Yin's son, and also inherit his new father's office.[50] Thus Ts'ao Fu became the fourth successive member of the Ts'ao family to hold the post of Nanking textile commissioner, and the family line had new hope of survival.

Li Hsü's memorial of thanks caught some of the pathos of Ts'ao Yung's early death, as well as the way the new son Ts'ao Fu was taking over under his tutelage:

I am humbly suggesting that Ts'ao Fu should pick a day in this month to take Ts'ao Yung's coffin out of the city, and place it in a temporary shelter at the ancestral tombs; and that when he has done that, he should memorialize for permission to take up his Nanking appointment. Because Ts'ao Fu's mother [Ts'ao Yin's widow] is nearly sixty, and has been all alone in the south attending to her husband's coffin, when she learns also that her son has

48. Evidence for Ts'ao Yung's death in Peking some time during 53/12 or 54/1 is in *Li Hsü Memorials*, p. 60, dated 54/1/18, and *Ts'ao Fu Memorials*, p. 30, dated 54/3/7. *HLMHC*, p. 404, suggests 54/1 as more likely.

49. Chou Ju-ch'ang thinks Ts'ao Yin may have had a son in his old age who died young (*HLMHC*, p. 50).

50. *Li Hsü Memorials*, p. 60, dated 54/1/18. This edict cannot have been issued in 54/2 (March 1713) as stated in *HLMHC*, p. 403, since Li Hsü acknowledged it on 54/1/18 (February 21, 1715).

died young, I fear that she will grieve terribly. Furthermore the costs of boat and carriage here and back will be hard for her to meet. The best thing that can be done is to order Ts'ao Fu to go on ahead and console her day and night. When the cold weather is over, then he and his mother can accompany Ts'ao Yin's coffin to its place of burial.[51]

Before Ts'ao Yin had been finally buried he had lost his only son and been granted a new one by imperial favor.

Ts'ao Yin's Adopted Son Ts'ao Fu

Ts'ao Fu left Peking on March 14, 1715, traveling south to Nanking with Li Hsü. While they were still on the road, Ts'ao Yin's widow learned of the Emperor's renewed favors to her family, and insisted on making the long journey to Peking so that she might thank the Emperor in person. Hearing of the old lady's journey, Ts'ao Fu and Li Hsü hurried to intercept her; the two parties met at Ch'u-chou in Anhwei province, and returned to Nanking together. She was dissuaded from traveling to Peking by being told that the Emperor had said she need not make the journey. By April 2 the family were assembled in the Ts'ao house in Nanking; three days later Li Hsü officially read them the Emperor's edict, which stated that Ts'ao Fu was henceforth to be regarded as Ts'ao Yin's son, that he was to succeed his father as textile commissioner, and that they should wait for fair weather before escorting Ts'ao Yin's coffin to the northern burial grounds. After this edict had been read (the family of course had known its contents for some weeks), Ts'ao Yin's widow led out the whole family to give ritual thanks to the Emperor; all faced toward the Emperor in Peking and prostrated themselves while she beat her head on the ground and wept, as incense burned on specially erected altars.[52] Four days later Ts'ao Fu collected his seals of office and began work as textile commissioner.

51. *Li Hsü Memorials*, p. 60, dated 54/1/18, with endorsement "So be it" (*shih*).

52. Composite sequence drawn from *Ts'ao Fu Memorials*, p. 29b, dated 54/3/7; and ibid., p. 30, same date. And from *Li Hsü Memorials*, p. 61, dated 54/3/10. In his memorial Ts'ao Fu also mentioned that the widow of his brother Ts'ao Yung, née Ma, was in her seventh month of pregnancy at this time, and that there was thus a hope of Ts'ao Yung's having a posthumous son, and Yin's direct male line being preserved. There is no later mention of the birth of this child, which might have been a girl, or else a boy who died in infancy. It is also possible that the son was born, survived, was adopted automatically by Ts'ao Fu, and was

Once again the family was on an even keel, with a working official —albeit also in his late teens [53]—at the helm. Though Ts'ao Yin had died so heavily in debt, owing to the Emperor's generosity in granting a further term as salt censor to Li Hsü the money had been collected, the accounts balanced, and a generous allowance been given to the Ts'ao family to take care of their personal debts. Ts'ao Yin should have been able to close his eyes and rest in peace, while his heirs continued happily at their work, freed from financial worries.

Such would have been the case had Ts'ao Yin's debts been calculated accurately, but subsequent examinations proved that matters were not so simple as they had appeared. The large debts had arisen because Ts'ao Yin had been compelled to use his salt revenues to pay for his textile works and his imperial commissions; the expenses were high and constant, but the revenue was irregular and only directly controlled by him once every two years when he was officially salt censor. It was obviously an unsatisfactory system, and the Emperor seems to have been aware of this; at least he did not criticize the Ts'ao family or Li Hsü for debts of this kind. In the last resort, the existence of the debts did not matter to the Emperor as long as he had a tight control over the salt merchants. For it was really the salt merchants who were paying the Emperor for his court fineries and his diversions.

Ts'ao Chan, the author of the *Dream of the Red Chamber*. This would accord perfectly with Wu Shih-ch'ang's belief that Ts'ao Chan was born "in the spring of 1715" (*On the Red Chamber Dream*, p. 118). For further discussion of this turbulent question, cf. appendix D below.

53. The problem of Ts'ao Fu's exact age is also a complex one. It is my belief that Ts'ao Fu was born not earlier than 1698, and thus was made textile commissioner when seventeen or eighteen. This is even younger than Chou Ju-ch'ang thinks, and of course far younger than Wu Shih-ch'ang believes, in *On the Red Chamber Dream*, p. 99. Wu Shih-ch'ang's thesis requires Ts'ao Fu to be fairly old, since he dates Ts'ao Chan's birth in 1715, and thinks that Ts'ao Fu was Ts'ao Chan's father. Chou Ju-ch'ang is content to have Ts'ao Fu young, since he dates Ts'ao Chan's birth in 1724. I think that Ts'ao Chan was born in 1715, and that Ts'ao Fu was young, very young. Hence Ts'ao Chan cannot have been his son. The evidence that Ts'ao Fu was very young at his assumption of office in 1715 is overwhelming. Apart from his own deprecatory remarks in his memorials of thanks, which could be dismissed as clichés, there is the fact that in 1718 the K'ang-hsi Emperor referred to him as a "child" (*hsiao-hai*). Cf. *Ts'ao Fu Archives*, no. 2859, dated 57/6/3, also cited *HLMHC*, p. 410. Such a term would surely not be applied to a man over twenty. Even more importantly, in 1727 the salt censor Ka-erh-t'ai memorialized that Ts'ao Fu was "young in years" (*nien-shao*), *YCCPYC*, *ts'e* 39, page 92b, dated Yung-cheng 5/1/18. Such a term is not likely to have been applied to a man over thirty.

The duty of Ts'ao Yin and his colleagues was to see that they continued to do so.

It must have been for this reason that when (only one year after the Emperor had made over the whole annual surplus from Liang-huai to clearing the Ts'ao family debts) Li Hsü admitted in a memorial that there were still serious uncleared deficits in the Nanking textile commissioner's yamen, the Emperor ordered the new salt censor Li Ch'en-ch'ang to take care of them from the 1715 surplus.[54] Li Hsü relayed this news of continuing imperial favor to the grateful Ts'ao family in Nanking, but only one year later he received a communication from the Board of Revenue that led him to send a flustered and apologetic memorial to the Emperor begging for further favor.

From Li Hsü's memorial, written on February 25, 1716, it is clear that officials from the Board of Revenue had been going through the various accounts submitted by the Liang-huai salt authorities—with incredible slowness, it is true, but also thoroughly enough to bring to light some of the grosser irregularities. What they had found was that Li Hsü had deliberately concealed a further debt of 110,000 taels: this was a sum that Ts'ao Yin should have furnished to pay off the merchant deficit. Li Hsü, acting as salt censor in Ts'ao Yin's place, had not paid this money into the treasury, but had used it to pay off further undeclared debts at the Nanking textile commissioner's yamen. It is not surprising that the unraveling of such complicated financial juggling had taken the Board a long time. They held that the Ts'ao family should furnish the additional money, since Ts'ao Yin had been theoretically responsible for the payment. The fact that Ts'ao Yin had been dead at the time does not seem to have worried them, any more than the fact that Li Hsü had falsified the accounts. The Ts'ao family were ordered to make good the sum of 110,000 taels, which of course they could not possibly afford to pay. Accordingly Li Hsü, with a dazzling example of evasive action, wrote that he risked death in begging the Emperor to extend his mercy to the Ts'ao family.[55]

In the same memorial Li Hsü added that though he had previously written that Ts'ao Yin's salt administration debts had been 263,000

54. *Li Hsü Memorials*, p. 60, dated 54/1/18. Chou Ju-ch'ang, in *HLMHC*, p. 405, points out that it is impossible to tell if this deficit was still Ts'ao Yin's or a new one of Ts'ao Yung's.

55. *Li Hsü Memorials*, p. 68, dated 55/2/3, with additional information in ibid., p. 87, dated 56/9/9.

taels, this figure must now be amended to 373,000 taels. This final assessment of salt administration debts makes it possible for the full extent of Ts'ao Yin's liability to be calculated. For there were in addition the textile commissioner's debts of 92,000 taels that had been declared in 1712, and the further debt of 110,000 that had been covered up by means of the misappropriated salt funds. There were also the private debts that the Emperor was aware of, and to pay off which he returned the 30,000 taels offered by Ts'ao Yin's son. It is therefore reasonable to assess Ts'ao Yin's debts at his death at about 600,000 taels.

The K'ang-hsi Emperor took care of the whole of this amount by allowing the surplus salt revenues for successive years to be used in paying them off. The debts were finally cleared in August 1717, five years after Ts'ao Yin's death, when Li Hsü had been made salt censor for an eighth term.[56] Though the Emperor seems to have been casual enough about the whole question of public debts, he showed a surprising interest in the exact state of the Ts'ao family finances, and to one of Ts'ao Fu's short memorials sending rice prices and weather reports he added this endorsement: "Why don't you send a report about the state of affairs in your family." [57] Ts'ao Fu clearly took this to be an order to report on their current resources, and did so as follows:

> Since my appointment I have made a detailed examination of the resources remaining. There are only two dwelling houses in the Inner City of Peking, and at Hsien-yü-k'ou in the Outer City there is one empty house. At T'ung-chou we have the mortgage on 600 *mou* of land. At Chang-chia-wan we have one pawnshop with a capital of 7,000 taels. In Chiang-nan at Han-shan-hsien we have over 200 *mou* of rice fields, and at Wu-hu-hsien over 100 *mou* of rice fields. In Yangchow we have one old house. Besides these there are no businesses or savings.
>
> I asked my mother, and the stewards in the house, and they all said: "When your father was alive his expenses were extremely large and he was not able to look after the houses. Concerning these properties, and our accounts, your elder brother Ts'ao Yung reported to the Emperor in person, and received everlasting favor

56. Ibid., p. 85b, dated 56/7/13. The figure of 263,000 shows that the earlier estimate of 230,000 was too low, and emphasizes Li Hsü's general casualness with figures.

57. Ts'ao Fu Archives, no. 2857, dated 54/6/3.

from the Emperor who granted Ts'ao Yung 30,000 taels. Only then was he able to pay off our private debts."

After I was appointed I sent memorials where fitting, but because there were so many other details, I did not dare introduce such trifling matters.[58]

Judging from later accounts of the Ts'ao family resources, this report was a considerable understatement. It gives, for example, no mention at all of the Ts'ao family mansions in Nanking and their valuable contents. These were probably taken for granted, since the Emperor had visited the family in Nanking on four occasions. But even if it underestimates, the report gives an inkling of the geographical spread of the Ts'ao family's commercial and agricultural operations—from T'ung-chou, east of Peking, to Wu-hu and Han-shan in southern Anhwei, and to Yangchow on the Grand Canal. Ts'ao Fu clearly thought it advisable to make some token offering to the Emperor in gratitude for favors received; accordingly, one month after the dispatch of his memorial on the family situation he sent the Emperor a present of 3,000 taels, to be used for the purchase of camels needed in the Western campaigns. The gift was accepted and handed over to the Boards.[59]

As textile commissioner, Ts'ao Fu's basic duty was managing the Nanking manufacturies and dispatching the silk quotas to Peking. Like his brother Ts'ao Yung before him, he sent regular short memorials on rice prices and harvest prospects—this had become a routine task for the textile commissioners.[60] In addition to these regular duties he also, like Ts'ao Yin before him, performed various commissions for the Emperor. The first of these on record, in early 1716, was to look after the children of the former grand secretary Hsiung Tz'u-li. This was the statesman whose death Ts'ao Yin had reported in such detail seven years before. Ts'ao Fu memorialized that there were three surviving male children: the eldest was seriously ill; the two young ones, aged nine and eight *sui*, worked away at their studies behind

58. *Ts'ao Fu Memorials*, p. 31, dated 54/7/16.

59. Ibid., p. 30b, dated 54/9/1.

60. He sent such brief price records in the fourth, sixth, seventh, ninth, tenth, and eleventh months of 1715, his first year in office. Cf. *Ts'ao Fu Archives*, nos. 2873, 2857, 2846, 2847, 2856, and 2848.

closed doors and did not go out. "The household makes a bare living. I have sent them 200 taels to take care of their household expenses," Ts'ao Fu wrote, earning the brief endorsement: "Good. Noted." [61]

Another time he and Li Hsü jointly brought a tablet, presented by the Emperor, to be hung in the P'u-chi hall. Both men recorded the reception of the present and the people's reactions in the effusive memorials customary upon such occasions. The K'ang-hsi Emperor was apparently bored enough by the repetitiveness of their language to depart from the normal endorsement "Noted." Instead he wrote: "There shouldn't be such a rumpus about this tablet." [62]

The two men also worked together on a project to restore the great T'ien-ning temple near Yangchow. The Emperor ordered them to furnish estimates of the work involved, and this they did in an enormous report which listed all expenses under fifteen heads. For each building they estimated the costs for bricks and tiles, stone and timber, paint and nails, as well as the wages of the carpenters and stonemasons. They concluded that the total cost would come to 14,243.36 taels, and added that the salt merchants of Yangchow had offered to donate all the money. Should they accept the offer? The Emperor's lengthy answer shows that when Ts'ao Fu sent such reports, they were definitely read; and also that the K'ang-hsi Emperor, never averse to accepting a donation to his exchequer, was still well aware of the value of making nominal official contributions to charitable works. He wrote:

> I have examined your palace memorial on materials and wages. The total is not large. Although the merchants are willing to make a general contribution it is also proper that some money from the treasury be used. Draw 500 taels from each of the textile commissioner's treasuries at Soochow, Nanking, and Hangchow. The rest can be paid for by the merchants, or by others

61. *Ts'ao Fu Memorials*, p. 32b, dated 55/2/5 and endorsement. In 1721 the K'ang-hsi Emperor issued a general appeal for support of the family of Hsiung Tz'u-li, a man who had had over 1000 disciples (men passed by him in examinations), yet whose family lived in poverty. Wang Hung-hsü and others gave a sum of 3,000 taels, which was handed over to Ts'ao Fu. He was ordered to use the interest from this sum to pay for the family's expenses. *Ch'ing pai lei-ch'ao*, section 49, pp. 82–83. Other references in *HLMHC*, p. 411.

62. *Ts'ao Fu Memorials*, p. 32, dated 55/6/13; and *Li Hsü Memorials*, p. 72, dated 55/6/15, with cited endorsement.

who want to make contributions. You must emphatically not take a penny more than what is needed for materials and wages.[63]

In addition to carrying out his duties as textile commissioner, and performing various extra tasks for the Emperor, Ts'ao Fu also began to edge into the role of secret informant. The way that he did has close parallels in the careers of Li Hsü and Ts'ao Yin; [64] he made initial reports on his own initiative, received at first vague and then specific imperial encouragement, and then sent detailed secret memorials.

Ts'ao Fu sent his first report of this kind in November 1715, at the end of his first year in office. The whole memorial was only eighty-eight characters in length:

> The mother of the Chiang-nan governor-general Ho-shou was eighty-one this year, and on November 20 she died in his yamen. All the townsmen, fearing that he would leave his post to observe the mourning period, closed the markets and would not let the governor-general hand over his seal; they implored him to remain. The Tartar general and others made repeated appeals and at last got the markets opened. As is fitting I send a palace memorial on the local situation, and beg the Emperor to examine it.[65]

Like the best of Ts'ao Yin's memorials in the past, this was a concise statement that covered most of the main issues and people involved; once he had read it, the Emperor would be well prepared to handle any excited reports of outbreaks of violence in Nanking, or laxity by the governor-general.

The Emperor did not comment on this particular memorial, but the following summer he sent specific orders for Ts'ao Fu to make an investigation on his own: "I hear that in Chekiang there has been heavy rain and that the people's life is difficult. I do not know whether this is

63. *Ts'ao Fu Archives*, no. 2852, dated 59/6/10, joint memorial with Li Hsü, with endorsement and enclosure. Ts'ao Fu's other commissions were sometimes paid for with surplus money received from Li Hsü, as in the case of 5,000 taels paid over in 1717 (*Li Hsü Memorials*, p. 87, dated 56/9/9), or 16,000 taels shared by the two men in 1716 (ibid., p. 78, dated 55/11/18).

64. Cf. the first part of chapter 6 above.

65. *Ts'ao Fu Memorials*, pp. 30b–31, dated 54/11/1, with endorsement "Noted."

so or not. You must make detailed inquiries and memorialize."[66] Ts'ao Fu replied that he had sent someone to make inquiries in Hang-chow, and that they had found nothing wrong. But Ts'ao Fu decided that this answer was inadequate, and he followed it up the next week with another memorial, in which he gave details of conditions and rice prices in six major Chekiang prefectures.[67] Ts'ao Yin and Li Hsü had never been instructed to memorialize on matters so far afield; the Emperor must have had his suspicions of the honesty of Chekiang local officials, and wanted an impartial report from an outsider.

In September 1716, however, Ts'ao Fu apparently lost whatever credit he might have gained by the thoroughness of his Chekiang report. For a greetings memorial in which he reported that the harvests were excellent and that the salt censor Li Ch'en-ch'ang had died in office, was returned with this angry endorsement:

> Noted. Prices of rice are still high; how could you say there was a hundred percent harvest? Also, writing about sickness and death in a greetings memorial to the Emperor is grossly improper.[68]

Ts'ao Fu had made a serious blunder, both reporting too hastily and offending the Emperor. For almost two years he stuck to his normal duties and received no special orders. Then suddenly, in July 1718, one of his short memorials on rice prices was returned with this cordial endorsement:

> I am well. Although you are an ignorant child, yet the things you manage are not simple ones. I remember that your father served me with all his strength for many years, and for this reason you have received special favors. Although you are not a local official, you also can send secret memorials about major or minor matters which you hear about, as your father used to do. I myself will make judgments as to their validity. If something turns out to be a joke that's O.K. Let your old Emperor have a good laugh and it will be all right.[69]

66. Endorsement in *Ts'ao Fu Archives*, no. 2853, dated 55/7/5.

67. Ibid., no. 2854, dated 55/7/14, with enclosure.

68. Ibid., no. 2858, dated 55/8/1, and endorsement.

69. Ibid., no. 2859, dated 57/6/3. Also quoted in *HLMHC*, p. 410. The endorsement ended with the extremely colloquial clause: "chiao lao-chu-tzu hsiao-hsiao yeh hao."

Presumably the Emperor meant that even matters that Ts'ao Fu might consider frivolous should be reported, and that if he made errors through youthful enthusiasm he would be forgiven. Strangely enough, the only lengthy memorial that Ts'ao Fu sent in answer to these orders was indeed calculated to make the Emperor laugh. The memorial described the machinations of two confidence men. One, a doctor named Hua Tzu-wen, cured the other, named Ho Ts'an-kung, of a serious illness. The two became friends, and Dr. Hua confided that he was planning a commercial venture beyond the seas. He produced forged seals and documents, and promised Ho Ts'an-kung a return of 50 taels if he would subscribe two taels now. Ho Ts'an-kung produced one and a half taels and two bolts of cloth; these he gave to the doctor, who promptly disappeared. Instead of brooding about his loss, Ho Ts'an-kung thought the ruse over and found it rather a good idea. He accordingly printed dozens of forged papers, which he sold to the gullible country folk at two taels each. The case was now being investigated by the senior provincial officials, Ts'ao Fu concluded, but it was obvious that only poor and ignorant people were involved, and that there was nothing to worry about.[70]

There may have been something of importance in the background of this case, or perhaps rumors had reached the Emperor that grossly exaggerated it, but it seems to have been a trifling affair. The only other case on which Ts'ao Fu memorialized, one in which an assistant district magistrate who was heavily in debt falsely accused the Anhwei judicial commissioner Nien Hsi-yao, involved more important people but was again a minor matter.[71] For whatever reasons, Ts'ao Fu did not use the license to report on local affairs that the Emperor had given him, and it cannot be claimed that he performed any outstanding services as a secret informant.

The most interesting project on which the K'ang-hsi Emperor employed Ts'ao Fu was the introduction of new rice types to Kiangsu. This called for a certain amount of agricultural knowledge, which Ts'ao Fu clearly did not possess, but after the first unfortunate year he acquitted himself fairly creditably. In the spring of 1715 the K'ang-hsi Emperor sent Li Hsü one picul (*shih*) of a new type of rice that

70. *Ts'ao Fu Archives*, no. 2849, dated 57/intercalary 8/1.
71. Ibid., no. 2851, misplaced in archives but possibly dated 59/2. For Nien Hsi-yao, the elder brother of the famous Nien Keng-yao, cf. *Eminent Chinese*, pp. 588 and 590.

grew fast enough to allow two sowings and harvestings each year; should this type prove successful, it would have profound effects on rice harvests, since previously early-ripening or late-ripening rice had been used largely in areas where natural conditions made normal rice planting impractical, or where rice was rotated with another crop such as wheat.[72] Now there was a chance of almost doubling rice production in an already prosperous rice-producing area. Li Hsü, as ordered, distributed the new rice to senior officials, to Ts'ao Fu, and to three members of the Soochow local elite. Ts'ao Fu received one peck (*tou*, 1/10 of picul); both he and Li Hsü planted their samples in the fourth month, and harvested them in the seventh. Ts'ao Fu's crop yielded the ratio of one unit of seed to seventy units of harvested rice, making 4.2 piculs per *mou*; Li Hsü's crop, sown on high ground, yielded one to sixty, 3 piculs per *mou*.[73] Both men reported that the local elite and peasants alike were amazed, and clamoring for samples of their own.

The experiment, which had started so well, ended in failure this first year. Ts'ao Fu, "unable to overcome my fear," had to report that his second crop had not yielded full grain; Li Hsü was more specific: the sprouts were tall but poorly grown, yielding under one picul per *mou*, a ratio of about one to twenty.[74] The Emperor calmed both men by pointing out that they had merely sown both crops far too late. Li Hsü, who happened to be in Peking after bringing a batch of dragon robes from the south, was sent off to consult with rice expert Li Ying-kuei.[75]

72. Ho Ping-ti, *Studies on the Population of China, 1368–1953* (Cambridge, Harvard University Press, 1959), pp. 169–76, discusses the spread of late- and early-ripening rice varieties. The rice seed distributed by the K'ang-hsi Emperor was apparently one that would grow both early and late; it was thus different from Champa and other varieties of early-ripening rice, which were alternated with a late-ripening variety. Cf. Katō Shigeshi, *Shina keizai shi kōshō* (Studies in Chinese Economic History) (2 vols. Tokyo, Toyo Bunko, 1952–53), 2, English abstract 20–21.

73. *Li Hsü Memorials*, p. 63, dated 54/5/16; p. 63b, dated 54/6/6; p. 65b, dated 54/8/20. *Ts'ao Fu Archives*, no. 2869, dated 54/8/20. Ts'ao Fu planted 6 *sheng* yielding 4.2 *shih*; Li Hsü 3 *tou* yielding 18.25 *shih*.

74. *Ts'ao Fu Memorials*, pp. 31b–32, dated 54/12/1. *Li Hsü Memorials*, p. 66b, dated 54/11/17. The figure of a one to twenty yield assumes that he sowed 6 *mou* as he had in the spring; thus 3 *tou* yielded 6 *shih*.

75. Endorsement to *Ts'ao Fu Archives*, no. 2869, dated 54/8/20; and *Li Hsü Memorials*, p. 65b, dated 54/8/20; p. 66b, dated 54/11/17; p. 67, dated 54/11/20. Li Ying-kuei, who was probably an official in the Imperial Household at this time, was a bondservant in the Plain

Li Hsü failed to benefit from Li Ying-kuei's instruction. In a puzzled memorial sent to the Emperor in the spring of 1716, he wrote that the local Soochow rice shoots and the imperial samples were growing at different speeds, and the latter were ready to be transplanted long before the former—"these types seem to be basically different." The Emperor was contemptuous: "You are not acquainted with the seasons and intercalary months. Your confused statements about the spring cold are incomprehensible. You are like a blind man groping down the road," he wrote in endorsement.[76] But after this unfortunate start, the season proved successful. Li Hsü reported yields of 3.7 piculs per *mou* on the first harvest, and a yield of 1.5 piculs per *mou* on the second. The second harvest was low because heavy gales in the early autumn had ruined many plants; even so the yield was far higher than local rice, which took from 140 to 150 days to ripen, and that year had yielded 3.9 piculs per *mou*. Ts'ao Fu reported yields of 3.7 piculs per *mou* on the first harvest, and from 2.2 to 2.8 on the second. The Emperor was pleased with these reports, and both memorialists were told to circulate the rice samples as widely as possible: Ts'ao Fu throughout Chiang-nan, and Li Hsü to Chekiang and Kiangsi. As much of the new rice as possible should be kept as seed, the Emperor added, and should not be wastefully eaten.[77]

In 1717 both Ts'ao Fu and Li Hsü obeyed the Emperor's injunctions. Ts'ao Fu sent a list of the yields of the new rice samples, giving details on the amount of land sown and the reported harvest registered by all individuals to whom seed had been issued in a fifty-mile belt of land along the Yangtze, stretching from Nanking to Wu-hu.[78] Li Hsü sent samples of the new rice to Chekiang, Kiangsi, and Anhwei, as well as to all the local elite, peasants, and salt merchants who requested it. In a succession of memorials he reported the fantastic success of the new rice: the eighty *mou* that he planted near Soochow

---

White Banner who became honorary vice-president of the Board of Revenue and a *ch'i-ku tso-ling*. Cf. *PCTC*, ch. 5, p. 40; *PCST*, ch. 74, p. 2b, which adds radical 167 to the "Ying" of his name.

76. *Li Hsü Memorials*, p. 70b, dated 55/intercalary 3/12, and endorsement.

77. *Ts'ao Fu Archives*, no. 2875, dated 55/7/14; and no. 2870, dated 55/10/1, with endorsement on circulation in Chiang-nan and against wasteful eating. *Li Hsü Memorials*, p. 72b, dated 55/6/25; and pp. 75b–76, dated 55/10/2, with endorsement on circulation locally and in Chekiang and Kiangsi.

78. *Ts'ao Fu Archives*, no. 2871, dated 56/7/20, with enclosure.

yielded 4.1 piculs per *mou* on the first harvest, and 2.5 on the second. Not surprisingly, there was a rising demand for sample seeds.[79] These figures may have been exaggerated to please the Emperor, but the regular lists of the yields of various rice types, including the new samples, furnished by Li Hsü over the next four years, show an average yield of about four piculs per *mou* on the first harvest, and two piculs on the second.[80] Ts'ao Fu, after a shaky start, had played a considerable part in a minor agricultural revolution in the Yangtze valley region. To put it mildly, in his own words of November 1716, "now that the common people can add one more crop a year, they will receive very great profit." [81]

This was the most successful episode in Ts'ao Fu's career, which on the whole was an undistinguished one. He had been overcautious as an informant; he was rash as a financier. In the summer of 1719 he sent a complex memorial to the Emperor in which he requested that he be given the monopoly for the purchase of copper. Ts'ao Fu's plan was that by saving on transport he would cut costs by 30,000 taels—"or if starting next year I am permitted to manage it for ten years, I will save in all 300,000 taels." At the present time, Ts'ao Fu continued, copper purchase was in the hands of eight governors-general and governors; every year forty foreign ships brought 40,000 piculs of red copper, and the officials drove up prices by competing against each other for its purchase. Ts'ao Fu would take advantage of a recent decision by the Boards that in times of dearth 30 percent of the copper quota might be provided in the form of old copper utensils; then, needing only 31,000 piculs of copper, he would confront the incoming foreign merchants with his monopoly. The merchants would bring 40,000 piculs as before. Ts'ao Fu would only want 31,000 piculs. Prices would tumble, and the government would save large sums of money. Perhaps the governors-general, Ts'ao Fu added, should still be allowed to provide the 30 percent of old copper utensils; he would handle everything else, with money drawn from the provincial treasury. If the money were given to him one year in advance, that would be even better. Ts'ao Fu did not neglect to mention that his

---

79. *Li Hsü Memorials*, p. 81b, dated 56/3/11; p. 84b, dated 56/6/29; p. 87b, dated 56/10/11.

80. Cf. appendix C below.

81. *Ts'ao Fu Archives*, no. 2870, dated 55/10/1.

father Ts'ao Yin had managed copper purchases for eight years, and that there had been no deficits or delays.

The Emperor's endorsement was unambiguous:

> It's absolutely out of the question to go ahead with this matter. In those days, if Ts'ao Yin had no deficit it was because he took money from Liang-huai. How could this commission be handed on to you? In later days you would have the deepest regrets.[82]

One of the Emperor's last endorsements, written in 1720, was equally discouraging on another topic. Ts'ao Fu had apparently been carrying out certain commissions for the Emperor that involved the dispatch of porcelain ware to Peking, and the application of cloisonné to such ware. The porcelain had been disappearing, and Ts'ao Fu received this endorsement:

> Now I do not know how many pieces of porcelain have been dishonestly removed, I really have no idea. From now on, if you get orders from anyone except me, you must make it known to me in a secret memorial, and memorialize their names. If you conceal such cases and fail to memorialize, when the matter is brought out into the open, I fear that you will be unable to bear the responsibility. And when you are punished with the others, you may regret it but it will be too late. If you receive the imperial commission on any other matters, the same applies.[83]

There is little doubt that at the end of his reign the K'ang-hsi Emperor's tolerance of the Ts'ao family was wearing thin.

The Fall of the Ts'ao Family

The K'ang-hsi Emperor died in December 1722, and almost immediately afterward Li Hsü was dismissed from his post as Soochow textile commissioner.[84] It was, for the Ts'ao family, an inauspicious be-

82. Ibid., no. 2850, dated 58/6/11, and endorsement.

83. *Ts'ao Fu Memorials*, p. 32b, endorsement to memorial dated 59/2/2.

84. CNTC, ch. 105, p. 10, says Li Hsü was *chih-tsao* until K'ang-hsi sixty-first year, his successor Hu Feng-hui taking office in Yung-cheng first year. Since such appointments were usually made rapidly, and CNTC does list successions taking place the same year, it may be presumed that Li Hsü left office in 61/11 or 61/12 (late December 1722 or January 1723). Evidence that he was dismissed is from *Yung-hsien lu*, p. 412, where he is described as "Li Hsü the degraded official" (*hsüeh-chi*).

ginning to the new reign. Admittedly Li Hsü was now in his seventies [85] and had not had a brilliant record, but he had been a favorite of the K'ang-hsi Emperor, and his dismissal meant definitely that the old order was changing.

The Yung-cheng Emperor had several attitudes to men and government that could not but hurt the Ts'ao family. As a disciplinarian he was for rigid control of household slaves and was often openly contemptuous of bondservants, whom he castigated as petty, dishonest, and disobedient.[86] He had a low opinion of the importance of the textile commissioner's office where men "did no more than listen to rumors and send on what they heard," [87] and felt that to be a salt censor "one need merely be clearheaded on handling finance." [88] He was bitterly opposed to cliques, and swift to punish incompetence and dishonesty.[89] In the first year of his reign he dismissed or shuffled around thirty-seven out of the forty-five senior Board ministers and censors.[90] He took a close interest in provincial finance, and especially in Kiangsu, with its large economic potential yet everpresent deficits.[91] And he backed up his attempts to regulate both the economy and his officials' conduct in two ways—institutionally, in bodies such as the office to control expenditure (hui-k'ao-fu), which functioned from 1723 to 1725; [92] and personally, by granting permission to many junior officials to send secret palace memorials reporting on their colleagues.[93] He thus greatly extended the system of informants that the K'ang-hsi Emperor had initiated, and went so far as to reprimand those allowed to send memorials on local affairs who failed to do so.[94]

The tribulations of the three textile commissioners in the early years

85. Cf. calculations on p. 212 above (note 157, chapter 5), that he was born in 1650.

86. Endorsements in YCCPYC, ts'e 8, pp. 14 and 16, on chia-jen; ts'e 13, p. 46, and ts'e 47, p. 37b, on bondservants.

87. Ibid., ts'e 50, p. 69, endorsement to Kao Pin memorial dated Yung-cheng 6/6/2.

88. Ibid., ts'e 39, p. 96, endorsement to Ka-erh-t'ai memorial dated Yung-cheng 6/5/10.

89. Examples of each in Yung-hsien lu, pp. 341–54, and 301–02, or throughout Eminent Chinese biographies of this period.

90. CS, p. 2609 (with two men on p. 2608, in the last month of the K'ang-hsi sixty-first year).

91. Examples are in Yung-hsien lu, p. 103; and in YCCPYC, ts'e 25, pp. 1–8; ts'e 60, p. 2; ts'e 38, pp. 102–03.

92. Wen-hsien ts'ung-pien, 43 (1937, no. 7). And later, of course, through the Grand Council.

93. YCCPYC, ts'e 48, p. 51; ts'e 47, p. 2; ts'e 2, p. 78b.

94. Ibid., ts'e 47, p. 40.

of the Yung-cheng reign are a good example of the way the new Emperor investigated and destroyed those whom he found wanting. Li Hsü's successor as Soochow textile commissioner, Hu Feng-hui, was in fact the first to go. Hu Feng-hui, a former district magistrate and department director in the Imperial Household, owed his position to the fact that his wife was the sister of one of the Yung-cheng Emperor's favored concubines.[95] He was thus appointed by court favor, exactly as his displaced predecessor Li Hsü had been. His first task was to check up on Li Hsü's various debts, and he did this competently, even disinterring one deficit that dated from 1693.[96] His second report was good enough for him to be told to work with the Kiangsu governor.[97] But when he turned to sending secret reports about fellow officials, the results were disastrous. Next to his first adverse comment about another official, the Yung-cheng Emperor wrote: "Most incautious. Look out for your head." And when Hu Feng-hui added that he had seen the erring official A-erh-fa and was teaching him the truth, he received the chilling endorsement: "Teaching A-erh-fa is secondary. It is teaching Hu Feng-hui that is the important thing." [98]

Things went from bad to worse. Further endorsements accused him of sending muddled memorials, of being careless, of being disobedient; [99] at the same time local officials kept an eye on him, and brought him further warnings from the Emperor.[100] Finally on March 15, 1726, the governor of Kiangsu and an Imperial Household official named Kao Pin called on Hu Feng-hui at his office to inform him that he had been relieved of his duties. At the end of March, Hu Feng-hui, his wife (née Nien), and his concubine Lu, all committed suicide.[101]

95. *Yung-hsien lu*, p. 265.

96. YCCPYC, *ts'e* 48, p. 101, memorial dated Yung-cheng 1/3/22.

97. Ibid., pp. 101b–02, dated Yung-cheng 1/4/5.

98. Ibid., p. 102, interlinear endorsements to memorial dated Yung-cheng 2/12/18. A-erh-fa was a Bordered Blue Banner bondservant, a *tso-ling* and later *ts'an-ling*. PCTC, ch. 10, p. 31b; and PCST, ch. 75, p. 6b.

99. YCCPYC, *ts'e* 48, endorsements to memorials on pp. 102b–03, dated Yung-cheng 3/7/26; p. 103b, dated 3/9/26; p. 104, dated 3/10/3.

100. Ibid., *ts'e* 12, p. 46; *ts'e* 8, p. 1b.

101. Ibid., *ts'e* 50, p. 61, Kao Pin memorial dated Yung-cheng 4/2/21, that they called on Hu on 4/2/12. (Kao Pin, bondservant and father of a Ch'ien-lung concubine, became a great official; cf. *Eminent Chinese*, pp. 412–13.) *Yung-hsien lu*, pp. 265–66, records that the suicides occurred in Yung-cheng 4/2. Hu was alive up to 4/2/21 when Kao Pin memorialized, so he must have killed himself almost immediately afterward.

Hu Feng-hui died with his family partly because he had been dishonest as textile commissioner, but mainly because he had become involved in the vicious political war that the Yung-cheng Emperor was fighting with those of his brothers whom he believed to be hostile to him. Both Yin-ssu and Yin-t'ang, the eighth and ninth sons of the K'ang-hsi Emperor, were to die in prison during 1726 after being degraded and arrested by the Yung-cheng Emperor, who was convinced that they would continue to resist his title to the throne.[102] Hu Feng-hui's wife Nien was the sister of the imperial concubine Tun-su, and her brother was the powerful official Nien Keng-yao. But late in 1725 the concubine fell seriously ill, and died soon after; then Nien Keng-yao was accused to having communicated with the Yung-cheng Emperor's brother Yin-t'ang. He was stripped of all his ranks, accused under ninety-two separate counts, condemned, and permitted to commit suicide.[103] The Ts'ao family must have watched this grim succession of events with alarm; for not only was Ts'ao Fu being rather unsuccessful as textile commissioner, but there were two gilt lions, over five feet high, standing in the family temple—and these lions had been presented to him by that same hated brother of the Yung-cheng Emperor, Yin-t'ang.[104]

The Ts'ao family held out a little longer. In the interim, Li Hsü was the victim again. Though he had been out of office since 1723, he must have remained under official surveillance, and in late March, 1727, he was arrested on the charge that he had been sending gifts to Acina's serving maid.[105] The word "Acina" means "cur" in Manchu, and was the humiliating name that the Yung-cheng Emperor had forced his brother Yin-ssu to adopt. Li Hsü was apparently involved with others in a clique, but it is not known what the specific charges against him were, nor what became of him.

In the meantime, the other two textile commissioners were not going unwatched. Sun Wen-ch'eng, Ts'ao Yin's old friend who had been commissioner at Hangchow since 1706, had come under suspi-

102. The subject is deftly covered by Fang Chao-ying in his three biographies of the brothers in *Eminent Chinese*, pp. 915–19, 926–27, 927–28.

103. *Yung-hsien lu*, pp. 265–66. *CS*, p. 3497 for short biography of concubine Nien (Tun-su). *Eminent Chinese*, pp. 587–90 for Nien Keng-yao biography.

104. Sui Ho-te memorial, dated Yung-cheng 6/7/3, cited in *HLMHC*, p. 420; translated in part in Wu Shih-ch'ang, *On the Red Chamber Dream*, p. 284.

105. *Yung-hsien lu*, p. 352. Cited *HLMHC*, p. 418.

cion in the first year of the Yung-cheng reign. The Emperor thought
that he had been taking forced extortions in order to pay for the repairs to a temple, and had been guilty of other irregularities. He ordered the governor of Chekiang to investigate and send a secret memorial on Sun Wen-ch'eng's conduct; but no definite evidence of mis-
conduct was forthcoming, and Sun Wen-ch'eng was left at his
post.[106] He spent the next few years at his administrative duties
without rebuke, but in 1726 he began to receive fresh imperial criticisms, especially with regard to the fact that he was not reporting
commodity prices accurately, and was trying to please the Emperor by
falsifying reports. In May 1727 he received a warning that, coming
from the Yung-cheng Emperor, must have been read as a condemna-
tion. It ran:

> In every hundred memorials, should there be even a slight inac-
> curacy, I fear you will suffer a punishment you will not recover
> from. You must know that I am not a ruler who was born and
> grew up deep in the palace. I had forty years experience of
> worldly affairs as Yung Ch'in-wang.[107]

No more of Sun Wen-ch'eng's memorials are on record, nor did the
Yung-cheng Emperor make any further comment. But eight months
later, in January 1728, Sun Wen-ch'eng was found guilty of unspecified charges and dismissed.[108] His fate is unknown.

Ts'ao Fu had managed not to cross the Yung-cheng Emperor in the
first years of his reign. There had been an awkward moment in December 1723, when the Board of Revenue had decided to cancel the
system by which the Liang-huai salt censor paid for the expenses of
the Kiangsu textile commissioners. The incumbent salt censor had already dispatched some money to Ts'ao Fu when he received the
Board's instructions; he accordingly wrote to Ts'ao Fu several times

106. YCCPYC, ts'e 47, p. 99, Emperor's warning to Sun Wen-ch'eng in endorsement to
memorial dated Yung-cheng 1/11/1. Instructions to Chekiang governor to investigate, ibid.,
ts'e 13, p. 46. No answering memorial is preserved in YCCPYC, but presumably Sun was
cleared. His case may have been lost sight of in the general confusion in Chekiang in 1724,
when five different men held office as governor (CS, p. 3053).

107. YCCPYC, ts'e 47, pp. 99b–101b, endorsements to his memorials dated Yung-cheng
4/6/1, 5/1/1, 5/3/1. Quoted endorsement ibid., p. 102b, to memorial dated 5/4/1. The
Yung-cheng Emperor was using some poetic license here; he had in fact been made Yung
Ch'in-wang in 1709, only eighteen years previously.

108. Yung-hsien lu, p. 390.

requesting that the money be returned, but got no reply. Finally he memorialized that Ts'ao Fu should be ordered to pay back the money to the Board of Revenue. The Emperor gave the order, but Ts'ao Fu was not punished for his recalcitrance.[109] He continued to make routine journeys to Peking to escort the silk transports, and was received in audience by the Emperor; on these occasions he conveyed greetings from the other commissioners. True, he was censured together with the others for extravagance in the preparation of objects for the palaces, but such rebukes were not usually taken very seriously.[110]

The immediate cause of Ts'ao Fu's fall was almost certainly a highly unfavorable report of his conduct which was sent to the Emperor. Such reports on others had been sent in by the Ts'ao family to the K'ang-hsi Emperor in their palace memorials. Now, ironically, the instrument was turned on them. Often the Yung-cheng Emperor merely noted such reports and kept them for future reference; it was unfortunate for Ts'ao Fu that he was reported on by an official who was riding high in the Emperor's favor. This man was Ka-erh-t'ai, who had been appointed Liang-huai salt censor in 1724 and was to hold the same post until 1729.[111] A serious and conscientious official, his memorials had received endorsements of a kind that Ts'ao Fu and his friends would never know: "Your good points are such that I cannot list them all. Best wishes (*mien-chih*). Best wishes." Or "All men can make a start, but few can bring things to completion. You must persevere in your fine ambitions, and never waver. Best wishes." [112]

On February 8, 1727, Ka-erh-t'ai sent a memorial reporting on the abilities of various local officials—his subjects ranging from salt merchants' sons, through the prefects of Nanking and Yangchow, up to the financial and judicial commissioners of the province. Third on the list was Ts'ao Fu, of whom Ka-erh-t'ai wrote as follows:

109. YCCPYC, *ts'e* 13, p. 33, Hsieh Tz'u-li memorial dated Yung-cheng 1/12/1.

110. Ibid., *ts'e* 50, p. 63b, Kao Pin memorial dated Yung-cheng 4/10/9, and p. 64, endorsement to his memorial dated 4/12/9. Both the K'ang-hsi and Yung-cheng Emperors frequently warned against extravagance, but the Ts'ao family had grown up with the K'ang-hsi Emperor and knew his tastes from the Southern Tours: he expected luxury. The Yung-cheng Emperor, however, meant what he said, and Ts'ao Fu would have done well to heed his warnings.

111. CNTC, ch. 105, p. 8b. He was previously Liang-che salt censor. In 1726 Ka-erh-t'ai had been made a special present of the Shun-chih Emperor's copy of the T'ang poet Wei Cheng's *Shih ssu shu* (cf. HLMHC, p. 165, cited passage on I-cheng salt memorial). Ka-erh-t'ai was made Anhwei financial commissioner in 1728.

112. YCCPYC, *ts'e* 39, pp. 91 and 91b, endorsements to memorials dated Yung-cheng 3/9/11 and 3/11/8.

On inquiry I found that Ts'ao Fu is young in years and without ability, and timorous in conducting his business. He has handed over the management of the textile commissioner's affairs to his household steward Ting Han-ch'en. I have seen him several times in Peking. He is of average ability.

Against this passage the Yung-cheng Emperor wrote two interlinear vermilion endorsements; next to Ts'ao Fu's name he wrote: "This man is really no good," and opposite the statement "He is of average ability" the Emperor wrote: "Why do you just say 'average' and leave it at that?" [113] When such a report was sent, and the Emperor read it with care and agreed with the informant's verdict, there can be little doubt that the career of the official involved must be in jeopardy.

When this memorial was sent, Ts'ao Fu was in Peking. He returned to the south on March 19 and visited Ka-erh-t'ai at his salt censor's yamen in I-cheng (I-chen) to relay to him one of the Emperor's often repeated prohibitions of extravagance.[114] It is strange to think of the two men going through the public ritual attendant upon the transmittal of the Emperor's edicts, while one of them knew that he had just damned his colleague in secret, and the other perhaps hankered after that same salt censor's post that his father and uncle had held for so long.

Ts'ao Fu was dismissed in January 1728, at the same time as the Hangchow textile commissioner Sun Wen-ch'eng. The official reason for the dismissal of Ts'ao Fu was that he had been in arrears.[115] Whether these arrears were still the dragging remains of Ts'ao Yin's past deficits, or the result of Ts'ao Fu's own tardiness in sending money to the Board of Revenue, or even in furnishing silk quotas to the court, is not specified. To these charges must be added the general attacks on his efficiency made by Ka-erh-t'ai and the Emperor's agree-

113. Ibid., *ts'e* 39, p. 92b, memorial dated Yung-cheng 5/1/18, with interlinear endorsements. The Emperor's reference to the word "average" (*p'ing-ch'ang*) could mean that he considered Ts'ao Fu below average, or it could be a reference to the fact that Ka-erh-t'ai had used the same phrase to describe another official two lines before. The K'ang-hsi Emperor had similarly expressed his agreement with secret condemnations, as in "I have long known that this man's reputation was not good" (in *Wang Hung-hsü Memorials*, p. 10).

114. YCCPYC, *ts'e* 39, p. 93, memorial dated Yung-cheng 5/3/10, stating that Ts'ao Fu had returned on 5/2/27. I-chen had been renamed I-cheng.

115. The only source for this is *Yung-hsien lu*, p. 390, though the fact that Ts'ao Fu left office in 1728 is corroborated by local histories; cf. CNTC, ch. 105, p. 9b.

ment with them. The continuing purge of all people connected with
the princes Yin-t'ang and Yin-ssu, which the Emperor was still conducting, was also probably a contributing factor. Sui Ho-te, the official who searched the Ts'ao family mansions in Nanking, reported
that he had found proof of a connection between the Ts'ao family and
Yin-t'ang, the brother of the Yung-cheng Emperor who had been
forced to take the name Seshe—meaning "pig."

> To the left of the Nanking textile commissioner's yamen, in the
> Wan-shou temple, were stored a pair of gilt lions, their bodies
> and attached bases being five feet six inches high. I made careful
> inquiries into their origin, and found that in 1716 Seshe had sent
> his guards officer Ch'ang Te to Nanking, to get them cast. After-
> ward, because the casting was poor, he handed them over to Ts'ao
> Fu, to be deposited in the temple. So much I have discovered; I
> do not know the original purpose of the casting, nor dare I con-
> ceal it. I humbly memorialize to ask for the emperor's instruc-
> tions as to whether I should send the lions to Peking to be exam-
> ined, or have them destroyed on the spot.[116]

All this memorial really shows is that Sui Ho-te was frightened by his
own discovery; there need have been no close contact between Yin-
t'ang and the Ts'aos over this business, nor is it likely that their own-
ership of the lions was public knowledge before Sui Ho-te's investigation. But it is quite possible that the Ts'ao family, like Li Hsü, were
enough in contact with members of the Yin-t'ang and Yin-ssu factions to make their dismissal justifiable to the Emperor.

No more is known of the Ts'ao family fall. A likely source of further information, the novel the *Dream of the Red Chamber*, gives no
direct descriptions of the family's fall, since Ts'ao Chan died before he
could write those closing sections of his story. There are merely hints
that members of the family were charged with certain grave offences,
and had been guilty either of some gross miscarriage of justice or were
involved with a group of local wealthy families that all fell together.[117]

116. Sui Ho-te memorial dated Yung-cheng 6/7/3, cited in *HLMHC*, p. 420. The officer
(*hu-wei, BH* 45) was probably the Ch'ang Te listed as a Chinese bondservant in the Bordered
Blue Banner, *PCST*, ch. 75, p. 16b. He rose to be a lieutenant (*hsiao-ch'i-hsiao, BH* 727).

117. Points discussed in Wu Shih-ch'ang, pp. 192, 163, 166. There is no direct support for

Certainly they were wealthy. After his investigation, Sui Ho-te reported the family resources as being:

> Living quarters and servants' dwellings numbering thirteen buildings, containing in all four hundred and eighty-three units (*chien*). Eight estates, totaling 1,967 *mou* [approx. 300 acres]. Household servants of all ages, male and female, numbering in all one hundred and fourteen people.

These were the basic units of the Ts'ao family wealth, but before the house was searched they had managed to remove much of the other items of great value that they must have owned; continuing his inventory, Sui Ho-te made no mention of their silks, their books and art objects, their Western curios and presents received from the Emperor. At some time during 1727 these must have been sent away for safety; Sui Ho-te listed merely "tables, chairs, beds, stools, old clothes, odds and ends, about a hundred pawnshop tickets, and nothing else." Household servants testified that Ts'ao Fu owed about 32,000 taels in local debts, and Sui Ho-te was taking care of these.

By imperial order, all the landed property, dwelling houses, and slaves that had belonged to Ts'ao Fu were given to his successor as Nanking textile commissioner, that same Sui Ho-te. By a special imperial dispensation, the Ts'ao family were allowed to keep some of their houses and slaves in Peking.[118]

With this disastrous episode, Ts'ao Fu disappears from history. But in the beginning of the Ch'ien-lung reign his family were apparently pardoned, and Ts'ao I, the youngest brother of Ts'ao Yin, who was still alive and serving as a bondservant company captain and concurrently colonel in the Guards Brigade, was granted posthumous honors for his ancestors. An imperial decree dated 1735 gave the founder of the family fortunes, Ts'ao Yin's grandfather Ts'ao Chen-yen, the

---

Wu Shih-ch'ang's new theory that the immediate cause of Ts'ao Fu's dismissal was a great fire at the *chih-tsao* yamen (p. 168 note 1). Such a fire would almost certainly have been mentioned by Sui Ho-te or the governor in their memorials.

118. Sui Ho-te, 1728 memorial. This important source is cited in *HLMHC*, p. 419, without date or origin, but comes presumably from the Palace Museum Archives. Problems arising from the confiscations are discussed by Wu Shih-ch'ang, pp. 115–16, and by Chou Ju-ch'ang in *HLMHC*, pp. 135–36. In ibid., pp. 142–43, Chou Ju-ch'ang advances the theory that Sui Ho-te might have given the Ts'ao family some of his *own* dwellings in Peking, to make up for the vast wealth he received in Nanking at their expense. This would have been a lordly gesture, of which there is no proof. It is more likely that the Ts'aos retired to their existing Peking houses, taking their Nanking movable property with them.

second-rank title of *tzu-cheng ta-fu*; and Ts'ao Chen-yen's two wives were given the comparable second-rank titles of *fu-jen*.[119] At this time also Ts'ao Fu was probably given the minor office of an assistant department director in the Imperial Household.[120] The family, however, made no permanent recovery and got no further offices. Their fortunes continued to decline, and by 1745 Ts'ao Chan, grandson of Ts'ao Yin, was living in bucolic poverty in the western suburbs outside Peking,[121] and had started writing a novel.

In the thirteenth chapter of the *Dream of the Red Chamber* Ts'ao Chan put these words into the mouth of a dying woman, who had married into the Chia family:

> Our family has lived in splendid style for nearly a century, but what if one day at the height of good fortune disaster strikes, or if the proverb that "when the tree falls the monkeys shall be scattered" should be fulfilled? Will not all our background of culture and the age of our clan prove vain? [122]

Next to the proverb in this passage, Ts'ao Chan's uncle, who was commenting on the manuscript, wrote these words:

> The remark that "when the tree falls the monkeys shall be scattered" is still ringing in my ears. Yet, counting up on my fingers, it is now thirty-five years since it was made. Alas, alas! How can one help grieving to death? [123]

Since this comment can be dated to about 1762, the writer must have heard the words around 1727, perhaps from the mouth of Ts'ao Fu, and they retained their poignancy for him because they were intimately connected with the happier times before the family's fall.

Ts'ao Fu had not discovered this proverb for himself. It had been well known to his adopted father, who was pleased to produce it in

119. *HLMHC*, pp. 41–42, 422–23. The honorary titles were *BH* 945. Ts'ao I's later ranks were *BH* 49 and 734.

120. *yüan-wai-lang*, *BH* 76. He is listed as holding this office in *PCST*, ch. 74, p. 9. However, on the same page Ts'ao Yung is listed as having been a *lang-chung*, department director, and there is no evidence from Ts'ao Yung's memorials that he was ever anything higher than a *chu-shih*, secretary. So in both his and Ts'ao Fu's cases the titles may have been honorary, or erroneous.

121. *HLMHC*, p. 425.

122. *Hung-lou meng pa-shih-hui chiao-pen*, p. 126.

123. *Chih-yen chai hung-lou meng chi-p'ing*, p. 161, translation adapted from Wu Shih-ch'ang, p. 109. For Chih-yen as Ts'ao Chan's uncle, cf. Wu Shih-ch'ang, pp. 97–101.

company. As Ts'ao Yin's friend Shih Li wrote at the end of one of his poems:

> Ts'ao Yin once selected these Buddhist words and declaimed them to his seated guests: "When the tree falls the monkeys shall be scattered." Now when I recall these words I am wracked with grief; for they show me the real depth of his understanding.[124]

It is a mournful proverb to echo through a family history, and Ts'ao Yin's adoption of it was doubly sardonic. For in the best-known story in which it occurs, a poem named from this proverb was sent to one Ts'ao Yung, who had been banished after the master in whose shadow he flourished had died.[125] Ts'ao Yin obviously felt for this other Ts'ao, whose name was so like his own.

The tree in whose encompassing branches the Ts'ao family flourished for some seventy years was a massive one, compounded of many elements: office, wealth, ability, astuteness, and not least the ambiguous bondservant status that was both servile and privileged, an amalgam of the Manchu and Chinese worlds. But the tree was never firmly rooted, and it stood only so long as the Emperor chose. Without his support, the tree must fall and the monkeys be scattered.

There is nothing pejorative in the metaphor—after all it was Ts'ao Yin himself who quoted it, and his family that repeated it after him. When the tree fell the monkeys would be scattered, and that was that. But for Ts'ao Yin's grandson then to write one of the greatest works in Chinese literature, the *Dream of the Red Chamber,* is the most curious twist of the whole family history. It also modifies the tragic nature of that history, since it adds an element of chance to the inevitability implicit in the family situation. It should therefore be legitimate to drive the metaphor to its logical conclusion, and take leave of the Ts'ao family with words from the mouth of the most engaging character in Chinese fiction:

> "We have promised to take on this job, and we have got to see it through. We've got to do the thing properly," said Monkey. "In any case we must wait till the king comes to eat us, or we shall spoil a good start by a poor finish." [126]

124. HLMHC, p. 393.

125. Tz'u-hai (1947, one vol. ed.), p. 720, under phrase "Shu tao, hu-sun san."

126. Wu Ch'eng-en, Hsi-yu chi; Eng. trans. Arthur Waley, Monkey (New York, 1943 ed.), p. 259. Composite quotation, ignoring Pigsy's interpolations.

APPENDIXES

Appendix A

Raw Silk Prices, 1712–26

Silk prices were quoted by Li Hsü in his memorials every year in the fifth or sixth month during this period. He gave prices of three qualities of silk thread: (1) twisted warp silk (*hsien-ching-ssu*), strong silk thread to run the length of the loom; (2) single warp silk (*tan-ching-ssu*), light silk thread to run the length of the loom; (3) woof silk (*wei-ssu*), shorter lengths of thread to be woven across the loom.

All prices were quoted by the ounce (*liang*), in *fen* (1/100 of a tael).

PRICES IN fen PER OUNCE

Date	Twisted Warp	Single Warp	Woof	Li Hsü Memorials
1712 (51/5/16)	8.4	—	7.5	p. 29b
1713 (52/int5/23)	8.9	8.2	7.8	p. 44
1714 (53/6/9)	8.5	8.1	7.7	p. 54
1715 (54/6/6)	8.0	7.0	6.6	p. 63b
1716 (55/5/12)	8.3	7.2	6.9	p. 71
1717 (56/6/3)	8.1	7.0	6.7	p. 83b
1718 (57/6/16)	8.2	7.6	7.2	p. 93b
1719 (58/6/24)	8.0	7.4	7.0	p. 103b
1720 (59/6/13)	7.9	7.0	6.5	p. 106b
1721 (60/6/6)	7.2	6.2	5.8	p. 111
1722 (61/6/7)	7.9	6.7	6.3	p. 114

In addition, Ts'ao Fu submitted these prices: (a) In 1715 (54/7/3), first-quality silk (*t'ou-teng*), 7.8 *fen* per ounce, second-grade silk (*tz'u-teng*), 7.2 *fen*. (b) In 1716 (55/6/13), first-quality silk, 7.9 *fen*, second-grade silk, 7.3 *fen*. Cf. *Ts'ao Fu Archives*, nos. 2846 and 2874.

In 1726 the Hangchow textile commissioner Sun Wen-ch'eng submitted these prices to the Yung-cheng Emperor:

Date	First-quality silk	Second-grade silk (shao-tz'u-che)
1723	7.8	7.2
1724	7.2, 7.3	6.7, 6.8
1725	7.0	6.5, 6.6
1726	7.0	6.5, 6.6

(Source: *Yung-cheng chu-p'i yü-chih, ts'e* 47, p. 100, memorial dated Yung-cheng 4/9/1.)

For comparative mid-eighteenth-century prices, cf. P'eng Che-i, "Chiang-nan chih-tsao," p. 110.

Appendix B

Kiangsu Rice Prices, 1706–22

Prices of rice were frequently reported by Ts'ao Yin and Li Hsü in their early memorials, and by 1713 such reporting had become routine for Li Hsü and Ts'ao Yin's sons. The regularity of these reports, and the fact that they are scattered throughout a large number of memorials, seems to justify an attempt to concentrate all prices here, so that we can see the kind of price fluctuations that occurred even at this period of great stability.

This appendix is offered to supplement the article by Ch'üan Han-sheng and Wang Yeh-chien, "Ch'ing Yung-cheng nien-chien-ti mi-chia" (The Prices of Rice of China during the Yung Cheng Period of the Ch'ing Dynasty), *Bulletin of the Institute of History and Philology*, Academia Sinica, 30 (Taiwan, 1959), 157–85. By filling out knowledge of the K'ang-hsi period prices, the appendix also modifies the picture of stability and slowly rising prices presented by the same two authors in "Ch'ing chung-yeh i-ch'ien Chiang-Che mi-chia-ti pien-tung ch'ü-shih" (Fluctuation Trends of the Rice Price in Kiangsu and Chekiang Before the Middle of the Ch'ing Dynasty), in the same *Bulletin*, extra volume no. 4 (Taiwan, 1960), 351–57. The K'ang-hsi reign figures show that besides the unusually high prices in 1706 and 1707 caused by droughts and the ensuing floods, there were considerable monthly fluctuations within any given year. In years when prices were steady, and figures for every month available, some definite conclusions can be drawn; for example the slowly rising price theory is contradicted by the fact that the average rice price of 1715-17 was definitely two or three *ch'ien* higher than the average price in 1719–21.

The sources for rice prices in this appendix are: *Ts'ao Yin Memorials, Ts'ao Yin Archives, Li Hsü Memorials, Ts'ao Yung Archives, Ts'ao Fu Memorials, Ts'ao Fu Archives*. In early memorials, Ts'ao Yin wrote that he was reporting on hulled and coarse rice prices, and Li Hsü that he was reporting on fine white and coarse rice prices. Later memorialists did not bother to specify the type of rice meant. When two prices are given for a certain month, it may be assumed that the two prices refer to finest quality and low quality rice, since this seems to have been common practice. When two memorialists report on prices in the same month, the lower variant is given in parentheses following the higher price. The number of the intercalary month in a given year is shown in brackets preceding the rice price for that month. All prices cited are from the areas of Soochow, Nanking, or Yangchow in Kiangsu province. All prices are in *ch'ien* (1/10 of a tael) per picul (*shih,* approx. 133 lbs. avoirdupois).

In years prior to 1706, these figures were listed by Li Hsü and Ts'ao Yin: 1693, seventh month, 9 and 7 *ch'ien;* 1693, tenth month, 10; 1697, tenth month, 8 and 7; 1698, eleventh month, 10 and 8.

Month	1706	1707	1708	1709	1710	1711	1712
First	—	—	—	—	—	—	—
Second	—	—	—	13	—	—	—
				12			
Third	14.3	—	13	14	12	—	—
	13.5		9	12	11		
Fourth	—	—	8	—	12	—	—
Fifth	—	—	—	—	—	—	—
Sixth	—	—	—	—	—	—	—
Intercalary	—	—	[3]10	—	—	—	—
Seventh	13	—	—	12	—	—	—
	8			11			
Eighth	—	14.7	—	8.4	—	—	8
		12					7
Ninth	—	—	13	8	7	—	—
			10				
Tenth	—	12	—	—	—	—	8
		11					7
Eleventh	—	—	—	—	—	—	—
Twelfth	—	17	—	—	—	—	8
		16					7

Month	1713	1714	1715	1716	1717
First	9(8)	10	11	7.4	11
	8(7)	9	10	6	10
Second	—	—	—	10	11
				9	10
Third	—	10	—	11	11.7(11)
		9		10	10.7(9)

Month	1713	1714	1715	1716	1717
Fourth	—	10	13	11	11.6(11)
		9	12	10	10.4(10)
Fifth	9	10	11.8	11(8.5)	11(10.4)
	8	9	10.5	10(7.8)	10(9.4)
Sixth	11(9)	11(10)	11.7(11)	11(8.6)	11(10.4)
	10(8)	10(9)	10.6(10)	9(7.8)	10(9.4)
Intercalary	[5]10	—	—	[3]11	—
	9			10	
Seventh	10	11.5(10)	12(11)	11(9.8)	9.4
	9	10.5(9)	11(10)	9(8)	8.2
Eighth	10(9)	10.6(11)	12	11(12)	11
	9(8)	9	11(7)	10	9.5(7.5)
Ninth	9	11	12(7.4)	11(11)	10(8.4)
	8	10	11(6.8)	10(9.5)	9(7)
Tenth	10(9)	10.5	7.4	11.5(11)	9
	9(8)	9.2	6	10	8
Eleventh	10(9)	—	7.4	11	9.5
	9(8)		6	10	8
Twelfth	10	—	7.4	11	9.5
	9		6	10	8

Month	1718	1719	1720	1721	1722
First	—	—	8.2	—	—
			7		
Second	—	—	8.2(7.5)	—	10.5
			7(6.4)		9
Third	—	—	8.6	—	12
			7.4		9.7
Fourth	10	9	8.4	9.7	12
	9	7.5	7.2	8.3	9.7
Fifth	10.5(9)	9	9	—	11.8
	9.5(8)	7.5	7.6		9.6
Sixth	10(9)	9	9.5	9.7	11.8
	9(8)	7.3	7.8	8.4	9.6
Intercalary	[8]9.5(8)	—	—	[6]9.7	—
	7(6.4)			8.4	
Seventh	9	8.7	9.5	9.8	12.5
	8	7.3	8	8.5	10.3
Eighth	10(8)	8.7	9.6	11	12
	9(7)	7.3	8.2	9.6	9.8
Ninth	—	8.7	9.2	—	11.4
		7.3	8		9.5
Tenth	8.5	8	9.4	—	11
	6.5	7	7.8		9.2
Eleventh	8.5	8	9	—	—
	6.5	7	8		
Twelfth	—	8	—	—	—
		7			

Appendix C

New Sample Rice Yields Reported By Li Hsü, 1715–22

Amount of land sown Soochow	Date 1st trans- planting	Date 1st harvest	Yield per MOU, in piculs (SHIH)	Date 2nd trans- planting	Date 2nd harvest	Yield per MOU, in piculs (SHIH)	Annual yield, piculs per MOU
6 mou	54/4/10	54/7/13	3.06	54/7/28	?54/11	under 1	—
50 mou	55/3/28	55/6/4	3.7	55/6/16	55/9/15	1.5 *	5.2
80 mou	56/3/9	56/6/21	4.1	56/6/29	56/10/2	2.5	6.6
80 mou	57/3/20	57/7/3	4.15	57/7/12	57/9/20	2.6	6.75
100 mou	58/3/1	58/6/15	4.25	58/6/23	58/10/3	2.2	6.45
100 mou	59/3/13	59/6/24	4	59/7/4	59/9/28	2	6
100 mou	—	60/int 6/6	4	60/int 6/16	—	—	—
100 mou	61/3/5	61/6/16	3 *	61/6/25	—	—	—

* Strong winds

Source: *Li Hsü Memorials*, pp. 65b–114 (p. 109, dated 59/10/3, has comparative performances of old and new seeds sown 5/12, harvest 9/25. Li Hsü enclosed detailed tables of the yields claimed by merchants and local elite at first and second harvest in 1718; all were lower than his [ibid., pp. 94–95, 99–100]. He was either a good farmer or a liar).

Appendix D

Author's Hypotheses on the Dream of the Red Chamber

I do not intend here to handle the intricacies of *Hung-lou meng* exegesis, but only those problems that arose in the course of preparing this book. The most vexed of these (and they are problems that have absorbed and are still absorbing *Hung-lou meng* scholars) are: first, the date of Ts'ao Chan's birth and the identity of his father; and second, the location of the Ta-kuan-yüan, the garden that figures so prominently in the novel. After comparing the historical and the literary records, I came to certain conclusions: first, that Ts'ao Chan was born in 1715, was the son of Ts'ao Yung but born after his father's death, and was therefore the paternal grandson of Ts'ao Yin (not the son of Ts'ao Yin's adopted son Ts'ao Fu); second, that the Ta-kuan-yüan was a literary reconstruction of both Ts'ao Yin's garden in the textile commissioner's yamen in Nanking *and* of a Ts'ao family garden in the hills above Nanking, which was later bought by Yüan Mei, who named it the Sui-yüan (a homophone after the name of its previous owner Sui Ho-te).

To say that these were "conclusions" is perhaps too strong; I should say rather that these were my working hypotheses, since they seemed to present plausible explanations of otherwise puzzling aspects of the novel. In an attempt to contribute modestly to the spate of current *Hung-lou meng* studies, the reasoning behind the formulation of these hypotheses is given herewith.

I agree with Wu Shih-ch'ang (*On the Red Chamber Dream*, pp. 117–18) that the most convincing date for Ts'ao Chan's birth was the spring of 1715. This means that Ts'ao Chan was thirteen when Ts'ao Fu was dismissed and the Ts'ao family left Nanking and moved to Peking; Ts'ao Chan had therefore had ample time to gather experiences of the lavish Ts'ao family life in Nanking.

Yet this does not necessarily mean that Ts'ao Chan was Ts'ao Fu's son. Remarks made by the Emperor in 1718 that Ts'ao Fu was "a child" (*Ts'ao Fu Archives*, no. 2859) and the statement by an official in 1727 that Ts'ao Fu was still "young in years" (*YCCPYC, ts'e* 39, p. 92b) mean that Ts'ao Fu cannot have been born much before 1698. It is unlikely that he could have been father of a Ts'ao Chan born in 1715, since there are no precedents for any of the Ts'ao family having children at such a young age.

Ts'ao Yung, only surviving son of Ts'ao Yin, died suddenly in 1714. When he died, his wife, née Ma, was pregnant (*Ts'ao Fu Memorials*, pp. 29b–30, dated 54/3/7). It is this child, born in the spring or early summer of 1715, who may well have been Ts'ao Chan the novelist. The theory that Ts'ao Chan was Ts'ao Yung's posthumous son is not original; it is discussed by Yü P'ing-po in his preface to *Hung-lou meng pa-shih-hui chiao-pen*, p. 29 note 6. Wu Shih-ch'ang dismisses the theory as "obviously wrong" (*On the Red Chamber Dream*, p. 115 note 4). But Wu Shih-ch'ang's reasons for dismissing the theory are surprising. He says that Ts'ao Chan had a younger brother, and that even if his mother had married again and had had another child, the child would still not have been his "brother" according to Chinese social custom. But we have a precedent for such terminology in the Ts'ao family itself! When Ts'ao Fu had been adopted as Ts'ao Yin's son, he always referred to Ts'ao Yung as "my elder brother." Why then could not Ts'ao Chan, after being adopted by Ts'ao Fu, refer to Ts'ao Fu's son as "my younger brother"?

One argument from the novel itself should be added. To a general reader there are three points about the hero Pao-yü that clamor for attention: (1) He is adored to distraction by his grandmother, the matriarch of the Chia house. (2) He has an extremely distant, almost hostile, relationship with his father Chia Cheng. (3) He is not close to any of his brothers, and spends most of his time in the company of the girls of the family or with outside friends. Nearly all critics of the novel agree that there is obviously a measure of autobiography in the novel, and that Ts'ao Chan identifies himself with Pao-yü. If we work from the hypothesis that Ts'ao Chan was Ts'ao Yung's posthumous son, and use the knowledge gained from a historical study of the Ts'ao family, all three of these points fit into place: (1) Ts'ao Yin's widow, née Li, lived on long after Ts'ao Yin's death. Her only son, Ts'ao Yung, had died tragically young.

As the matriarch of the Ts'ao family living on in Nanking, naturally she adored Ts'ao Chan, the only surviving child from Ts'ao Yin's line and her only real grandchild, and favored him above all the other children. (2) Ts'ao Fu was not Ts'ao Chan's father but his adopted father. Ts'ao Fu had no particular affection for Ts'ao Chan, and resented the extent to which the matriarch (whose adopted son Ts'ao Fu was) favored Ts'ao Chan over Ts'ao Fu's own children. (3) Ts'ao Chan was orphaned and an only child. He relied on his grandmother's protection and was never really at ease with Ts'ao Fu's children, who were younger than he and regarded him as something of an outsider.

None of these arguments is final, and the debate still rages. Nevertheless one of the essays in a recent collection of essays on the *Dream of the Red Chamber* starts off with the words, "Ts'ao Hsüeh-ch'in [Chan] was probably Ts'ao Yung's son" (cf. Wu En-yü, "Ts'ao Hsüeh-ch'in sheng-p'ing wei-jen hsin-t'an" [A New Discussion of Ts'ao Hsüeh-ch'in's Style of Life], in Wu Shih-ch'ang et al., *San-lun Hung-lou meng* [Miscellaneous Essays on the *Dream of the Red Chamber*] [Hong Kong, 1963], p. 90). So this view may yet become orthodoxy, and Ts'ao Yin be reinstated as the true grandfather of Ts'ao Chan, a position he had long occupied until recent research revealed that Ts'ao Fu was his adopted son only. Now even more recent research confirms Ts'ao Fu as Ts'ao Yin's adopted son and offers Ts'ao Chan as Ts'ao Fu's adopted son.

(Writings on the *Dream of the Red Chamber* are coming out of China so fast at present that there is little point in trying to offer a bibliography; the best lead into the literature on the subject remains Wu Shih-ch'ang, *On the Red Chamber Dream*, Oxford University Press, 1961. One useful new work is I Su, *Hung-lou meng chüan*, 2 vols., Peking, 1963; this is a collection of all discoverable writings about Ts'ao Chan and the *Dream of the Red Chamber* that appeared between the Ch'ien-lung reign and the May Fourth Movement (1919). In conjunction with I Su's *Hung-lou meng shu-lu*, Shanghai, 1958, a bibliographical study of the *Dream of the Red Chamber* and of critical works on the novel, this gives a comprehensive base from which to advance into contemporary critical literature.)

One of the most important factors concerning the interrelationship between Ts'ao Chan's novel and historical fact is the location of the action of the novel. The setting for the visit of Yüan-ch'un to her parents was the Ta-kuan-yüan, the specially prepared garden within the Chia mansion. The poet Yüan Mei claimed that his own famous garden, the Sui-yüan in Nanking, was the site of the Ta-kuan-yüan in the novel; this claim was dismissed as boasting by critics, but further research has now shown that Yüan Mei based his claim upon the remark of a friend of Ts'ao Chan's that "the so-called Grand View Garden (Ta-kuan-yüan) was the old site of the present Sui-yüan." (Wu Shih-ch'ang, *On the Red Chamber Dream*, p. 111.)

Chou Ju-ch'ang, the foremost scholar on the *Dream of the Red Chamber*, believes that Ts'ao Chan spent all his conscious life in Peking, that the Ta-kuan-yüan was in Peking and that it was probably on a specific site, which he has located, in the northwest part of the city (*HLMHC*, pp. 134, 144). Yet the modern critic Wu Shih-ch'ang, having gone carefully through Chou Ju-ch'ang's arguments, finally rejects both Chou's dating of Ts'ao Chan's birth and his location of much of the novel's action, and concludes that the Ta-kuan-yüan was definitely in Nanking, in the yamen of the textile commissioner, and that it later passed into the hands of Yüan Mei. (Wu Shih-ch'ang, pp. 142–44. Both he and Chou Ju-ch'ang qualify these rather strong statements elsewhere in their works, but their basic views are clear.)

Study of the life of Ts'ao Yin casts some doubt on both these interpretations, and justifies the offering of a new one. After examining the records of the Southern Tours and the part that Ts'ao Yin played in them, it seems almost certain that Ts'ao Chan drew his inspiration for the visit of Yüan-ch'un to the Chia family from family memories of the glories of the K'ang-hsi Emperor's visits to the textile commissioner's yamen in Nanking. Yet in the early Ch'ing dynasty the homage due to the Emperor was such that it is inconceivable to think of a garden in which the Emperor had had his temporary palace (*hsing-kung*) being allowed to fall into decay and being sold only forty years later to a local poet. This is not to deny the pervasiveness of what has been called "planned ephemerality" in Chinese cities and buildings (cf. Arthur Wright, "Symbolism and Function, Reflections on Changan and Other Great Cities," *Journal of Asian Studies*, 24 (1965), pp. 667–79); it is merely "inconceivable" in the context of seventeenth- and eighteenth-century Ch'ing imperial attitudes. These temporary palaces were shrines to an Emperor's memory, and were not for use by other men.

This is simply illustrated in the present case. The Nanking temporary palace of the K'ang-hsi Emperor, with its surrounding gardens, was inside the walls of the textile commissioner's yamen. It was to decorate this garden that the Emperor sent Ts'ao Yin ten rare saplings in 1711. (*Ts'ao Yin Archives*, no. 2713, dated 50/3/1. The Emperor sent twenty saplings and told Ts'ao Yin to distribute the remainder, which he did by sending two each to the five main Buddhist temples in the Yangchow area.) Sixteen years later the Yung-cheng Emperor recalled his father's practical and symbolic action, writing that those trees in the yamen "were a token of the K'ang-hsi Emperor's love; you should pay special attention to rearing them, and not let them be damaged." (*YCCPYC, ts'e* 47, p. 100, vermilion endorsement to memorial of Sun Wen-ch'eng dated Yung-cheng 5/1/1. The trees he referred to were in fact a similar batch in the Hangchow *chih-tsao hsing-kung*, but it seems legitimate to assume that equal importance was attached to those in the Nanking yamen.) Finally, in 1751 the Nanking yamen was made into a permanent palace for the Ch'ien-lung Emperor, and the textile commissioner had to move elsewhere. (Cf. ch. 4, note 66, above.)

There was one beautiful garden within the textile commissioner's yamen in Nanking which Ts'ao Yin called the Hsi-t'ang, the West Court, in memory of a garden of the same name in Peking. One of Ts'ao Yin's fanciful names was "The flower-sweeping traveling monk of the West Court," and friends referred to him as "Lord of the West Court." (Wu Shih-ch'ang, pp. 135 and 79, *HLMHC*, p. 161.) When Ts'ao Chan wrote in his novel that there was a flower garden at the back of the house, the commentator Chih-yen added: "Why did the author use the word 'back' instead of 'West'? He was afraid that the gentleman might shed tears." (Wu Shih-ch'ang, pp. 79–80.) This was probably the garden that was worked over and perfected for the K'ang-hsi Emperor. It was partly the model for the Ta-kuan-yüan in the novel, and in the eighteenth chapter of *Hung-lou meng*, Yüan-ch'un wanders in and out of the garden on the way to the various buildings that made up the Chia mansion.

Yet Yüan Mei was perhaps not totally wrong in saying that his Sui-yüan was the Ta-kuan-yüan. As it is described in the novel, the

Ta-kuan-yüan was of enormous extent, considerably larger than the space available within the textile commissioner's yamen, which was in the city of Nanking proper next to the governor-general's yamen. (*HLMHC*, pp. 159, 162.) In his *Sui-yüan shih-hua* (p. 587) Yüan Mei wrote that he bought the garden that became the Sui-yüan when it was in ruins, and that it had been in the possession of the Nanking textile superintendent Sui Ho-te. In *Hsiao-ts'ang-shan-fang wen-chi*, ch. 12, Yüan Mei further described the location of the garden as being two *li* to the west of the North Gate of Nanking, on the hill known as the Hsiao-ts'ang-shan. From the top of this hill there was a splendid view out over the city, to the Chi-ming temple in the northeast, and the Mo-ch'iu lake in the southeast. None of this corresponds at all to the known locations of the textile commissioner's yamen. Yüan Mei continues his description:

> There, in the time of the K'ang-hsi Emperor, a certain textile commissioner named Sui raised a pavilion on the northern peak of the hill, and planted around trees and shrubs, and surrounded the whole with a wall. All the inhabitants of Nanking came to walk there and to admire nature in this place. It was called the Sui-yüan after the name of its owner. Thirty years later, when I was named a magistrate in Nanking, this garden was almost entirely deserted, and the pavilion was transformed into a vulgar cabaret, where carters and chair-porters rowdied all day long. . . . I pitied the garden and asked the price of the land, which was 300 taels, one month's salary. I became a garden owner, and surrounded it with a new wall. (Translation adapted from Gaillard, *Nankin*, p. 253.)

Obviously this was not a former Emperor's residence in the heart of the city.

What it may well have been, however, was a private garden of the Ts'ao family, bought by them in their days of affluence. It would be natural for them to have a garden in the hills where they could retire to escape the heat and enjoy the view. Sui Ho-te, mentioned by Yüan Mei as a textile commissioner in the K'ang-hsi reign, was not in fact appointed until 1728, in the sixth year of the Yung-cheng Emperor's reign. From 1692 until 1728, all the Nanking textile commissioners were members of the Ts'ao family. It is very likely that when the

Ts'ao family were dismissed in 1728, and their property taken over and inventoried by Sui Ho-te, he also got hold of their garden in the hills, which by this time was associated with the holdings of the textile commissioner. (Chou Ju-ch'ang in *HLMHC*, p. 419, and Wu Shih-ch'ang, *On the Red Chamber Dream*, p. 143, both suggest this possibility, but without working from the known location of the Sui-yüan.) If the above be a correct analysis, then Ts'ao Chan would have been well acquainted with this garden, and as a creative writer could have added its size and general layout to that of the Hsi-t'ang to make up his composite Ta-kuan-yüan.

One last point is worth considering. The original title of Ts'ao Chan's novel was *Shih-t'ou chi*, which is commonly translated as *The Song of the Stone* or *The Record on a Stone*, and taken to refer to that stone on which the novel was written in the author's fanciful introduction. Later, the alternative title of *Hung-lou meng*, the *Dream of the Red Chamber*, was adopted, and the earlier title discarded. Yet Shih-t'ou (identical characters) had long been in use as a name for that area of Nanking in which Yüan Mei's garden was located, as can be seen from maps of Nanking printed in the Ch'ing and preceding dynasties. Also, in poems written for Ts'ao Yin by his friends Singde and Tu Chieh, Shih-t'ou is used as the name of the place in which they are saying farewell to Ts'ao Yin. Both are referring to the area of Nanking, and add the idea of height to their descriptions: Singde writes of the waters *below* Shih-t'ou; Tu Chieh writes of gazing from the water's edge *up* to the ramparts of Shih-t'ou. (The poems are quoted in *HLMHC*, pp. 233 and 238.) This would be explainable if they were referring to Ts'ao Yin's garden in the hills above the city. To eighteenth-century Chinese readers, *Shih-t'ou chi* must have meant "records from the Nanking hills" as much as it meant "the record on a stone."

It should therefore be safe for readers of the *Dream of the Red Chamber*, as they wander down the luxuriant paths of the Ta-kuan-yüan, to reflect that Ts'ao Yin must once have strolled through very similar gardens and, among some of them at least, the K'ang-hsi Emperor also.

Bibliography

This bibliography contains only works of general importance in the writing of this volume. Works used merely to substantiate minor points are cited in full in the relevant footnotes; the characters for Chinese works in this category, and for works mentioned in quotations or in the text, are given in a separate list at the end of the bibliography.

Works are listed in alphabetical order in the form in which they are cited. For ease of reference they are all listed together. The abandonment of the customary practice of subdividing the bibliography by classification (manuscript, primary source, secondary work) and by language seems justified on the grounds both of simplicity and of accuracy. The distinction in the Chinese works consulted between primary and secondary material is often impossible to make. Major "primary sources" like the *Shih-lu*, the *Ch'ing-shih*, or even the *Hui-tien shih-li* were carefully edited and highly selective; the same applies to such major documentary collections as the *Yung-cheng chu-p'i yü-chih* or the more recent *Wen-hsien ts'ung-pien* and *Ming-Ch'ing shih-liao*. On the other hand, "secondary works" such as *Yung-hsien lu*, *Yang-chou hua-fang lu*, and *Ch'ing pai lei-ch'ao* contain invaluable material that was never included in government compendiums. A book like Chou Ju-ch'ang's *Hung-lou meng hsin-cheng* contains so much citation from rare early Ch'ing sources that it can be used as a book of documents. The novel *Dream of the Red Chamber*, though technically fiction, is also a primary source for material on the Ts'ao family. It is only by combining the various categories of official compendiums, memorials, and private writings that the historian of China can reach toward the truth; in this process no one category is more important than any other.

BH. H. S. Brunnert and V. V. Hagelstrom, *Present Day Political Organization of China*, Eng. trans. A. Beltchenko and E. E. Moran, Shanghai, 1912. (Cited as *BH* followed by the compilers' numbering of the office concerned; e.g. *chih-tsao* is *BH* 845.)

Chang Chung-li, *The Chinese Gentry, Studies on Their Role in Nine-*

teenth-Century China, Seattle, University of Washington Press, 1955.

Chang Po-hsing Archives. The original palace memorials of Chang Po-hsing 張伯行 , stored (in 1963) in the National Palace Museum, Wu-feng, Taichung, Taiwan, crate 76, package 81, memorials numbered 2168–98.

Chang Ying 張英 , *Nan-hsün hu-ts'ung chi-lüeh* 南巡扈從 紀略 [Records from the Retinue on the Southern Tour of 1689], printed in *Chao-tai ts'ung-shu* 昭代叢書 , collection 5.

Chao Hung-hsieh Memorials. A selection of the palace memorials of Chao Hung-hsieh 趙弘燮 , "Ch'ing K'ang-hsi chu-p'i yü-chih" 清康熙硃批諭旨 [Vermilion Endorsements of the K'ang-hsi Emperor], pp. 33–40, in *Wen-hsien ts'ung-pien, 12,* (1931).

Che-chiang t'ung-chih 浙江通志 [The Gazetteer of Chekiang Province], 280 *chüan,* 1899.

Cheng T'ien-t'ing 鄭天挺 , *Ch'ing-shih t'an-wei* 清史探微 [Studies in Ch'ing History], 1946.

Chih-yen chai hung-lou meng chi-p'ing 脂硯齋紅樓夢輯 評 [The Collected Commentaries of Chih-yen on the *Dream of the Red Chamber*], ed. Yü P'ing-po 俞平伯 , Shanghai, 1960.

Chin Te-ch'un 金德純, *Ch'i-chün chih* 旗軍志 [Monograph on the Banner Forces], 6 leaves, 1715, printed in *Hsüeh-hai lei-pien* 學海類編 , *ts'e* 40, Shanghai, 1920 ed.

Ch'ing pai lei-ch'ao 清稗類鈔 [Miscellaneous Records Concerning the Ch'ing Dynasty], ed. Hsü K'o 徐珂 , Shanghai, 1918.

Ch'ing-shih, cf. *CS.*

Ch'ing-shih kao 清史稿 [Draft History of the Ch'ing Dynasty], ed. Chao Erh-sun 趙爾巽 , 536 *chüan,* Peking, 1928.

Ch'ing-shih lieh-chuan 清史列傳 [Ch'ing Dynasty Biographies], 80 *chüan* in 10 vols. Taipei, 1962 reprint.

Chou Ju-ch'ang, cf. *HLMHC.*

Ch'ü T'ung-tsu, *Local Government in China under the Ch'ing,* Harvard East Asian Studies, 9, Cambridge, Harvard University Press, 1962.

CNTC. Chiang-nan t'ung-chih 江南通志 [The Gazetteer of Chiang-nan (Kiangsu and Anhwei)], 200 *chüan,* 1736.

CS. *Ch'ing-shih* 清史 [History of the Ch'ing Dynasty], 8 vols. Taipei, 1961.

Du Halde, Jean Baptiste, *Description géographique, historique, chronologique, politique, et physique de l'empire de la Chine*, 4 vols. Paris, 1735; Eng. trans. R. Brookes, *The General History of China*, 4 vols. London, 1741.

Eminent Chinese of the Ch'ing Period, ed. Arthur W. Hummel, 2 vols. Washington, U.S. Government Printing Office, 1943–44.

Fairbank, John K., and Teng Ssu-yü, *Ch'ing Administration, Three Studies*, Harvard-Yenching Institute Series, 19, Cambridge, Harvard University Press, 1960.

Gaillard, Louis, *Nankin d'alors et d'aujourd'hui, aperçu historique et géographique*, Variétés Sinologiques, 23, Shanghai, 1903.

Gale, Esson M., and Ch'en Sung-ch'iao, "China's Salt Administration, Excerpts from Native Sources," *Journal of Asiatic Studies* (*Asea Yon'gu*, Asiatic Research Center, Korea University), *1:1* (1958), 137–217; *1:2* (1958), 193–216; *2:1* (1959), 273–316.

Hall, John W., "Notes on the Early Ch'ing Copper Trade with Japan," *Harvard Journal of Asiatic Studies*, *12* (1949), 444–61.

HLMHC. Chou Ju-ch'ang 周汝昌, *Hung-lou meng hsin-cheng* 紅樓夢新證 [New Studies on the *Dream of the Red Chamber*], Shanghai, 1953.

Ho Ping-ti, "The Salt Merchants of Yang-chou: A Study of Commercial Capitalism in Eighteenth-Century China," *Harvard Journal of Asiatic Studies*, *17* (1954), 130–68.

——— *The Ladder of Success in Imperial China, Aspects of Social Mobility, 1368–1911*, New York, Columbia University Press, 1962.

HT. *Ch'in-ting ta-Ch'ing hui-tien* 欽定大清會典 [The Ch'ing Statutes], 100 *chüan*, Shanghai, 1899; Taiwan, 1963 reprint with continuous pagination, in one vol.

HT (1732). The *Yung-cheng hui-tien*, 1732.

HTSL. *Ch'in-ting ta-Ch'ing hui-tien shih-li* 欽定大清會典事例 [The Collected Statutes and Precedents of the Ch'ing Dynasty], 1220 *chüan*, Shanghai, 1899; Taiwan, 1963 reprint with continuous pagination, in 19 vols.

Hu-pu tse-li 戶部則例 [The Regulations of the Board of Revenue], 100 *chüan*, 1874.

Hu Shih 胡 適, "Hung-lou meng k'ao-cheng" 紅樓夢考證 [A Study of the *Dream of the Red Chamber*], printed in *Hu Shih wen-ts'un* 胡 適 文 存 [The Collected Essays of Hu Shih], 4 vols. Taipei, 1953 reprint, 1, 575–620.

Huang-ch'ao wen-hsien t'ung-k'ao 皇朝文獻通考 [Imperial Encyclopedia of the Ch'ing Dynasty], 300 *chüan*, Taipei, 1963 reprint, with continuous pagination.

Hung Lou Meng, or the Dream of the Red Chamber. A Chinese Novel, trans. H. Bencraft Joly, 2 vols. Hong Kong, 1892, and Macao, 1893. (This is an almost literal translation of the first fifty-six chapters of the *Hung-lou meng*.)

Hung-lou meng pa-shih-hui chiao-pen 紅樓夢八十回 校本 [The Original Eighty-Chapter Version of the *Hung-lou meng*], ed. Yü P'ing-po 俞平伯, 4 vols. Peking, 1958.

Index to Thirty-Three Collections of Ch'ing Dynasty Biographies, ed. Tu Lien-che and Fang Chao-ying, Harvard-Yenching Institute Sinological Index Series, 9, reprint by the Japan Council for East Asian Studies, Tokyo, 1960.

K'ang-hsi nan-hsün pi-chi 康熙南巡秘記 [A Private Record of the K'ang-hsi Emperor's Southern Tours], by "Yin-fu lao-jen" 蟫伏老人, Shanghai, 1920.

Kuo-ch'ao kung-shih 國朝宮史 [A History of the Ch'ing Palaces], 36 *chüan*, 1759; Tientsin, 1925 reprint.

Lang T'ing-chi Memorials. A selection of the palace memorials of Lang T'ing-chi 郎廷極, "Ch'ing K'ang-hsi chu-p'i yü-chih" 清 康熙硃批諭旨 [Vermilion Endorsements of the K'ang-hsi Emperor], pp. 40–43, in *Wen-hsien ts'ung-pien*, 12 (1931).

Lettres édifiantes et curieuses, écrites des missions étrangères, nouvelle édition, Paris, 1781.

Li Hsü Memorials. A selection of the palace memorials of Li Hsü 李 煦, "Su-chou chih-tsao Li Hsü tsou-che" 蘇州織造李 煦奏摺 [The Palace Memorials of the Soochow Textile Commissioner Li Hsü], pp. 1–116, in *Wen-hsien ts'ung-pien*, 29–45 (1935–42). (The pagination of the memorials is continuous through successive numbers of the journal, with the exception of vols. 29–32 (1935), where the repetition of identical page numbers made confusion easy. The pagination was corrected in a Palace Museum reprint of 1937; this reprint covered seventy-

eight pages of Li Hsü memorials that had already appeared in
Wen-hsien ts'ung-pien. I have used the pagination of the reprint
in all citations up to *Li Hsü Memorials,* p. 26, and thereafter the
continuous pagination adopted in the later numbers of *Wen-
hsien ts'ung-pien.* The Taipei 1964 reprint of *Wen-hsien ts'ung-
pien* unfortunately reproduces the early confusing pagination,
instead of the 1937 revisions. The 1964 reprint also omits the last
eleven pages of Li Hsü's memorials.)

Li Hsüan-po 李玄伯, "Ts'ao Hsüeh-ch'in chia-shih hsin-k'ao" 曹
雪芹家世新考 [A New Study of Ts'ao Hsüeh-ch'in's
Family], *Ku-kung chou-k'an* 故宮週刊, 84–85 (1931).

Liang-huai yen-fa chih 兩淮鹽法志 [The Salt Gazetteer of
Liang-huai], 40 *chüan,* 1748.

Liu Chia-chü 劉家駒, Ch'ing-ch'ao ch'u-ch'i-ti pa-ch'i ch'üan-ti
清朝初期的八旗圈地 (The Allotted Land Policy
for the Eight Banners in the Early Ch'ing Dynasty), Taipei, 1964.

Marsh, Robert M., *The Mandarins. The Circulation of Elites in China,
1600–1900,* Glencoe, Ill., The Free Press, 1961.

Meng Sen 孟森, "Pa-ch'i chih-tu k'ao-shih" (PCCTKS) 八旗
制度考實 [An Examination of the Organization of the
Eight Banners], *Bulletin of the Institute of History and Philology,
Academia Sinica,* 6 (1936), 343–412. This article is also printed
in Meng Sen, *Ch'ing-tai shih* 清代史 [Essays in Ch'ing His-
tory], ed. Wu Hsiang-hsiang 吳相湘, Taipei, 1960, pp.
20–100.

Ming-Ch'ing shih-liao 明清史料 [Historical Materials on the
Late Ming and Early Ch'ing Dynasties], Institute of History and
Philology, Academia Sinica, Shanghai and Taiwan, 1930 ff.

Mo Tung-yin 莫東寅, *Man-tsu shih lun-ts'ung* 滿族史論
叢 [Collected Essays on the History of the Manchu Clans],
Peking, 1958.

Nan-hsün sheng-tien 南巡盛典 [A Record of the Ch'ien-lung
Emperor's Southern Tours], 120 *chüan,* 1771; Shanghai, 1882
ed.

Pa-ch'i i-wen pien-mu 八旗藝文編目 [List of Literary Works
by Members of the Eight Banners], ed. Pao-hsi 寶熙, no date
or place of publication.

PCST. *Pa-ch'i Man-chou shih-tsu t'ung-p'u* 八旗滿洲氏族

通 譜 [Genealogy of the Manchu Clans in the Eight Banners], 80 *chüan*, 1745.

PCTC. *Pa-ch'i t'ung-chih* 八 旗 通 志 [General History of the Eight Banners], 1739.

PCTC (*1795*). As above, edition of 342 *chüan*, undated but listing officials through the year 1795.

Pei-chuan-chi 碑 傳 集 [Collection of Funerary Inscriptions], 160 *chüan*, 1893.

P'eng Che-i 彭 澤 益, "Ch'ing-tai ch'ien-ch'i Chiang-nan chih-tsao ti yen-chiu" 清 代 前 期 江 南 織 造 的 研 究 [A Study of the Chiang-nan Textile Offices in the Early Ch'ing], *Li-shih yen-chiu*, 82 (1963, no. 4), 91–116.

Pfister, Louis, *Notices biographiques et bibliographiques sur les Jésuites de l'ancienne mission de Chine, 1552–1773*, 2 vols. Variétés Sino-logiques, 59, Shanghai, 1932, and 60, Shanghai, 1934.

Saeki Tomi 佐 伯 富, *Shin-dai ensei no kenkyū* 清 代 鹽 政 の 研 究 (The Salt Administration under the Ch'ing Dynasty), Kyoto University Oriental Research Series, 2, 1962 ed.

Shang Yen-liu 商 衍 鎏, *Ch'ing-tai k'o-chü k'ao-shih shu-lu* 清 代 科 舉 考 試 述 錄 [A Study of the Examination System in the Ch'ing Dynasty], Peking, 1958.

Shao Wen 少 文, "Chi Lien-t'ing t'u yung chüan" 記 棟 亭 圖 咏 卷 (Notes on the Handscroll of Painting and Poems Dedicated to Ts'ao Lien-t'ing [Yin]), *Wen-wu* 文 物, 1963 (no. 6), pp. 23–25.

Sheng-tsu wu-hsing Chiang-nan ch'üan-lu 聖 祖 五 幸 江 南 全 錄 [A Complete Record of the K'ang-hsi Emperor's Fifth Southern Tour], anon., printed in *Chen-ch'i t'ang ts'ung-shu* 振 綺 堂 叢 書, ed. Wang K'ang-nien 汪 康 年, 1st series.

Shih-liao hsün-k'an 史 料 旬 刊 [Historical Materials Published Every Ten Days], 40 *ts'e*, Peiping, Palace Museum, 1930–31; 1 vol. reprint with continuous pagination, Taipei, 1963.

Shih-lu. Ta-Ch'ing Sheng-tsu Jen huang-ti shih-lu 大 清 聖 祖 仁 皇 帝 實 錄 [Veritable Records of the K'ang-hsi Reign], 300 *chüan*, Tokyo, 1937.

Sinica Franciscana, 5. Relationes et epistolas illmi D. Fr. Bernardini della Chiesa O.F.M., ed. PP. Anastasius van den Wyngaert et Georgius Mensaert, O.F.M., Rome, 1954.

Sirén, Osvald, *Chinese Painting, Leading Masters and Principles*, 7 vols. New York, Ronald Press, 1956–58.

Su-chou fu-chih 蘇州府志 [Gazetteer of Soochow Prefecture], 150 *chüan*, 1883.

Sun, E-tu Zen, *Ch'ing Administrative Terms*, Harvard East Asian Studies, 7, Cambridge, Harvard University Press, 1961.

Sung Lao Archives. The original palace memorials of Sung Lao 宋犖, stored (in 1963) in the National Palace Museum, Wu-feng, Taichung, Taiwan, crate 76, package 87, memorials numbered 2400–43.

Tōdo meishō zue 唐土名勝圖會 [Collected Illustrations of China's Scenic Areas], 1st collection in 6 *ts'e*, 1806.

Ts'ao Fu Archives. The original palace memorials of Ts'ao Fu 曹頫, location as in *Ts'ao Yin Archives*, memorials numbered 2845–90.

Ts'ao Fu Memorials. A selection of the palace memorials of Ts'ao Fu, title as in *Ts'ao Yin Memorials*, pp. 29b–32b, in *Wen-hsien ts'ung-pien*, 11 (1931).

Ts'ao Yin Archives. The original palace memorials of Ts'ao Yin 曹寅, stored (in 1963) in the National Palace Museum, Wu-feng, Taichung, Taiwan, crate 76, package 98, memorials numbered 2709–2827.

Ts'ao Yin Ch'ih. An unnumbered document dated K'ang-hsi 47/9/10 included in the six rolls (containing 125 items) of K'ang-hsi imperial commands (*ch'ih-yü*) in the Institute of History and Philology, Academia Sinica, Taiwan. These documents were classified (in 1966) as "Nei-ko ta-k'u ts'an-yü tang-an" 內閣大庫殘餘檔案 [Miscellaneous Archives from the Grand Secretariat].

Ts'ao Yin, Li-hsüan tz'u 荔軒詞 [The *Tz'u* Poems of Ts'ao Yin], printed in *Pai ming-chia tz'u ch'ao* 百名家詞鈔, 1st series.

Ts'ao Yin Memorials. A selection of the palace memorials of Ts'ao Yin, "Ch'ing K'ang-hsi chu-p'i yü-chih" 清康熙硃批諭旨 [Vermilion Endorsements of the K'ang-hsi Emperor], pp. 1–26, in *Wen-hsien ts'ung-pien*, 9 and 10 (1931).

Ts'ao Yin Shih. Lien-t'ing shih-ch'ao 棟亭詩鈔 [The *Shih* Poems of Ts'ao Yin], 8 *chüan*, printed in *Lien-t'ing chi* 棟亭集, 15 *chüan*, 1712.

Ts'ao Yin Tz'u. Lien-t'ing tz'u-ch'ao 楝亭詞鈔 [The *Tz'u* Poems of Ts'ao Yin], 1 *chüan*, location as in *Ts'ao Yin Shih.*

Ts'ao Yin Wen. Lien-t'ing wen-ch'ao 楝亭文鈔 [The Essays of Ts'ao Yin], 1 *chüan*, location as in *Ts'ao Yin Shih.*

Ts'ao Yung Archives. The original palace memorials of Ts'ao Yung 曹頫, location as in *Ts'ao Yin Archives*, memorials numbered 2828–44.

Ts'ao Yung Memorials. A selection of the palace memorials of Ts'ao Yung, title as in *Ts'ao Yin Memorials*, pp. 27–29b, in *Wen-hsien ts'ung-pien, 11* (1931).

Tung-hua lu 東華錄 [Ch'ing History], 160 *ts'e*, 1884 ed.

Waley, Arthur, *Yuan Mei, Eighteenth Century Chinese Poet*, London, 1956.

Wang Hung-hsü Memorials. A selection of the palace memorials of Wang Hung-hsü, "Wang Hung-hsü mi-shan hsiao-che" 王鴻緒密繕小摺 [The Small Secret Memorials of Wang Hung-hsü], pp. 1–36, in *Wen-hsien ts'ung-pien, 2* and *3* (1930).

Wen-hsien ts'ung-pien 文獻叢編 [Miscellaneous Ch'ing Historical Documents], Palace Museum, Peiping, 1930 ff., and 2 vols. Taipei, 1964 reprint.

Wu Shih-ch'ang, *On the Red Chamber Dream*, Oxford, Clarendon Press, 1961.

Yang-chou hua-fang lu 揚州畫舫錄 [A Descriptive History of Yangchow], by Li Tou 李斗, Peking, 1960 ed.

YCCPYC. *Yung-cheng chu-p'i yü-chih* 雍正硃批諭旨 [The Vermilion Endorsements of the Yung-cheng Emperor], 60 *ts'e*, Shanghai, 1887 ed.

YFTC. *Yen-fa t'ung-chih* 鹽法通志 [Gazetteer of the Salt Regulations], 100 *chüan*, 1918.

Yu T'ung 尤侗, *chüan Ken-chai-kao wen-chi* 艮齋倦橐文集, printed in *Hsi-t'ang yü-chi* 西堂餘集, 1691, *chüan* 4–10.

Yung-hsien lu 永憲錄 [A History of the Years 1722–28], by Hsiao Shih 蕭奭, Shanghai, 1959 ed.

Yüan Mei 袁枚, *Sui-yüan shih-hua* 隨園詩話, 2 vols. Peking, 1960 ed.

Other Chinese and Japanese works mentioned in the text
or the footnotes.

Abe Takeo 安部健夫, *Hakki Manshū niru no kenkyū* 八
    旗滿洲ニルの研究
Ch'ang-lu yen-fa chih 長蘆鹽法志
Chao Hsüeh-min 趙學敏, *Pen-ts'ao kang-mu shih-i* 本草綱
    目拾遺
Ch'en Chieh-hsien 陳捷先, *Man-chou ts'ung-k'ao* 滿洲叢考
Ch'en-feng-ko ts'ung-shu 晨風閣叢書, *Ch'ien-ts'ai t'ang shu-
    mu* 潛采堂書目
Chi-chou ch'üan-chih 吉州全志
Ch'in-ting chung-shu cheng-k'ao (pa-ch'i) 欽定中樞政考
    （八旗）
Ch'in-ting ta-Ch'ing hui-tien t'u 欽定大清會典圖
Ch'ing hua-chia shih-shih 清畫家詩史
Ch'ing shih-lu ching-chi tzu-liao chi-yao 清實錄經濟資料輯
    要
Ch'üan Han-sheng 全漢昇 and Wang Yeh-chien 王業鍵,
    "Ch'ing Yung-cheng nien-chien-ti mi-chia" 清雍正年間
    的米價 , and "Ch'ing chung-yeh i-ch'ien Chiang-Che mi-
    chia-ti pien-tung ch'ü-shih" 清中葉以前江浙米價的
    變動趨勢
Ch'üan T'ang shih 全唐詩
Fang Chao-ying 房兆楹 and Tu Lien-che 杜聯喆, *Tseng-chiao
    Ch'ing-ch'ao chin-shih t'i-ming pei-lu* 增校清朝進士題
    名碑錄
Fang Hao 方豪, *Chung-Hsi chiao-t'ung shih* 中西交通史
Fu-chien yen-fa chih 福建鹽法志
Haneda Toru 羽田亨, *Manwa jiten* 滿和辞典
Ho Ch'ang-ling 賀長齡, *Huang-ch'ao ching-shih wen-pien* 皇
    朝經世文編
Ho-tung yen-fa chih 河東鹽法志
Hsiao I-shan 蕭一山, *Ch'ing-tai t'ung-shih* 清代通史
Hsiao t'ao-yüan tsa yung 小桃園雜咏
Hsiao-ts'ang-shan-fang wen-chi 小倉山房文集
Hsü-tsuan Chiang-ning fu-chih 續纂江寧府志
Hsü Shih-ch'ang 徐世昌, *Wan-ch'ing i-shih hui* 晚晴簃詩滙

Huang-Ch'ing k'ai-kuo fang-lüeh 皇清開國方畧

Huang P'ei 黄培, "Yung-cheng shih-tai ti mi-tsou chih-tu" 雍正時代的密奏制度

I Su 一粟, *Hung-lou meng chüan* 紅樓夢卷, . . . *shu-lu* 書錄

Inaba hakushi kanrekikinen Mansenshi ronsō 稻葉博士還曆記念滿鮮史論叢

Inaba Iwakichi 稻葉岩吉, *Shinchō zenshi (Ch'ing-ch'ao ch'üan-shih)* 清朝全史

Katō Shigeshi 加藤繁, *Shina keizai shi kōshō* 支那經濟史考證

Kuang-tung t'ung-chih 廣東通志

Kuo-ch'ao hua-shih 國朝畫識

Kuo-ch'ao shu-hua-chia pi-lu 國朝書畫家筆錄

Li-tai chih-kuan piao 歷代職官表, *Ts'ung-shu chi-ch'eng* 叢書集成

Liang-che yen-fa chih 兩浙鹽法志

Lien-t'ing shih-erh chung 楝亭十二種, . . . *wu-chung* 五種

Lin Yutang 林語堂, "P'ing-hsin lun Kao E" 平心論高鶚

Liu Chün-jen 劉鈞仁, *Chung-kuo ti-ming ta tz'u-tien* 中國地名大辭典

Man-wen lao-tang 滿文老檔

Na-lan tz'u 納蘭詞

Nieh Ch'ung-ch'i 聶崇岐, "Man-kuan Han-shih" 滿官漢釋

Pa-ch'i wen-ching 八旗文經

P'ei-wen yün-fu 佩文韻府

Pen-ts'ao kang-mu 本草綱目

Rikubu seigo chukai 六部成語註解

Shang-Chiang liang-hsien chih 上江兩縣志

Shang yü pa-ch'i 上諭八旗

Shih-t'ou chi 石頭記

Ssu-k'u ch'üan-shu tsung-mu t'i-yao 四庫全書總目提要

Su-chou fu-chih 蘇州府志

Ta-Ch'ing T'ai-tsu Kao huang-ti shih-lu 大清太祖高皇帝實錄

Tz'u-hai 辭海

Wada Sei 和田清, *Tōashi kenkyū: Manshū hen* 東亞史研
　　究 滿洲篇, *Tōashi ronsū* 東亞史論藪
Wang Ch'ang 王昶, *Kuo-ch'ao tz'u-tsung* 國朝詞綜 in *Ssu-
　　pu pei-yao* 四部備要
Wei Cheng 魏徵, *Shih ssu shu* 十思疏
Wu Ch'eng-en 吳承恩, *Hsi-yu chi* 西遊記
Wu En-yü 吳恩裕, "Ts'ao Hsüeh-ch'in sheng-p'ing wei-jen hsin-
　　t'an" 曹雪芹生平為人新探 in Wu Shih-ch'ang 吳
　　世昌 ed. *San-lun Hung-lou meng* 散論紅樓夢
Yang-chou shih-jih chi 揚州十日記

Index–Glossary

Names and terms are in alphabetical order of first syllables, ignoring aspirate marks and umlauts. The Chinese characters for offices mentioned only in the footnotes with *BH* identifying numbers are not given. Place names can be found in the frontispiece map.

A-erh-fa 阿爾法, 284

Acina. *See* Yin-ssu

An-ch'a-shih 按察使, bondservants as, 15

An-t'ai 安泰, 104 n.

Ao-fu-ho 敖福合, 83 n., 118 n.

Appointments: as governors-general, 4–5, 72; as governors, 5, 72; of bondservants, 13–16; in provinces, 72–75

Artisans: numbers, 90; specialization of labor, 91; wages, 91, 94

Asan 阿山, 112, 141 n., 146 n., 147–49, 186, 188–90, 193

Bamboo: for musical instruments, 117, 217 n.; without knots, 215, 217

Banner elite, 46, 71, 80, 81, 145; defined, 45; proportion of offices held by, 72–74. *See also* Chang Po-hsing; Gali

Banner system: formation, 6; basic organization, 2–3; and Imperial Household, 11, 34, 38; office holders, 70–75; examinations, 75–76; hereditary succession in, 3; personal allegiances in, 76; obscured in local histories, 72 n. *See also* Banner elite; Bondservants; Chinese bannermen; Manchus

Board of Civil Office, 30, 33 n., 40, 93, 159, 162, 229, 252, 312

Board of Punishments, 40

Board of Revenue, 89, 95, 100–02, 107–10, 125, 169 n., 171–78, 190–91, 197, 207, 208, 272, 286

Board of Rites, 29, 143, 242, 243 n.

Board of War, 30, 40, 93, 216

Board of Works, 88–95, 100, 125, 154

Bondservants (*pao-i*): origins of, 7–9; in Banners, 10–11, 39; in Imperial Household, 11, 34–35; replace eunuchs, 17, 33, 86; legal status, 17, 46; hereditary succession, 21–22; ending status, 38; examination quotas, 30 n., 76; general offices held by, 13–16, 166; as textile commissioners, 86 n.; as customs directors and Hoppos, 104 n.; as salt censors, 174–75, 191; as secret informants, 240; and Westerners, 120; despised by Yung-cheng, 283

Booi amban 包衣昂邦, 11

Bouvet, 124, 136

Buddhism: monks, 121 n., 123, 148, 159, 234, 236; recluse, 122; nuns, 140, 154; temples, 121, 148, 158–59; gifts to temples, 121–22, 305; repairs to temples, 275, 286

Cammann, Schuyler, work discussed, 96 n.

Catty (*chin*), passim as unit of measure, approx. 1.3 pounds avoirdupois, 1/100 of a picul (*shih*)

Centers, Richard, quoted, 43–44

Ch'ang 場, 169

Chang Ch'ao-chen 張朝珍, 71 n.

Chang Chia-mo (mou) 張嘉謨 (謨), 86 n., 87 n., 89 n.

Chang Ch'un 張純, 229

Chang Ch'un-hsiu 張純修, 69

Chang Kuang-ssu 張廣泗, 5 n.

Chang P'eng-ko 張鵬翮, 140 n., 143, 232 n.; criticized by K'ang-hsi, 133; and corruption cases, 243–51, 253 n.

Chang Po-hsing 張伯行: eulogy for Ts'ao Yin cited, 28, 39–41, 49 n., 96, 262–63; palace memorials, 224–25; on examination-hall case, 242; and Gali, 243–53; persecution mania, 239

Ch'ang-shang 場商, 169

Ch'ang Shou 常壽, 174 n.

曹寅(1658-1712)は漢人でありながら早くから滿洲族に降ってこれに仕え、「包衣」ではあったが、かなり優越な地位にいた。と言うのは、都した都市以外の各地方で新王朝に仕える連中がかなり必要であり、異族の王朝が漢語を解する好意を持たない滿洲人が十七世紀初期の清王朝に仕え、彼等の織造の役割で宦官の責任とし、先祖代々内務府、江寧織造の職は明朝では宦官の職についていた。其れ故に高地位について没落をつとめた。曹寅一家は此れらの漢軍を通じて必要の政治腐敗などに通じていたが、かなり優越な都市が高かった。曹寅一家が此れらの政治をつとめたなどにあった。

曹寅は江寧織造、兩淮塩運使等の役人として巨万の富を貯えた。これは康熙帝の南巡や、全唐詩の編纂、地方官を帝に通じて呈し、康熙帝の南詩の編纂官を帝に通じて異わる。時、皇帝が彼を保持と默認し、融通利く独裁一族、曹霑事懷旧的として重要として描寫されている。江蘇の行告す康熙故に王朝史家達の行政方針の此れらの現存皇帝、歴官吏の此れが清皇帝の鋭きが廉潔を解傭して中國重要的々描寫される。運使等も默認していたので、迎えて款待期間に王朝に特殊役割と密切な生涯し、王朝特殊役割と曹寅を鞏固に幸い方針の密奏して仕えたので、雍正帝の独裁的一族、曹霑を重要として懷旧的に描寫される。

曹寅は貯えた。この富を貯えるため全穫の企曹寅。其の收穫の外報に、又逆定、反。信上の密奏處理の帝詩し通事物実も創作家の最盛期。曹寅は厚かつ行政上幾分の問題から、且つの問題も曹寅。友學生れ、康熙帝度は夢は正制落樓で。

曹寅（一六五八——一七一二）的祖先原是漢人，在滿清入關以前，已經入了旗籍了。在異族統治下的中國，因為身居優越的地位，所以能夠不腐敗，滿洲人最初對他們這種人既有戒心。曹家這十七世、七個官宦的父親，並且担任成朝計富地成的……因為新朝居高位，卒致於覆亡，當時一般人頗有反感。曹寅為人認為內務府原都是由宦官担任的差事。「包衣」既有明文應官官的父親，並且担任成朝計富地成的謠言……本江寧織造這些工作和他的兩個兒子都曾在明朝。關以前，衣的身份，又能通漢語，晚年其璽，曹都曾作過的。

曹寅利用康熙許多次，為了黙在蘇州局地方匪等些特殊政家，特於曹寅可保持雍時，為孫曹紅樓夢的重要性，利用作江寧織造的時候，都由他執行的。他酬報許多大旱米價的起康熙之點。他同時又因和為帝的親信，同時許多好機會處理批語的儒，一方面說廉，由時受於期，盛於這一點。康熙達成了一些的寫密奏，以及可能危害邦國安全的事業。淮鹽運使等官的駕就是他斂任經，報告國安全……

顯示著滿洲人密奏時期的財政，由於他存在，作情報一生於他對帝，乃不感為中本身……清朝利用親信奏至今吏項的性格，一可相屬作，也污黙寫了一最也是……上吏間怎麼了裡面看容一家小大有政官人怎時所品以當制了，曹部偉是在方可專了一個最……某單使樣帝解，我仍出忍部曹說的它。